AF739663

An Introduction to Automated Data Acquisition

Ben E. Cline

PBI
a petrocelli book
new york / princeton

Designed by Liz Waite
Composition by Eastern Graphics

Published in the United States of America.
1 2 3 4 5 6 7 8 9 10

Library of Congress Cataloging in Publication Data

Cline, Ben E.
An introduction to automated data acquisition.

Bibliography: p.
Includes index.
1. Automatic data collection systems. I. Title.
II. Title : Automated data acquisition.
TS158.6.C57 1984 001.64 83-26309
ISBN 0-89433-192-2

To Sue Ellen

Contents

Preface

The field of automated data acquisition deals with the use of instrumentation to measure and record values of one or more physical quantities over a period of time without direct human intervention. The types of physical quantities that can be measured include temperature, light intensity, and duration. The number of applications to which data collection systems can be successfully applied are practically endless. The fields of endeavor that can benefit from data acquisition instrumentation include engineering, the traditional sciences, and the social sciences.

Due to the current availability of inexpensive digital computers, almost all data acquisition systems are built around microcomputers or minicomputers. To understand all aspects of a data collection system, an individual must understand electronics, digital computer hardware and software, traditional instrumentation techniques, and the physical system being measured. The interdisciplinary nature of this field adds to both the complexity and the appeal of implementing a data acquisition system.

The major emphasis of this book is to provide an introduction to the techniques and tools used to address data acquisition problems. Because a wide variety of commercial hardware is available for use in data acquisition projects, a discussion of basic electronics, standard interfaces, and application techniques is given as opposed to a detailed presentation of interface design. The reader is assumed to have a knowledge of computer programming and basic computer architecture. An overview of software techniques for data acquisition systems is presented with an emphasis on the design of interrupt software for use with data acquisition interfaces.

In addition to the technical aspects of data acquisition systems, managerial aspects are discussed. The selection of equipment and a discussion of the real costs associated with system implementation are presented.

This book is not meant to be a data acquisition cookbook for two reasons. First, the variety of situations in which a data acquisition system is applicable are too diverse to be covered in a cookbook fashion. Second, rapid changes in technology make current hardware obsolete. Thus, a detailed example of the use of a popular interfacing integrated circuit may be outdated in a short time. Examples, however, are provided in this text, although particular hardware is generally not emphasized.

Acknowlegement

The aid, encouragement, and sacrifice of my wife, Sue Ellen J. Cline, during the production of the manuscript for this book are greatly appreciated. I am also grateful to Dr. A. L. Ritter of the Physics Department at Virginia Polytechnic Institute and State University for the description of his research which is the basis of an example used in this text.

1

Introduction to Automated Data Collection

Automated data collection is the process whereby measurements are taken from a physical system and stored or displayed without direct human intervention. A human operator may be present to supervise and interact with the data collection system, but he does not directly record data. In addition to the data collection function, the data acquisition equipment may perform data analysis and data presentation functions.

With today's declining computer hardware costs, many data collection instruments contain computing equipment. Low hardware costs allow more laboratories and industrial processes[1] to be automated. The implementation of computer-based data acquisition systems using microcomputers and minicomputers is the focal point of this book.

There are three primary reasons for using automated data acquisition systems. First, the use of such equipment can relieve human personnel from mundane tasks such as converting strip chart graph information into numeric quantities for computer analysis. Second, data collection equipment reduces human errors such as digit transposition while recording figures manually. Third, some processes to be measured generate large amounts of data that cannot be handled directly by humans.

Figure 1.1 illustrates automated data acquisition systems. Connected to a process to be monitored are transducers, devices that produce an electrical signal (voltage amplitude, frequency, etc.) that corresponds to the value of some physical quantity. Transducers are available for the measurement of a variety of quantities including temperature, pressure, flow, and force.

Interfaces are required to connect the transducers to the computer. The interface (internal to the computer) and related interfacing circuitry (external to the computer) translate the electrical signal from the transducer into a form readable by the digital computer. The interfacing circuitry is not needed in many cases where the transducer and interface are directly compatible. For a given computer, a variety of interfaces of differing type and complexity are generally available.

The function that the central processing unit (CPU) of the computer performs with the data generated by the transducers depends on the software designed for the computer. The computer might simply monitor a process and turn on an alarm if some process quantity exceeds a present limit. It might store the data for later analysis or provide graphic output of the monitored data for the operator.

A large number of computer systems in use today interact only with computer peripherals (e.g. disk drives). The only interface to the "outside world" is via a computer terminal that a human operator uses. In the realm of automated data collection, the computer hardware is directly interfaced to devices that measure some "real world" quantities in real time. (Real-time data collection refers to the measurement of process parameters as they change over time. The term "real-time" typically refers to measurements that must be performed in a time-critical fashion to prevent loss of information). The added dimension of data acquisition systems associated with interfacing to "real world" systems and that of taking measurements in real-time requires that data acquisition system designers be familiar with computer programming, with computer hardware and interfacing, and with the process that is being measured. Normally in such projects, individuals will be familiar with a single aspect of the project. System designers with an interdisciplinary background are essential in the field of data acquisition to coordinate the effort, provide communications between specialists, and to reduce the number of design errors.

The types of decisions facing the implementor of a data acquisition system are illustrated by an example. A scientist wishes to monitor the

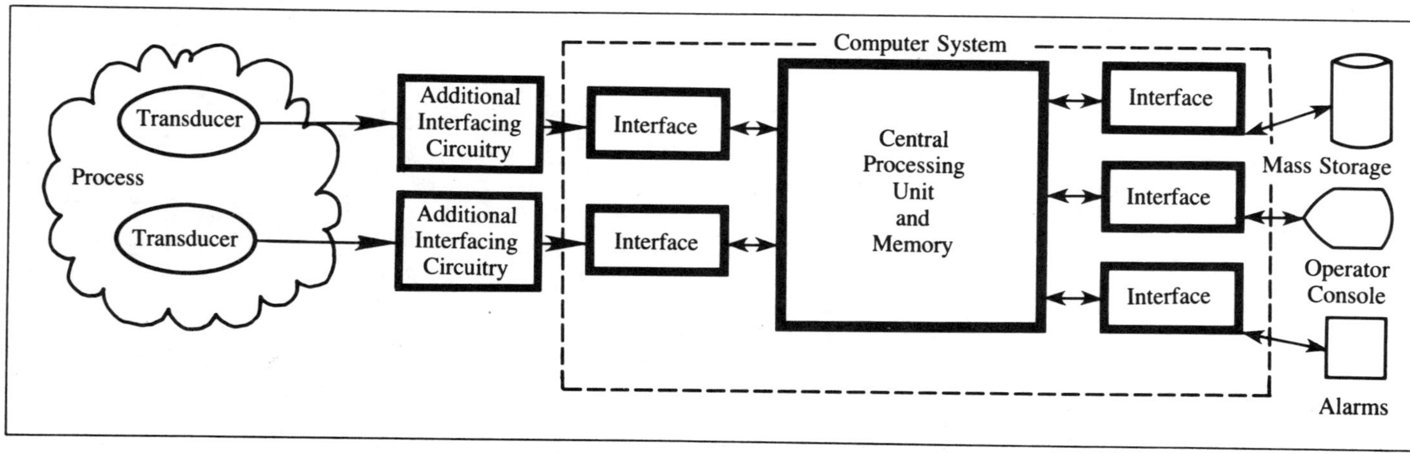

Figure 1.1. Block diagram of an automated data acquisition system.

temperature in five houses heated by solar energy. He wishes to record the temperature every ten minutes. Data are to be collected over a period of four months and then analyzed on a large computer system.

The scientist, being a university professor with a limited budget, decides to implement the project himself. He must decide which transducer to use to sense temperature. He must decide what computer hardware to use, and he must interface it to the transducer. A media must be chosen to store the data that will allow the data to be easily transferred to a large computer system for analysis. Software must be written or purchased to direct the hardware to perform the task of collecting temperature data. If the software is developed by the professor, development tools must be purchased. (A solution to this problem is given in Chapter 12.)

All of the decisions a system implementor makes relate to two goals. The first goal of any data collection system is that the system properly perform the task it was designed to do. The second goal is to minimize costs. Overrall costs are influenced by hardware costs, software costs, expected lifetime of the project for which the system is developed, flexibility of the equipment for use in other projects, and so forth.

System Planning

The task that a data acquisition system is designed to perform should be well specified. There is a tendency for both the user for whom a system is designed and the system implementor to develop a data acquisition system in steps. In this case, each step is analyzed and implemented without regard to later steps or with later steps only partially analyzed. Such an implementation technique tends to require longer development times than for projects where planning is well organized and thorough. When a system is planned in steps, implemented software usually has to be modified to incorporate functions needed by software developed in later steps. If planning is poor, it may be found that the computer hardware purchased is too limited to perform the required task.

If the system implementor and the user for whom the system is to be constructed are not the same individual, the system implementor must be persistent in making the system user describe in detail what he wishes the system to do. If the system implementor is also the end user, he must discipline himself to plan in detail.

There are, however, some research projects that do not lend themselves to full planning. In such cases, the system implementor should pay close attention to making the system software flexible and easily modifiable.

Care must be taken when a system designer who is not familiar with the physics of the process to be measured communicates with a scientist who is describing the process. If the scientist is not acquainted with instrumentation techniques, he may unknowingly mislead the system designer. Signals may be described as they might appear in a textbook without regard to electrical noise or signal components not important to the task at hand. If it is possible, the system designer should verify signal shape, frequency, and noise content with existing instrumentation before designing the measurement system.

Costs

The cost of a data acquisition system includes analysis and planning costs, computer hardware costs, hardware interfacing costs, software costs, and documentation costs. All but the cost of the most tangible items (the hardware components and the software development tools, e.g. programming languages) are easily underestimated. Software design and implementation, interfacing hardware, hardware and software maintenance, testing costs, and documentation costs are sometimes even overlooked. Even if these costs are estimated, allowances may not always be made for unforeseen circumstances such as the time needed by a software developer to diagnose a hardware problem during development.

The system planner must analyze, at least in part, the required functions of a system before he can even begin to estimate costs. A system planner can only accurately estimate costs after much experience.

There are some fallacies in estimating costs. The first of these is the fallacy of the $7.64 interface. An engineer once described how for $7.64 worth of hardware he created a computer interface that would perform a particular function. With great delight he described how it worked and how it could be modified by others to perform even greater tasks.

The fallacy of the $7.64 interface is that the designer did not explain that the cost of special purpose hardware, especially for a one-of-a-kind system, is much greater than the cost of the parts used to construct it. The time required by the implementor to design, build, test and document a circuit should be included in the cost. If the designer is not trained in hardware design, extensive training costs can be incurred. One chemist became aware of how deceiving computer hardware costs can be when he realized the microcomputer system he was troubleshooting cost 1/20 of the price of the test equipment he was using to debug it.

A second cost estimation fallacy is an over-reaction to the fallacy of the $7.64 interface. This fallacy comes from the belief that expensive, industrial grade, factory-assembled hardware devices are required to solve all interfacing problems. A designer afflicted with this belief will overlook those cost-saving design decisions where inexpensive hardware, applied with skilled hands and mind, are the best solution to a particular problem. For example, in many data acquisition projects, a minimal microcomputer configuration can perform the same function as a large minicomputer system that may cost 100 times as much. Although software development costs are usually more expensive on small systems, many problems are more appropriately solved with inexpensive hardware.

A third fallacy related to project cost estimation is that the cost of software development is relatively inexpensive. Because software is more intangible than hardware and because it can be duplicated for almost no cost, software development costs are greatly underestimated. In the area of data acquisition systems, the hardware required to solve a large number of problems costs less than the salary for one year of a single computer specialist writing data acquisition software.

2

Review of Basic Computer Principles

This chapter is a review of computer basics. It is assumed that the reader is already familiar with the digital computer and computer programming. The topics presented are a needed foundation for discussions in following chapters.

Data Representation

The typical stored program digital computer uses groups of binary digits, called bits, to represent data items. Each bit in the computer has a value of either zero or one. For many computers, the smallest unit of addressable storage is the byte. A byte is most typically defined as a data item of eight bits (see Figure 2.1). The bits in a byte are labeled

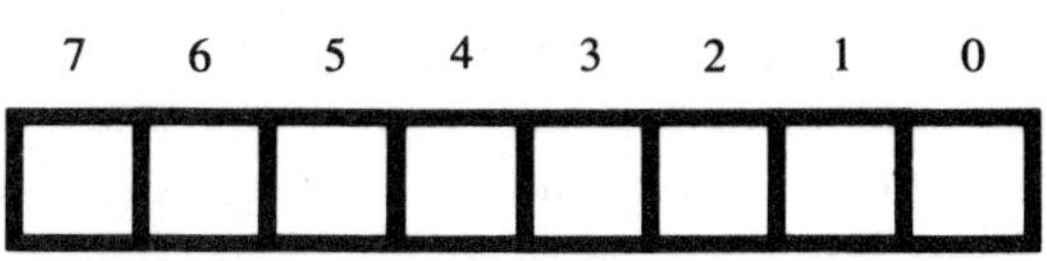

Figure 2.1. A schematic representation of a byte with individual bits labeled.

zero through seven. Bit zero is also called the low-order bit or the least significant bit (LSB). Bit seven is called the high-order bit or the most significant bit (MSB).

The complement of a bit value is the opposite binary state. The complement of a bit with the zero value is one, and the complement of a logic one is logic zero. The complement of a byte value is obtained by complementing each bit in the byte.

Since each bit can represent either a logic zero or a logic one, there are 256 different bit combinations in a byte. If the byte value is treated as an eight-bit binary value, its equivalent value in decimal can be computed as follows:

$$\sum_{i=0}^{7} b_i 2^i$$

where b_i is the value, zero or one, of bit i. Using this unsigned integer representation, a byte can contain the integer values between 0 and 255.

Two's complement notation is the most widely used scheme to represent signed integers in digital computers. The high-order bit is zero for positive numbers and one for negative numbers. Positive numbers in a byte format are represented using the low-order seven bits. The positive integers 0 to 127 can be represented.

Negative numbers are represented so that $i+(-i)=0$ using unsigned, modulo 2^n arithmetic where n is the number of bits in the representation (2^n is equal to 256 for an eight-bit representation). Mechanically, the representation of $-i$ can be found by taking the representation of $+i$, complementing it, and adding one with addition being performed as if the byte were treated as an unsigned quantity. A carry out of the high-order bit position is ignored. Figure 2.2 represents two's complement notation.

Note that the negative range is from -128 to -1. Because one of the positive representations is used for zero, $+128$ cannot be represented. It should also be noted that two's complement notation is widely used because an inexpensive, n-bit, unsigned adder performs signed arithmetic on two's complement quantities without additional hardware.

Some additional numeric representations are used in digital computers. The one's complement notation is similar to the two's complement notation except that the addition of one is not performed when negating a number. The negative of a number is obtained by complementing the bits in the representation of the number. (See Figure 2.3.)

$00000000_2 = 0_{10}$

$00000001_2 = 1_{10}$

$11111111_2 = -1_{10}$ $(00000001_2 + 11111111_2 = 00000000_2$ using unsigned, modulo 256 arithmetic)

$01111111_2 = 127_{10}$

$10000001_2 = -127_{10}$ $(10000001_2 + 01111111_2 = 00000000_2$ using unsigned, modulo 256 arithmetic)

Figure 2.2. Sample two's complement, eight-bit integers.

$00000000_2 = +0_{10}$

$11111111_2 = -0_{10}$

$00000001_2 = +1_{10}$

$11111110_2 = -1_{10}$

$01111111_2 = +127_{10}$

$10000000_2 = -127_{10}$

Figure 2.3. Sample one's complement, eight-bit integers.

Note that the range for one's complement representation using eight bits is -127 to $+127$. There is both a positive zero and a negative zero.

The signed magnitude representation of i and $-i$ is the same except that the high-order bit indicates the sign (zero for positive and one for negative). See Figure 2.4 and note the two representations for zero.

Excess notation is another method of representing signed integers. For a binary value represented with n bits, excess 2^{n-1} is typically used. For $n = 8$, excess 128 is common. To represent i in excess 128 notation, 128 is added to i using unsigned arithmetic to form the bit pattern to be associated with i. Figure 2.5 represents this notation.

All the notations discussed can be used with any number of bits.

$00000000_2 = +0_{10}$

$10000000_2 = -0_{10}$

$00000001_2 = +1_{10}$

$10000001_2 = -1_{10}$

$01111111_2 = +127_{10}$

$11111111_2 = -127_{10}$

Figure 2.4. Sample signed magnitude, eight-bit integers.

$10000000_2 = 0_{10}$

$10000001_2 = 1_{10}$

$01111111_2 = -1_{10}$

$11111111_2 = +127_{10}$

$00000000_2 = -128_{10}$

Figure 2.5 Sample excess 128 integers.

Most microcomputers perform arithmetic on eight-bit bytes and 16-bit words. Some 16-bit microprocessors also perform 32-bit arithmetic.

Another representation for integers, binary coded decimal (BCD), uses groups of four bits to encode the decimal digits zero to nine. The remaining six representations of this four-bit code are either not used or are used to represent an arithmetic sign. BCD digits may be packed into bytes by placing two digits in a byte. Figure 2.6 represents BCD notation.

Floating point representation is similar to scientific notation on a calculator. It is a notation for representating real numbers using a mantissa and an exponent. Figure 2.7 is a typical 32-bit floating point representation. The mantissa is a 24-bit value that is less than one. Its value is computed as follows:

$$\sum_{i=0}^{23} b_{23-i} 2^{-(i+1)}$$

$0000_2 = 0_{10}$

$0001_2 = 1_{10}$

$0010_2 = 2_{10}$

$0011_2 = 3_{10}$

$0100_2 = 4_{10}$

$0101_2 = 5_{10}$

$0110_2 = 6_{10}$

$0111_2 = 7_{10}$

$1000_2 = 8_{10}$

$1001_2 = 9_{10}$ (a)

$10010011_2 = 93_{10}$

(b)

Figure 2.6. BCD representation (a) and 93_{10} in packed BCD format (b).

This value is a binary fraction with the binary point directly to the left of bit 23. The bit value of bit 23 is weighted by 2^{-1}, that is, 1/2. Bit 22 is weighted by 2^{-2} (or 1/4) and so forth.

The seven bits of the exponent field are encoded in excess 64 notation. The sign bit is the sign of the mantissa in signed magnitude format.

The decimal equivalent of a floating point number in the given format can be computed as follows:

$$(-1)^S \cdot M \cdot 2^{-24} \cdot 16^{(E-64)}$$

where S is the value of the sign bit, M is the value of the mantissa treated as an unsigned integer, and E is the value of the exponent treated as an unsigned integer. A base of sixteen is used to expand the range covered by the representation. The range covered by the exponent is 16^{-64} to 16^{63} (approximately 10^{-76} to 10^{76}). Note that very small numbers with an exponent of 16^{-64} have a resolution of $2^{-24} \cdot 16^{-64}$

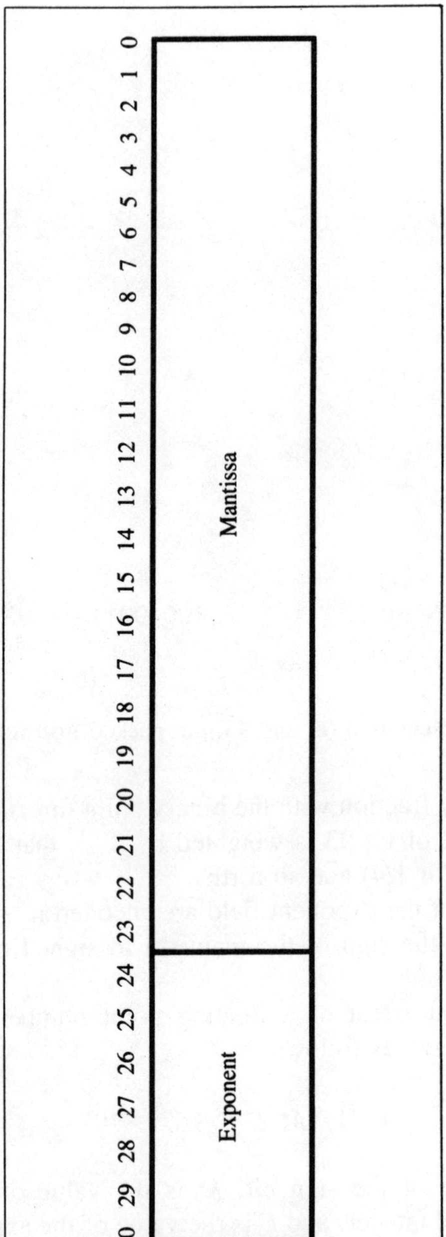

Figure 2.7. Typical 32-bit floating point representation.

1	1000000	100000000000000000000000	= −1/2
0	1000001	110010000000000000000000	= 12 1/2
0	1000000	110100000000000000000000	= 13/16
1	1000001	010100000000000000000000	= −5

Figure 2.8. Sample floating point numbers.

or 32^{-88}. Very large numbers with exponents of 16^{64} have a resolution of $2^{-24} \cdot 16^{63}$ or 32^{39}. The resolution refers to the difference between adjacent representable numbers. In other words, floating point representation allows good resolution around zero with diminishing resolution as the magnitude increases. Figure 2.8 shows some floating point examples.

Binary strings (groups of bits) can also be used to encode non-numeric data. Typically, single characters are stored in bytes, and character strings are stored in successive bytes. The byte allows 256 different characters to be defined. The seven-bit ASCII (American Standard Code for Information Interchange) code (Appendix A) is used with most small computers. The first 32 representations in the ASCII code set are control characters. These characters do not have a printable representation. The control characters include the carriage return and linefeed characters and characters used in electronic communications (see Chapter 11). The remaining 96 characters are printable characters.

Since the ASCII code set uses only seven bits, a second set of 128 special nonstandard graphics characters can be defined if an eight-bit byte is used to store characters. When ASCII characters are transmitted electronically, the eighth bit may be used as an error checking bit. In an even parity system, the number of logic one bits in each character is even. In an odd parity system, the number of logic one bits in each character is odd. (See Figure 2.9). The receiver of characters transmitted electronically in a parity system verifies that the character received has the proper number of logic one bits. If the character is not valid in

Character	7-bit ASCII	Decimal	Even parity	Odd parity
A	1000001	65	01000001	11000001
B	1000010	66	01000010	11000010
C	1000011	67	11000011	01000011

Figure 2.9. Even and odd parity examples using ASCII characters.

the parity system, the receiver knows that the character was modified, perhaps by noise, during transmission. It should be noted that if two or more bits are modified by noise, the parity scheme may not detect the error.

Digital Computer Organization

Figure 2.10 shows the parts of a digital computer. The divisions are conceptual in nature. A single microcomputer integrated circuit may contain elements of each part. In a large minicomputer, the divisions may be more distinct.

Primary Memory

Primary memory is used to store data and instructions. Data are numeric and non-numeric values encoded as binary strings. Instructions are encoded actions that the computer is to perform. A set of instructions makes up a computer program.

When a binary string is written in a memory cell, this value, called the contents of the cell, is retained until the computer writes a new value in the cell. Writing a new value in a cell forever destroys the old value. The computer can read the cell contents without altering the contents.

The memory unit is made up of addressable cells of *n* bits each. In microcomputer systems, eight-bit bytes are typically the smallest addressable units. Figure 2.11 shows the most common addressing technique.

The primary memory cells may be accessed in any order by supplying the address of the cell to be accessed. The time required to access a cell is not dependant upon the order in which cells are accessed (as was the case in some early forms of primary memory that were rotational magnetic devices). This type of primary memory is called a random access memory (RAM).

A form of RAM is the read-only memory (ROM) in which data or instructions are written into memory using a special process. Normally, the memory contents can be read by the computer, but the contents cannot be altered by the computer. The current usage of the terms RAM and ROM, although not exactly correct, are used in this and following chapters. RAM refers to primary memory that can be read or written by the computer. ROM refers to memory that can only be read by the computer.

Memory elements can be classified as to their behavior when power is removed from the computer system. Volatile memory does not

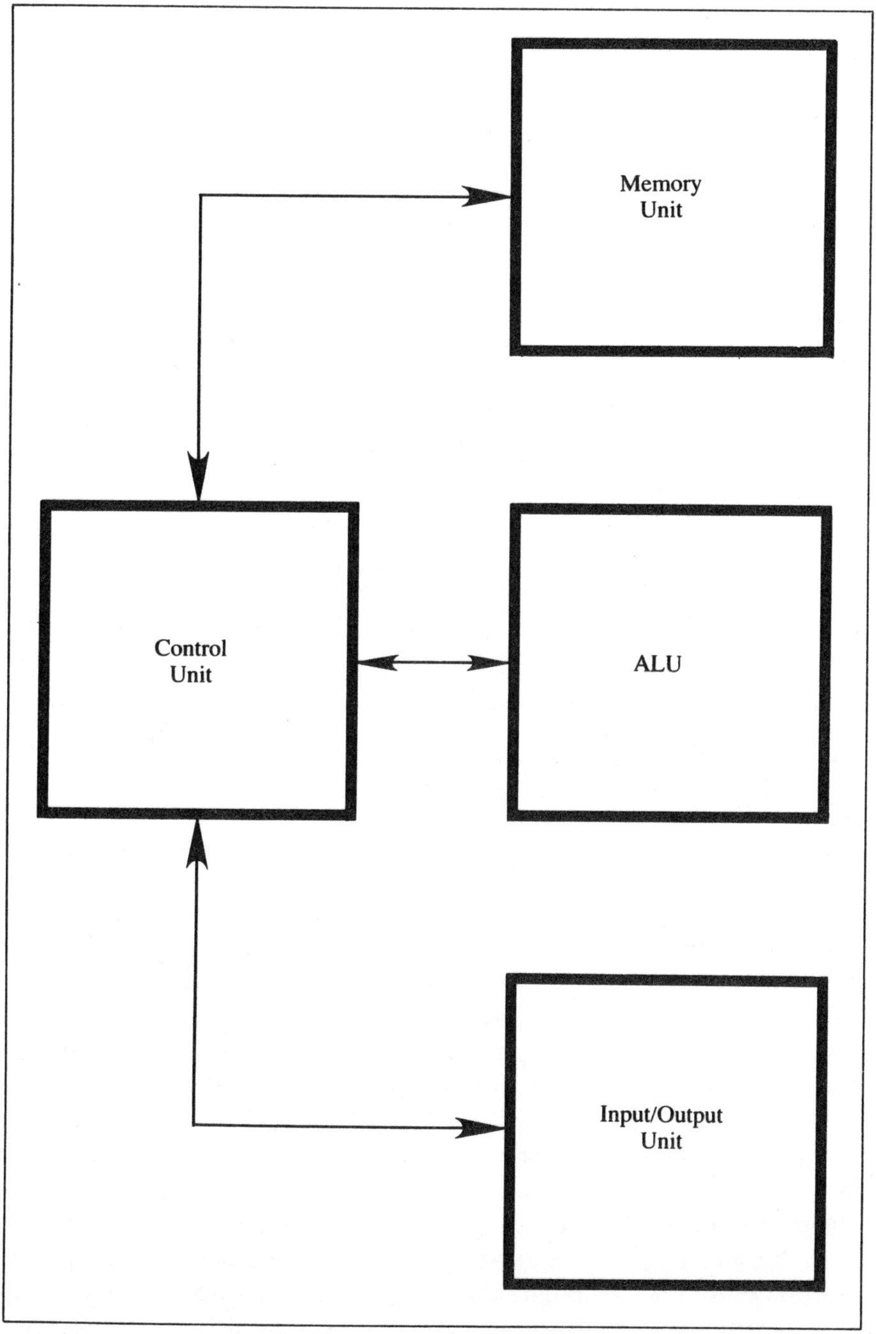

Figure 2.10. Conceptual parts of a computer.

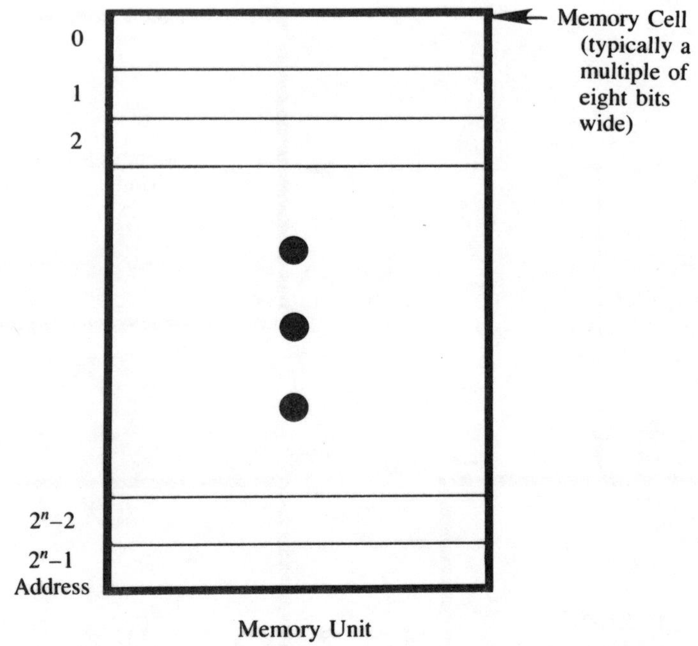

Figure 2.11. A typical memory addressing technique where an n-bit address is used to access 2^n memory cells.

retain its contents when power is removed from the system; however, nonvolatile memory does retain its contents. ROM is nonvolatile. Most RAM integrated circuits are volatile. Low power RAM circuits can be made nonvolatile using a battery to power them during periods when power is removed from the system in which they reside.

ROM is typically used to store the only program in a small dedicated system or to store a loader program in a larger system where the loader can be used to copy a program from some external source into RAM for execution.

Standard ROM's are either manufactured with the memory contents in place or can be programmed in the field once. Erasable programmable read-only memories (EPROM) can be programmed a number of times by a computer using a special programming circuit. The EPROM must be erased before programming by subjecting it to ultraviolet light of a specific wavelength and intensity for a certain period of time (typically ten minutes). The computer can then program the EPROM. The programming operation requires a much longer access time than is normal for accessing memory. After programming, the circuit retains its contents until erased.

Electrically alterable read-only memories (EAROM) and electrically erasable read-only memories (EEROM) are nonvolatile memory circuits that behave as ROM's except that they can be placed in a special mode where the contents can be erased and reprogrammed. Unlike EPROM's, there is no need to remove the EAROM from the computer and erase it with ultraviolet light before reprogramming it. Some chips allow all or part of the contents to be erased electrically. The write operation of an EAROM is much slower than for a standard RAM. The EAROM is best used in situations where a nonvolatile memory is needed that requires its contents changed infrequently.

Arithmetic and Logic Unit

The arithmetic and logic unit (ALU) is the part of the computer that manipulates data values. It performs arithmetic (e.g. addition) and logical (e.g. the logic AND) functions. It can also compare two data elements.

As part of the ALU, there are typically several registers. A register is a high-speed storage device one or more bytes wide. The registers are used to hold temporary data values and primary memory addresses during the execution of a program.

Input/Output Unit

The input/output (I/O) unit is the part of the computer where external devices are connected to the computer. The I/O unit contains a set of interfaces, circuits used to connect external devices to the computer.

A computer may be connected to a terminal for communication with an operator. Both printing (or hardcopy) and cathode ray tube (CRT) terminals are typical. A computer may also be connected to one or more mass storage devices. Mass storage devices are typically rotational magnetic devices used to store large amounts of data or programs in a nonvolatile manner. These units use magnetic tape or a magnetic disk to store information. The capacity of a mass storage device typically greatly exceeds the capacity of primary memory. Programs and data can be stored on a mass storage device until needed and then read from the magnetic media into primary memory. Data and new programs can be stored on the mass storage device by the computer.

In laboratory applications, interfaces are needed to connect the computer to devices and instruments used to read the parameters of some physical system. The types of interfaces typically used is the topic of Chapter 5. Storage devices are discussed in Chapter 8.

Control Unit

The control unit consists of the circuits needed to read instructions from primary memory and to execute them. Executing an instruction may require that data elements be read from primary memory, may require that the ALU or I/O unit perform some action, and may require that data be written into a memory unit cell.

Typically, a computer executes instructions from memory in a sequential manner. A program counter register (PC) contains the primary memory address of the next instruction in memory to be executed. If the instruction is not a sequence modifying instruction (a branch), the PC is incremented by the length of the instruction during its execution so that the PC contains the address of the next sequential instruction. If the instruction is a branch instruction, it causes a new value to be placed in

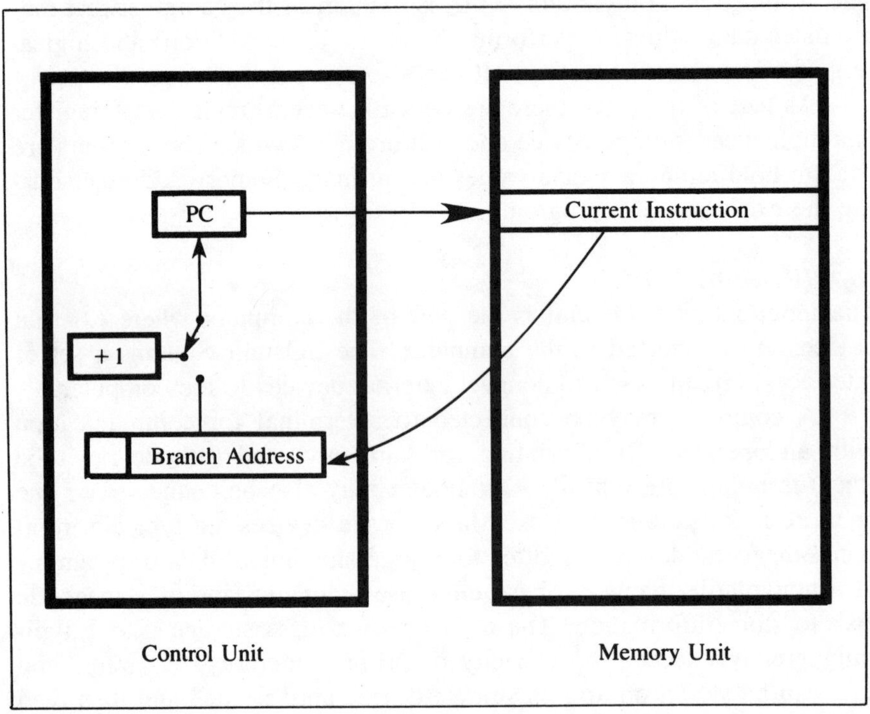

Figure 2.12. PC address sequencing. The address in memory of the current instruction is held in the PC. The instruction is placed in a temporary register in the control unit where it is executed. If the instruction does not cause a branch, the PC is incremented by the length of the instruction (one in the example). If a branch is performed, the branch address part of the instruction is placed in the PC.

the PC. A conditional branch is an instruction that tests some condition and branches if the condition is true. If the tested condition is not true, normal sequential instruction execution occurs by incrementing the PC. Figure 2.12 illustrates instruction sequencing.

Conditional branches test conditions related to the state of the computer. These conditions include ALU flags (single bit status indicators) that indicate characteristics about the last ALU result, such as "result equal to zero". The ALU flags and other status flags are typically kept in a processor status word register (PSW) in the control unit.

A special type of branch instruction is used to invoke a subroutine. This subroutine call instruction saves the current updated PC value (address of the instruction following the subroutine call instruction, called the return address) and performs a branch to the subroutine. The subroutine is a program that performs some function and then executes a subroutine return instruction that places the saved PC value back in the PC (see Figure 2.13).

A stack is typically used to save the return address. Figure 2.14 shows a typical implementation of a stack. A stack pointer (SP) register

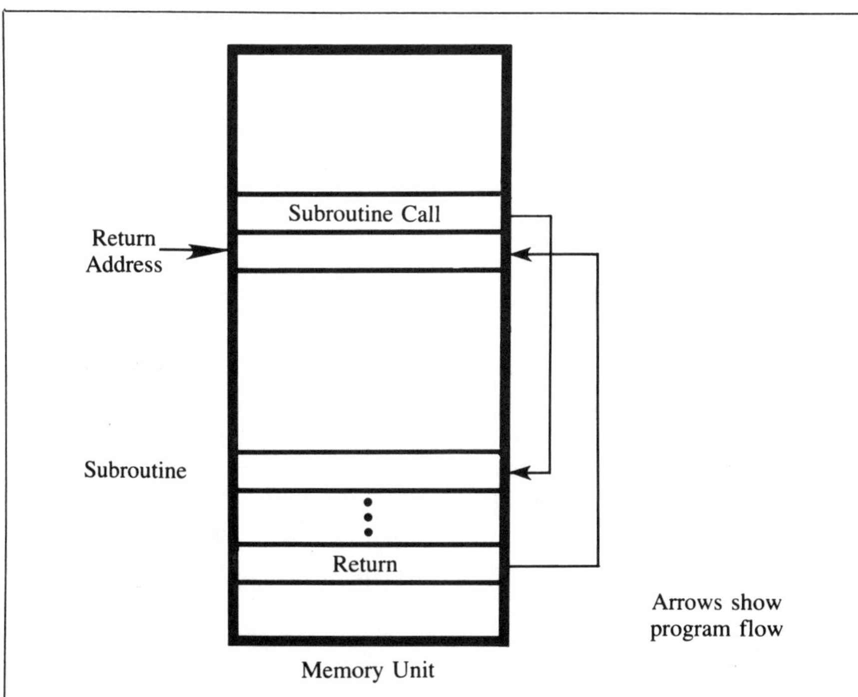

Figure 2.13. Subroutine call example.

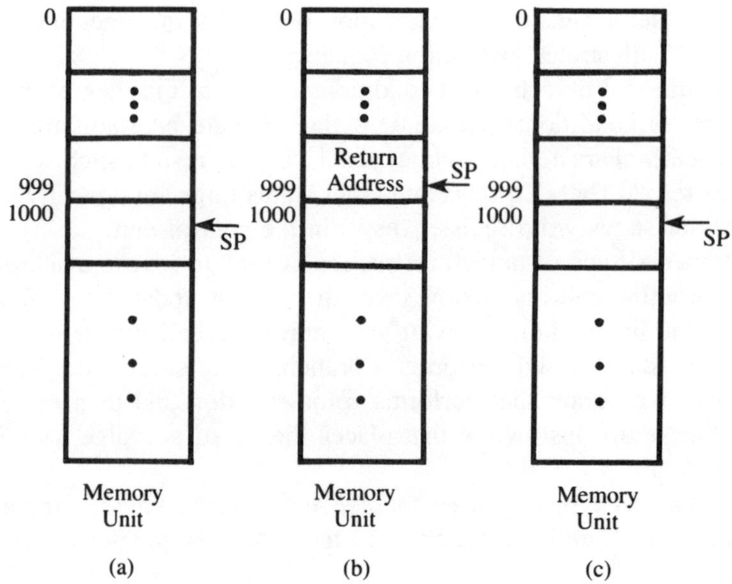

Figure 2.14. Stack usage during a subroutine call. Before the call, the SP points to location 1000 (a). When the call is executed, the return address is placed on the stack (b). When the return from subroutine instruction is executed, the return address is removed from the stack (c).

has the memory address of the top stack element. A subroutine return address is pushed onto the stack by decrementing the SP and writing the return address at the memory location whose address is contained in the SP. A subroutine return instruction is performed by popping the stack into the PC. This operation is performed by reading the memory cell whose address is in the SP and placing the memory cell contents in the PC. The SP is then incremented to remove the return address from the stack. Several levels of subroutine calls can be made using the stack. The stack can also be used to store temporary data. The stack always makes available the most recent value pushed onto it.

Pointers

Assume that a data value is pushed onto the stack. The SP does not contain the data item, but it does contain the address in primary memory of

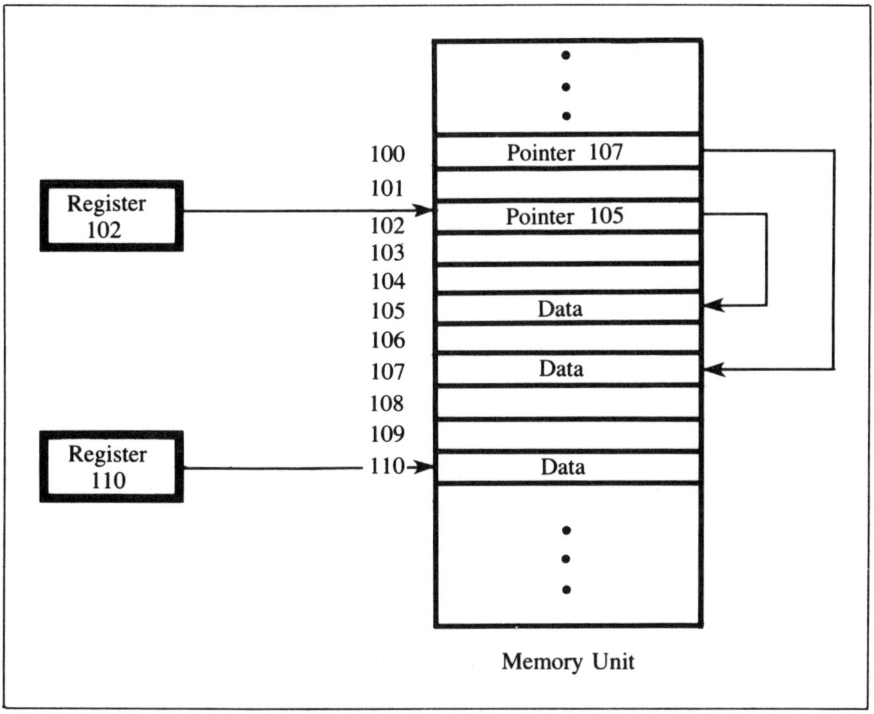

Figure 2.15. Registers and memory locations used as pointers.

the data value. It is said that the SP is a pointer to the data item because the contents of the SP locates the data value in memory. Memory locations can also be used as pointers. Such a memory location contains the address of another cell in memory where the data element of interest is stored. See Figure 2.15.

I/O Techniques

Data is transferred between an I/O device and the computer. Depending on the device and how it is used, an area of memory may be used to hold data to be transferred to the device. Data transferred to the computer may be placed in an area of memory before it is processed. In both cases, the memory area is referred to as a buffer.

A bus is a communications path in a computer. Typically, a number of data sources (suppliers of data) and a number of data sinks (receivers of data) are connected to a bus. A data transfer operation can occur on each bus cycle. During each cycle that data is transferred on the

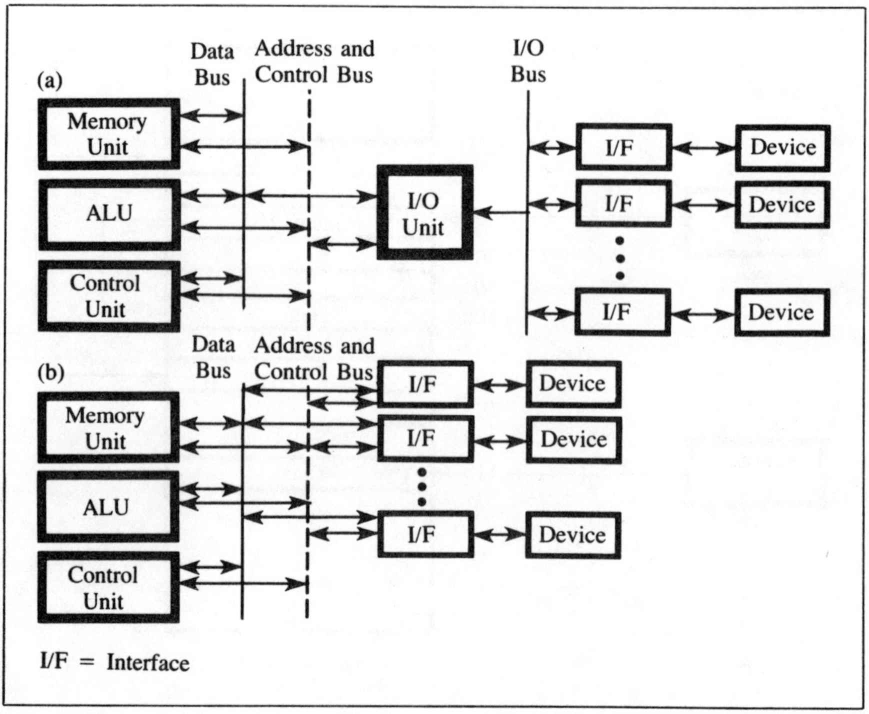

Figure 2.16. Dedicated I/O bus (a) and memory-mapped I/O (b) systems.

bus, one data source and one or more data sinks are involved in the transfer. On another bus cycle, a different data source and sinks may be involved in a data transfer. In many cases, a data source during one transaction may be a data sink on another transaction.

Figure 2.16 shows two common bus implementations. In 2.16a, I/O interfaces are connected to a dedicated I/O bus. When I/O instructions are executed, the control unit directs the I/O unit to control a device (e.g. start some I/O operation) or to transfer data between an I/O device interface and the data bus via the I/O bus and I/O control circuits.

In 2.16b, the I/O devices and memory unit are addressed in the same address space. I/O devices connected in this fashion are said to be memory-mapped.

Figure 2.17 shows a typical memory-mapped I/O addressing technique. The memory unit responds to addresses in a certain range while I/O devices respond to addresses in another range. Due to the relatively small number of I/O devices in a computer, many addresses in the I/O portion of the address space are not used.

Figure 2.17. A typical minicomputer memory-mapped I/O addressing scheme with a 4K I/O address space.

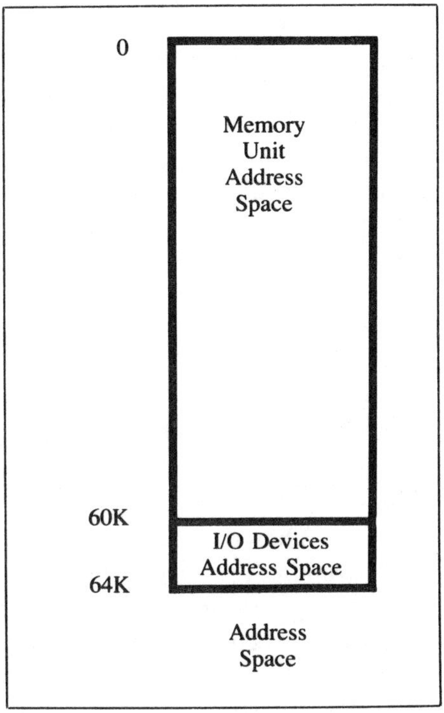

Each device interface must respond when it is addressed. There are typically no I/O instructions in a memory-mapped system. The same instructions used to access memory locations are used to access devices. A device interface appears as one or more memory locations to the program accessing it. Each of these memory locations is a device register. Writing data to one device register may perform control functions, while reading or writing data to another device register may cause data to be transferred between the interface and the computer.

Regardless of the I/O system used to implement a computer, the techniques used to write I/O software are similar.

I/O operations are typically slower than the instruction rate of the computer. The computer program directs an I/O device to perform some operation. The computer is then free to execute other instructions until the I/O operation is complete. During the time the I/O device is active, the computer must not attempt to give it data or instructions to perform another operation. The computer, therefore, must be able to determine when an I/O operation is complete.

There are two methods of synchronizing the computer and an I/O device. The simpler method is called status checking or polling. The computer executes an instruction to determine if the operation is complete. In a dedicated I/O bus system, this instruction would typically be a conditional branch instruction specifying the I/O device to be tested. In a memory-mapped system, status flags in an I/O device register would be tested using the same instructions used to determine the status of individual bits in a memory location.

If the device is busy when tested, the software performs some other instructions not associated with the I/O device and later checks the state of the device again, or the software remains in a loop that continuously checks the device until it is no longer busy. The latter method is called a busy wait loop.

A second method for synchronizing a program to the operation of an I/O device is the interrupt. Figure 2.18 diagrams interrupt operation. The program starts an I/O device operation and continues performing some task. When the I/O device completes its function, it requests an interrupt. When the control unit is in a state to respond to interrupts and an interrupt is requested, an interrupt acknowledgement sequence occurs. During this sequence, it is determined which device will be serviced. The execution of the program currently executing is suspended,

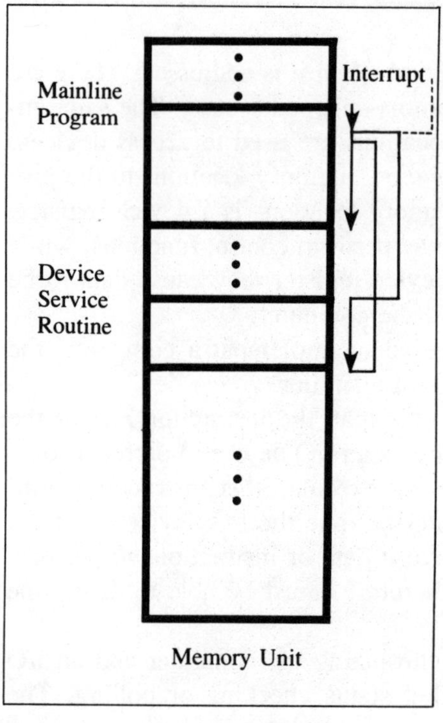

Figure 2.18. Flow of control showing interrupt processing.

and the service routine for the interrupting device is given control. The service routine is a program that performs functions related to the I/O device. In most cases, when the service routine completes, it will resume execution of the suspended program.

During the interrupt acknowledgement sequence, several operations are performed by hardware and software, depending on the design of the machine. The address of the next instruction to be executed in the suspended program is saved. The contents of any registers that will be modified by the interrupt routine are saved. Either during the interrupt acknowledgement sequence or by code in the service routine, the condition causing the interrupt to be requested is cleared (i.e. the computer responds only once to any I/O event). On exit from the service routine, the saved registers are restored, and a branch is made to the next instruction in the suspended program.

The interrupt service routine saves the state of any registers it modifies including the PSW so that the state of the system when the suspended program was interrupted can be restored. This requirement is necessary to allow the suspended code to execute properly. Certain memory locations are accessible by both the mainline code and the service routine for communications. In a small, dedicated system, some registers may be shared between the mainline code and an interrupt service routine for communications. In this case, the values in the shared registers are not saved and restored by the service routine.

The use of status checking, interrupts, and service routine and mainline code communications are discussed in Chapter 6.

Direct Memory Access

Direct memory access (DMA) is a technique whereby I/O data transfer operations can be performed without intervention of the processor. A DMA transfer is initiated by a program by accessing the DMA unit as an I/O device. The DMA device is given the parameters of the transfer including the direction of the transfer (into memory from a device or out of memory to a device), the number of bytes to be transferred, and the memory address of the data buffer. The processor then performs other tasks while the DMA interface performs the transfer.

Each time the DMA interface must access memory, either to retrieve a byte to transfer to the device or to place a byte from the device into memory, it requests access to the memory unit. When the memory unit is available (i.e., the DMA interface will not interfere with a memory access in progress), the DMA unit is given access to the memory unit, and the processor must wait until the DMA memory access is complete before it can use the memory unit.

Normally the processor is faster than the I/O device connected to the DMA unit. In this case, the DMA interface only accesses memory (and thus delays the program being executed) at a rate that is much slower than typical processor accesses. Alternatively, special DMA processors connected to intelligent devices may operate in burst mode where the processor is suspended from execution during an entire data transfer. In either case, the DMA operation is transparent to the program being executed although the execution time of the program is slower than if a DMA transfer were not in operation. Completion of a DMA transfer is determined by the processor either by status checking or by an interrupt.

3

Introduction to Data Acquisition Electronics

Individuals implementing a data acquisition system must be knowledgeable in the field of electronics. Even if interfacing is to be done by a specialist, system designers must be able to communicate with hardware specialists to specify transducers, interfaces, and related hardware.

The material presented here is an overview for the system designer. More in-depth information can be found by consulting texts cited in the bibliography.

Basic Electronics

According to modern physics, electricity is the movement of charged particles. The unit of charge is the coulomb. The charge of one electron is 1.602×10^{-19} coulombs.

Electrostatic potential is the measurement of the work required to move a coulomb charge from infinity (zero potential) to a point in space against the electric field at the point. The measure of potential is the volt. One volt is equivalent to one joule/coulomb. (One joule is the work done when a one newton force is required to move a mass one meter. A newton is the force required to accelerate a one kilogram mass at a rate of one meter per second squared.) Electrostatic potential difference is a measure of the work required to move a unit charge from one point in an electric field to another. The unit of potential difference is the volt.

A source of electromagnetic force (EMF) such as a battery creates an electrical potential. It has the ability to move charged particles through a conductor. In electric circuits, voltage is measured in terms of the potential difference between a point of interest and some reference point defined to be at zero potential. The zero reference point is called the circuit ground. Because the earth is often used as this reference point, the term *ground* is used; however, the ground of a given circuit may be at a different potential than some point on the earth.

Electric current is defined as the amount of charge moving past a point in a circuit over a given time. Electrons flow from a point of lower potential to a point of higher potential; however, by convention, current is said to flow from the higher potential to the lower potential. The unit of current is the ampere. One ampere is one coulomb/second.

The measure of a material's performance as a conductor is electrical resistance. Good conductors (e.g. gold, silver, copper) have low resistances. Poor conductors (e.g. glass, mica) have high resistances. Resistance is measured in ohms. A conductor with a resistance of one ohm will allow one ampere to flow between a potential difference of one volt.

Figure 3.1a is a graph of several direct current (DC) signals. The voltage polarity of a DC signal is constant over time. (The output of a battery is a DC signal.) Figure 3.1b illustrates three alternating current (AC) signals. The voltage value of an AC signal varies with time. The polarity of the AC signal changes periodically. The signal may be repetitive as in the figure, but this repetition is not required. In describing AC signals, the frequency, amplitude, and waveform are of interest.

The potential of an AC signal can be expressed in terms of its peak amplitude or its root-mean-squared (RMS) value. The RMS value of a sinusoidal wave is the peak amplitude of the signal divided by the square root of 2. The RMS value relates to the effectiveness of an AC signal. An AC signal of one volt RMS delivers the same power as one volt DC. The RMS value of waveforms other than the sine wave may be difficult to compute. As an example of an AC signal, 120-volt AC power has a peak amplitude of approximately 170 volts. It is a sinusoidal wave with a

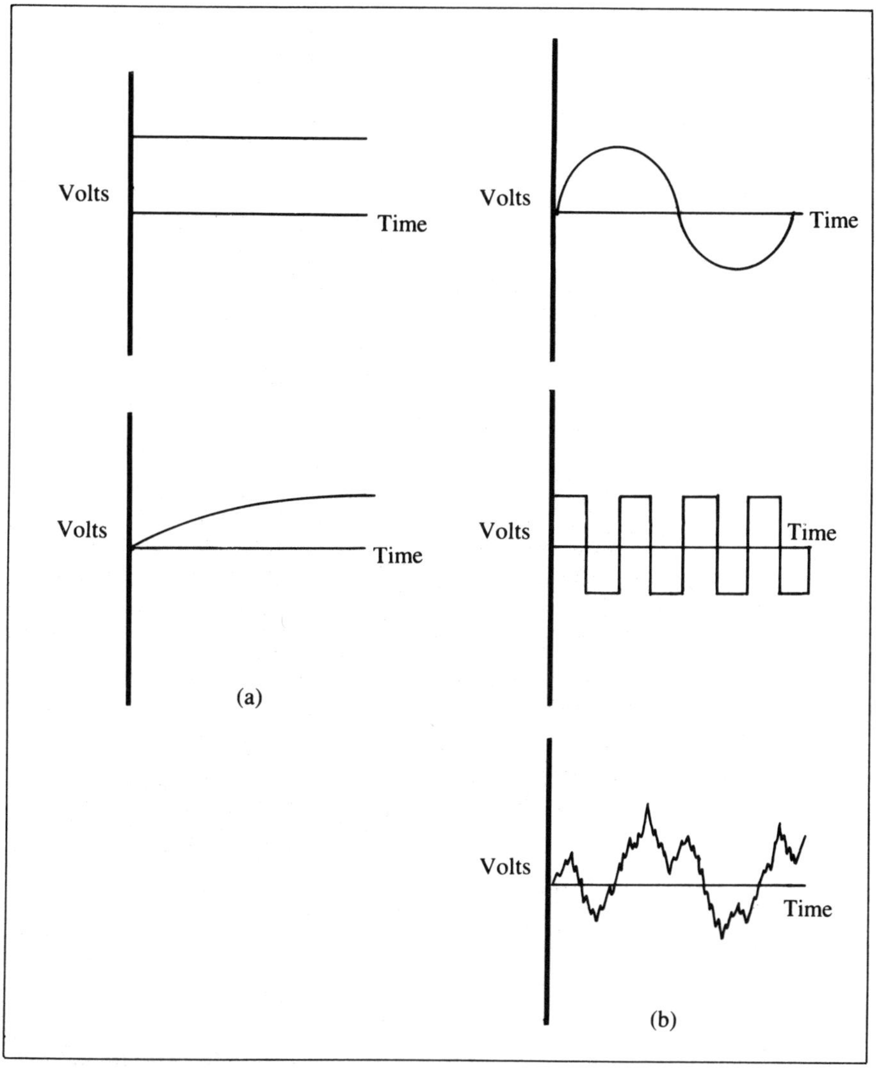

Figure 3.1. Example DC signals (a) and AC signals (b).

frequency (in the U.S.A.) of 60 Hertz (Hz.) (One Hz. is one cycle/second).

Ohm's law, a relationship between voltage, current, and resistance for a DC circuit, is given by

$$E = IR$$

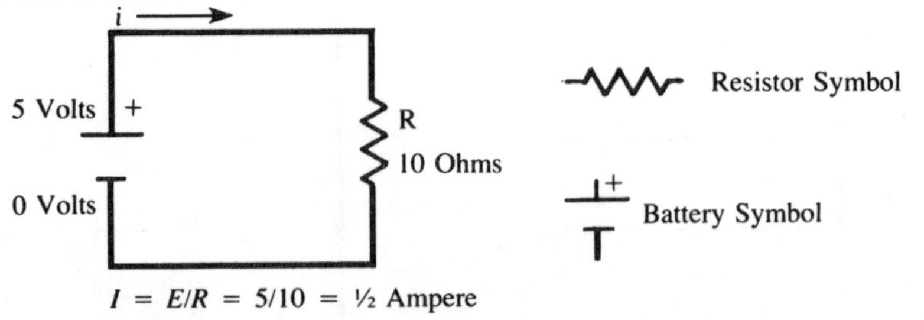

Figure 3.2. Simple DC circuit illustrating Ohm's law.

where E is voltage, I is current, and R is resistance. Figure 3.2 illustrates this relationship.

Power is the rate of doing work and is expressed in watts. Power, P, is defined by $P = IE$. Using Ohm's Law and algebraic manipulation, power can be expressed as E^2/R or I^2R.

Resistances in series are additive. Resistances in parallel follow a reciprocal relationship. See Figure 3.3.

Kirchoff's two laws are used to analyze complex resistor networks in which current flows. The first states that the sum of potential rises and drops in a loop equals zero. Potential rises are created by batteries, power supplies, and some transducers. Voltage drops occur across resistors in which current flows.

Figure 3.4 illustrates the law. The current flow in the loop is computed using Ohm's law to be 0.001 amps. Also by Ohm's law, a potential difference of 3 volts is required for a current of 0.001 amps to flow in a 3K resistor. A potential difference of 2 volts is required to produce a current flow of 0.001 amps through a 2K resistor. The sum of the voltage drops around the loop is equal to the rise produced by the battery.

The second law states that the sum of the currents flowing into a node is equal to the sum of the currents leaving the node. Figure 3.5 illustrates the current law. Note that the current flowing into point A, $I1$, is equal to the sum of the currents flowing out of the point, $I2 + I3$.

The Kirchoff laws are useful for understanding circuits and for computing unknown values of voltage, current, or resistance in complex circuits.

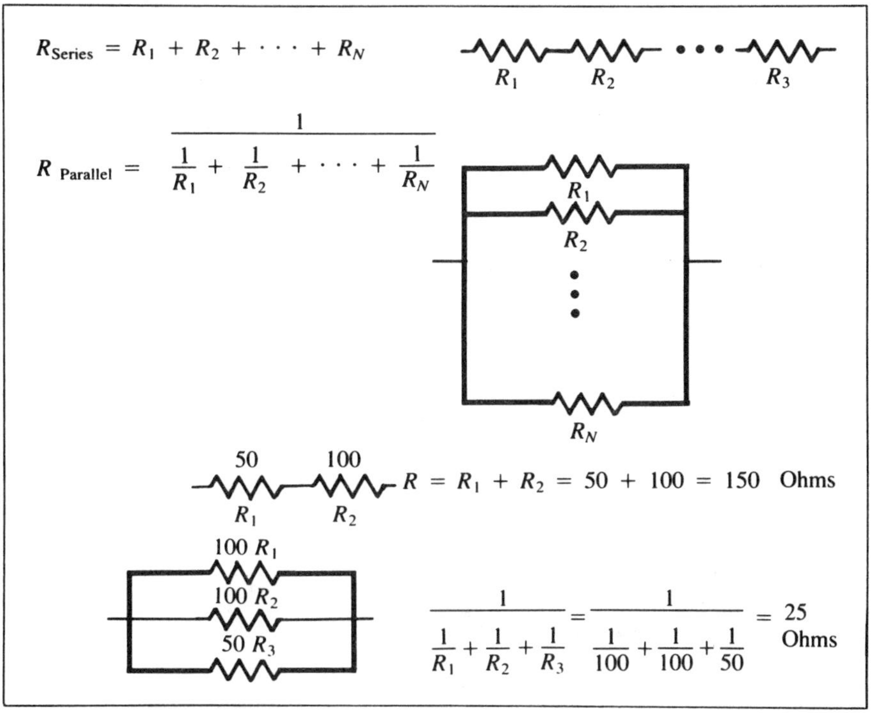

Figure 3.3. Series and parallel resistance computation.

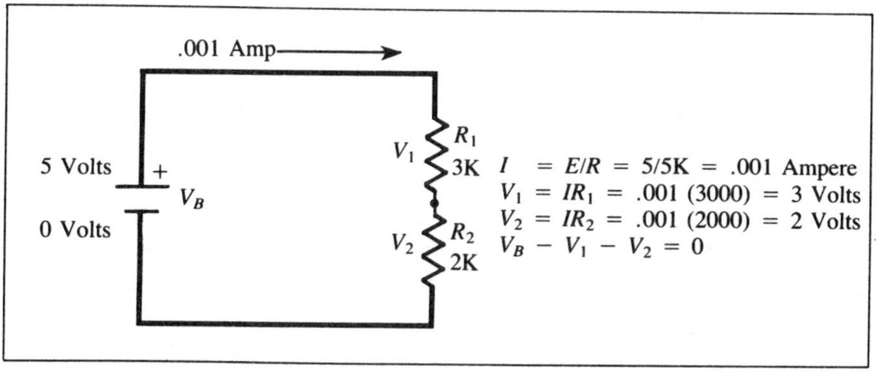

Figure 3.4. Kirchoff's voltage loop law example.

Phase Relationships

It is sometimes necessary to refer to the relationship of two AC signals in time. If the same part of both cycles occurs at the same time, the signals are said to be in phase. If the same part of both cycles occurs at a

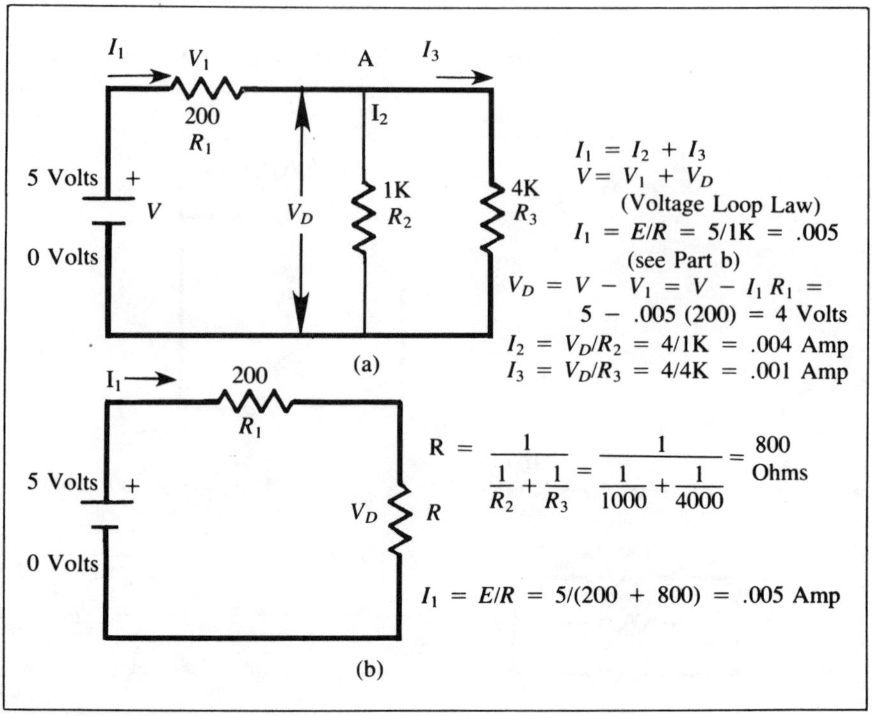

Figure 3.5. Example of Kirchoff's current node law (a) and simplification of the circuit to find I_1 (b).

different time, the signals are out of phase. The phase difference may be specified as an angle or as a time delay. Figure 3.6 illustrates phase relationships.

It is common to discuss the phase relationship between the voltage and current of an AC signal. When an AC signal is applied to a purely resistive load, the current and voltage are in phase. When an AC signal is applied to a capacitor or a coil (see following sections), the current and voltage in the circuit are out of phase.

It may also be useful to discuss the phase relationship between two signals (e.g. voltages from two different transducers). The phase relationship of two signals may be altered by the data collection process and by signal conditioning circuitry. In some cases, the phase relationship between the signals must be preserved to allow meaningful data to be extracted from the collected data.

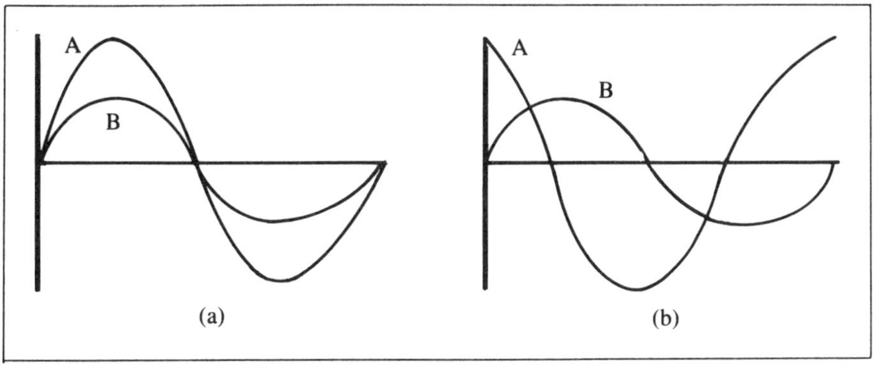

Figure 3.6. Signals A and B in phase (a) and A and B out of phase with A leading B by 90° (b).

Capacitors and Inductors

A capacitor is a device that can store energy in an electric field. It is constructed of two conductive plates separated by an insulator (high resistance material). Capacitance, which is measured in farads, is a measure of how much charge can be stored in a capacitor per volt of potential difference across the plates. Standard capacitors are rated in microfarads (10^{-6} farads) and picofarads (10^{-12} farads).

Figure 3.7a illustrates what occurs when a DC voltage is applied to a discharaged capacitor. When the voltage is initially applied, the capacitor appears as a low resistance, and the current flow is determined by the DC voltage value and the resistance of the circuit. As the plates of the capacitor are charged, the current flow decreases. The capacitor becomes 63.2% charged in one time constant (RC). Once the capacitor is charged, the charge is retained. If the DC voltage is removed, the capacitor will eventually lose its charge because the insulating material used in the construction of the capacitor is not a perfect insulator.

If a resistor is connected across the plates of a charged capacitor, the capacitor discharges. The capacitor looses 63.2% of its charge in one time constant. The voltage and current equations for a discharging capacitor are given in Figure 3.7b.

If an AC signal is applied to a capacitor, the capacitor behaves much as a resistor to a DC signal; however, the phase of the AC signal is altered by the capacitor. Resistance to an AC signal by a capacitor is called capacitance reactance and is measured in ohms. The reactance of a capacitor is a function of the frequency of the applied signal and the value of the capacitor. Due to the capacitor behavior, it can be used to

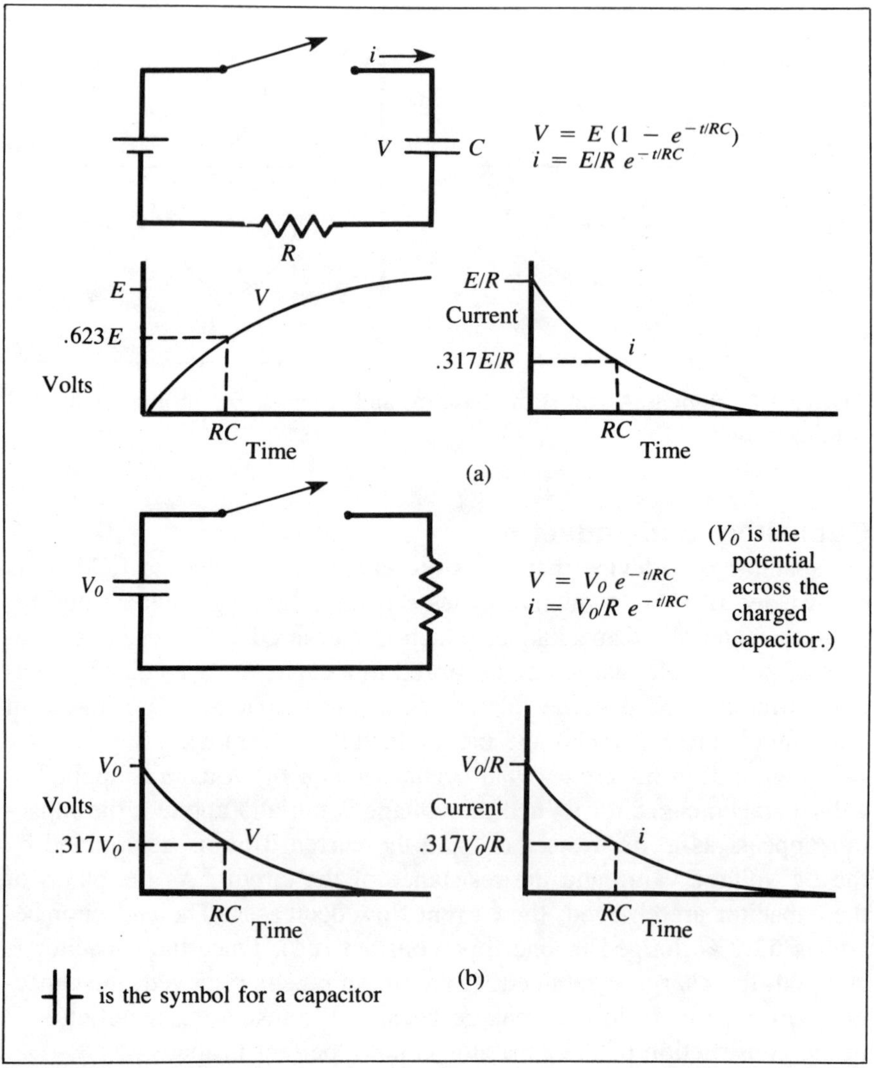

Figure 3.7. Capacitor charging characteristics (a) and capacitor discharging characteristics (b).

block DC signals while passing AC signals. Capacitance reactance can be determined by the following relationship (f is frequency; C is capacitance):

$$x_C = \frac{1}{2\pi f C}$$

An inductor, a coil of wire, stores energy in a magnetic field. The measure of inductance, the *henry*, is related to the amount of energy that can be stored in the coil's magnetic field. A henry is the inductance required to produce one volt of EMF when the inducing current changes at one ampere per second. Standard inductors are rated in henrys and millihenrys. Behavior of inductors when a DC signal is applied is illustrated in Figure 3.8. The inductor opposes a change in the current flow through it as is illustrated by the graph in the figure. When the DC signal is removed from the inductor, the magnetic field created by the inductor collapses, creating an EMF of reversed polarity across the coil. The duration of this "back EMF" is very short as illustrated by the formula in the figure.

The inductor displays inductive reactance to an AC signal. The reactance of an inductor is a function of the inductance and the frequency of the signal applied. Inductance reactance, X_L, is given by the following equation (f is frequency; L is inductance):

$$X_L = 2\pi fL$$

An inductor causes a phase shift in an AC signal applied to it.

Impedance is the combined effect of resistance and reactance. Impedance, Z, is the square root of the expression $R^2 + X_L{}^2 - X_C{}^2$.

Amplifiers

There are many active devices that can be made to amplify a signal. Commonly, amplifiers in data acquisition systems are constructed from discrete solid state devices (e.g. transistors) or integrated circuits. For this discussion, amplifiers will be treated without regard to their construction.

Figure 3.9 illustrates the diagram for an amplifier. The ability of an amplifier to boost a signal is its *gain*, the ratio of the input voltage or current to the output voltage or current (V_o/V_i or I_o/I_i). Gain is normally expressed in decibels (dB). The gain of an amplifier expressed in decibels is 20 log V_o/V_i or 20 log I_o/I_i. (The decibel is related to loudness as perceived by the human ear. The smallest change in loudness detectable by the ear is approximately one decibel.)

Amplifier gain begins to decrease at some frequency. Above this cutoff frequency, the decrease in gain can be expressed in dB/octave (the decrease in gain if the frequency is doubled).

The amplifier in the figure is single-ended (one signal input). The

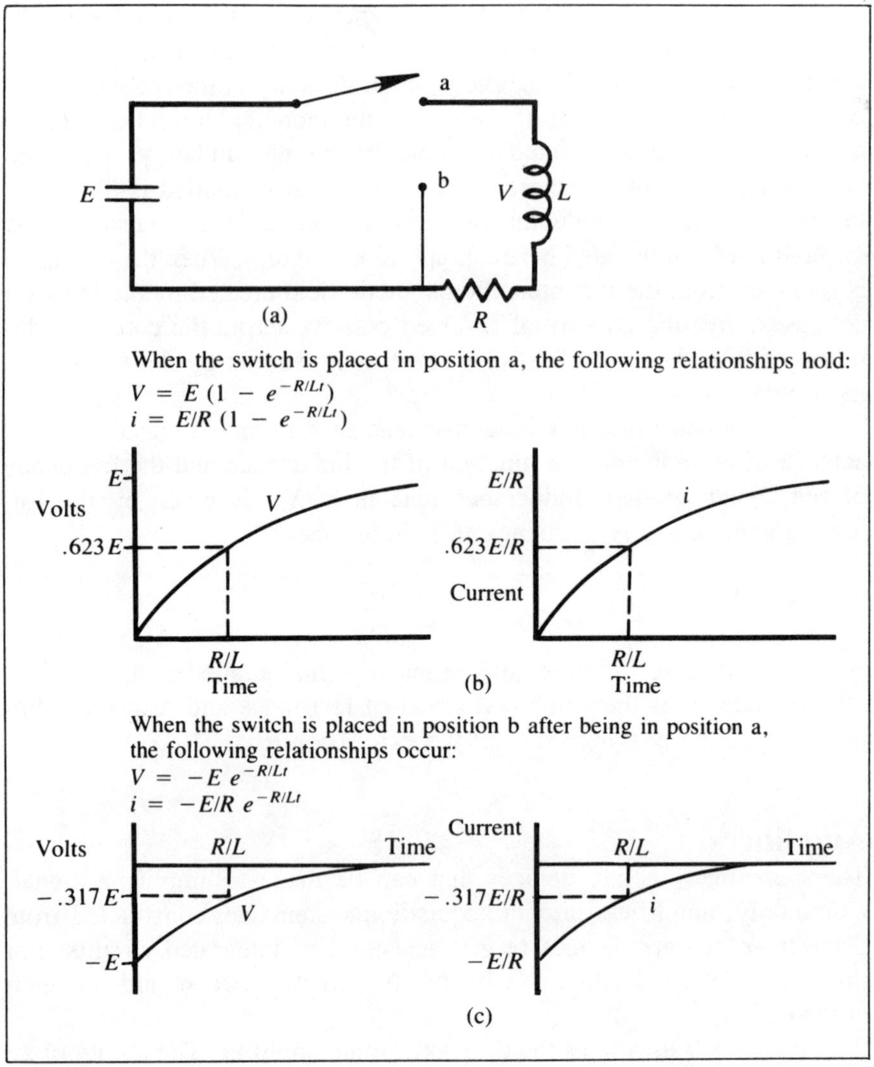

Figure 3.8. Inductor characteristics. The schematic in (a) allows current to be applied to the inductor when the switch is in position "a." Part (b) shows the circuit behavior when the switch is placed in the "a" position. When the switch is moved to the "b" position, the magnetic field decays, and a "back emf" (opposite polarity of the applied voltage) is induced in the circuit (c). The magnetic field decays rapidly.

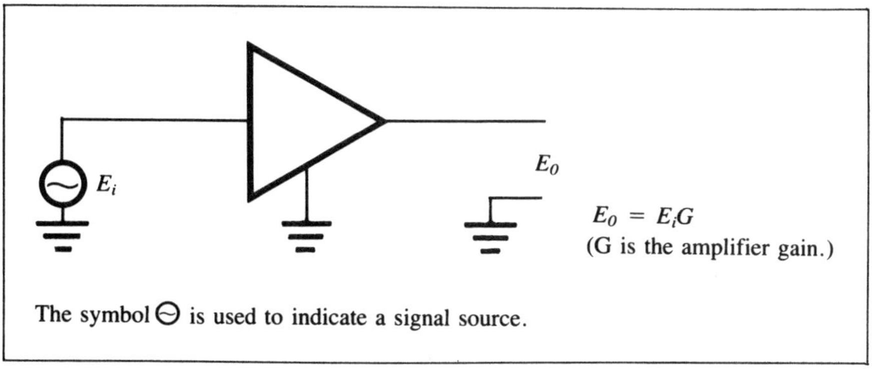

Figure 3.9. Single-ended amplifier.

signal amplified is referenced to ground. Current flowing from the signal source connected to the input of the amplifier returns to the device through the ground connection. The return path for the current flow, called the return, may be through a wire grounded at the device and the amplifier or through another ground path such as the AC power system.

Figure 3.10 shows a special type of amplifier called the differential amplifier. It amplifies the difference between two input signals. The figure illustrates differential amplifier operation.

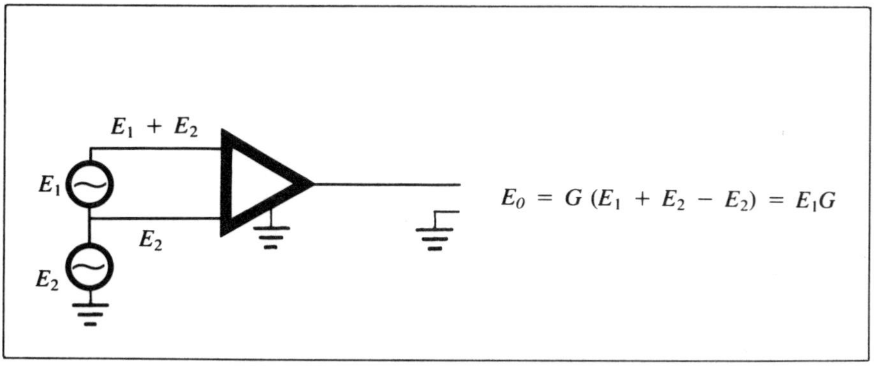

Figure 3.10. The differential amplifier amplifies the difference between its inputs.

The operational amplifier (op amp) is an amplifier module (commonly an integrated circuit) which can be configured (gain, inverting/non-inverting, etc.) by external components. The op amp has differential inputs (an op amp could be used to construct a differential

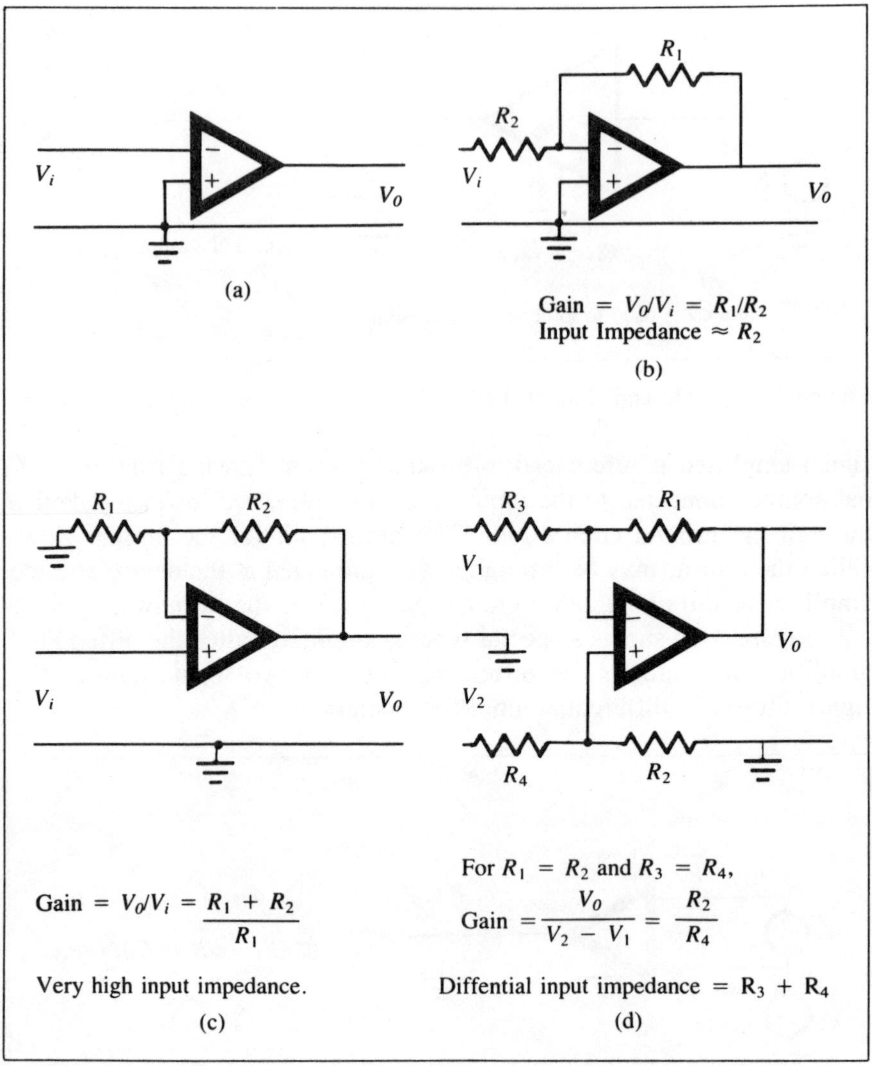

Figure 3.11. Four op amp configurations. The open loop circuit (a), the inverting amplifier (b), the noninverting amplifier (c), and the differential amplifier (d).

amplifier) and typically has very high gain. Figure 3.11 shows some common op amp configurations.

The open-loop circuit is rarely used. Due to the high gain of the op amp, this circuit can easily become nonlinear as the output of the circuit is driven into its maximum value (saturation). The gain of the inverting and non-inverting amplifier is determined (for frequencies below the cutoff frequency) by an external resistor network. The maximum gain is limited by the quality of the amplifier.

Op amps can be used to construct high gain amplifiers, voltage comparators, and other circuits useful in a data acquisition environment. An op amp text should be consulted for more information.

Filters

A filter is an electronic circuit which attenuates signals of certain frequencies while passing others. Figure 3.12 shows the ideal response of three common filter types. Filters are constructed using capacitors and inductors. To improve filter performance, active elements (devices that amplify) are added to the circuit.

Filter performance can be described in terms of the ratio of the output voltage to the input voltage (V_o/V_i) at different frequences. It is common to discuss this ratio on a logarithmic scale. For this reason, the decibel is used (20 log V_o/V_i).

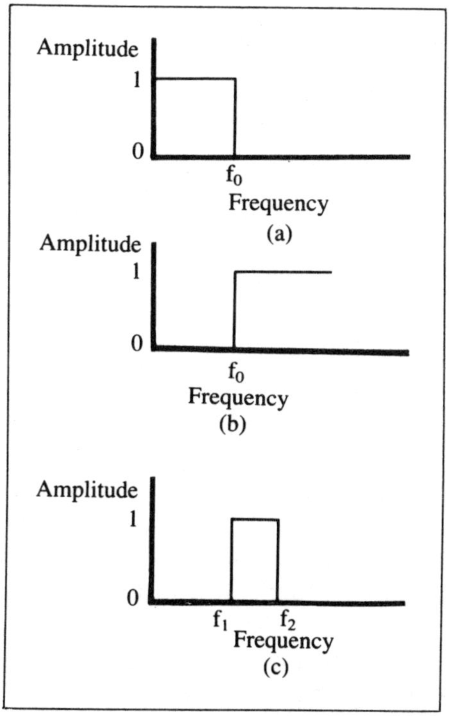

Figure 3.12. Response of ideal filters: low-pass (a), high-pass (b), and bandpass (c).

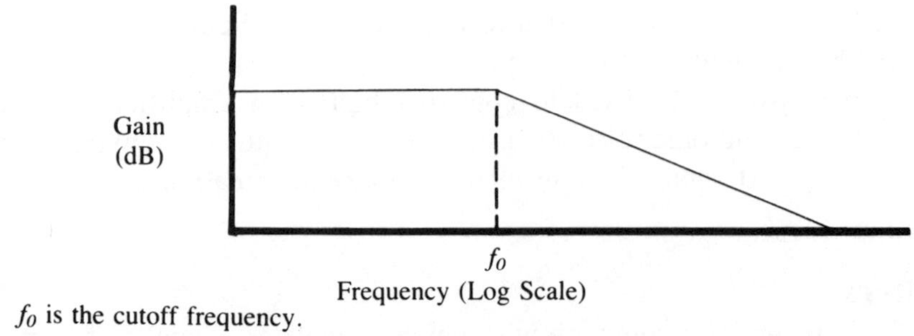

Figure 3.13. Typical low-pass filter performance.

Figure 3.13 shows the performance of a typical low-pass filter. The filter passes signals up to the cutoff signal ($V_O = V_i$). Beyond this frequency, the signal is attenuated (or rolls off) more and more as the frequency increases. The steeper the roll-off curve, the more the filter is like the ideal filter of Figure 3.12.

The slope of most roll off curves is a multiple of six dB/octave (a change in frequency of one octave occurs when the frequency is doubled.) A first-order filter has a roll off of six dB/octave; a second-order filter has a roll off of 12 dB/octave; and so forth. The higher the order, the better the filter.

Digital Electronics

An analog signal in the laboratory generally is a voltage or current whose amplitude is directly related to some physical quantity. Such a signal is continuous over its range. Figure 3.14 illustrates an idealized representation of the output of a temperature transducer as the temperature is varied.

Typical digital signals are restricted to certain discrete values. Normally each digital signal will be allowed to exist in one of two states. This sytem is called a two-valued logic system. One state is called logic zero or false, and the other state is called logic one or true. Several digital signals can be combined to carry more complex information by encoding the information as a set of two-valued signals.

The complement of a digital signal is the opposite logic state. The complement of a zero is a one, and the complement of a one is a zero.

For this discussion, it is assumed that the value of the voltage of a signal indicates its state. Figure 3.15 shows two methods of encoding a

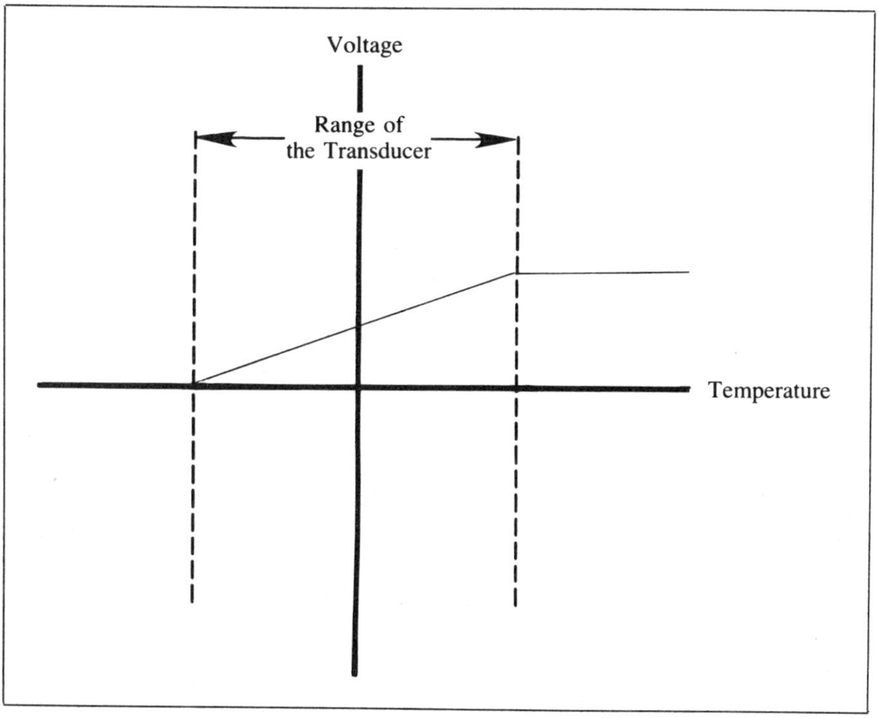

Figure 3.14. Output of an ideal temperature transducer to illustrate a continuous signal.

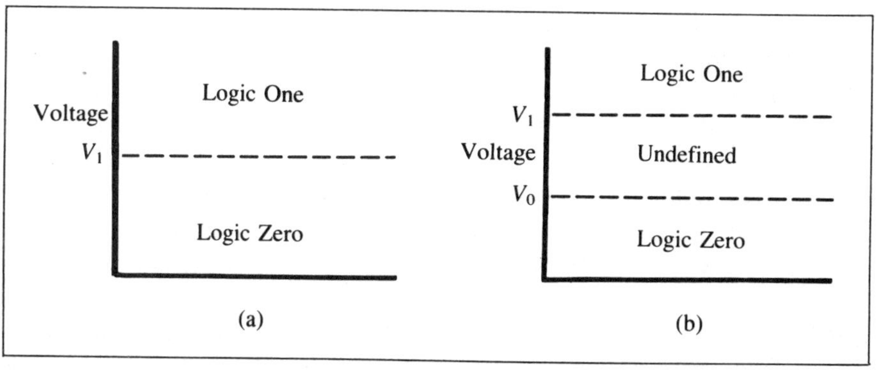

Figure 3.15. Two schemes for encoding binary states as a voltage.

digital signal using voltages. In 3.15a, any voltage less than V_1 is a logic zero. Any signal greater than or equal to V_1 is a logic one. Figure 3.15b illustrates a second encoding method. Any signal with a voltage greater than V_1 is a logic one, and any signal below V_0 is a logic zero.

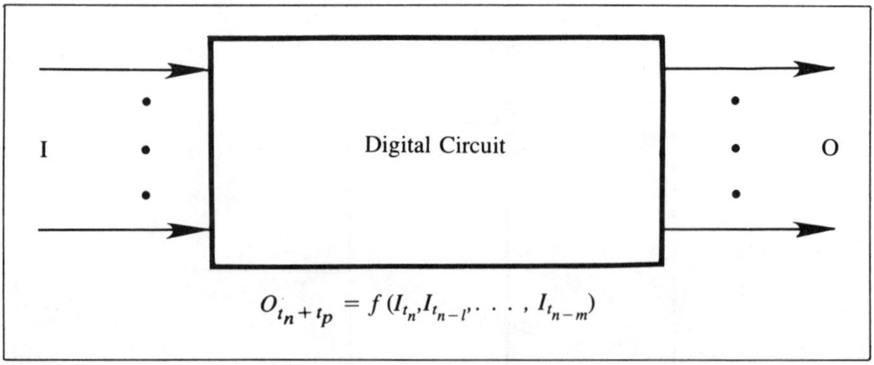

Figure 3.16. Model of a digital signal.

The region between V_0 and V_1 is an undefined state. Circuits are designed to avoid this state. As a signal switches from a one to a zero or vice versa, its voltage value should move through the undefined state rapidly. By segregating the logic states and by requiring signals to pass rapidly through the undefined region, digital signals are afforded some immunity to noise.

Digital circuits input one or more digital signals and output one or more digital signals based on the input. Figure 3.16 shows a model of a digital circuit in which t_p represents the propogation delay associated with the circuit. If the input of the circuit changes at time t, the output does not change until time $t+t_p$ due to delay in the circuit.

The output at time t_n+t_p is based on the current input at time t_n and on previous inputs. If m, the number of previous inputs in the function produced by the circuit, is zero, the output of the circuit at time t_n+t_p is only dependant on the input at time t_n. This type of digital circuit is a combinational circuit. The propagation delay may or may not be important depending on circuit use. In the following discussion, the propagation delay is assumed small enough to be negligible.

Figure 3.17 shows the four possible single input, single output combinational logic circuits for a two-valued logic system (signals are either logic zero or logic one). The first three circuits are trivial. The fourth circuit is an inverter and produces the complement of the input.

There are sixteen possible two-input, one-output circuits as shown in Figure 3.18.

Using a combination of the AND, OR, and inverter functions, any of the sixteen two input functions can be produced. (Mathematically, the AND, OR, and inverter functions and the binary values logic zero and

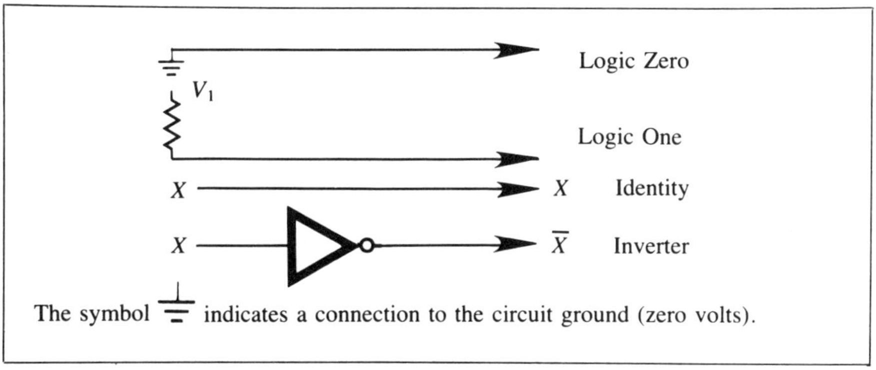

Figure 3.17. Single input logic functions.

logic one form a Boolean algebra which can be shown to be complete.) Figure 3.19 illustrates the circuit to form an exclusive or (EXOR) function from AND and OR gates. (A circuit that performs a logic function is commonly called a gate. This terminology is due to the fact that a typical usage of logic circuits is to pass or block a signal. This function is analogous to opening or closing a fence gate.)

It is also possible to generate all functions using only the NOR function or the NAND function. Figure 3.20 illustrates how, by using one of these simple functions as a common building block, more complex functions can be produced.

It is common to find integrated circuits with a number of NAND or NOR gates on a single chip. Not only is it possible to construct any two-value logic function from a number of these gates, but in many logic families these are the fastest gates (smallest propogation delay). Other functions require more inverter stages and therefore have a larger propogation delay.

DeMorgan's Law states that in a Boolean algebra, $\overline{(a + b)} = \bar{a}\cdot\bar{b}$ and $\overline{(a\cdot b)} = \bar{a} + \bar{b}$. These equivalences are illustrated in Figure 3.21. By $\overline{(a + b)} = \bar{a}\cdot\bar{b}$, a NOR gate is equivalent to a NAND gate with inverted inputs and inverted output. By $\overline{(a\cdot b)} = \bar{a} + \bar{b}$, a NAND gate can be replaced by a NOR gate with inverted inputs and output.

There are a number of popular integrated circuit logic families. TTL (transistor-transistor logic), CMOS (complementary metal oxide semiconductor), and ECL (emitter coupled logic) are some examples. TTL is moderately fast and widely used. CMOS is slower than TTL, requires less current, and can operate over a wider range of power supply voltages.

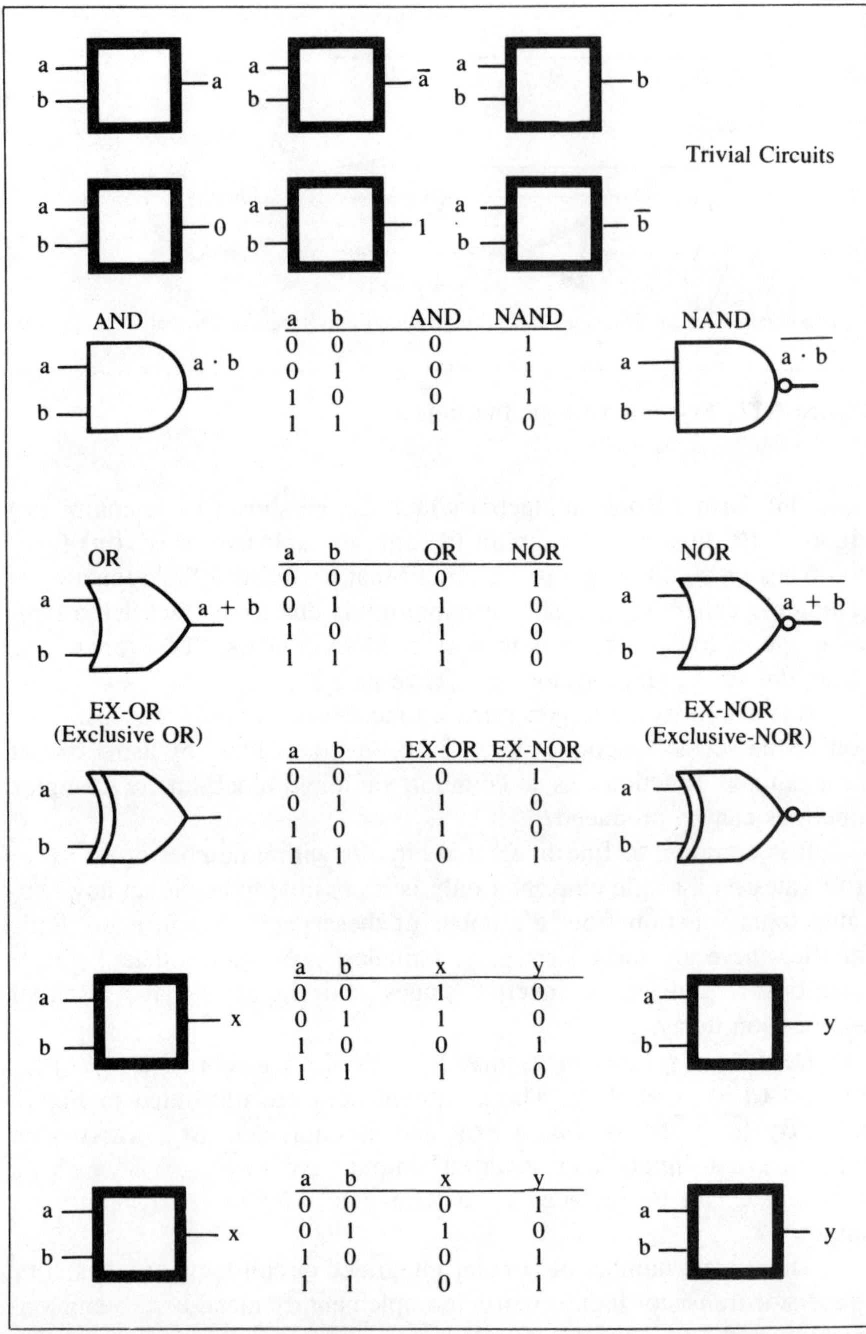

a	b	AND	NAND
0	0	0	1
0	1	0	1
1	0	0	1
1	1	1	0

a	b	OR	NOR
0	0	0	1
0	1	1	0
1	0	1	0
1	1	1	0

a	b	EX-OR	EX-NOR
0	0	0	1
0	1	1	0
1	0	1	0
1	1	0	1

a	b	x	y
0	0	1	0
0	1	1	0
1	0	0	1
1	1	1	0

a	b	x	y
0	0	0	1
0	1	1	0
1	0	0	1
1	1	0	1

Figure 3.18. The 16 two-input binary functions.

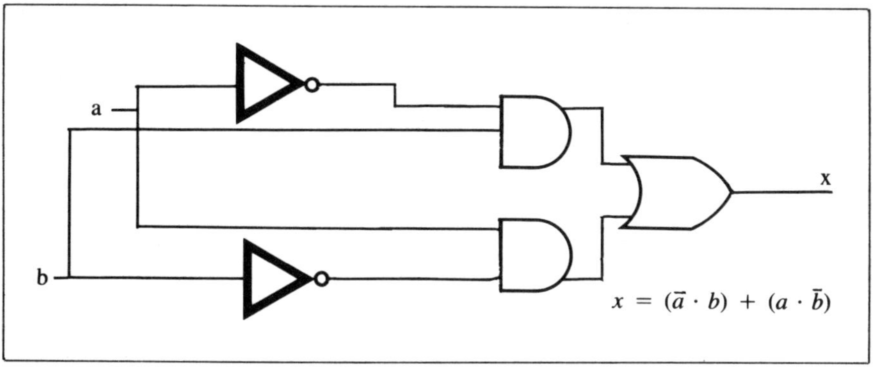

Figure 3.19. Exclusive or (EXOR) gate constructed from AND, OR, and inverter gates.

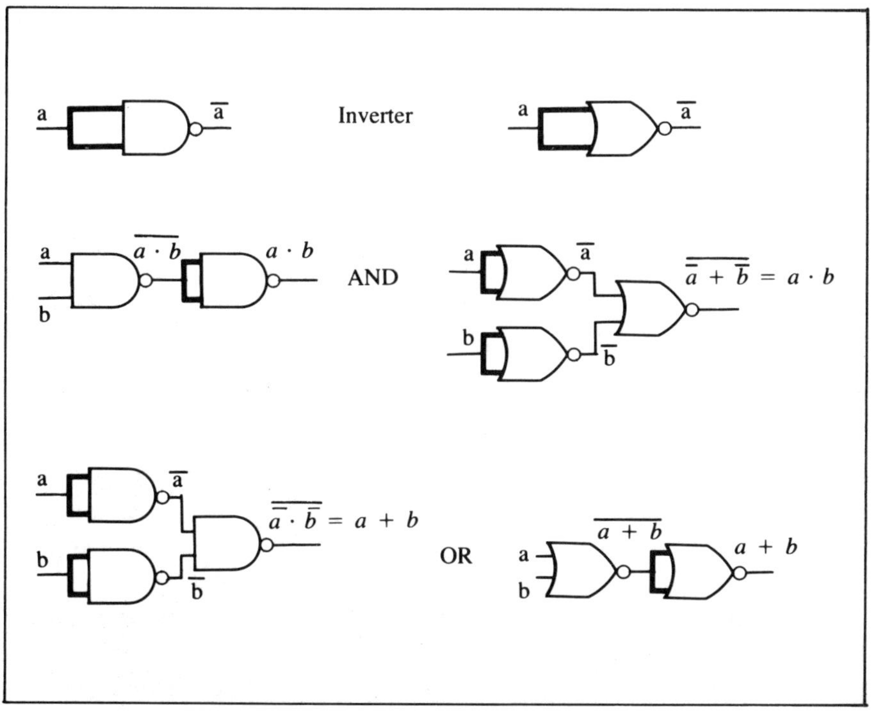

Figure 3.20. Construction of other gates using either NAND or NOR gates exclusively.

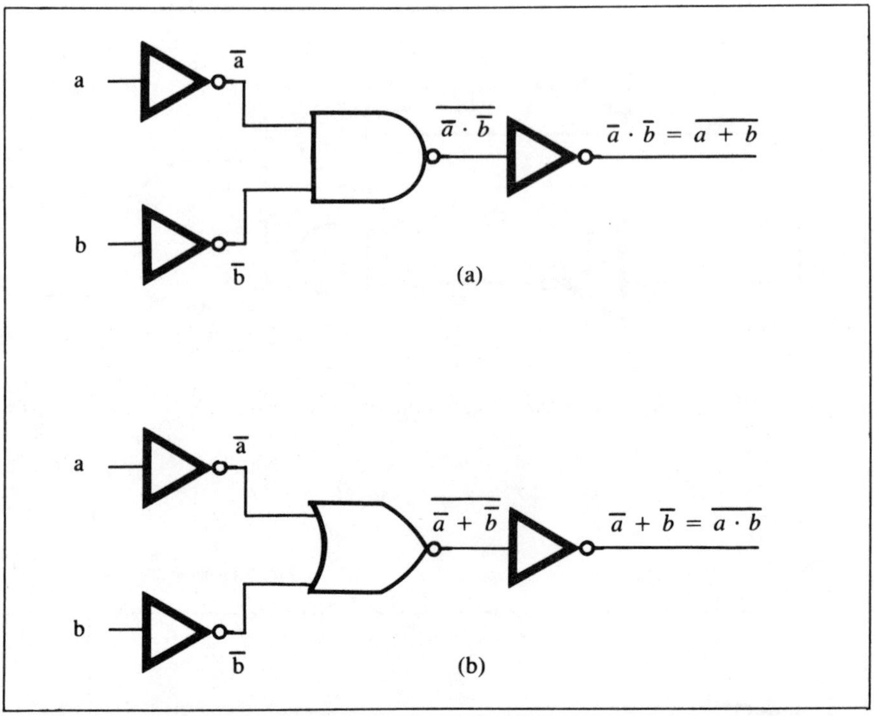

Figure 3.21. Example of DeMorgan's law showing construction of a NOR gate using NAND and inverter gates (a) and construction of NAND gates using NOR and inverter gates.

As an example of a popular logic family, TTL integrated circuits are powered by a five-volt power supply. A TTL logic zero is produced by a voltage between 0 volts and .8 volts which can carry or "sink" 1.6 milliamps of current. A TTL logic one is produced by a voltage between 2.4 volts and 5 volts and produces or "sources" 40 microamps of current. Leaving a TTL input open (unconnected) produces a logic one on the input. Leaving inputs unconnected is not recommended due to noise considerations. A constant logic one is normally produced by connecting a register (to limit current) to the positive side of the power supply. A logic zero is produced by connecting the input to ground.

Due to the implementation of TTL circuits, high switching rates can produce spikes—fast changing variations—on the power supply output which can generate false pulses in near circuits. Decoupling capacitors are used to suppress these spikes. Each capacitor is located near a group of integrated circuits.

The flip-flop (bistable mulitvibrator) is the simplest memory circuit. It stores one bit of information. There are a number of flip-flop types; however, only the D flip-flop is discussed. The D flip-flop has a D (data) input, a clock input, and, optionally, one or more initialization inputs. It has two output lines, Q and its complement, $\bar{Q}$.

At any time, the output is either in the Q=1 or Q=0 state. This state is retained until a clock pulse occurs, at which time Q is set to the value of the D input when the clock pulse occurred, and $\bar{Q}$ is set to its complement. For this discussion, the flip-flop is clocked by the leading edge (zero to one transition) of the clock pulse. The rise-time (time to make the zero to one transition) of the clock pulse must be very small.

The initialization inputs can be used to set or clear the Q value independently of the clock. A common usage of these inputs is to place the flip-flop in a known state when power is applied to the circuit. Figure 3.22 diagrams flip-flop operation.

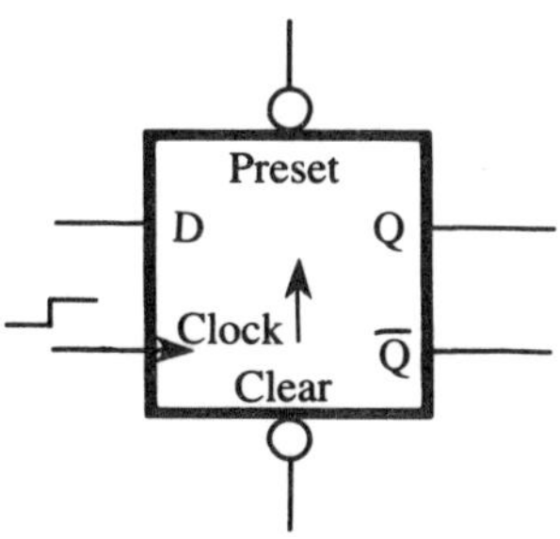

Preset	Clear	Clock	D	Q	$\bar{Q}$
0	1	–	–	1	0
1	0	–	–	0	1
1	1	↑	1	1	0
1	1	↑	0	0	1
1	1	0	–	Q_t	$\bar{Q}_t$

↑ indicates the leading edge of the clock. Q_t is the value of Q at the end of the last clock cycle, preset, or clear.

Figure 3.22. D flip-flop operation.

A sequential circuit is a circuit whose output is based on its current input and the previous *m* inputs.

$$O_{t_n + t_p} = f(I_{t_n}, I_{t_{n-1}}, \ldots, I_{t_{n-m}})$$

The sequential circuit therefore contains memory elements to contain the input history.

Flip-flops are used to contain the history of the input signal. Counters, which are constructed from flip-flops, are an example of sequential circuits. The digital computer is a very complex sequential machine.

The typical data acquisition system designer need not be concerned with the design of sequential machines from a traditional point of view.

Due to decreased hardware costs, problems once requiring efficiently designed sequential circuits are now being solved using ad hoc circuits or microcomputer systems. The overall costs of such solutions are typically less expensive than optimized traditional solutions due to their flexibility and decreased time requirements on the part of the designer.

Switches

Mechanical switches are very noisy. When a switch is opened or closed, it takes several milliseconds for the device to stabilize mechanically. If a switch is connected to high-speed digital logic, this mechanical instability may appear as several openings and closings to the digital circuit. If the circuit must only be triggered once each time the switch is activated, signal conditioning circuitry to "debounce" the switch must be constructed. (In some applications where a switch is connected to a computer, the debounce function can be performed in software.) Figure 3.23a illustrates a typical circuit used to condition mechanical switches

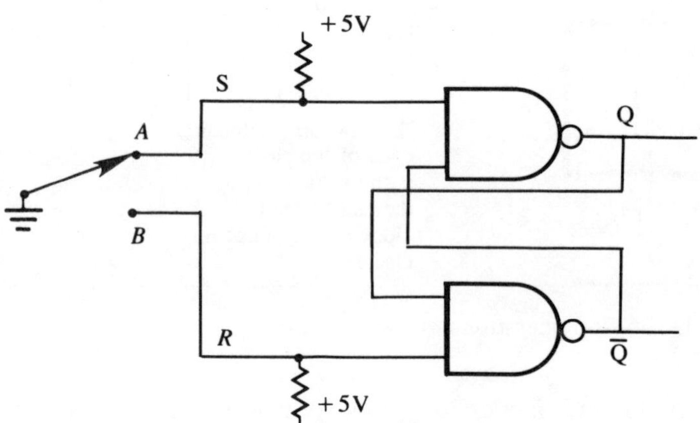

(a)

S	R	Q	$\overline{Q}$	
0	0	1	1	Not used
0	1	1	0	Set
1	0	0	1	Reset
1	1	Q_t	$\overline{Q_t}$	Retain

(b)

Figure 3.23. Circuit to debounce a switch using a set-reset flip-flop (a), and set-reset flip-flop operation (b).

using TTL logic. The circuit uses a set-reset flip-flop constructed of NAND gates. Operation of the flip-flop is illustrated in 3.23b. If the switch is in position A and switched to position B, point A will be placed in the logic one state by the pull-up resistor, and point B will be grounded. Because of switch bounce, B will be grounded, then placed in the logic one state several times before the switch settles; at which time, it will remain at the ground potential. The first time that point B is grounded, the flip-flop will change states; and, due to the feedback connection of the flip-flop, the state change will remain stable while the switch is stabilizing. An analogous situation occurs when the switch is again moved to position A.

The detailed discussion of solid state devices is not included in this text; however, a simple example of the use of a transistor in a practical circuit is useful. Figure 3.24 shows a transistor connected to form a switch. The transistor switch is useful in that a small current flow in the control circuit can be used to control a larger current in the switched circuit.

There are a number of types of solid state devices that can be used as switches depending on the intended application. Bipolar transistors are available for switching DC signals over a wide range of current values. Field effect transistors (FET) are useful where the control signal must not be loaded (field effect transistors have a high input impedance.) Silicon controlled rectifiers (SCR) and TRIACS are solid state devices used to switch high currents.

In some cases, it is necessary for the control voltage of an electronic switch to be isolated from the switched voltage. For example, the switched voltage may control a very large voltage and isolation is desired to prevent a circuit malfunction in the high voltage circuit from damaging the control circuit. A useful isolation device is the opto-isolator shown in Figure 3.25.

In the figure, the light emitting diode (LED) is a solid state device that produces a light when a current flows through it in the proper direction. The phototransistor is a simple solid state switch that only conducts when it is illuminated. In an opto-isolator, the LED and phototransistor are optically connected and isolated from outside light sources. When current is removed from the LED, the phototransistor does not conduct. When the LED is lighted, the phototransistor conducts and allows current to flow in the output circuit. There is no electrical connection between the input and output circuits.

Digital signals that are noisy, have a slow rise time, or are produced by mechanical means can be cleaned up using a special circuit

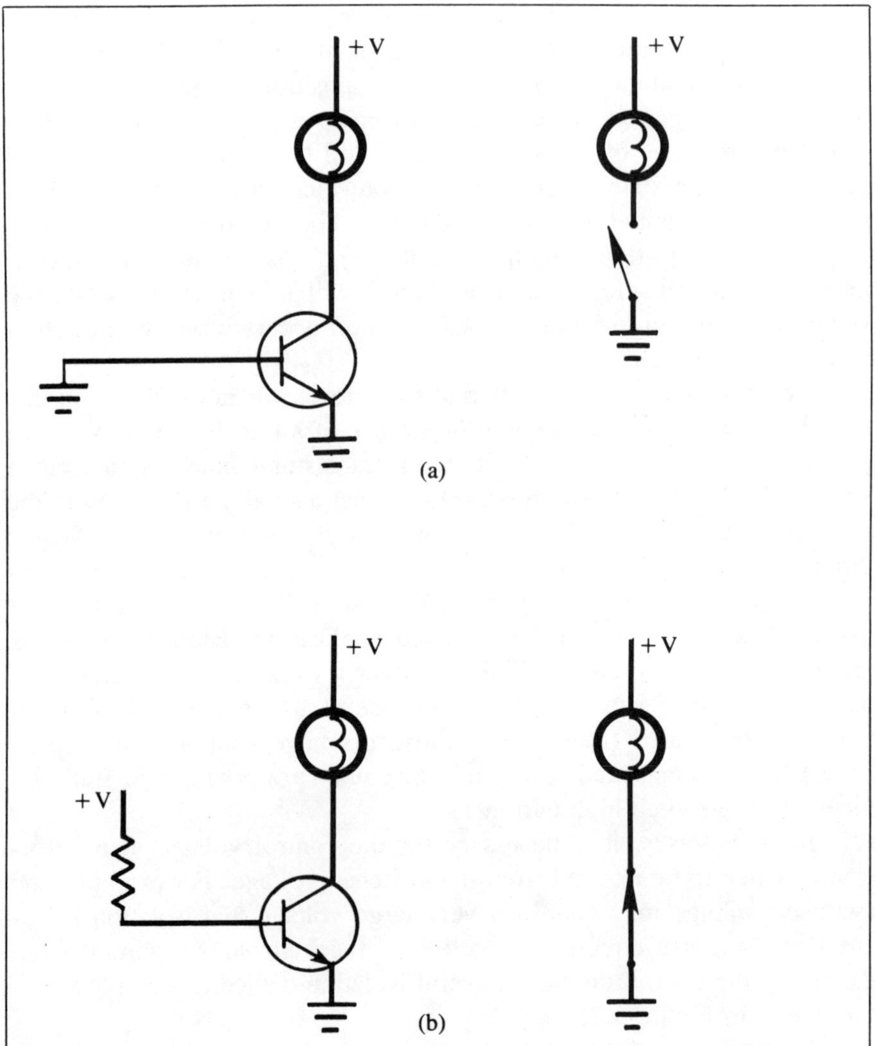

Figure 3.24. Simple transistor switches and equivalent circuits: switch open due to control voltage equal to zero (a) and switch closed with small positive control voltage (b).

called the Schmitt trigger. The "snap" action of this device gives it greater noise immunity than standard logic circuits. Figure 3.26a shows the hysteresis effect of the circuit. As the input of the Schmitt trigger rises from zero to point a, the output of the circuit changes to indicate the logic one state. The point of transition is lowered to point b. The in-

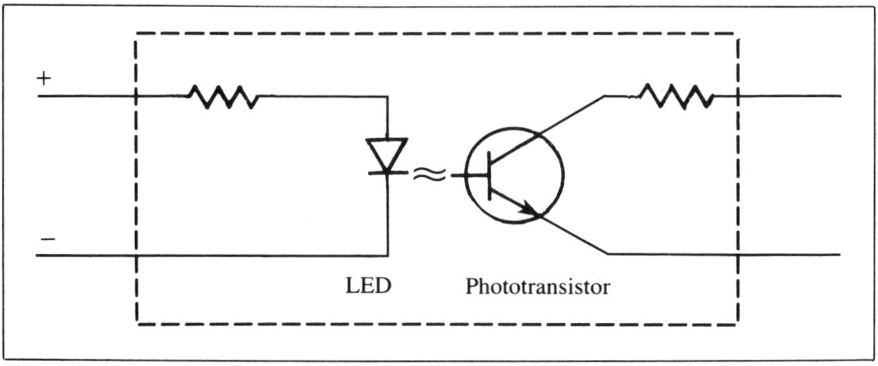

Figure 3.25. The opto-isolator.

put must fall below point b before the output changes to a logic zero state. Figures 3.26b and 3.26c illustrate typical Schmitt trigger uses.

RC Networks and Related Circuits

The RC (resistor-capacitor) time constant was previously discussed. RC circuits are useful in both analog and digital circuits.

Figure 3.27 shows an RC circuit that can be used to initialize a flip-flop when power is applied to a circuit. The flip-flop clear input is active when it is at a logic zero state (termed a negative assertion signal). When the clear input is at logic zero, the flip-flop is brought to the Q=O state and is held there until the clear input becomes a logic one. When CLEAR is one, the other flip-flop inputs can be used to change the state of the circuit.

When power is applied to the input circuit, the discharged capacitor begins to charge. The capacitor appears as a small resistance while it is charging. The voltage at the clear input (which is also the voltage across the capacitor) rises from zero exponentially. At one time constant, the voltage is 63.2% of the maximum value. The clear input is at logic zero while the voltage across the capacitor is below V_0, the maximum voltage for a logic zero. By choosing the value of R and C, the clear input can be held low during the time the power supply is stabilizing.

Figure 3.28 shows a block diagram of an astable multivibrator. A multivibrator is an oscillator which has two output states. Multivibrator integrated circuits are available so circuit details are not discussed. The circuit may be implemented such that the two state outputs correspond to the logic zero and the logic one states of a particular logic family.

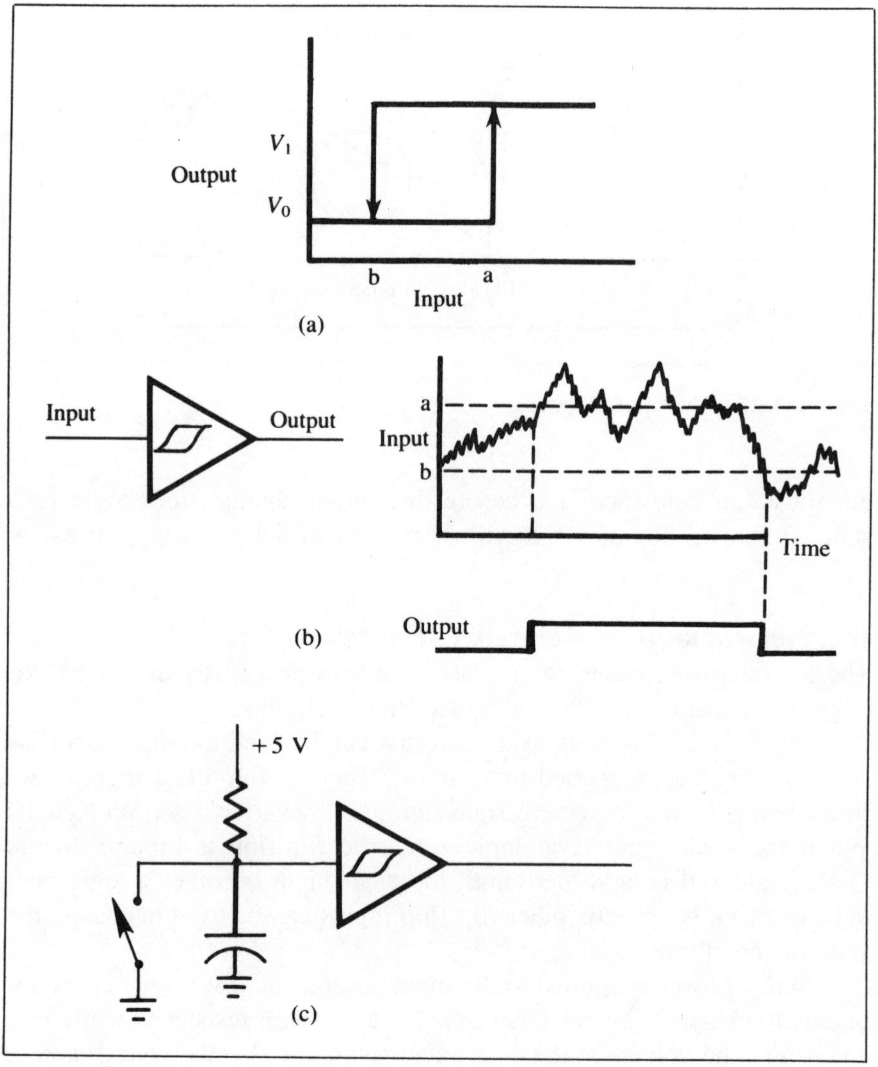

Figure 3.26. Schmitt trigger operation (a), a Schmitt trigger circuit to clean up a noisy signal (b), and a Schmitt trigger switch debouncing circuit (c).

A monostable multivibrator has two output states. The circuit remains in one state, the stable state, until it is triggered. The circuit output enters the unstable state for a predetermined amount of time set by circuit components and then returns to the stable state. The triggering pulse may have some variation in pulse width; however, the pulse width

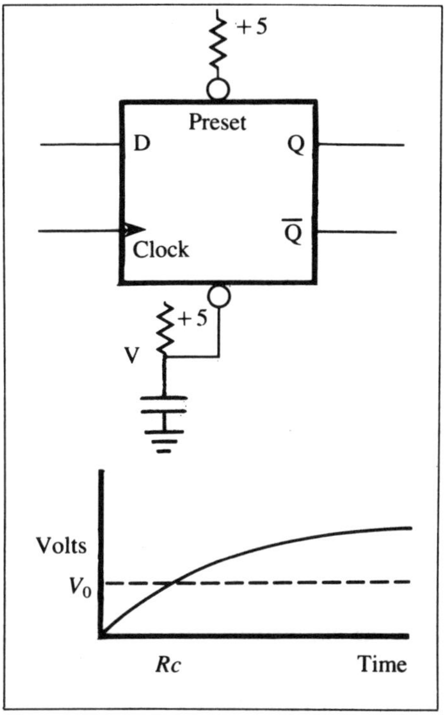

Figure 3.27. RC circuit used to initialize a flip-flop when power is applied to the circuit. Clear is active at logic zero as long as $V < V_O$.

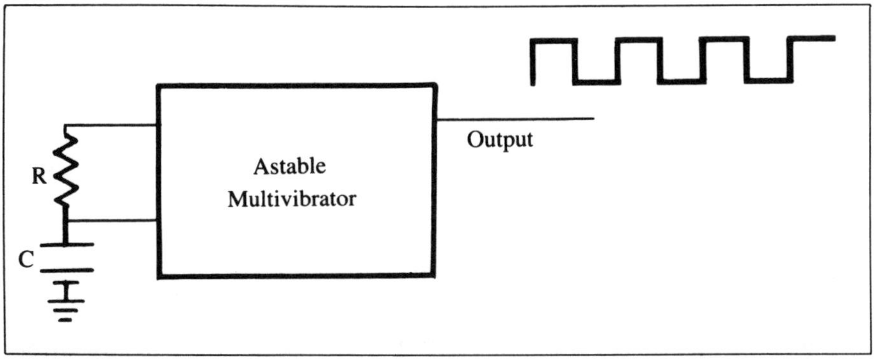

Figure 3.28. Block diagram of an astable multivibrator. Frequency of the output is set by R and C.

of the output of the monostable is constant. A monostable can be used to produce a pulse of predetermined duration when some event occurs. Figure 3.29 illustrates monostable operation.

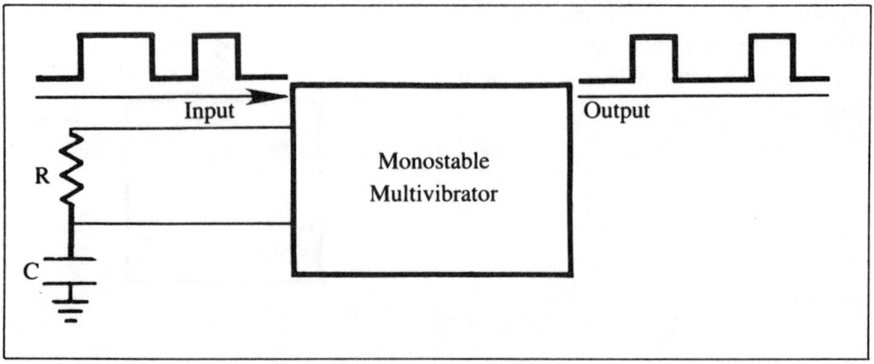

Figure 3.29. Block diagram of a monostable circuit. An input pulse of varying width will produce an output pulse of a width set by R and C.

Sources of Noise

Electrical noise is interference which distorts a signal being measured. A common source of noise is the 60 Hz. AC power lines. Suppose a device produces the signal shown in Figure 3.30a. If a one volt, 60 Hz. noise signal is combined with the data signal, the result is 3.30b. If an attempt is made to measure the signal at point X, the result will be four volts instead of three volts due to the noise.

Causes of noise and techniques to diminish the effect of noise are discussed in later chapters; however, the data acquisition system designer should always be aware that noise, and the fact that electrical circuits are not perfect, cause the ideal signal that we envision and the measured signal to differ.

Ideally, the output of a transducer is related to the physical quantity it measures:

$$p = f(x)$$

Given x, the electrical output of the transducer (e.g. voltage), the physical quantity affecting the transducer (e.g. force) can be determined by application of the function.

Unfortunately, signals in the "real world" are affected by interference or electrical noise. Noise has a number of sources and can be random or coherent. The frequency components of random noise are randomly distributed. Coherent noise, such as noise produced by the 60 Hz. power lines, has some frequency components with higher probability than others. If a signal that contains noise component x_n is mea-

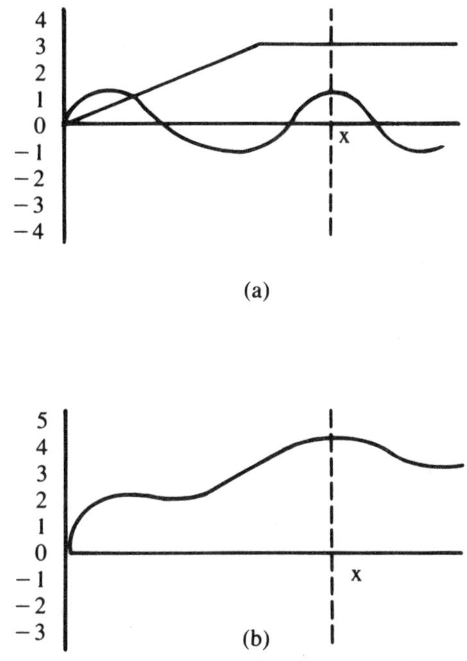

Figure 3.30. Graph (a) shows a signal to be measured and a one volt peak to peak, 60 Hz. noise signal. Graph (b) shows the summation of the signals and the error associated with making a measurement at point x.

sured, the physical quantity predicted by applying the translation function is in error:

$$\acute{p} = f(x + x_n)$$

The signal-to-noise ratio is

$$S/N = \frac{x}{x_n}$$

The signal-to-noise ratio can also be expressed as a ratio of the electrical power of the signal and the noise. If the signal-to-noise ratio is high, the error in measurement caused by noise is low. If the *S/N* ratio is not large enough to insure reasonable accuracy in measurement, techniques must be applied to reduce the effect of noise.

Thermal noise, produced by thermal energy affecting subatomic particles, is present in all transducers and conductors. In most cases, thermal noise is relatively small in amplitude. The frequency content of thermal noise is random in nature.

Electrostatic or capacitive noise is produced by capacitive coupling between conductors carrying signals. When a signal carrying conductor is in close proximity with other signal carrying conductors or ground, two plates of a capacitor are formed. If the conductors are at different potentials, the charging and discharging of the capacitor formed between the conductors causes current flow.

The interference due to capacitive coupling is more severe as signal frequencies increase (capacitance reactance decreases with frequency). The magnitude of the noise due to capacitive coupling increases with the impedance of the circuits. Long signal leads form a larger capacitance between conductors and thus produces more noise than shorter signal leads.

Noise can also be induced between signal leads magnetically. Signal leads running near wires carrying large amounts of current, such as 60 Hz. AC power lines or a conductor carrying rapidly changing currents, can pick up interference by inductance. Low impedance circuits are more susceptible to inductive coupling. The severity of inductance noise increases with the frequency of the current carrying conductors.

Radio frequency (RF) noise is electromagnetic radiation that can interfere with signal carrying conductors. RF energy travels through space as waves. The source of the RF energy need not be in close proximity with the signal carrying conductors to cause interference. RF signal sources include radio transmitters, flourescent lights, thunderstorms, and high frequency digital circuits.

The coupling of signals between adjacent signal carrying wires is called crosstalk. It may be caused by static, magnetic, and RF coupling or a combination of these effects. The coupling of independent signals is as undesirable as the coupling of a noise signal to an information signal. Because crosstalk and noise coupling are similar, similar methods are used to reduce their effects.

The ground of a circuit is the part in the circuit chosen to be at zero volts. All potentials in the circuit are measured with reference to the ground. Sometimes, the ground point is connected through the AC power line to earth ground.

Two circuits grounded via the AC power line may not reference the same ground potential. The resistance of the wires leading to earth ground may not be the same (due to wire size and length), and the points of earthing may be at different potentials (due to soil type and moisture content). Figure 3.31 illustrates grounds at different potentials.

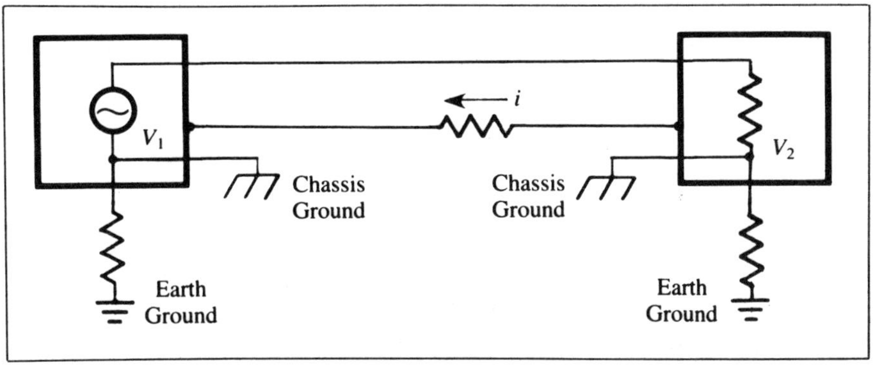

Figure 3.31. A ground loop is created because both chassis ground points are at different potentials due to different resistances of the paths to earth ground. Due to the different ground potentials, a current flows in the signal return lead, thus creating a voltage drop in the ground lead and inducing noise in the signal carrying wires.

The current flow between grounds at different potentials can induce noise into the system. Ground loop noise can be induced in a circuit where multiple signal carrying wires use a common return to ground. If a return line carries large amounts of current, the voltage drop associated with the line can also cause a ground loop. The impedance of thermocouple (temperature transducer) wire can also be a factor in creating ground loop noise.

4

Data Collection Fundamentals

Transducers are devices which convert some physical quantity into an electrical signal whose value (amplitude, frequency, etc.) is related to the physical quantity. If an ideal transducer existed and its output could be measured perfectly, the physical quantity being detected by the transducer could be determined from the measured output. Ideal transducers do not exist; however, a wide variety of accurate transducers are in use today.

A majority of transducers produce a voltage proportional to the physical quantity being measured. In this catagory are thermocouples for measuring temperature and strain gauges for measuring load. Due to the large number of voltage-producing transducers, many computer analog interfaces are designed to measure voltage.

A transducer that produces a current related to some physical quantity can be used with a standard voltage measuring interface if the current is first translated to a proportional voltage. Figure 4.1a is a simple current to voltage translation network. For the translation network to provide an accurate translation of current to voltage, a precision resistor must be used and the measuring circuit must have a high impedance in-

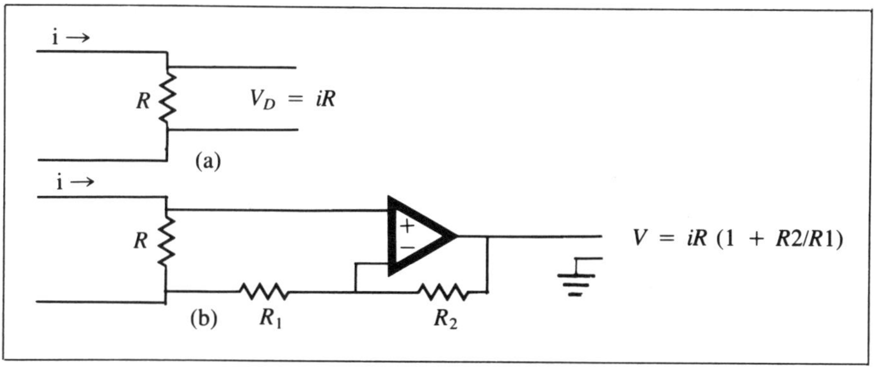

Figure 4.1. Current to voltage converter (a) and current to voltage converter with isolation (b).

put (or the voltage drop across the resistor is proportional to only part of the current being measured). If the measuring device does not have a high impedance input, the op amp circuit of 4.1b may be used to condition the signal.

Some transducers, such as temperature measuring thermistors and photoconductive cells, are variable resistors. To measure the resistance of such a transducer with a standard voltage interface requires a known voltage be applied to the transducer as in Figure 4.2. The resistance, and therefore the physical quantity being measured, can be computed from the voltage drop.

The information produced by the transducers discussed so far is related to the amplitude of a voltage, current, or resistance. Some transducers produce outputs whose frequency is related to some physical quantity. The simple angular velocity transducer of Figure 4.3 illustrates such a transducer. The output of the circuit is digital. The speed of the rotating shaft can be determined by counting output pulses over a known time interval.

In general, the type of transducer used is determined by the particular application. The choice of computer interface is less restrictive but limited by the product line of vendors producing equipment for a particular computer. Translation circuits that transform the output of a particular transducer into a signal suitable for the interface can be used to match transducers to standard interfaces. The translation circuit may not be required, may be simple such as a resistor network, or may be complex. If the translation circuit is complex, a better approach may be to construct a special interface which accepts the transducer input directly.

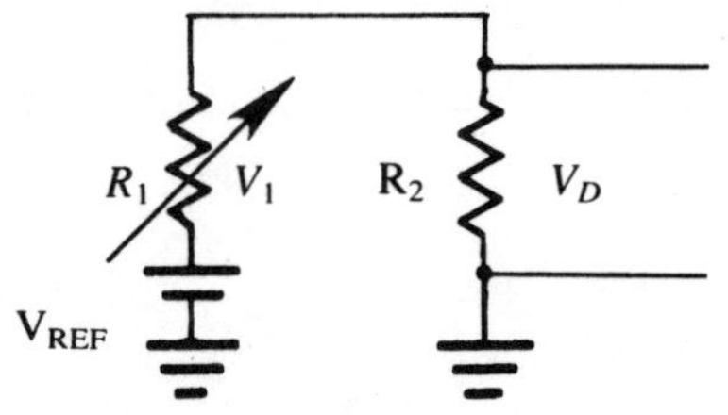

$$V_{REF} = V_D + V_1$$
$$V_1 = V_{REF} - V_D$$
$$iR_1 = V_{REF} - V_D$$
$$R_1 = \frac{V_{REF} - V_D}{i}$$

$$R_1 = \frac{R_2\,(V_{REF} - V_D)}{iR_2}$$

$$R_1 = \frac{R_2\,(V_{REF} - V_D)}{V_D}$$

Figure 4.2. By measuring the voltage drop, V_D, across R2, the resistance associated with transducer R1 can be determined. R2 can be chosen to limit the maximum current in the loop.

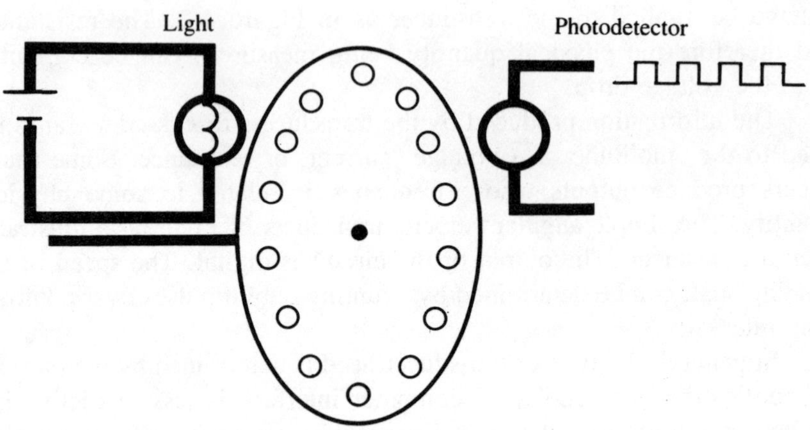

Figure 4.3. An angular velocity transducer using a light, disk, and photodetector.

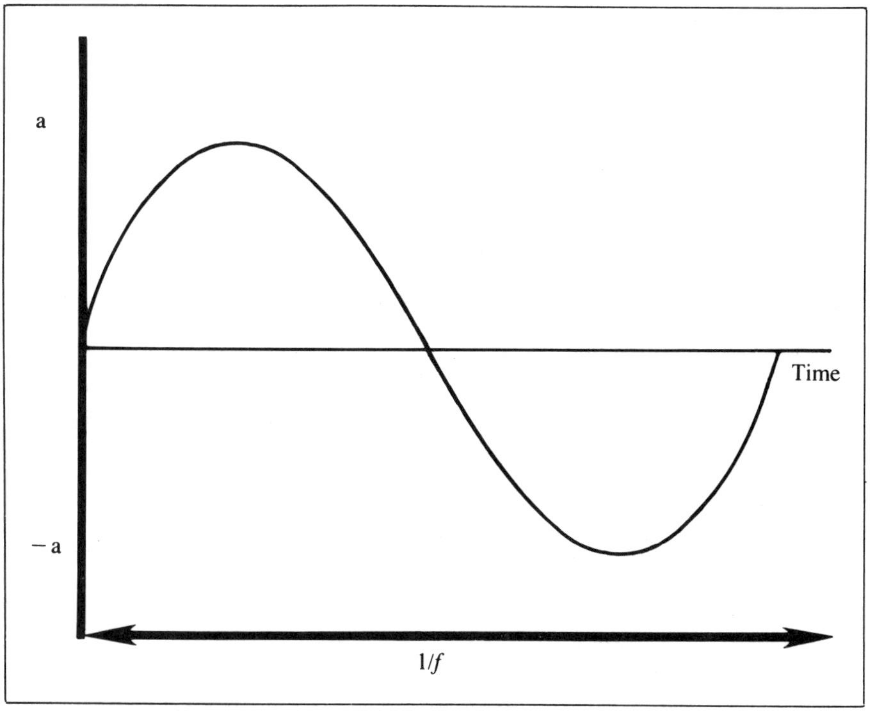

Figure 4.4. An ideal process variable that is a sinusoidal wave of amplitude *a* and frequency *f*.

Sampling Theorem

In many cases in data acquisition systems, data is collected from a process variable. The computer is limited as to how fast a particular signal can be sampled. The speed of the interface, the speed of the computer, and the software controlling the sampling all determine the maximum rate at which a signal can be sampled.

Figure 4.4 shows an ideal process signal plotted against time. The sinusoidal waveform has frquency f and peak amplitude a. The process signal produces a voltage that is proportional to some physical quantity. This signal is connected to a suitable computer interface that converts the voltage to a binary number. The maximum rate of conversion is f_s. The computer may thus sample the signal at any rate up to f_s.

Figure 4.5 shows the results of sampling the signal at various rates. The reconstructed signal is a plot of the converted values with a smooth curve drawn through the points; f_c indicates the sample rate used.

As the figure shows, the ability to accurately reconstruct a wave-

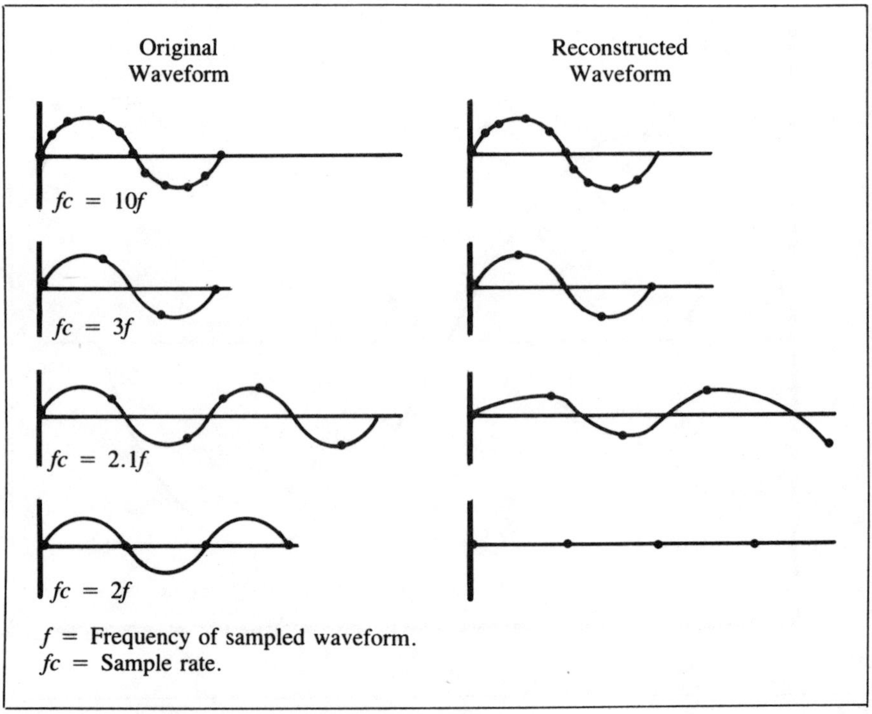

Figure 4.5. The effect of sampling a sinusoidal wave of frequency f at different sample rates.

form is related to the sample rate. If the frequency of the signal is the only characteristic of the waveform desired, a smaller sample rate is permissible than would be required if the waveform had to be reconstructed accurately.

In a data acquisition system where more than one process variable is sampled or when the computer must perform a number of tasks, the optimum sample rate should be selected. This sample rate allows the required information to be extracted from the signal without wasting computer power collecting unnecessary information.

Figure 4.6 shows an ideal process signal plotted against time. Any complex waveform can be broken down into components of sinusoidal waves which when added together will produce the complex waveform. (For more detail, consult a text on Fourier analysis.) Figure 4.7 illustrates this principle for the waveform of Figure 4.6.

A plot of the frequency content of the waveform of Figure 4.8 (a power spectrum—see Chapter 6) shows that the waveform contains si-

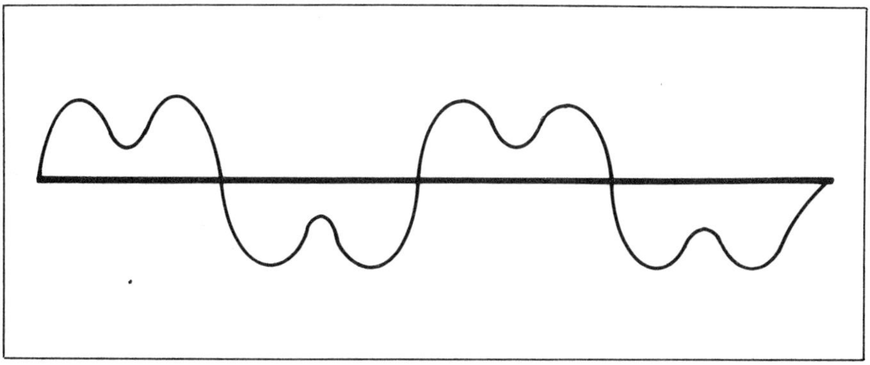

Figure 4.6. A complex waveform.

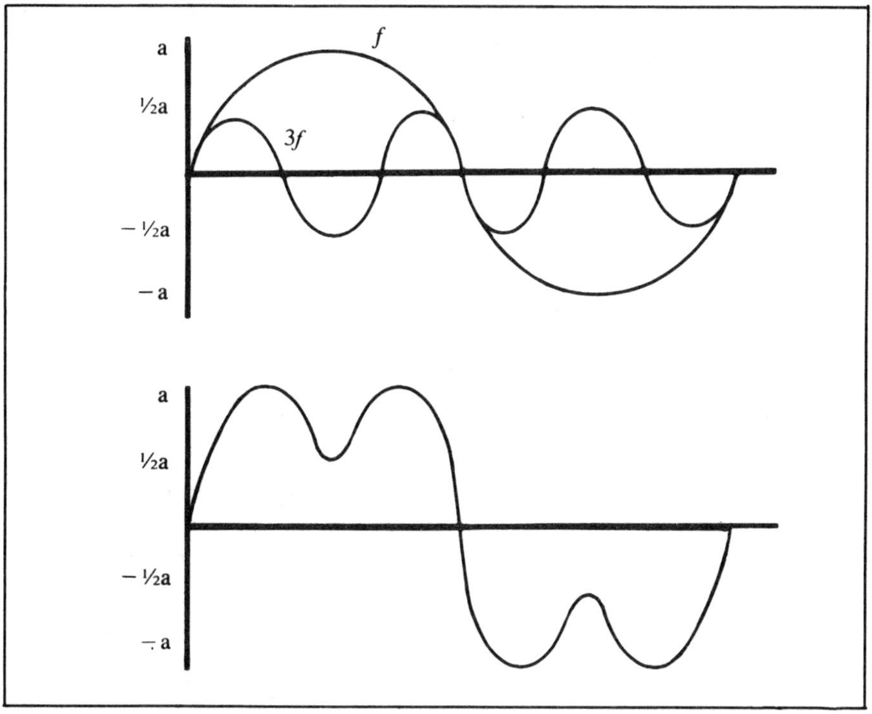

Figure 4.7. The complex waveform of Figure 4.6 is the sum of two sinusoidal waveforms.

nusoidals of two frequencies, f and $3f$. The amplitude of the $3f$ component is one-half the amplitude of the f component.

Suppose that only the signal component of frequency f is of concern. According to Figure 4.5, it appears that a sample rate of greater

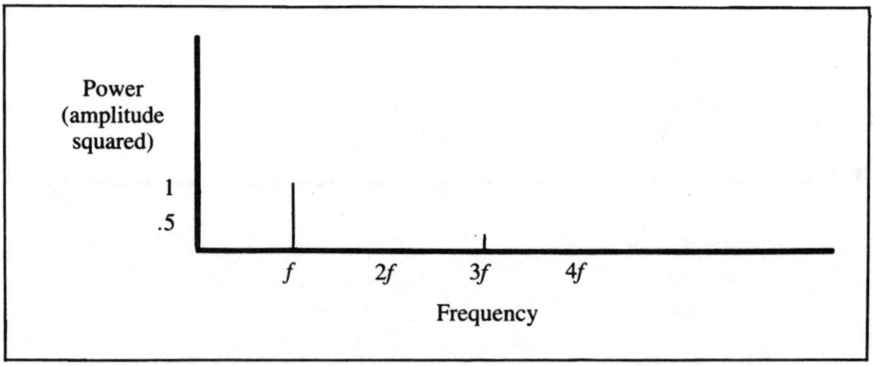

Figure 4.8. Power spectrum of the waveform in Figure 4.6.

than $2f$ would allow the signal to be roughly reconstructed. A sample rate of $4f$ should be adequate to reconstruct a signal of frequency f. Figure 4.9 shows the result of sampling at $4f$. The $3f$ signal appears to be a waveform component of frequency f 180 degrees out of phase with

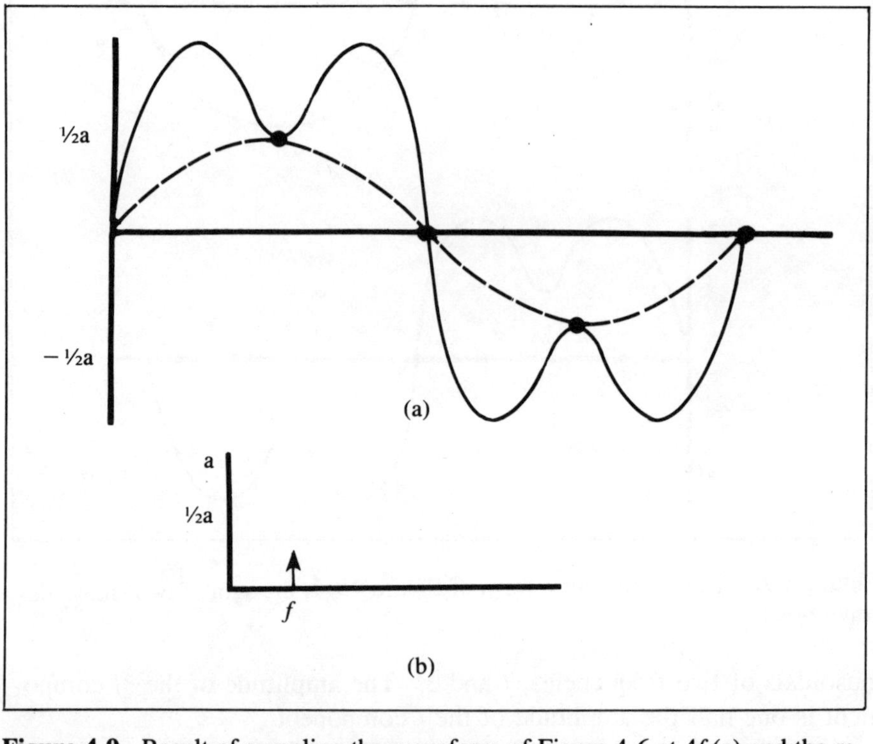

Figure 4.9. Result of sampling the waveform of Figure 4.6 at $4f$ (a) and the resulting power spectrum (b).

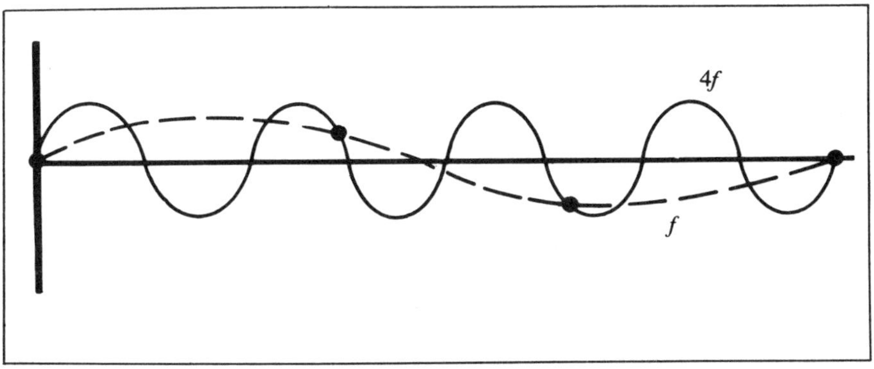

Figure 4.10. Sinusoidal waveform of frequency $4f$ being sampled at $3f$. The frequency of the reconstructed waveform is f.

the real signal component of frequency f. The reconstructed waveform appears as a signal of frequency f and amplitude one-half when the waveform is sampled at frequency $4f$. This phenomenon is called aliasing or frequency folding. Figure 4.10 illustrates aliasing with a simple case of a sine wave of frequency $4f$ being sampled at frequency $3f$.

This discussion leads to the sampling theorem (accredited to both Shannon and Nyquist). The sampling theorem states that the sample rate must be greater than twice the highest frequency component of the waveform being sampled to allow the signal being sampled to be reconstructed accurately. As can be seen in Figure 4.5, a sample rate several times greater than $2f$ is needed to extract the waveform as well as the frequency of the process signal. This rate depends on the waveform complexity and the accuracy desired.

In some cases, the investigator is only interested in signals with a frequency of f_x or less; however, he must take into account components of frequency greater than f_x to avoid aliasing. In a few cases, it may be permissable to ignore the error due to aliasing. If the amplitude of the signal components above f_x is small and if the error produced from the aliasing of these components is not critical, the signal can be sampled at a rate appropriate to recover signals below f_x. Care should be taken to insure that the aliasing error is small before ignoring signals above f_x.

There are two ways to limit aliasing. The first method is to determine the highest frequency component of the signal being measured and to sample at a rate greater than twice this frequency. This method is appropriate if the additional sample rate does not burden the processor and if the system does not prohibit the additional data storage and processing time required.

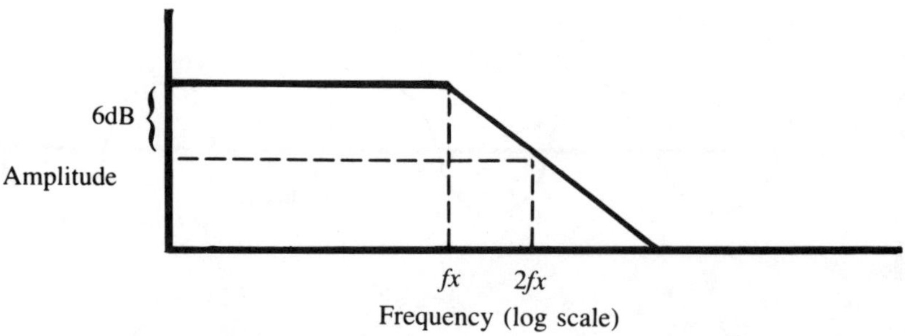

Figure 4.11. Attenuation of a signal of frequency $2f_x$ by a low-pass filter. The attenuation is 6 dB (approximately 50%).

The second method is to use a low-pass filter to attentuate frequency components above f_x. Such an anti-aliasing filter is placed between the transducer and the computer interface used to sample the process variable.

The quality of the anti-aliasing filter can be critical. If the components of the process signal to be filtered are close to f_x, the filter will not attentuate them completely. Figure 4.11 shows the action of a first-order filter on a waveform with components f_x and $2f_x$ of equal amplitude. The $2f_x$ signal is attenuated by six dB. The amplitude of the $2f_x$ component is approximately 50% after filtering. If a sample rate of $2f_x$ is used to measure the output of the filter, this 50% amplitude, $2f_x$ signal is folded and appears as a constant DC signal.

Higher order filters are generally more expensive than first-order filters. The quality of the filter required depends on the relationship of the cut-off frequency to the frequencies being filtered and to the amount of error due to aliasing that can be tolerated.

It is important to note that aliasing must be handled at data collection time, either by increasing the sample rate or by filtering. After data is collected that contains ambiguous frequency components due to aliasing, the true waveform cannot be recovered by software filtering. There is no way to distinguish a true signal component of frequency f and a signal component of a higher frequency that is folded to f by aliasing. These components are identical when collected data is analyzed.

Noise Reduction

Sources of noise are discussed in Chapter 3. The practice of keeping cables short and cables and connections neat should be followed in all applications, even if noise is not a major problem. When the signal-to-noise ratio is small, steps must be taken to identify the sources of noise and to reduce them. All systems contain noise, and noise produces errors. Techniques must be employed to reduce the error due to noise to an acceptable level. Hardware techniques to reduce the noise level are discussed in this section. Software techniques to deal with noise error are discussed in Chapter 6.

Electrostatic noise is produced by capacitive coupling between signal-carrying wires and other conductors or ground. High impedance circuits carrying high frequency signals are most susceptible.

The primary defense against electrostatic noise is to shield signal-carrying wires by wrapping them in a conductor that is grounded. The shield should be grounded at only one point. In most cases, the shield should be grounded at the signal source. The wires inside the shield are protected from capacitive coupling to potentials outside the shield.

If the transducer and any signal conditioning circuitry between the transducer and the interface are all electrically isolated (i.e. floating, not grounded) and the interface has a single-ended input, the shield may be used as the ground connection. Coaxial cable can thus be used to make shielded connections to floating transducers. (If the transducer is grounded, a ground loop may be formed which causes noise-producing current to flow in the coaxial cable shield.) It should be noted that some transducers, such as strain gauges, may be grounded through part of the structure they are connected to and are, thus, not floating. At frequencies above 1 MHz., a phenomenon known as skin effect allows coaxial cable to be used with grounded transducers to provide electrostatic shielding. At high frequencies, the current due to electrostatic coupling flows on the outside of the shield while the signal return current flows on the inside of the shield. This effect produces the same result as two conductors surrounded by a shield. Figure 4.12 shows accepted shielding techniques to reduce electrostatic noise.

Signal leads that pass near strong magnetic fields can pick up noise by induction. Motors and AC power lines carrying large currents are sources of magnetic interference. Separating signal-carrying wires and AC power lines can reduce magnetic noise. Signal-carrying wires that are twisted together with their return line are less subceptible to mag-

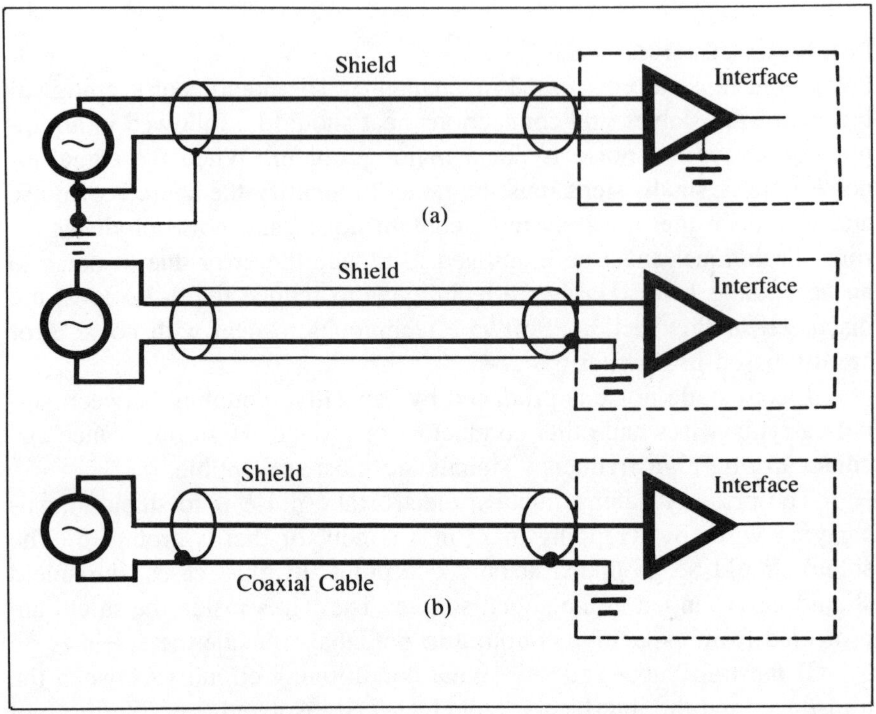

Figure 4.12. Connection of shield to ground for a grounded transducer (a) and for a floating transducer (b). The shield is only grounded at one point.

netic pickup. Noise induced in each of the small loops created by the twists tends to be cancelled by opposite voltages induced in other twists.

Electromagnetic or RF (radio frequency) noise may be picked up by signal-carrying wires. Radio waves from flourescent lights or high frequency switching circuits are possible RF sources. Electromagnetic noise can affect circuits over a considerable distance.

A separate conductive RF shield, which may be grounded in several places, can be placed over groups of electrostatically shielded cable to form RF noise protection. Signal-carrying leads should be close to their return signals.

Wires that carry high frequency signals must be terminated properly to avoid signals from being reflected back toward the signal source and interfering with the signal following it. RF energy does not travel in the conductors but between the two conductors of a cable. An RF signal traveling in a cable "sees" a characteristic impedance based on the capacitance and inductance of the cable. At the receiver of the signal, the cable is terminated in some circuit with some impedance. If the characteristic impedance and the termination impedance are the same, the driver (signal sender) of the cable "sees" a cable of infinite length. If the cable is not terminated at the proper impedance, the cable no longer appears electrically infinite, and energy is reflected back down the cable toward the driver. Impedance mismatch can occur if signal return lines are not grounded close to the source. Care must be taken in high frequency, low impedance cables, driven by circuits such as TTL, that impedance matching and good grounding are observed. Coaxial cable or shielded twisted pairs should be used to carry RF signals.

Ground loops occur when the zero voltage reference point (ground) for a transducer is different than the ground of the computer interface. Because the grounds are at different potentials, current flows through the signal return wire, inducing noise into the system. Similar noise can be induced when signal wires share a common return wire, when large currents flow in the return line, and in thermocouple circuits (due to the resistance of thermocouple wire).

The type of noise induced by ground loops is called common mode noise. Common mode noise is an interference signal injected into both the signal-carrying wire and its return. A differential amplifier subtracts the voltage on the signal-carrying wire and the return, thus reducing common mode noise. The ability of a differential amplifier to reduce common mode noise can be expressed as common mode rejection. A common mode rejection factor of 120 dB means that a common mode signal of x volts is reduced by a factor of 10^{-6} at the output of the differential amplifier while normal mode signals are not attentuated. The common mode noise rejection ability decreases as the frequency of the common mode signal increases.

Sixty Hz. AC power interference can enter a data acquisition signal by electrostatic means, induction, ground loops, or directly through an excited (powered) transducer. Signals at the first harmonic, 120 Hz., can also cause problems. If 60 Hz. noise cannot be significantly reduced by the means discussed so far, it may be possible to use a high-pass filter to remove the 60 Hz. and 120 Hz. frequencies. Filtering cannot be used if the signal contains meaningful frequency components in this frequency range. Noise of other frequencies can also be removed by filtering as long as the filtering does not distort meaningful signal components. Filtering may also be performed in software.

It is possible for mechanical vibration to induce noise into transducers. Strain gauges and optical systems are some of the transducers that may pick up mechanical noise. Sources of mechanical noise include

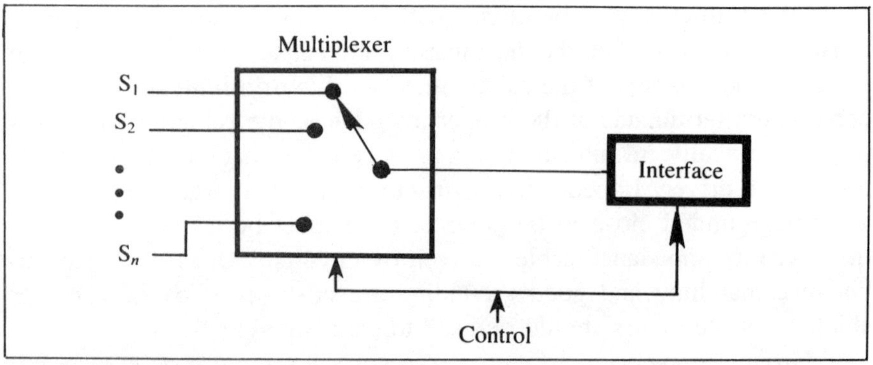

Figure 4.13. Interface multiplexing.

pressure variations in water pipes used to cool equipment and motor vibration.

Sampling Errors

Errors other than from noise can occur in the sampling process. Many of the errors discussed pertain to the sampling of analog signals.

In many applications, it is desirable to sample more than one signal at a time. In order to save hardware costs, the computer interface that performs the sampling is shared by several signals (Figure 4.13).

In the figure, the multiplexer is directed to connect signal s_1 to the interface. S_1 is sampled, and the result of the sampling is made available to the computer. Next, the multiplexer is directed to select s_2, and then s_2 is sampled. This process continues until all the channels are sampled. For example, the multiplexer requires time t_m to select a channel and deliver it to the interface which requires time t_s to convert and buffer it for the computer. In the simple case, the multiplexer will not begin to select a new channel until the interface is finished processing the signal. When the system is directed to begin sampling at time t_0, signal s_1 is selected by the multiplexer and sampling is performed. The completed sampling of s_1 occurs at time $t_0+t_m+t_s$. If the hardware either automatically or under computer control samples successive channels, the s_2 signal is available at time $t_0+2(t_m+t_s)$. S_3 is available at $t_0+3(t_m+t_s)$. S_n is available at $t_0+n(t_m+t_s)$.

In a typical application, the computer would sample all n channels every period of time t_d. Figure 4.14 illustrates this sampling arrangement. The process of sampling all the channels once is called a sweep.

The figure illustrates that the time skew between the time the signals are sampled in each group can be up to $(n-1)(t_m+t_s)$ time

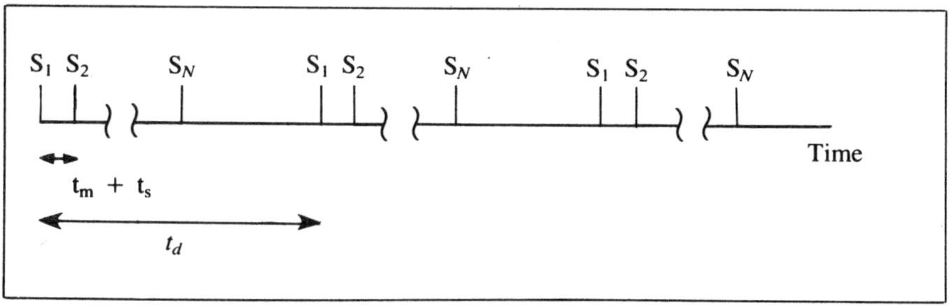

Figure 4.14. Typical sampling arrangement. A sweep of n channels is taken every t_d time period. The time skew between two adjacent channels is $t_m + t_s$.

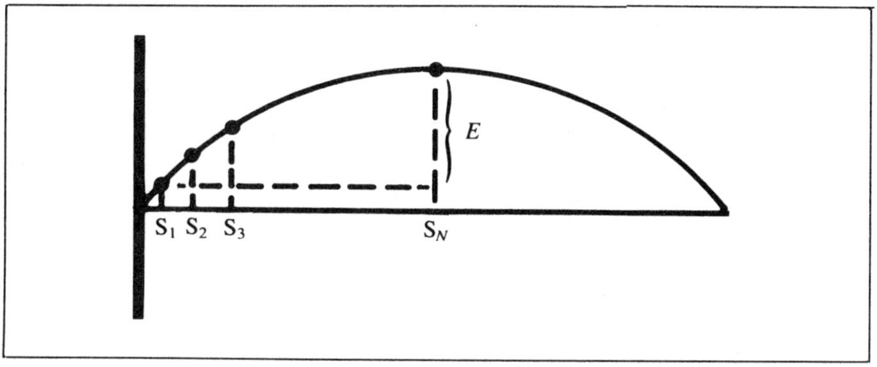

Figure 4.15. The result of sampling n multiplexed channels all connected to the sample input signal. E is the error due to time skew between channel 1 and channel n.

units. The computer program cannot determine the value of all the channels at the same time. Figure 4.15 illustrates the error. To simplify the figure, the result of connecting all the multiplexer inputs to the same signal is shown.

As shown in the figure, the effect of time skew depends on the frequency of the signals being measured and the values of t_m and t_s. The importance of the phase relationship of the signals also relates to importance of reducing time skew.

Figure 4.16 illustrates one method of reducing time skew. Before beginning the sampling process, the storage circuits (sample and hold circuits) are strobed by the control logic to store the current values of analog signals s_1 through s_n. The storage circuits may drift and introduce some error.

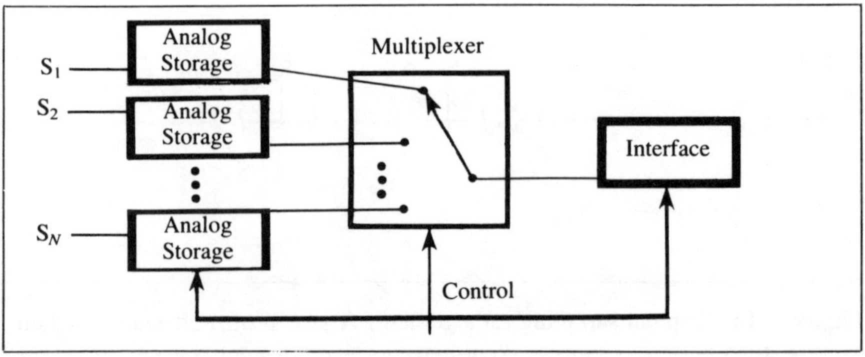

Figure 4.16. A method of reducing time skew.

Time skew may also occur if multiple interfaces are used without a means of synchronizing the units.

Interfaces that convert analog signals into digital signals are called analog-to-digital converters (A/D converters). The construction of these interfaces is discussed in Chapter 5. A/D converters quantize continuous values into discrete binary values. Figure 4.17 illustrates a possible encoding scheme for an ideal converter.

In the figure, each binary combination covers a two volt range. Any output voltage between -5 volts and -3 volts will cause an output of the binary value 110 which corresponds to -4 volts. The maximum error due to quantization in the example is one volt.

In the example, the least significant bit (LSB) of the output is weighted by a factor of two volts. Each successive bit combination covers a two volt range. Any input voltage between the center value of the range minus one volt and the center value of the range plus one volt gives an output equal to the center value.

The error due to quantization is therefore $\pm 1/2$LSB. To lower this error requires that the LSB correspond to a smaller voltage input. To cover the same input range, a converter with a smaller LSB value requires more output bits and is more costly.

Figure 4.18 represents offset error in an A/D converter. Ideally, any input in the range $-1/2$LSB to $+1/2$LSB should produce a zero output. If the range is offset, some voltage other than zero is at the center of the $\pm 1/2$LSB range.

The output of an ideal A/D converter changes once every time the input changes by the value corresponding to one LSB. Real A/D converters do not display such a linear relationship across their entire range.

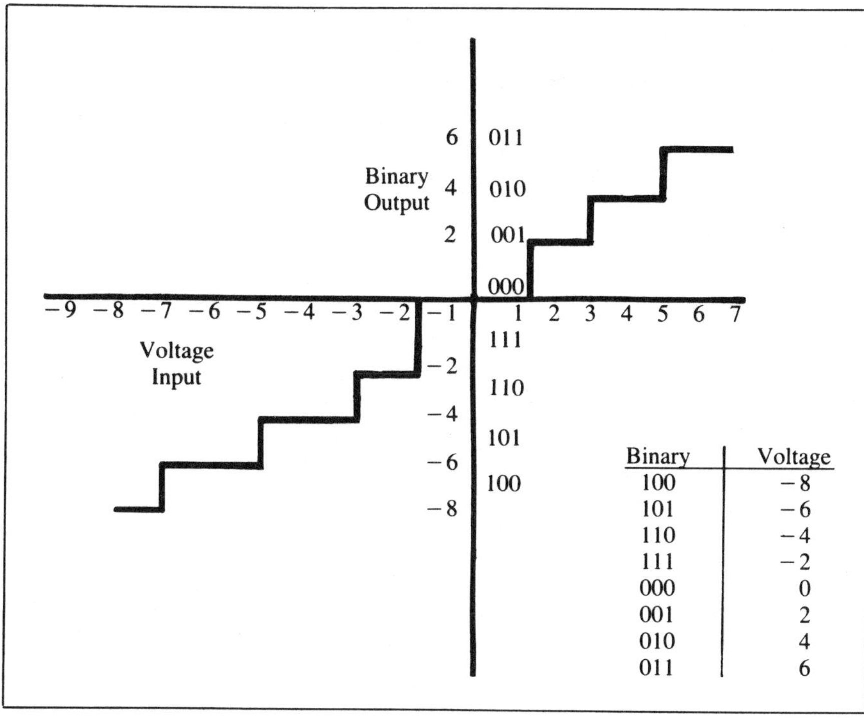

Figure 4.17. A/D converter binary output based on voltage input. The error due to quantization is one volt.

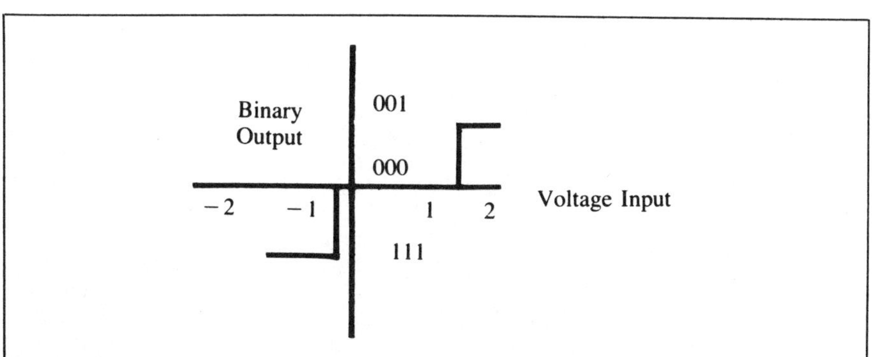

Figure 4.18. A/D converter offset error. Input voltage of −1/2 to 1 1/2, instead of −1 to 1, corresponds to an output of 000.

Depending on the input voltage value in relationship to the A/D converter range, the input change required to produce a one LSB change can be more or less than is expected based on the range covered.

The maximum error due to offset and linearity depends on the quality of a particular A/D converter. The manufacturer's data sheet should be consulted when selecting an A/D converter for a particular application.

5

Interfaces, Special Instruments, and Clocks

There are a wide variety of transducers and laboratory instruments. To acquire data from any device by a computer requires that data from the device be presented to the computer as an encoded binary string. Figure 5.1 shows the general methods of connecting a transducer to a computer. The technique in Figure 5.1a requires a computer interface that directly converts transducer output to a digital form readable by the computer. Figure 5.1b shows a signal conditioning circuit between the transducer and the computer interface. The network performs some translation of the data (e.g. a conversion from current to voltage) but provides little or no data storage. Figure 5.1c shows an instrument connected to the transducer. The instrument may be very sophisticated and even include some computing power of its own. The instrument stores data and possibly performs complex transformations on the data. Such instruments perform specialized functions and typically are connected to a data acquisition system for further data processing and permanent storage.

The types of interfacing shown in Figure 5.1 are broad categories. The actual physical separation of the components may not be as clear.

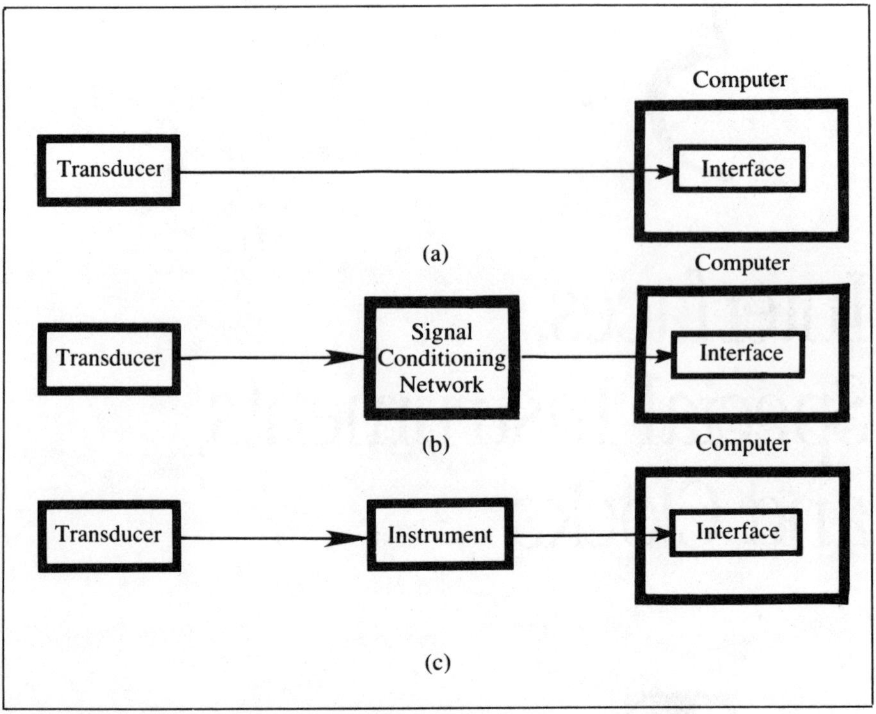

Figure 5.1. Methods of connection of a transducer to a computer: direct connection (a), with signal conditioning (b), and using an intelligent instrument (c).

For example, a laboratory balance designed to connect to a computer contains the transducer and the translation network of 5.1b in a single enclosure.

Signal Conditioning

Signal conditioning networks perform two functions. The first function is to perform some necessary signal conversion to match the transducer output to a standard computer interface. As an example, Figure 5.2 illustrates a network to translate a 0 to 10-volt signal into a 0 to five-volt signal required for a particular A/D converter.

The second primary function of a signal conditioning network is to provide a means for a transducer signal to be propagated over a length of cable. This function is required if transducers are placed throughout a factory and are to be read by the same computer. Even if the cable lengths are relatively short, it may be desirable to condition low-level

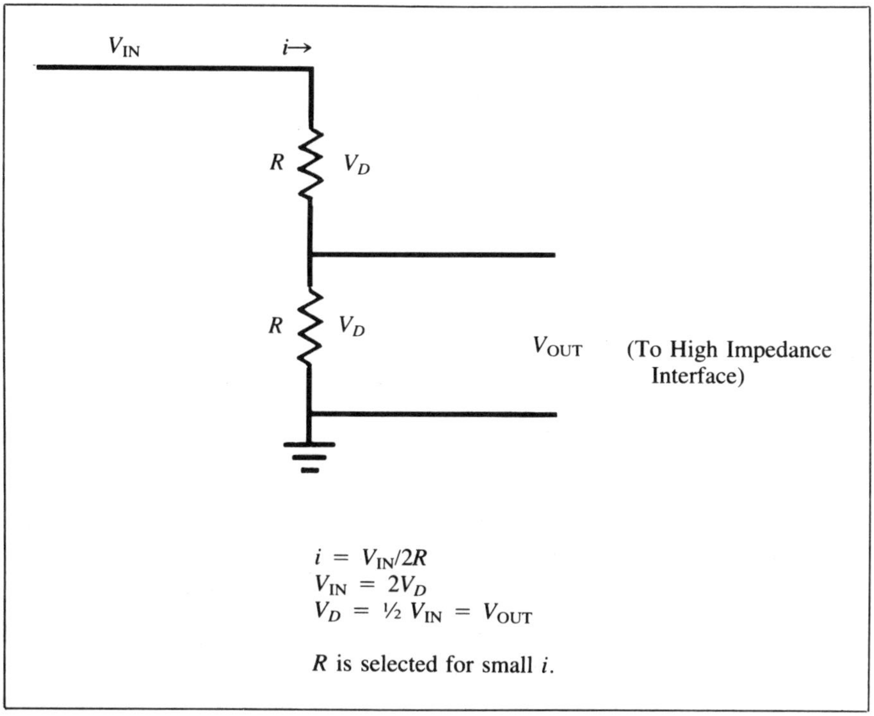

Figure 5.2. Circuit to convert a 0 to 10 volt signal (V_{IN}) to a 0 to 5 volt signal.

signals near their source to prevent signal degradation due to noise. Signal conditioning units should be purchased that exceed the accuracy requirements of the measurement to be performed.

One way to condition a low-level signal is to amplify it. The use of a differential amplifier in such a signal conditioner is typical. The gain of the amplifier must be accurate. Amplifier errors such as drift are typically minimized. The use of an amplifier can improve the signal-to-noise ratio of a signal propagated over a cable; however, signal losses due to the resistance of long cables cause an error.

The conversion of the voltage output of a transducer to a current that is proportional to the voltage provides a means of propagating a signal over long lengths of cable without experiencing loss. A standard signal conditioner translates a specified voltage range into a four to 20 milliamp signal. A signal equal to the lower voltage of the range produces a current of four milliamps, and a signal equal to the high end of the range produces a 20 milliamp signal. The current flows in a loop as shown in Figure 5.3.

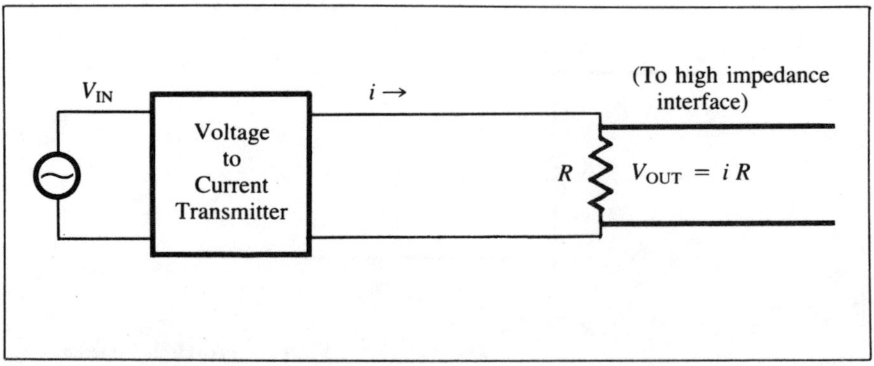

Figure 5.3. Transducer voltage output is converted to a current for transmission over a length of cable. The voltage drop across R is a voltage directly proportional to the transducer voltage.

The signal conditioner is designed so that it modifies its output voltage in order to maintain the appropriate current in the loop. In this manner, it compensates for the effects of long lengths of cable and measuring devices that are in its operating range. The current in the loop can be translated back to a voltage by putting a precision resistor of known resistance in the loop and measuring the voltage drop across the resistor.

Signal conditioning units are available for a wide variety of transducers. Selection of a signal conditioner is based on desired input and output, common mode rejection, gain, and accuracy.

Parallel Interfaces

The simplest type of interface, shown in Figure 5.4, is the parallel interface. The number of signal lines depends on the interface. Each signal line can carry one bit of digital data. Typical parallel interfaces are available in eight, 16, and 32-bit models. The data lines may be input lines, output lines or programmably selected to be either input or output lines depending on the interface. Some additional lines are used to provide handshake (control information) between the interface and the device connected to it.

Since parallel interfaces transfer digital data, the signals connected to the device or transducer from which data is read or written are typically implemented using a standard logic family such as TTL.

Figure 5.5 shows a simple use of a TTL, eight-bit input parallel interface. The interface is connected to eight switches so that if a switch is closed, a binary zero is read for the switch. A logic one indicates an

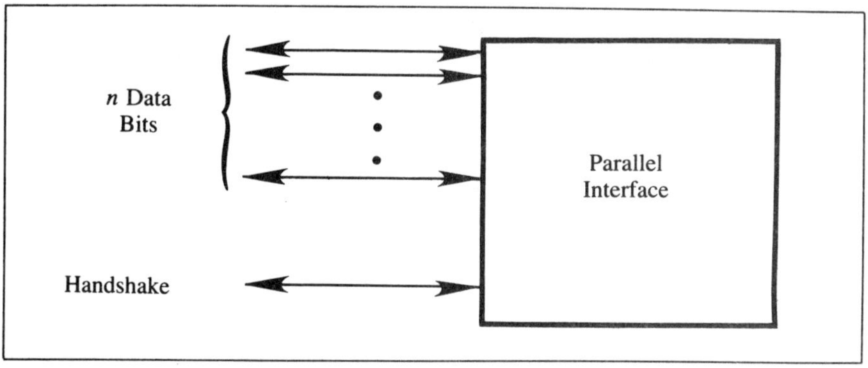

Figure 5.4. An *n*-bit parallel interface. Each data line carries binary information.

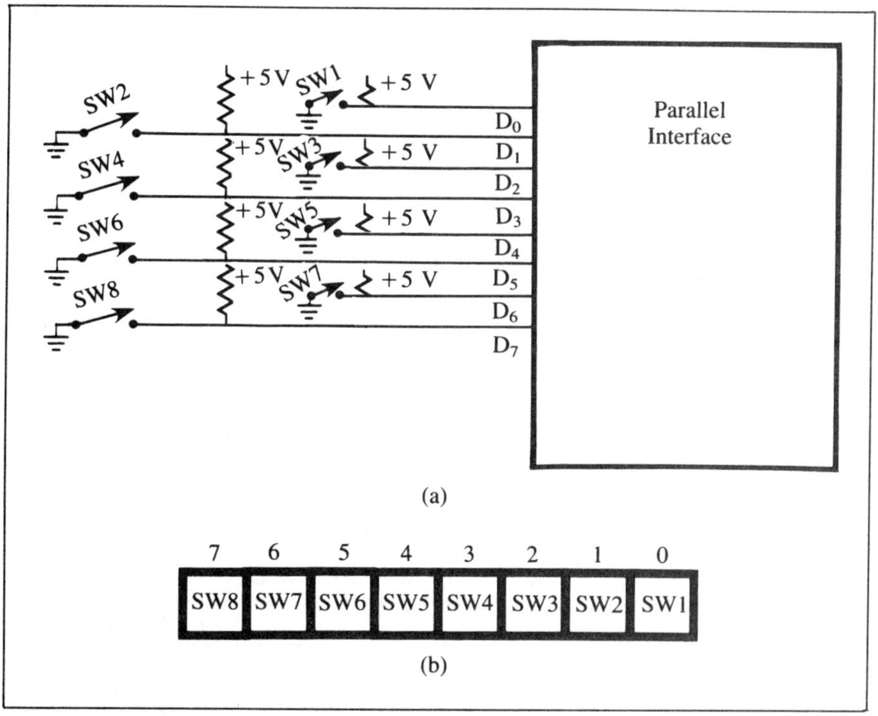

Figure 5.5. Eight switches connected to an eight-bit parallel interface (a) and corresponding input register (b).

open switch. The bit map in the figure shows the correspondence between the switch and the input value presented to the computer by the interface. This particular switch interface uses no handshaking. The computer must periodically read the switch setting since no handshake is available to indicate when the switch state changes. It should also be noted that switch bounce (mechanical instability when the switch changes state) must be handled by the software using the interface. The debounce operation is performed by ignoring the parallel interface for a small period when a switch change is detected. After the delay, mechanical instability of the switch has stopped, and the switch state can be read.

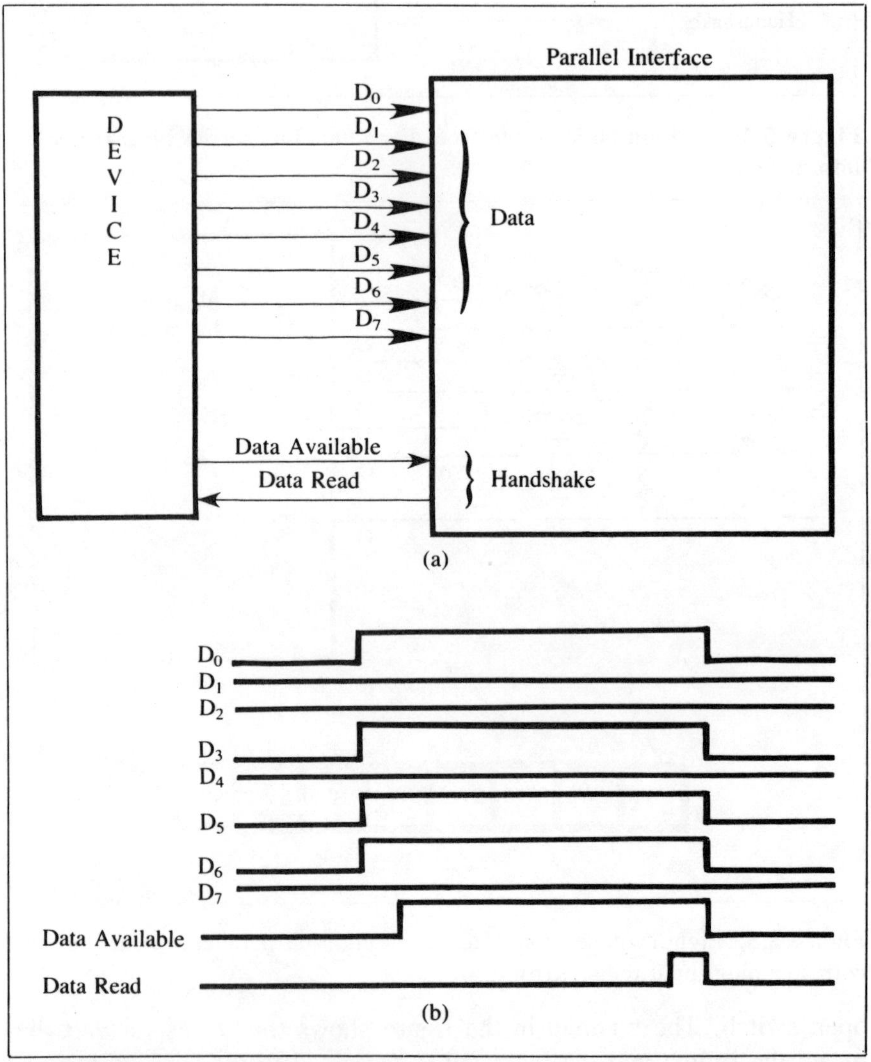

Figure 5.6. A device connected to a parallel interface (a) and a timing diagram of a data transfer (b).

Figure 5.6a shows a typical input parallel interface connected to some device, and 5.6b shows a timing diagram for a typical input transfer. The device presents data to the interface, and when the data is stable, the data available line is asserted. The computer detects the data available condition by performing a status checking operation on the interface or by an interrupt, and then reads the data. When the data has been read, the interface generates the data read signal that informs the device that the data has been read, and the device can remove the data from the interface.

A more complex interface might include a latch for the data in the interface. In this case, the device need not output the data until the data read signal is produced. Instead, the data is saved in the latch on the interface.

If the device is intelligent, it may produce information at a rapid rate that must be read by the computer at a corresponding rate to prevent data loss. If the computer does not read the data fast enough, it is desirable to indicate this overrun condition to the computer. A sophisticated interface will indicate an overrun when the data available line is asserted twice before the computer reads the data corresponding to the first assertion.

Figure 5.7 illustrates a simple output interface. When a 1 is written to a bit in the output interface register, the corresponding LED (light emitting diode) lights.

Figure 5.8 shows a possible parallel interface handshake when the interface is used to output data to an intelligent device. When the computer outputs data to the interface, the data is placed on the data lines; and when the data is stable, the data available line is asserted to indicate to the device that valid data is on the output data lines. The interface continues to output the data until the device strobes the data accepted line. The computer can sense that the data has been accepted by status checking the interface or by an interrupt generated by assertion of the data accepted line. In practice, the data remains on the output data lines until the computer writes new data to the interface.

A typical eight-bit interface appears as two registers to the computer (Figure 5.9a). The data register for an input interface reflects the current value placed on the data lines or the value in the latch of a latched interface. The control/status register for an input interface contains two usable bits. The DATA AVAILABLE bit reflects the state of the data available line. It is set when a device asserts the data available line. It is cleared when the data register is read.

The computer can set or clear the ENABLE INTERRUPT bit.

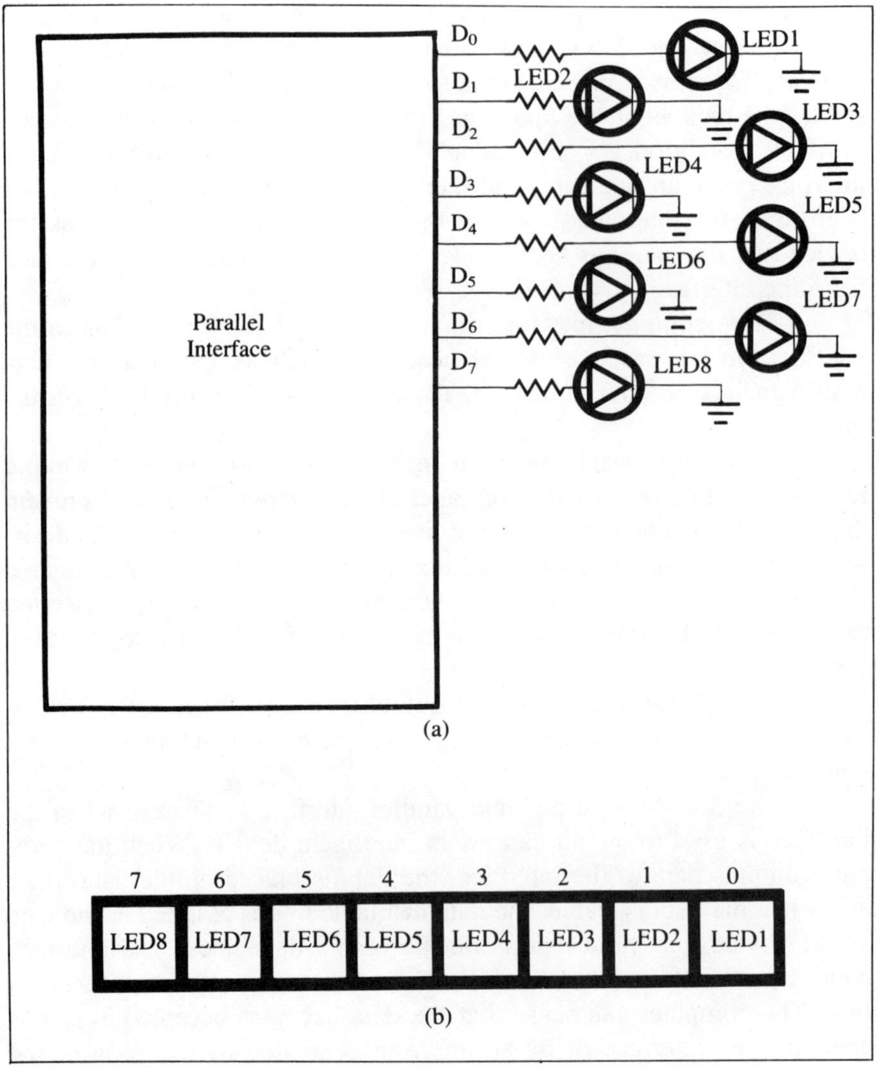

Figure 5.7. An output parallel interface driving eight LEDs (a) and a bit map showing the correspondence of the output value to the LEDs (b).

When either of the two bits is set, a low to high transition on the other bit requests an interrupt. Clearing the ENABLE INTERRUPT bit masks (disables) the interrupt operation. Figure 5.10a shows a possible conceptualization of interrupt generation for an input interface.

Figure 5.9b shows typical registers for a parallel output interface. When data is written to the data register, it is output on the data lines,

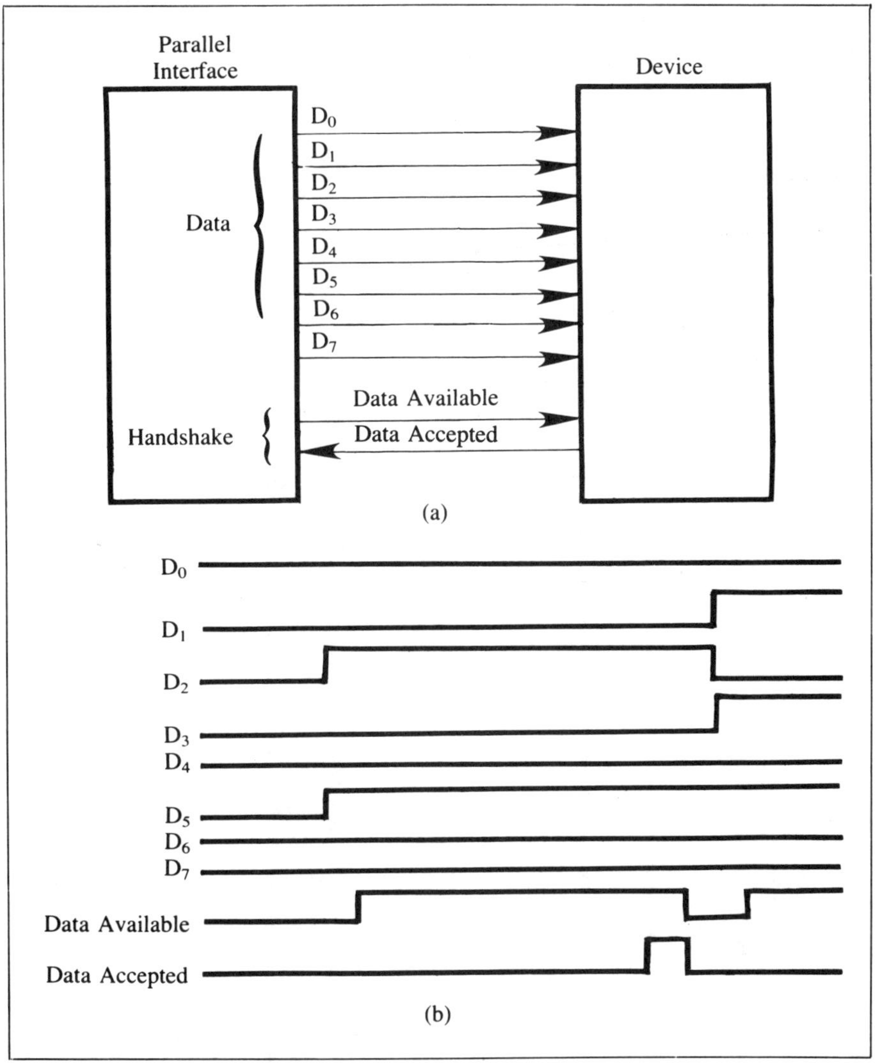

Figure 5.8. An output parallel interface connected to a device (a) and a timing diagram showing a data transfer (b).

and the data available line is asserted. The data register can also be read by the computer as a means of obtaining the last value written to the interface (i.e., the current data line values). This feature allows different program segments to be aware of the interface output value in a simple manner.

When the data accepted signal is strobed, the DATA ACCEPTED

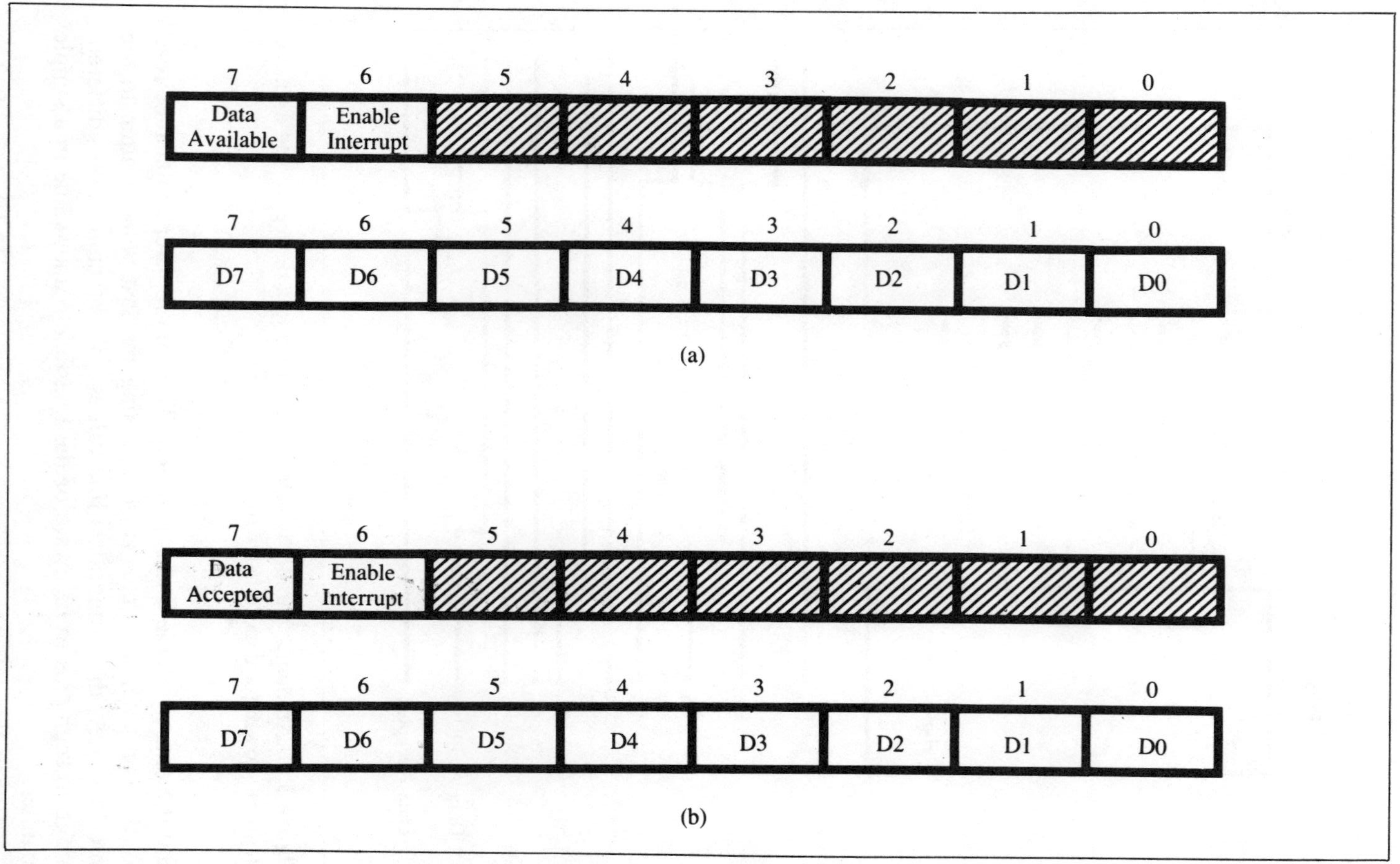

Figure 5.9. Typical registers for an input parallel interface (a) and an output parallel interface (b).

bit in the control/status register is set. It remains set until a new value is written to the data register. This signal may also be used to generate an interrupt (Figure 5.10b).

In both the input and output interfaces, the setting of the status bit (DATA AVAILABLE or DATA ACCEPTED), or the interrupt generated by the setting of the status bit informs the computer that it must

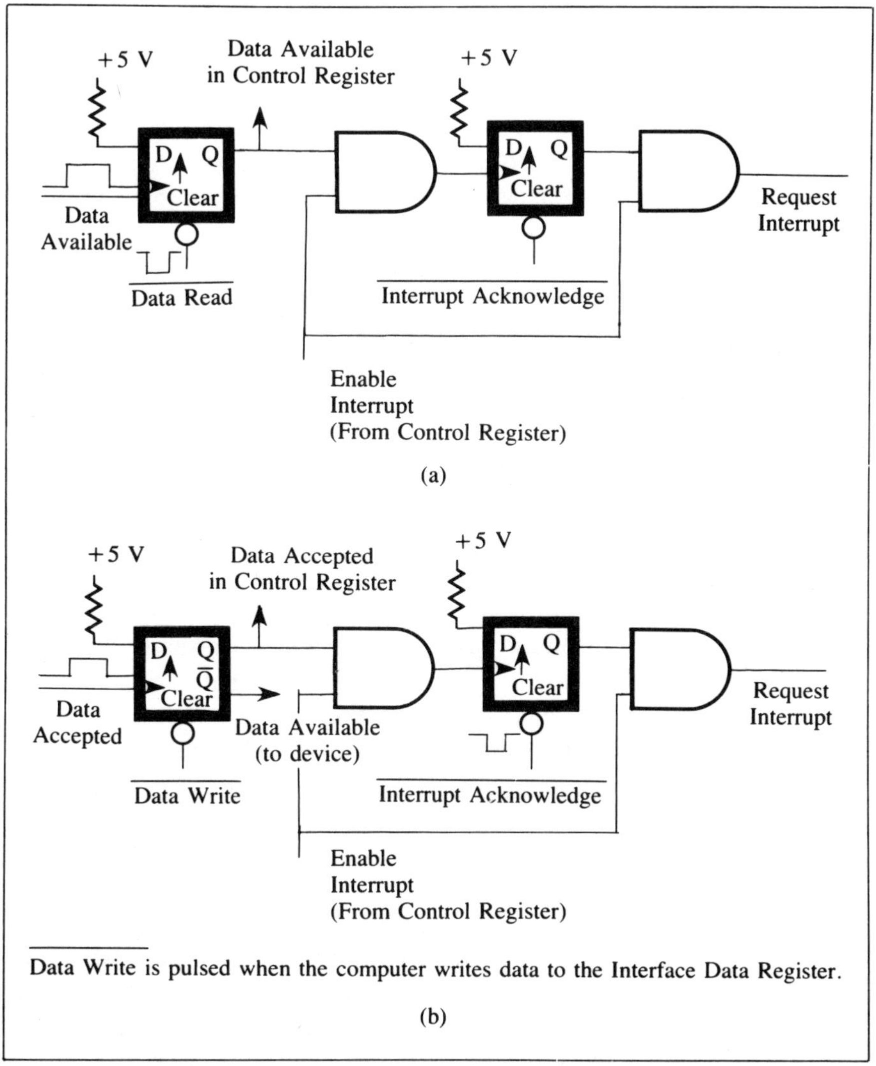

Figure 5.10. Conceptual interrupt control circuits for an input parallel interface (a) and an output parallel interface (b).

perform some action. It must either read data from an input interface or is free to write data to an output interface.

Several added features are available on some interfaces. If the interface can detect a data overrun condition (input data not read before new data is available, or a device does not read output data before new data is output), a bit in the status register is used to indicate the condition. This condition may possibly generate an interrupt.

A special feature of some input interfaces allows any selected input data lines to detect a transition and to generate an interrupt when the transition occurs. A third interface register contains a bit for each line. If the bit for a corresponding line is set, a transition on the line causes an interrupt. If such an interface were used to implement the switch circuit of Figure 5.5, an interrupt could be generated when the state of any switch changed. The computer would then not have to repeatedly read the interface to check for switch state changes.

Another possibility is to combine the input and output interfaces into a single programmable interface. A register contains a bit for each data line. The computer writes programming information to the register to select the function, input or output, for each line. The handshake logic must provide enough flexibility to perform both input and output control.

A programmable interface is useful in a number of circumstances. First, it is flexible and can be used in a variety of applications. Second, it can be connected to a device that requires data transfer in both directions (as an example, see the digital oscilloscope description in this chapter). Third, a programmable interface can be used to form a bidirectional bus for communications with a number of devices and computers.

There are a wide variety of parallel interfaces that vary greatly. To connect devices and computer interfaces made by different vendors may require some external logic. This logic may be as simple as inverting handshake signals or as complex as generating handshake signals not provided by a device.

IEEE-488 Interfaces

The IEEE-488 interface is a standard interface used in some laboratory equipment and digital voltmeters. This interface contains 16 signal lines. Eight data lines pass command information, address information, and data between devices. The other eight are used for control.

A number of instruments, up to 15, can be connected to the bus. A single device is the bus controller. Bus devices that can send data are called talkers, bus devices that can receive data are called listeners. Some devices can perform both functions.

Bus devices are assigned unique addresses in the range of 0 to 30. Each device may also respond to secondary addresses in the 200 to 230 range. Secondary address meaning is a unique function based on device design.

The bus controller sets up data transfers by making one device a talker and one or more devices listeners. The bus controller selects talkers and listeners by activating the bus ATN (attention) line. When this line is active, control messages are passed on the data bus. Commands to select and unselect talkers and listeners are included in the command set.

After the talker and listeners are selected and the ATN line is made a logic zero, the talker begins to transmit data to the one or more listeners. A bus control line is set by the talker when its message is complete.

The controller may also send a trigger command to the selected listeners. The trigger function is instrument dependent. In the case of a voltmeter, for example, the trigger function may cause the voltmeter to take a new reading and to hold it.

The controller may check the status of bus devices by executing a serial poll or a parallel poll. To conduct a serial poll, the bus controller performs a serial poll enable command. Each device to be polled is sequentially made a talker. As each instrument is placed in talk mode, it reports a byte of status information. The controller exits serial poll mode by executing a serial poll disable command.

Before a device can participate in a parallel poll, it must be enabled to do so by the bus controller. When it is enabled, the device is assigned one of the eight data lines to respond on and assigned the status information to be reported. If the instrument addressed as 2 is enabled to present its data available status condition on data line 6, it will do so when a parallel poll function is performed by the controller. The parallel poll function allows the bus controller to determine the status of one condition for each of eight instruments rapidly.

There is a service request line on the IEEE-488 bus. A bus instrument asserts this line if it needs service. The controller can then respond to the service request function by doing a serial poll to determine which device needs servicing.

Figure 5.11 shows a typical IEEE-488 application. The IEEE-488 interface in the computer is the bus controller. Three devices are connected to the bus: a printer, a plotter, and a digital voltmeter.

The printer and plotter can only perform the listener function. The

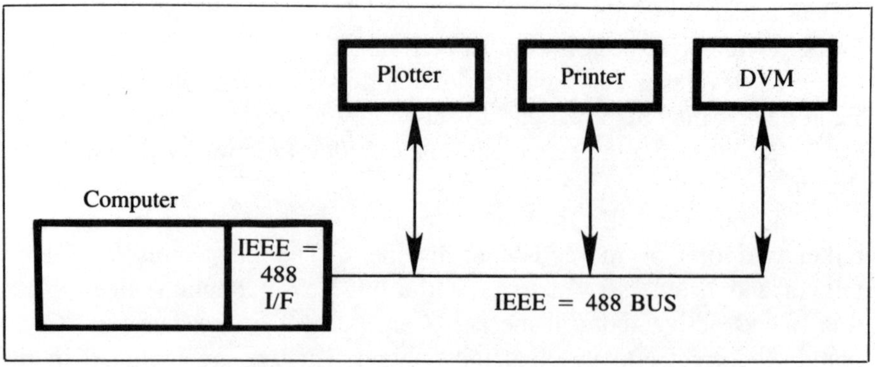

Figure 5.11. IEEE-488 bus connecting a computer, plotter, printer, and digital voltmeter (DVM).

DVM can only be a talker. For the computer to use the plotter, it would place the plotter in the listen mode, enter talk mode itself, and transfer the data to be plotted.

The computer could trigger the DVM to take a reading, place both the printer and itself in listen mode, and accept the data provided by the DVM. The data value would also be printed.

The advantages of the IEEE-488 interface are its well-defined characteristics and its ability to connect a computer to a number of devices using one interface.

Compared to the parallel interface, the software required to drive the IEEE-488 interface is complex. Due to the complex bus protocol, several bus cycles are required to set up a transfer, thus reducing the speed of IEEE-488 transfers. Another disadvantage is that only one device can be talking at a time, meaning that the computer can only effectively communicate with a single bus device at a time. The need for polling also increases device service time in a multiple device environment.

Asynchronous RS-232C Interfaces

The RS-232C is a standard defining the physical and electrical connection of terminals to modems. This standard is also widely used for connecting computers to terminals. Many laboratory instruments can be purchased with RS-232C interfaces.

The RS-232C standard is for use with devices that transmit and receive data serially (one bit at a time). Interfaces used with such devices are thus called serial interfaces. Data bits are either in the mark state, a logic one, or in the space state, a logic zero. Mark is defined as a signal in the range of −3 volts to −25 volts. A space is in the range of +3 volts to +25 volts. Control signals are considered in the logic zero state if the signal is between −3 volts and −25 volts, and in the logic one state when the signal is between +3 volts and +25 volts. Signals in the region between −3 volts and +3 volts are in the undefined state. This region is provided for noise immunity.

RS-232C terminal cables terminate in a 25-pin male connector. Modems terminate in a 25-pin female connector. Figure 5.12 lists RS-232C signal line functions. For the laboratory environment, many of the control lines are not used.

Data generated by a terminal is transferred to the modem on the wire connected to pin 2 of the connectors. Data received from the modem is transferred to the terminal via pin 3. If two devices that are cabled to connect to a modem (e.g., a typical computer interface and a terminal) are to be connected, a "null modem" or "modem eliminator" is required. The "null modem" is comprised of two female connectors wired as shown in Figure 5.13. The cabling arrangement allows data generated on pin 2 of each device to be routed to pin 3, the receive line, of the other device. The "null modem" also interconnects control lines such that each device "sees" a modem whose control lines indicate it is connected to another modem that is ready to receive and transmit data. Some interfaces will not operate unless this modem ready condition exists.

Most laboratory equipment and computer interfaces used in the laboratory transfer data in the asynchronous mode. (The RS-232C standard does not address data format. It can be used with asynchronous, synchronous, and bit-oriented devices—see Chapter 11.) If data is not being transmitted, the transmit data line is in the mark state. When a character is to be transmitted, a string of bits are placed on the line sequentially at a specified rate. Typical transmission rates are 110, 300, 1200, 2400, 4800, and 9600 bits per second (bps). The first bit in the character is a start bit. The start bit is at the space level, indicating a character is being transmitted. The actual character data bits follow the start bit. Most laboratory instruments use the seven-bit ASCII code (Appendix A) with an additional parity bit for error checking. In cases where parity is not used, an eighth bit in the space state is commonly transmitted to preserve the typical eight-bit format. Following the character are one or two stop bits at the mark level. The stop bits allow the receiver to verify that a character has probably been received (as opposed to noise that caused the line to enter the space condition for a time

Pin	Function	Originator
1	Protective Ground	—
2	Transmit Data	Terminal
3	Received Data	Modem
4	Request to Send	Terminal
5	Clear to Send	Modem
6	Data Set Ready	Modem
7	Signal Ground	—
8	Carrier Detect	Modem
9	(Test Function)	—
10	(Test Function)	—
11	—	—
12	Secondary Received Line Signal Detect	Modem
13	Secondary Clear to Send	Modem
14	Secondary Transmit Data	Terminal
15	Transmit Clock	Terminal
16	Secondary Received Data	Modem
17	Receive Clock	Modem
18	—	—
19	Secondary Request to Send	Terminal
20	Data Terminal Ready	Terminal
21	Signal Quality Detector	Modem
22	Ring Indicator	Modem
23	Rate Selector	Terminal or modem
24	Transmit Clock	Terminal
25	—	—

The secondary channel control lines are used in a system where high speed transmission occurs in one direction at a time. The secondary channel is a slow speed communications path in the opposite direction. The clock signals, test leads, secondary channel control lines, and most of the other control lines are not used in a laboratory environment. Serial data is passed on lines two and three.

Figure 5.12. RS-232C signal functions.

longer than a character). The BREAK condition is created by putting the line in the space condition for more than one character time (no stop bits). The BREAK condition is usually generated by a terminal connected to a computer when the operator presses the BREAK key to re-

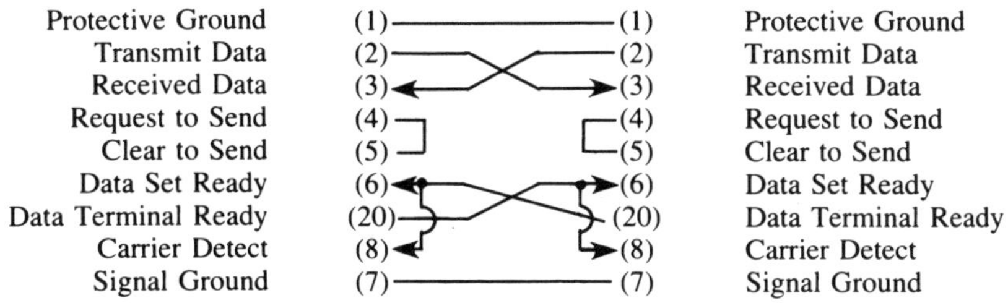

Figure 5.13. An RS-232C null modem for connection of two devices when each is cabled for connection to a modem.

quest the attention of the computer. (Most laboratory instruments do not use the BREAK facility.)

Most computer interfaces, terminals, and laboratory instruments operate in full-duplex mode (as opposed to half-duplex mode). When full-duplex devices are connected, both can transmit simultaneously. Some laboratory instruments, such as a balance with an RS-232C interface, can only transmit data. They do not receive information from the device to which they are connected.

Intelligent laboratory devices, e.g. digital oscilloscopes (described below), receive commands or commands and data from the device they are connected to as well as transmitting data.

The advantage of RS-232C interfaces in the laboratory is that standard interfaces are readily available. The two primary disadvantages of serial transmission as compared to parallel transmission is speed and complexity. At 9600 bps, the time to transmit an eight-bit asynchronous mode character is one millisecond. An average eight-bit parallel interface can transfer the same information one thousand times faster.

Most modern laboratory instruments store data internally in parallel format. To transmit the data serially requires circuitry more complex than needed to transfer the data in parallel format. UART (Universal Asynchronous Receiver Transmitter) integrated circuits perform the parallel to serial and serial to parallel conversions. These chips greatly reduce the complexity of serial interfaces.

Digital Panel Meters (DPM)

A digital panel meter (DPM) is a small, relatively inexpensive device that inputs an analog signal and displays a numeric value related to the input. The DPM is essentially a digital voltmeter capable of reading one voltage range.

Most DPMs have BCD outputs that reflect the value being displayed. These outputs can usually be directly connected to a parallel interface of a computer.

A typical DPM has a display range of 3½ digits (−1999 to +1999). The time to convert the analog input to a display value is relatively long (in the range of 50 samples/second). Most DPMs sample continuously (not on demand by a computer connected to it). Some handshake signals are provided by the BCD interface so that the computer can read the converted value when the panel meter is not in the process of changing its outputs. (This handshake is more necessary when two eight-bit ports are used to read the information. The situation where one port is read, the DPM changes its output, and the second port is read must be avoided.)

Many DPMs have one input. The voltage input to produce a full-scale output is fixed. External logic is required if the DPM must be switched between input sources and if multiple input ranges are needed. More sophisticated DPMs are also available with multiple input channels and multiple ranges. Typically the selection of channel and range can be performed manually or under computer control via a parallel interface.

DPMs are important to the data acquisition system designer for two reasons. First, many laboratory instruments contain a DPM that can be connected to a computer using a parallel interface. Second, the DPM can be used in some applications to cheaply interface a slowly changing analog signal to a parallel interface. Greater speed, accuracy, and flexibility can be obtained when sampling analog signals by using an analog-to-digital converter (described below); however, analog interfaces are typically more expensive than DPMs.

A typical DPM application is to measure room temperature in a controlled environment. The computer monitoring the environment might only need to check the temperature every ten minutes or so. The accuracy of the reading is not critical. By connecting a resistive temperature sensor (e.g. a thermistor), a voltage source, a DPM, and a parallel interface as shown in Figure 5.14, an inexpensive temperature interface is constructed.

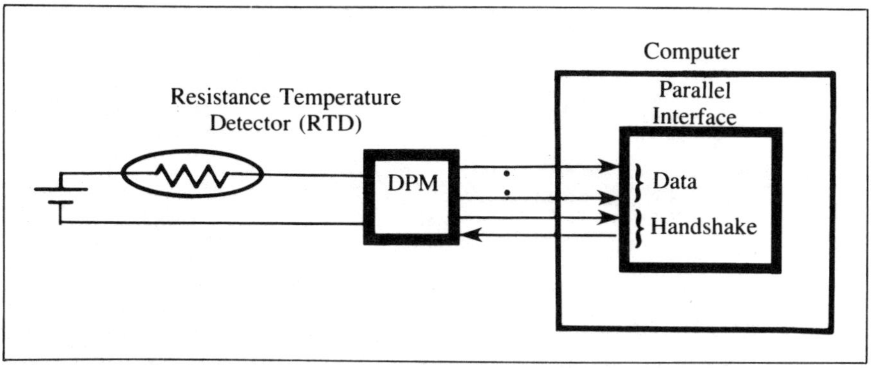

Figure 5.14. An inexpensive temperature measuring device that interfaces to a parallel interface using a DPM.

Digital Oscilloscope

A digital oscilloscope captures analog data, stores it in digital form in a buffer, and displays it on a CRT (see Figure 5.15). Typically, a digital oscilloscope allows the operator to zoom and pan through the data. Stored data can commonly be transferred to a computer.

A typical digital oscilloscope can store several thousand points. Storage and display is rapid. The power of the digital oscilloscope is in its extensive trigger features. In pretrigger mode, the buffer is filled until the trigger condition is met (the input signal reaches a certain level, or possibly a certain level is reached by a separate trigger signal). This mode allows the operator to determine signal behavior before the trigger event occurs. Other trigger and storage modes allow viewing of a signal during and after the trigger.

Typical digital oscilloscopes allow the data buffer to be transferred to a computer using a common interface (parallel, IEEE-488, or serial). The digital oscilloscope may accept data from the computer for display. Floppy disks or cassette tape units may also be connected to some digital oscilloscopes for storage of the data buffer.

The digital oscilloscope is useful when one or possibly two signals must be digitized and displayed. The digital oscilloscope is suited for capturing a randomly occurring signal. The display feature allows immediate analysis by the operator. A particularly useful feature allows the operator to move a cursor along the displayed curve. As the cursor is moved, the digital value of the point under the cursor is displayed as a number on the digital oscilloscope screen.

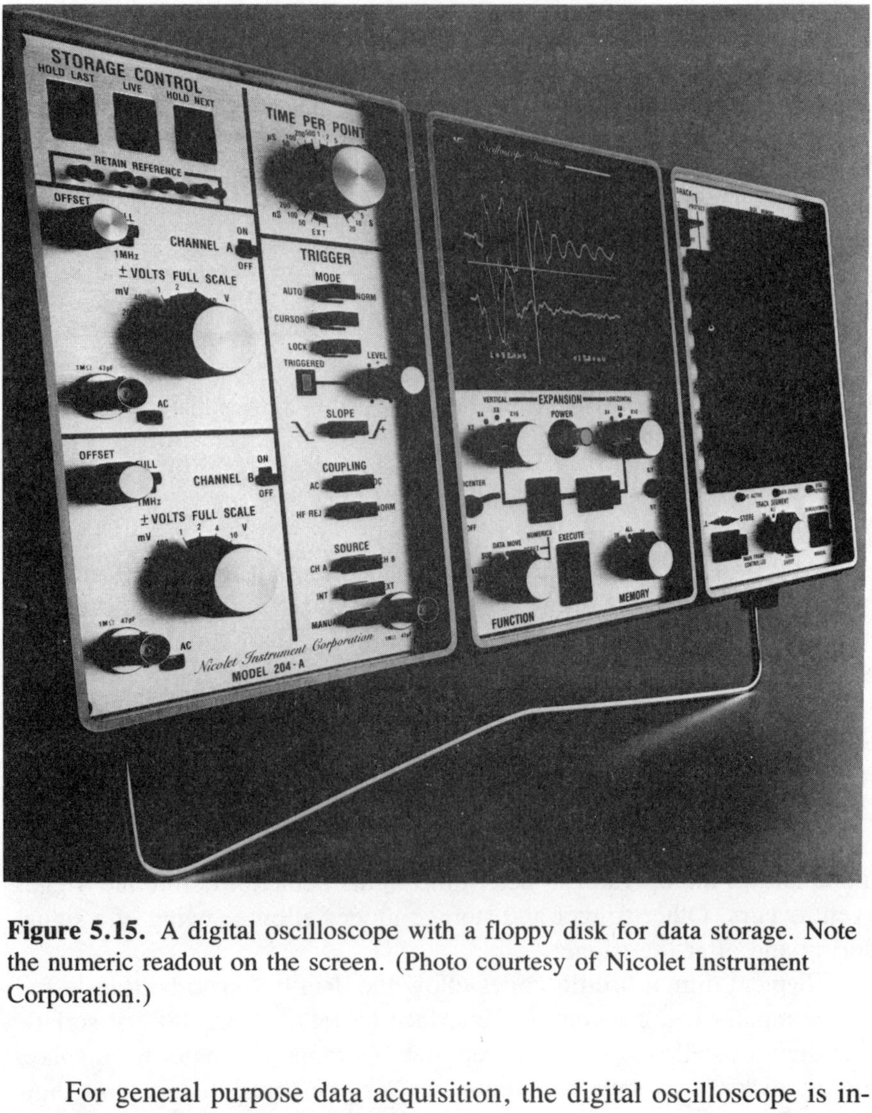

Figure 5.15. A digital oscilloscope with a floppy disk for data storage. Note the numeric readout on the screen. (Photo courtesy of Nicolet Instrument Corporation.)

For general purpose data acquisition, the digital oscilloscope is inflexible. It is limited by the number of signals that can be sampled concurrently. Since the digital oscilloscope is not programmable, it can not be made to transform the data or to perform control functions. The size of the buffer limits the number of points that can be stored. (A computer with access to a mass storage device has a much larger storage size provided that the sample rates involved do not prohibit mass storage usage).

It should be noted that the digital oscilloscope is a highly specialized data acquisition system. It includes an analog-to-digital converter, data storage, and control circuits. Depending on the speed required, the control circuits of the digital oscilloscope could be implemented using a microprocessor, bit-slice integrated circuits, or logic circuits.

Analog to Digital Converters

The designer of a data acquisition system normally has a wide variety of A/D converters from which to choose. Although he need not be able to design an analog to digital converter, he should understand their workings in order to be able to make wise selections.

Figure 5.16 shows a block diagram of an A/D converter subsystem with many typical features. The actual A/D converter portion of the A/D converter subsystem (A/D converter interface) converts a single analog input in a particular range to a binary value. Additional subsystem components are required to provide multiple channels, multiple ranges, input stability, and computer bus interfacing. The typical A/D converter subsystem consists of a multiplexer, an amplifier, a sample and hold, an A/D converter, and control circuitry. In other literature and in following sections where A/D converter subsystem hardware is not being described, the terms "A/D converter" and "A/D converter subsystem" both refer to the entire analog interface.

We shall examine the converter section first. There are a number of methods used to construct an A/D converter. Some of the methods use a digital-to-analog converter (DAC) as a major component. The DAC is described in greater detail in Chapter 10. For the current discussion, it is described as a device that outputs an analog voltage that is a function of a digital value input.

The integration method of A/D conversion is shown in Figure 5.17. To start a conversion, the counter is cleared, and the capacitor is discharged and allowed to begin charging. As the capacitor of the integrator charges, the counter is incremented at a known frequency.

The output of the integrator is a ramp function. This ramp value is compared to the signal to be digitized. When the input signal and ramp signal are equal, counting is stopped, and the counter value is proportional to the input value. If the reference voltage and counter clock rate are known, the correspondence between a digital counter value and the input value can be computed.

There are improvements on the basic integration converter that can be used to improve converter speed and accuracy. One of these methods, the counter-comparator method, is shown in Figure 5.18. To start a conversion, the counter is cleared and then is incremented by a clock. Each count value is applied to a DAC which produces an analog value corresponding to the digital count. The output of the DAC is compared

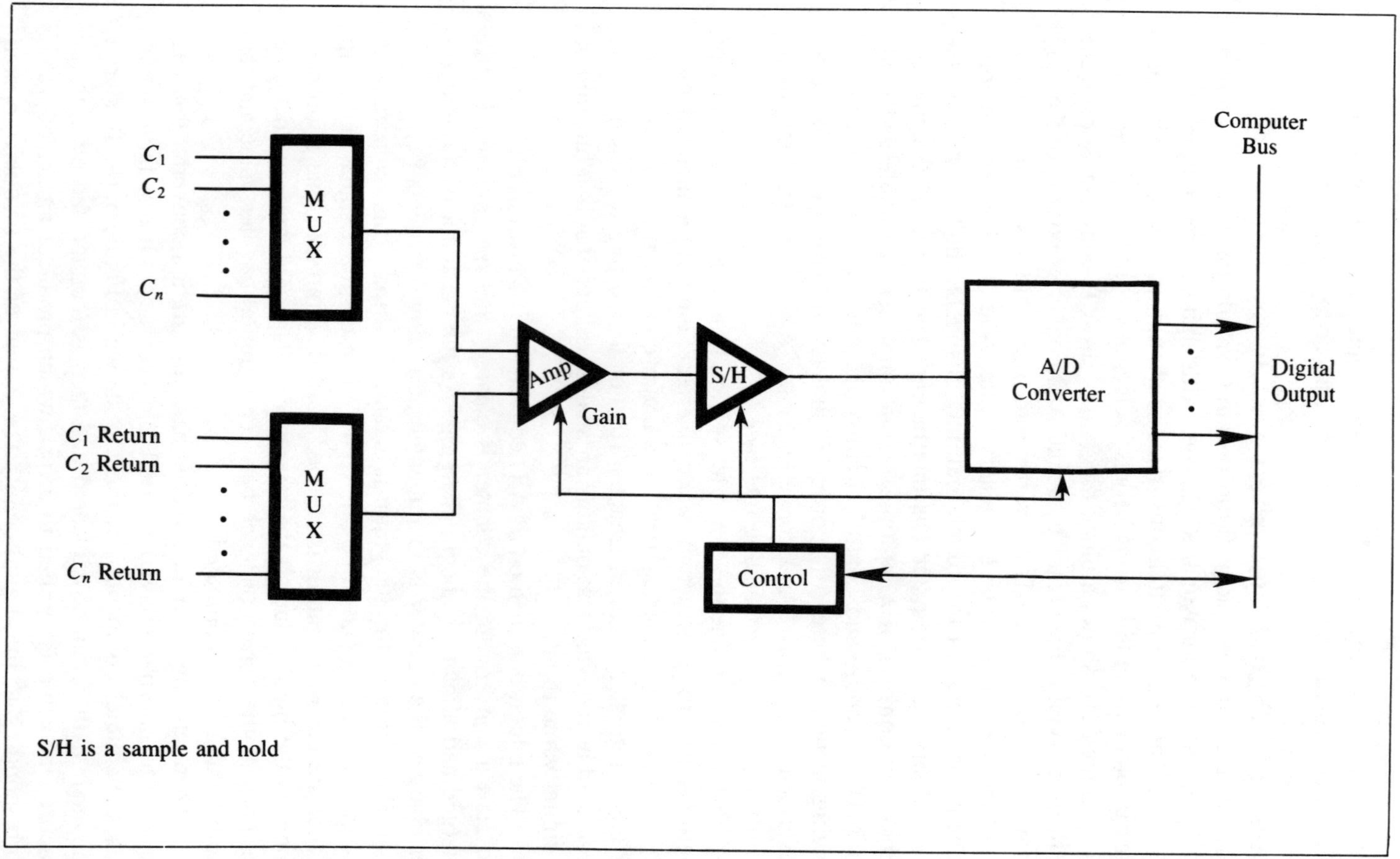

Figure 5.16. Block diagram of an A/D converter subsystem with differential inputs and programmable gain.

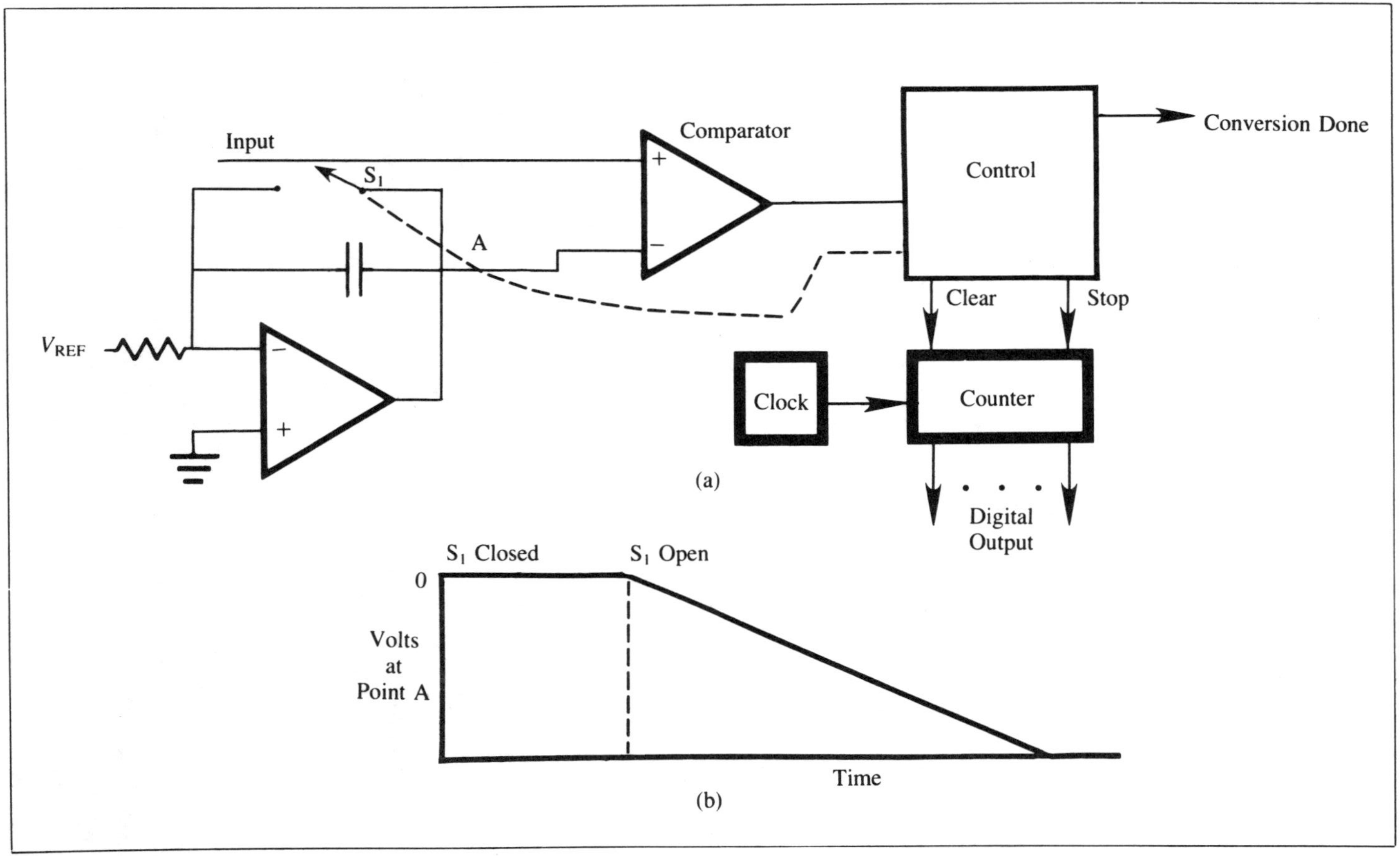

Figure 5.17. The integration method of A/D conversion: a block diagram (a) and output of the integrator (b).

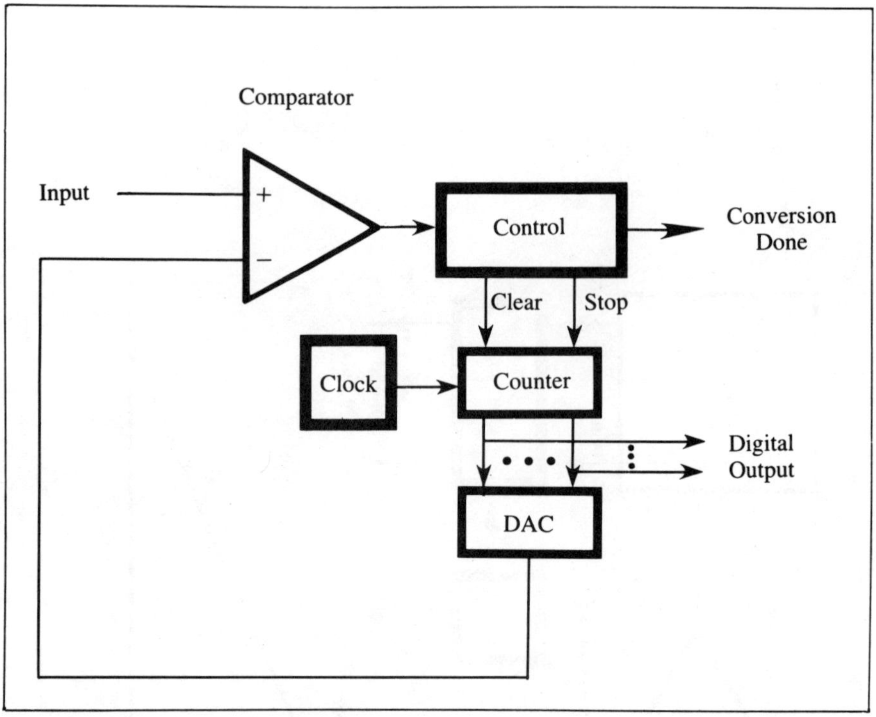

Figure 5.18. A block diagram of a counter-comparator A/D converter.

with the input value. If the input and output values are equal within the significance of the converter, counting is stopped, and the counter contains the digital equivalent of the input value.

The primary disadvantage of this type of converter is that conversion time required for full-scale values is large since the counter must be incremented through its entire range. Improvement on the counter method of conversion uses a counter that can be both incremented and decremented. Control logic either increments or decrements the counter based on which counting method will produce the faster conversion for a particular input.

The successive approximation method of analog-to-digital conversion is shown in Figure 5.19. When conversion is started, the register is cleared. In a loop starting with the most significant bit of the register, each bit is set to one. If the value generated by the DAC connected to the register is less than the input value, the bit remains set. If the DAC value is larger than the input value, the bit is cleared. In either case, the steps are repeated for the remaining bits in the register, proceeding toward the least significant bit.

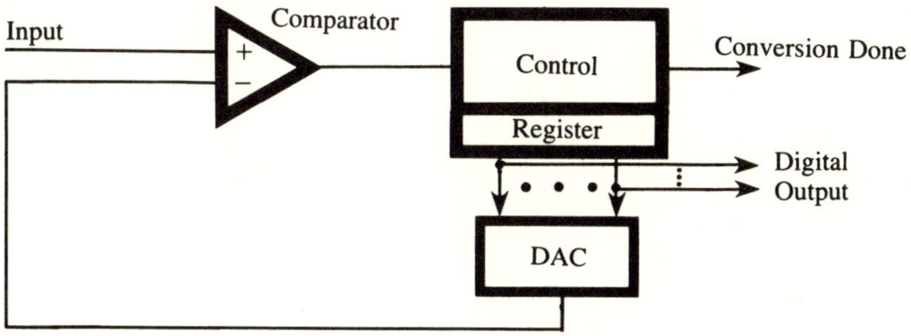

Figure 5.19. Block diagram of a successive approximation A/D converter.

Regardless of the input, the conversion always takes a fixed amount of time. Figure 5.20 shows the output of the DAC during the conversion operation for an example input value. The successive approximation converter requires that the input to the converter remain

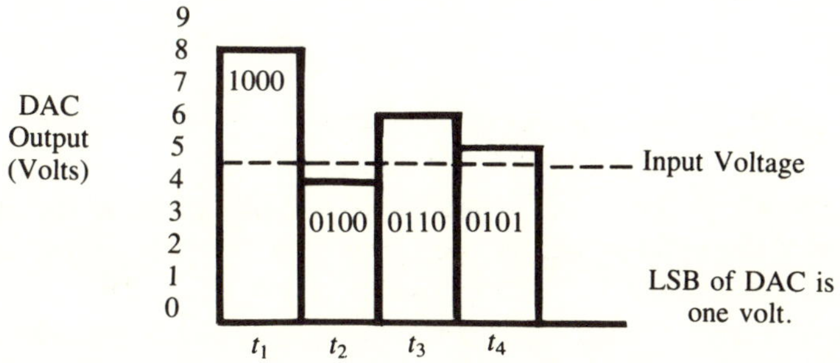

At t_1, DAC bit 3 is set: $V_{DAC} > V_{IN}$ so bit 3 is cleared.
At t_2, DAC bit 2 is set: $V_{DAC} < V_{IN}$ so bit 2 remains set.
At t_3, DAC bit 1 is set: $V_{DAC} > V_{IN}$ so bit 1 is cleared.
At t_4, DAC bit 0 is set: $V_{DAC} > V_{IN}$ so bit 0 is cleared.

Digital output is 0100_2 (4_{10}). (The resolution of the converter is one volt.)

Figure 5.20. The action of a successive approximation A/D converter during conversion of an input voltage of 4.5 volts.

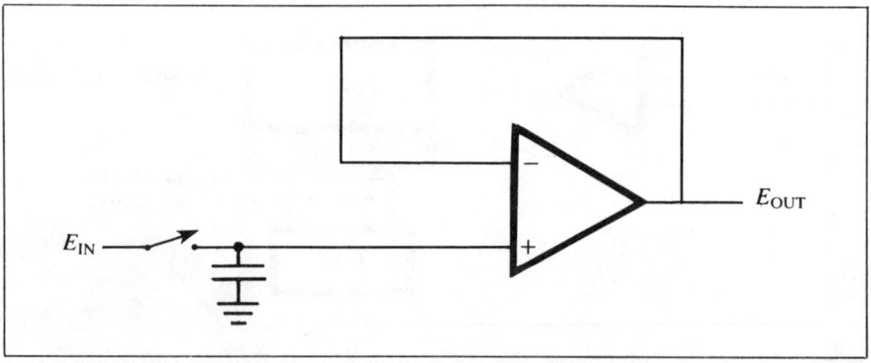

Figure 5.21. Simplified diagram of a sample and hold. Op amp feedback loop as shown forms a voltage follower configuration with unity gain.

constant during the conversion. This condition was not necessary in the other converter types; however, most general purpose converters are implemented such that the input signal is held constant during the conversion by using a sample and hold circuit (described below). (For other converter applications such as in digital voltmeters, it may be desirable to average the signal over the conversion time. Certain types of integration type converters, where an integrater is driven by the input value, perform a conversion on the average input signal during the integration period.)

Figure 5.21 shows a simplified diagram of a sample and hold circuit. When the switch is closed, the output voltage is the same as the input ($E_{out} = E_{in}$). The sample and hold is said to track the input in this mode. When the switch is open, the output of the sample and hold is the last input value before the switch was opened. This value is retained as a charge on the capacitor. The high impedance of the op amp allows the charge to be retained for long periods.

In practice, the switch is constructed using a solid state device such as a field effect transistor (FET). Much faster switching speeds are obtainable using transistors instead of mechanical switches. In addition, a FET buffer may be placed between the capacitor and the op amp to reduce leakage (current flow out of the capacitor).

The purpose of the sample and hold in the typical converter (Figure 5.16) is to sample the signal for a short period of time and to store the sampled value long enough for the value to be converted. Depending on the frequency of the signal being sampled, the type of converter, and the speed of the converter, the need for a sample and hold can be determined. Most general purpose A/D converter subsystems provide a sample and hold circuit.

Many general purpose A/D converter subsystems include an amplifier with a number of discrete, selectable gains. The gains may be manually selectable with straps or switches on the A/D converter printed circuit board, or the gain may be selected under program control. Programmable gains allow the computer to vary the gain from channel to channel, while in manually controlled systems all channels are sampled at the same gain.

Programmable gains add to the flexibility of an A/D converter subsystem. In some instances, the value of a signal must be measured accurately over a wide input range. The software can select a gain, read the value of the signal, and, if necessary, increase or decrease the gain and perform another conversion. This autoranging function can be performed as long as the need to take multiple samples does not interfere with other desired functions.

An n-bit A/D converter must divide the input range into 2^n possible digital values. If the signal to be sampled occurs over a range much smaller than the A/D converter input range, some potential accuracy of the converter is lost. By amplifying the input signal to match the A/D converter input range more closely, the signal can be read with greater accuracy.

The quality of the amplifier is important. A special high quality amplifier called an instrumentation amplifier is usually used in A/D converter subsystems requiring differential inputs with high common mode noise rejection. Instrumentation amplifiers are used when low-level (millivolt signals) must be amplified.

Figure 5.22 illustrates schematically how programmable gains can be implemented. By writing a two-bit gain code into a register in the A/D converter subsystem, one of four solid state switches is closed to select a gain controlling resistor. Another method would be to allocate a control register bit for each switch, thus allowing any combination of resistors to be selected.

Without a multiplexer, the A/D converter can sample only one signal. By using a multiplexer, multiple channels can be sampled by a single converter, thus reducing cost over replicating A/D converters. Figure 5.23 shows a multiplexer configuration for use with a single-ended A/D converter. Only the non-grounded side of the signal is switched, and the input is connected to a single-ended amplifier. The single-ended configuration is used when the input signals do not contain

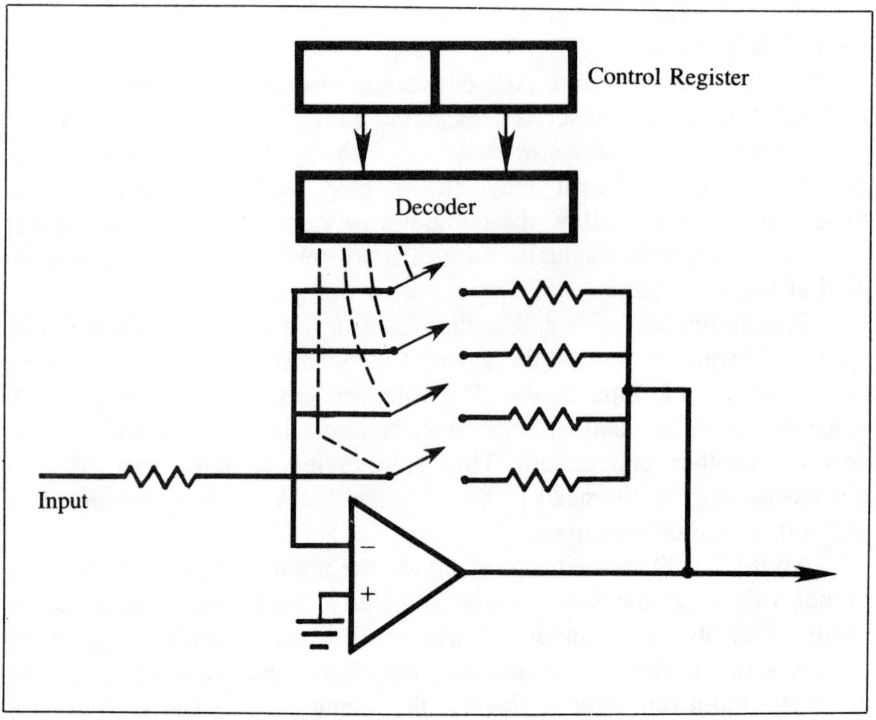

Figure 5.22. Schematic diagram of computer controlled gain circuit.

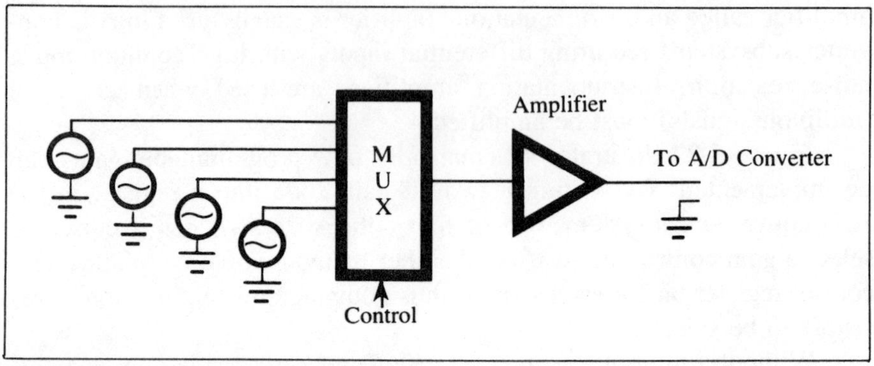

Figure 5.23. Multiplexer configuration for a single-ended A/D converter subsystem.

enough common mode noise to reduce the accuracy of the measurements below desirable limits.

Figure 5.24 shows a multiplexer for a differential input A/D converter subsystem. To perform a conversion operation, multiplexer A se-

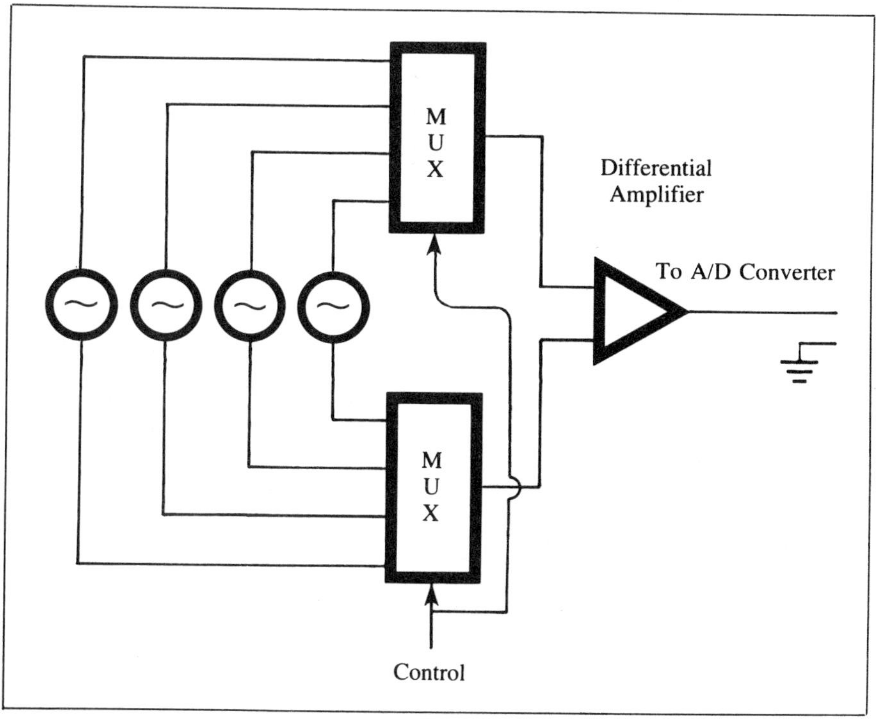

Figure 5.24. Multiplexer configuration for a differential input A/D converter subsystem.

lects the high-level input of the desired channel, and multiplexer B selects the low-level input.

A reduction in multiplexer hardware is possible with the pseudo-differential system of Figure 5.25. In this system, all the transducer return lines are connected together. The pseudo-differential configuration provides common mode noise rejection if the low-level signal side of the sources are at the same potential and if the transducers are relatively close together.

Digital Equipment Corporation has coined the term "quasi-differential" to describe a technique which provides high common mode noise rejection at DC levels but whose common mode noise rejection falls off rapidly as input frequency increases. Figure 5.26 shows a simplified diagram of a quasi-differential converter. This configuration attempts to reduce A/D converter subsystem cost by removing the need for a differential amplifier.

To perform a conversion, the multiplexers select the high-level and low-level signal components of a particular signal. The high-level com-

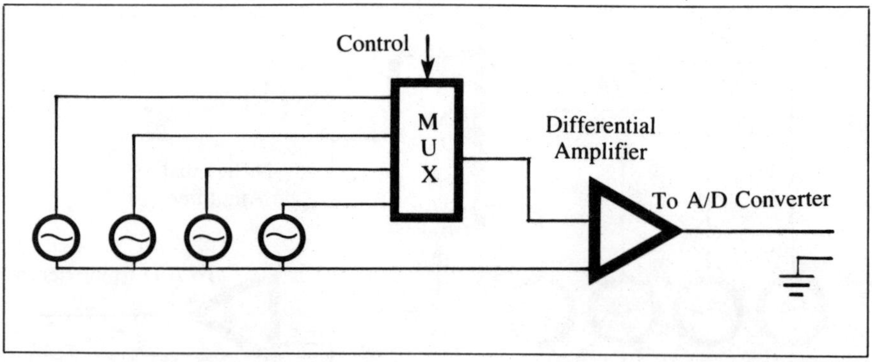

Figure 5.25. Multiplexer configuration for a pseudo-differential input A/D converter subsystem.

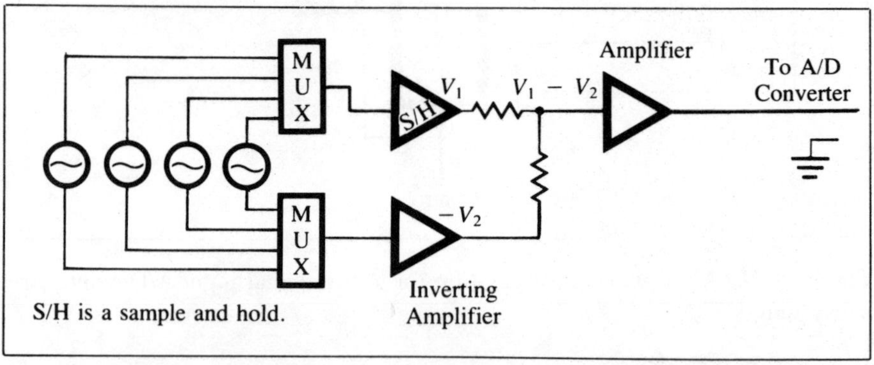

Figure 5.26. Block diagram of a quasi-differential input section of an A/D converter subsystem.

ponent is sampled by a sample and hold circuit. The held signal is algebraically summed with the negative of the low-level signal component. The low-level signal will contain only common-mode noise. If the common mode noise is at a DC level, the output of the summing amplifier is the normal mode signal after the common mode noise is subtracted out. If the common mode noise is an AC signal, the output of the summing amplifier varies during the conversion. This condition reduces the accuracy of the conversion.

Multiplexer design becomes more critical if low-level signals in the millivolt range must be switched. Differential techniques become more important. Also, another multiplexer may be added to multiplex the cable shield for each channel. This technique allows the shield of the selected channel to be connected to the differential amplifier shield to satisfy shielding requirements for preventing capacitive coupling of noise. In most cases, the shield for each channel would be grounded only at the signal source.

A common technique for multiplexing low-level signals is shown in Figure 5.27. The flying capacitor technique connects the signal to be measured across a capacitor, where it is charged by the potential difference between the high-level and the low-level of the input. When the capacitor is charged, it is disconnected from the signal source. The capacitor is then connected to the A/D converter. Because the A/D converter processes the potential difference across the capacitor, common mode signals are removed.

The flying capacitor technique averages the input during the capacitor charge time. Although the common mode rejection is high, the flying capacitor technique has poor normal mode noise rejection. If normal mode noise is included in the signal, it is averaged as part of the signal and is difficult to remove at later stages of the converter. Another disadvantage of the flying capacitor technique is that a single channel cannot

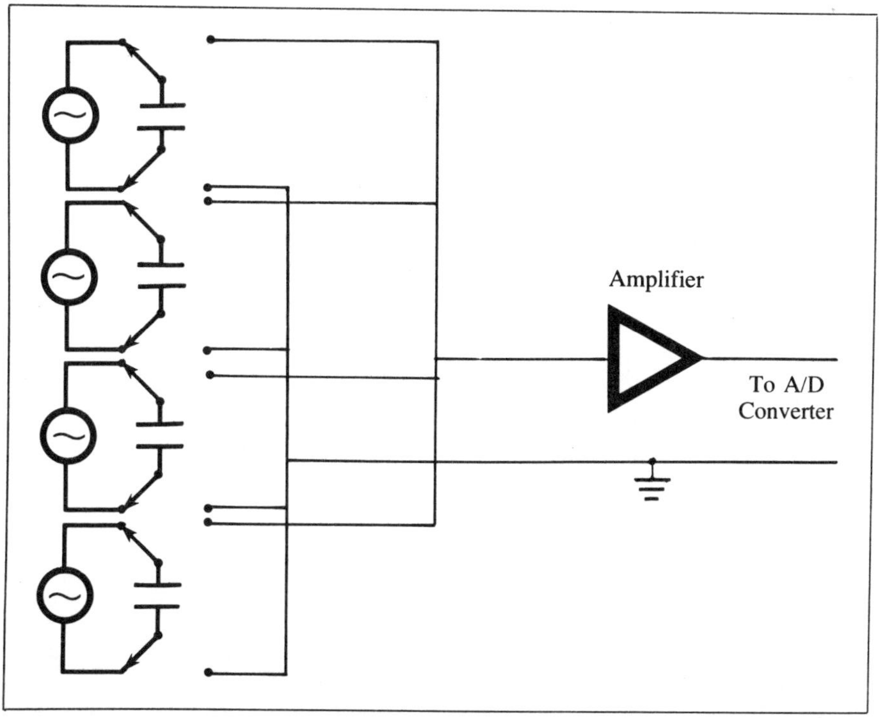

Figure 5.27. Flying capacitor multiplexing technique for a low-level A/D converter subsystem.

be sampled continuously as each channel requires a recovery time between conversions.

One problem with the multiplexed A/D converter is that it is impossible to sample all the channels at the same instance. This time skew error (see Figure 4.17) may be highly undesirable if phase relationships between channels is important. The magnitude of the time skew error is affected by the number of channels sampled, the frequency of the signals sampled, and the conversion rate.

Figure 5.28 illustrates a time skew reduction technique whereby each channel contains its own sample and hold. When sampling is initiated, all the channels are sampled in parallel by the sample and hold circuits. The output of each sample and hold is then converted to its corresponding digital value one channel at a time. The only time skew is due to sample and hold drift which is a function of the quality of the sample and hold and the conversion rate.

Another A/D converter subsystem enhancement is an externally

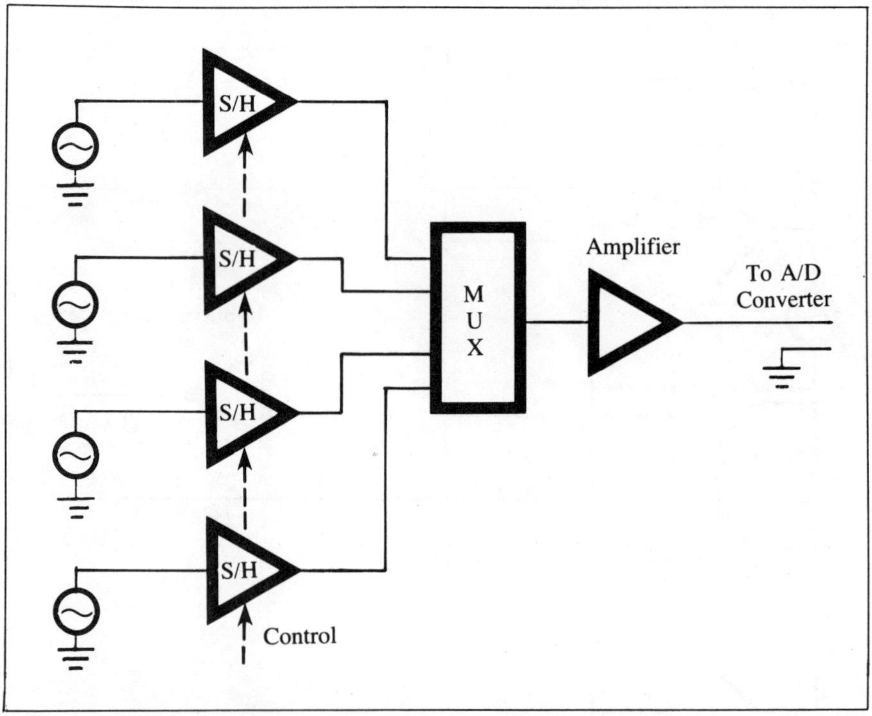

Figure 5.28. Technique to allow channels to be sampled simultaneously by using a sample and hold circuit for each channel.

generated control signal that can be used to initiate a conversion. Without this feature, the computer controls when sampling is to begin. With the external trigger feature, the computer readies the A/D converter and then is free to perform other unrelated tasks. The converter remains idle until the trigger condition is met; at which time, a conversion is started. At the end of the conversion, an interrupt is generated. The computer can continue to sample other channels under program control.

The external trigger allows the start of sampling to be accurately synchronized with some external event or an internal clock. Trigger inputs may be digital or analog level triggered or digital or analog edge triggered, depending on the design of the particular interface.

A similar capability could be implemented using a standard A/D converter and a separate trigger interface; however, delays from a trigger to the start of conversion are added by the computer in acting on the trigger signal and starting the conversion.

Some converters can be made to automatically sample sequential channels. The computer selects the first channel to be sampled and starts the A/D converter subsystem. When the first conversion is completed, the converter buffers the digital value, informs the computer that the value is available, increments the channel number, and starts another conversion. The computer must read the buffered value before the second conversion ends. The converter continues to sample successive channels (modulo the number of channels) until stopped by the computer. Since the computer is not required to select each channel and initiate each conversion, the A/D converter subsystem operates at maximum speed. The method does not allow random channel ordering or random gain selection on a channel basis. A typical converter using this technique can usually be operated in a mode whereby the computer can initiate each conversion if necessary.

Another special feature of A/D converter subsystems is the inclusion of anti-aliasing filters. One set of filters may be multiplexed for use by all channels, or each channel may have its own filters. The cutoff frequency of the filters may be selected programmatically on some converters.

An A/D converter subsystem feature which is used to improve computer performance uses a DMA channel to transfer converter data into computer memory. The computer initiates a conversion by informing the A/D converter subsystem of the channels to be scanned and the address of the memory buffer in which to store the data. The A/D converter then performs a conversion for each channel and places the digital values in the memory of the computer. During the sampling operation, the computer performs other tasks. The computer is delayed during memory cycles when the converter is transferring data.

The DMA technique relieves the computer from handling interrupts after each conversion. If a range of channels are to be converted, the computer need only be involved in initiating the first conversion and processing the data after the last channel is sampled.

The most advanced type of A/D converter subsystem contains its own memory and computing system separate from the main computer. The main computer instructs the A/D subsystem of such parameters as the channels to be sampled and the sample rate. The subsystem can collect data from the specified channels (a sweep), delay a specified period (the sample period), and collect data from the channels again. The subsystem can collect data from many such sweeps, each separated by the sample period time (Figure 5.29).

The subsystem may buffer the data in its own memory and transfer it to the main computer memory after all the data is collected. It may buffer the data and transfer it during the sampling operation. A DMA technique could also be used to transfer the data between the subsystem and the computer.

Some subsystems are implemented to perform other tasks such as optimally choosing a gain factor for each channel. It could be programmed to perform calibration and to supply collected data in scientific units. Such complex A/D subsystems perform tasks that could be performed by a suitable computer and a simple A/D converter subsystem. By implementing the functions as an A/D converter subsystem, the main computer is relieved of many time-consuming tasks. The computer is re-

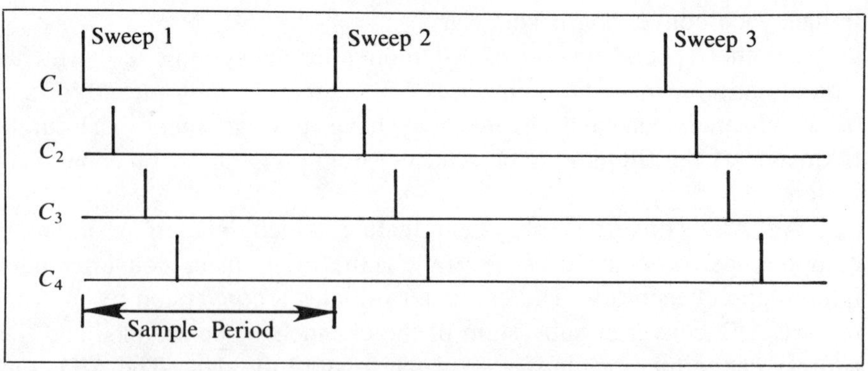

Figure 5.29. Timing diagram showing A/D converter subsystem collecting data from channels c1 to c4 at a specified sample rate.

quired to inform the subsystem of data collection parameters and then to receive the data and process it.

If the power of the A/D converter subsystem exceeds the power of the computer it is connected to, the A/D converter subsystem must be operated at a rate that is slower than its fastest possible rate, or the A/D converter subsystem can be operated in burst mode. In burst mode, the subsystem collects a certain amount of data up to the capacity of its own buffer memory. The data is then transferred to the main computer and processed (e.g. stored on disk and plotted). The A/D converter subsystem can then collect another set of data. This mode of operation is suited to collecting data from processes that are sampled intensively for short intervals.

The main disadvantage of a complex A/D converter subsystem is that the computer element that is part of the subsystem is usually not directly programmable. This condition limits the flexibility of the subsystem. For example, if large amounts of data are buffered before it is transferred to the main computer, the A/D converter data may not be received by the computer fast enough to allow time dependant control information to be generated.

A/D Converter Subsystem Specifications

The performance and quality of an A/D converter subsystem can be specified by a number of parameters. It is important to be knowledgeable about converter parameters when selecting an interface for a particular application.

Acquisition time is the time required to select a particular analog channel, convert the analog signal to its corresponding digital value, and to present the digital value to the computer. This time includes sample and hold and multiplexer settling times, and the actual conversion time of the converter. The acquisition rate is the reciprocal of the acquisition time and is the number of samples per second that can be processed. The acquisition time reflects the maximum performance of the hardware. To acquire data at this maximum rate requires appropriate software.

The resolution of an A/D converter is the smallest analog change that can be represented. It is a function of the number of bits of digital information used to express the analog input. An n-bit converter has a resolution of 1 part in 2^n. If the analog input range is E_{range} volts, the smallest representable voltage change is $E_{range}/2^n$.

For example, a 12-bit converter (4096 digital combinations) with an input range of −10 volts to +10 volts can represent a change of 20/4096 or .049 volts. The least significant bit (LSB) represents this value.

There is a quantizing error associated with the resolution of a converter of ±1/2 LSB. All analog values within ±LSB of the input that corresponds to a particular digital output are all represented by this output.

Common converters have a resolution of eight, 10, and 12 bits. Noise and internal A/D converter errors cause the useful resolution to be less than the theoretical value.

The range covered by a converter is specified by the full scale value and whether the converter is unipolar (measuring either positive or negative voltages only) or bipolar (measuring from the negative full scale value to the positive full scale value). Varying the gain of an A/D converter subsystem with programmable gains effectively changes the range.

The digital output of an A/D converter may be one of a number of codes. Common coding techniques are binary, two's complement binary, and excess binary. Excess binary codes are usually converted in the computer to two's complement notation before much calculation is performed. If the word size of the computer is greater than a two's complement A/D converter value, it may be necessary to extend the sign bit in software before performing calculations. Some converters perform the sign extension.

The number of channels is an important parameter of an A/D converter subsystem. Some A/D converter interfaces can be expanded to more channels using an external multiplexer.

The absolute accuracy of a converter relates to the converter's performance in measuring a standard volt as defined by the National Bureau of Standards.

The relative accuracy of an A/D converter is a function of the linearity of the converter. Figure 5.30 shows a "best fit" straight line drawn through the ideal transfer function between analog input and digital output values. Relative accuracy is defined as the maximum deviation of the actual analog to digital transfer function from the straight line. For a quality converter, the relative accuracy is less than ±1/2 LSB.

Ideally, each digital output should represent a range of analog inputs of width one LSB. Figure 5.31 illustrates differential nonlinearity, a deviation of the width of analog input values covered by one LSB. The differential nonlinearity is typically ±1/2 LSB for a quality converter.

With the input terminals of an A/D converter subsystem connected

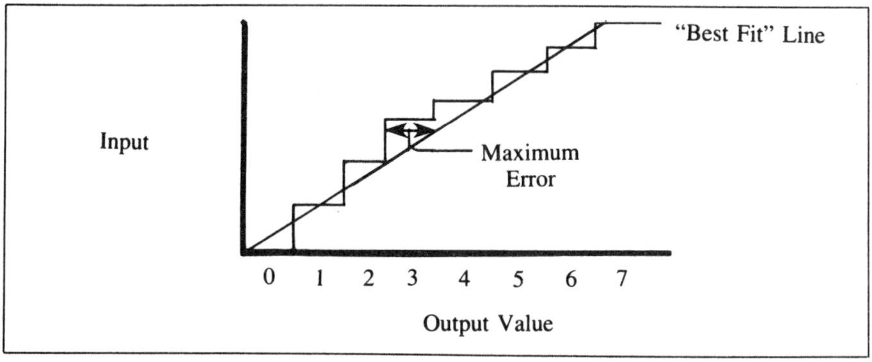

Figure 5.30. Relative accuracy defined as the maximum deviation of the A/D converter transfer function from a "best fit" straight line.

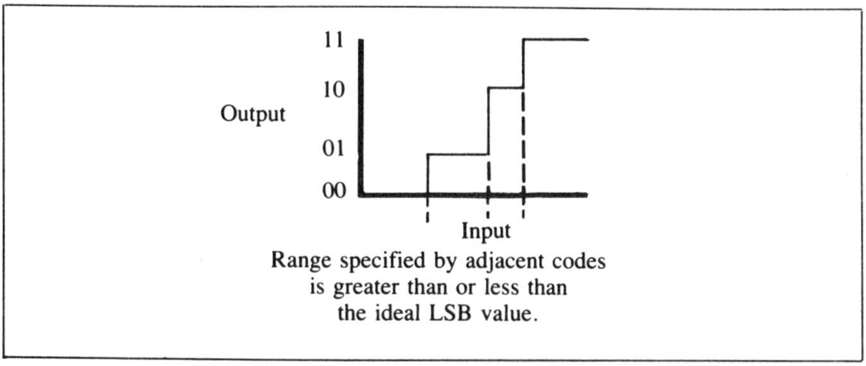

Figure 5.31. Differential nonlinearity error.

together, the digital output after conversion should be zero in the code of the converter. Any deviation from the zero output is offset error. Quality A/D converters can be adjusted for zero offset error over a specified temperature range. More sophisticated converters have a technique for eliminating offset error by using a solid state switch to connect the A/D converter subsystem inputs together and measuring the deviation from zero. This deviation is used to automatically adjust the output of the converter.

The ability of a differential input amplifier to reject common mode noise can be expressed as the ratio of the magnitude of the common mode input voltage to the magnitude of the output caused by this common mode input voltage. This common mode rejection ratio (CMRR) can also be expressed in dB units (20 times the log of the CMRR). The higher the CMRR value, the better common mode signals are rejected.

Other errors include crosstalk (the error due to interaction between channels), gain error (inaccuracy due to gain of the front-end amplifier), and errors based on temperature effects. Errors related to anti-aliasing filters that are part of the A/D converter subsystem or connected externally must be considered. Transformation networks (e.g. current to voltage converters) and range-setting circuits external to the A/D converter subsystem add errors to the overall conversion process.

The worst case error of an A/D converter subsystem can be estimated by summing all the maximum error limit values. It is advisable to select a converter subsystem that exceeds the necessary accuracy.

Data Loggers

A data logger is a device similar to an intelligent A/D converter subsystem. A typical data logger can operate in stand-alone mode by recording data on some magnetic media, or it can transfer data to a computer system. A typical data logger can be programmed to collect analog and digital data at a variety of rates and trigger conditions. The data is typically recorded on a magnetic cassette or a printer. Programming is accomplished using a keypad or by a computer connected to the data logger.

The interface between the data logger and the computer system is typically an asynchronous communications line using the ASCII code. Commands can be sent to the data logger and data can be sent to the computer using the communications link.

The advantages of a data logger are its ease of programming and its ability to easily connect to a variety of computers using a standard interface. The disadvantages are the speed of data transfer using an asynchronous communications link and its inflexibility due to the high-level commands it accepts.

For some applications, a commercial data logger combined with an inexpensive personal computer is a viable solution to a data acquisition problem. The personal computer is used to store data and to control the data logger.

Real-time Clocks

Real-time clocks are I/O devices used to allow a computer to measure intervals accurately. Figure 5.32 is a block diagram of a real-time clock. The clock is made up of a crystal controlled oscillator, a programmable divider network, and a counter. The oscillator outputs a signal whose

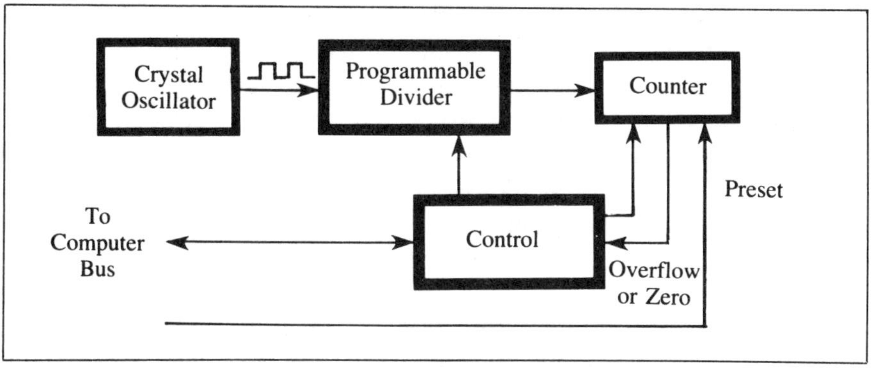

Figure 5.32. A block diagram of a real-time clock.

frequency is accurately controlled. The signal is divided by the divider network to one of several frequencies that are less than or equal to the oscillator frequency. Selection of the frequency output by the divider is under computer control. A typical clock might have selectable frequencies of 100 KHz., 10 KHz., 1KHz., and 60 Hz.

The selected signal drives an *n*-bit counter. For each clock cycle (output of the divider), the counter is decremented (or incremented). When the counter reaches zero, a status flag is set and may be used to request an interrupt. The counter may be loaded to some *n*-bit value by the computer. After the interval (in seconds) equal to the counter value divided by the frequency output by the divider network, the status flag is set.

An improvement to the clock is the addition of a buffer register connected to the counter (see Figure 5.33). The computer can then load

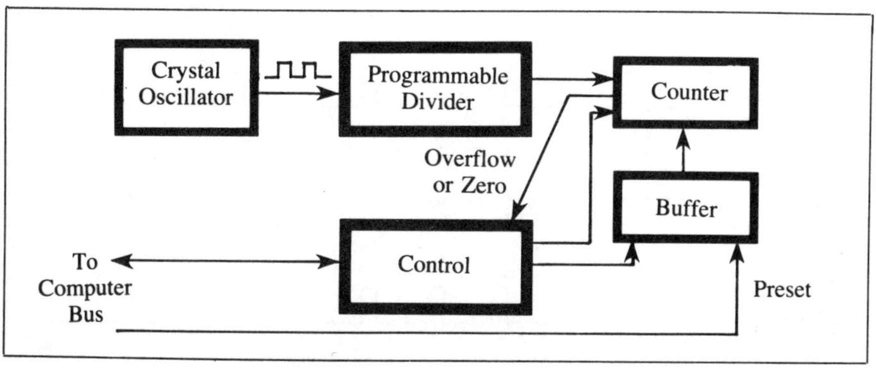

Figure 5.33. A block diagram of a real-time clock with a counter buffer register.

the count value once. Every time the counter reaches zero, the clock requests an interrupt. The value in the buffer register is loaded into the counter by clock circuitry, and the counter is decremented at the clock frequency. As long as the computer services the interrupt before the counter reaches zero again, accurate timing is maintained, and the computer is interrupted at a rate defined by the selected clock frequency and the value placed in the counter buffer register. Use of a buffer register relieves the computer of the task of reloading the counter after each interrupt.

A typical clock has a status bit that is set if the computer does not acknowledge an interrupt request before the counter again reaches zero. This status bit allows the software driving the clock to determine when a timing inaccuracy occurs.

Some clocks allow the counter register to be read by the computer. This feature allows the software driving the clock to determine intervals shorter than the interrupt rate. For example, when an asynchronous event is detected, the computer can read the current counter value to determine when the event occurred with finer resolution than with respect to the interrupt rate.

Some clocks may be started under software control or under control of an external event. The external event may be in the form of a digital signal or a voltage level. When the trigger condition is met, the clock begins to decrement or increment the counter. This feature allows timing to be synchronized to an external event. A second external trigger may be available to stop the clock.

Figure 5.34 illustrates clock timing errors. The start condition is out of phase with the clock oscillator signal that drives the counter. The

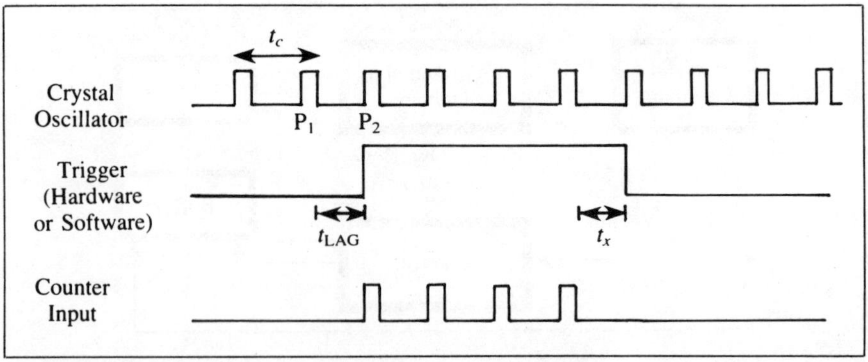

Figure 5.34. Clock timing errors due to the asynchronous trigger event not being synchronized to the time base of the real-time clock.

start signal lags clock pulse p_1 by t_{lag}. When clock pulse p_2 occurs, the clock is decremented indicating the passage of t_c seconds ($t_c = 1/f$ where f is the frequency of the signal driving the counter). Since only $t_c - t_{lag}$ seconds have elapsed since the starting condition, the error is t_{lag} seconds.

A similar condition exists at the end of a timing interval. The portion of time after the last clock pulse to the end of the interval (t_x) is not included in the count.

The effect of timing errors at both ends of an interval tend to cancel each other. The total error in timing an asynchronous event is thus less than t_c. (The error in delaying a specified interval initiated by some asynchronous event is t_{lag}, and is also less than t_c.) If the counter is not accessed and only clock interrupts are accessed by the computer, the maximum error is less than the interrupt rate.

6

Data Acquisition Software Techniques

This chapter discusses a variety of techniques and concepts related to the software elements of a data acquisition system. The system designer may not be directly exposed to all elements of such a system if he designs data acquisition software that runs under a purchased real-time operating system.

Device Handlers

I/O devices normally operate at a rate slower than the instruction rate of the computer they are connected to. The computer will typically initiate an I/O operation and then perform some other task until the device completes its action. The action initiated may be simple—such as starting an analog-to-digital conversion—or more complex—such as starting a DMA operation that will transfer many bytes of data. The device may not complete an operation in a fixed amount of time, especially when it is connected to some external device (e.g., the receive side of an RS-232C interface).

The computer can determine when a device has completed an operation either by status checking or by the use of interrupts. Status checking requires that the computer periodically perform an I/O instruction to test a status flag that is set if the device is ready for service.

In the interrupt method, the device is placed in the interrupt mode by executing a set of I/O instructions. Each time the device needs servicing, it requests an interrupt. When the computer is in a state that the device interrupt can be acknowledged (computer in interrupt enabled mode and no higher priority device requesting an interrupt), the computer suspends execution of the current program and executes an interrupt service routine for the device. The interrupt service routine will service the device, and normally it will return to the program that was interrupted. Interrupt service routines are also referred to as device handlers.

In a small data acquisition system where there is only one I/O device active during data collection or where there is only one device that must be serviced rapidly, status checking is simpler and faster for the primary device than the use of interrupts. Figure 6.1 shows a macro flowchart of a simple status checking system that reads a DPM every clock tick (clock rate is one pulse every ten seconds) and prints the DPM value on a terminal. If a key has been depressed on the terminal, the program stops.

The assumption is that the DPM is ready for data transfer except for a small period when its output is being updated. The terminal keyboard is only checked once every ten seconds. The main status checking loop is the one that waits on the clock pulse.

Figure 6.2 shows a macro flowchart for a program using the status checking technique. The program services two devices while performing some computation. The computation code interacts with the devices either by supplying or receiving data.

In the case of Figure 6.2 and many of the following figures, a requirement is that a device must be serviced in a manner such that no data is lost. A device that supplies data bytes or words serially at a certain rate must be serviced such that each data element is read by the computer before the next data element becomes available. Output devices may have to be serviced similarly to supply data to an external process at a critical rate.

In Figure 6.2, the block labeled "perform some computation" requires explanation. Periodically through the program, both devices must be checked. Instead of a loop, this requirement means that interspersed throughout the computation part of the program are instructions to determine if the devices need servicing. Although the construction of Figure

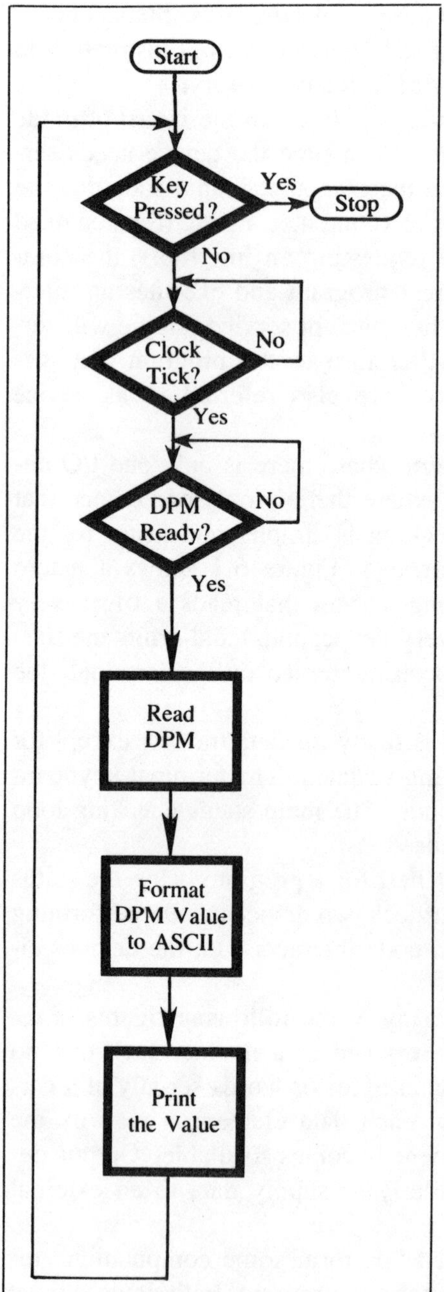

Figure 6.1. A macro flowchart of the status checking I/O example. The DPM value is read and printed every clock tick (one clock tick every 10 seconds). If a keyboard key is depressed, the program stops.

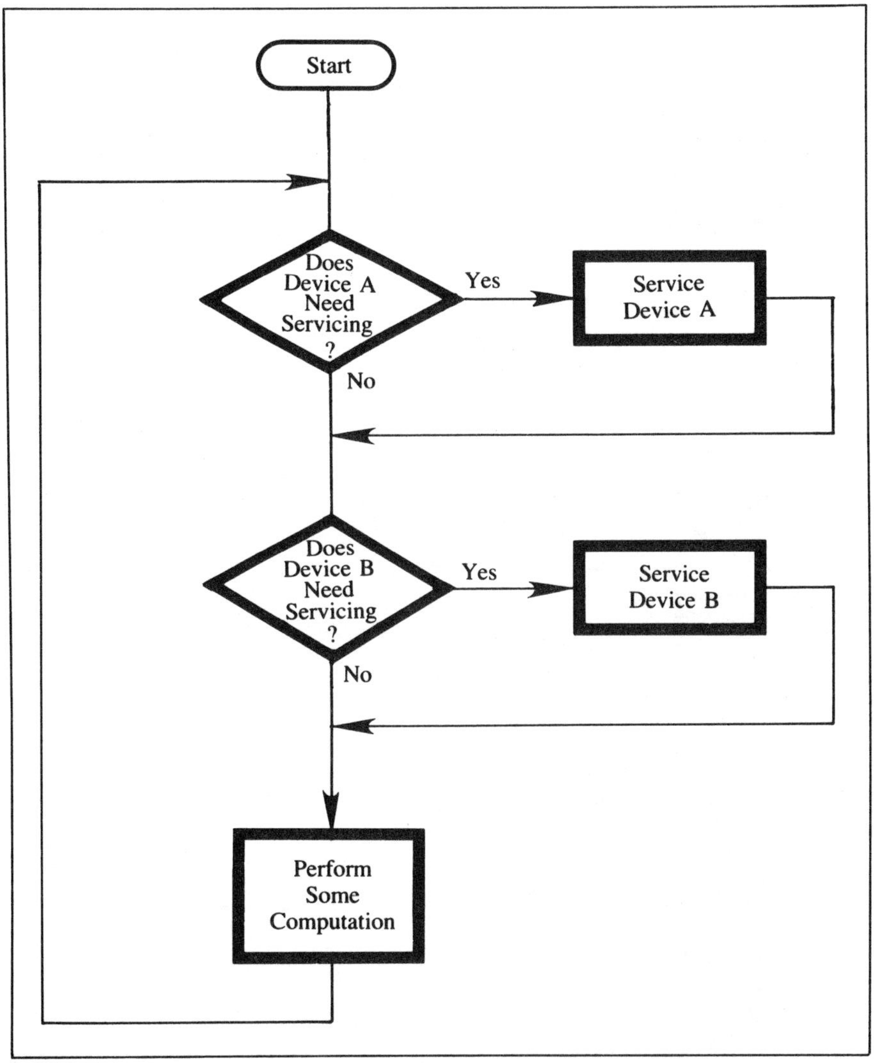

Figure 6.2. A macro flowchart of a program using the status checking technique for two devices. See the text for a description of the box labeled "perform some computation."

6.2 will be used in subsequent figures, Figure 6.3 better illustrates this technique.

The maximum delay that can occur before a device needing service is serviced is the time required to execute the longest executing program segment between device status checks. It is difficult to design such a

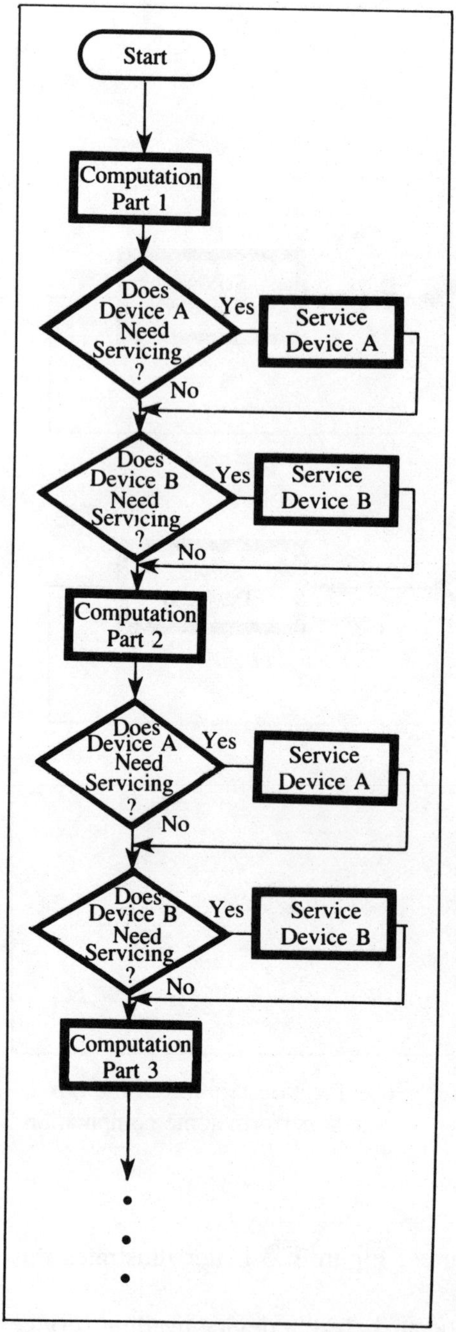

Figure 6.3. A macro flowchart illustrating the complexity of a program that uses status checking for two devices.

program since the maximum execution time of each loop must be determined so that the device status checks can be included in the program properly. A complex program using status checking on one device or almost any program using the status checking technique on more than one device is generally difficult to debug and maintain.

Figure 6.4 illustrates a program similar to Figure 6.2 except that status checking is replaced with interrupt processing. The requirement to intersperse device service request tests throughout the program is no longer required.

In the technique shown in Figure 6.4, the device service routines run with the interrupt system disabled. With interrupts disabled during execution of the service routines, interaction between interrupt routines is reduced; however, device response is limited by the execution time of the service routines. When one service routine is executing, service for the second device is delayed until the executing service routine completes.

Devices operating at a high rate must be serviced rapidly. After servicing, the device stays busy performing the next operation for a relatively long period of time. For example, after collecting data from a channel, data must be read from the A/D converter and a new channel must be selected before starting a new conversion. For the A/D converter to operate at a high rate, the service routine must perform the above functions immediately after the device requests service. After starting the next conversion, the service routine can then perform less time-critical tasks, such as buffering the data. During this part of the service routine, the time-critical portion of other device service routines can be allowed to execute as long as the service routine completes before the device interrupts again.

Figure 6.5 shows device handlers with a time-critical section and a low priority section. The time-critical section performs those functions needed to keep the device operating at a high rate, while the low priority section contains data manipulation and storage functions that need not be executed immediately. If the time-critical sections of all interrupt handlers are executed with interrupts disabled, the longest the highest priority device will have to wait for service is the time required to execute the longest executing time-critical section.

The low priority sections may be interrupted by the time-critical part of the other interrupt handlers. The low priority sections must complete before the device they service interrupts again. Figure 6.6 shows a typical scenario. In the figure, device A requires servicing. The time critical portion of the device A handler, TC_A, is given control. The en-

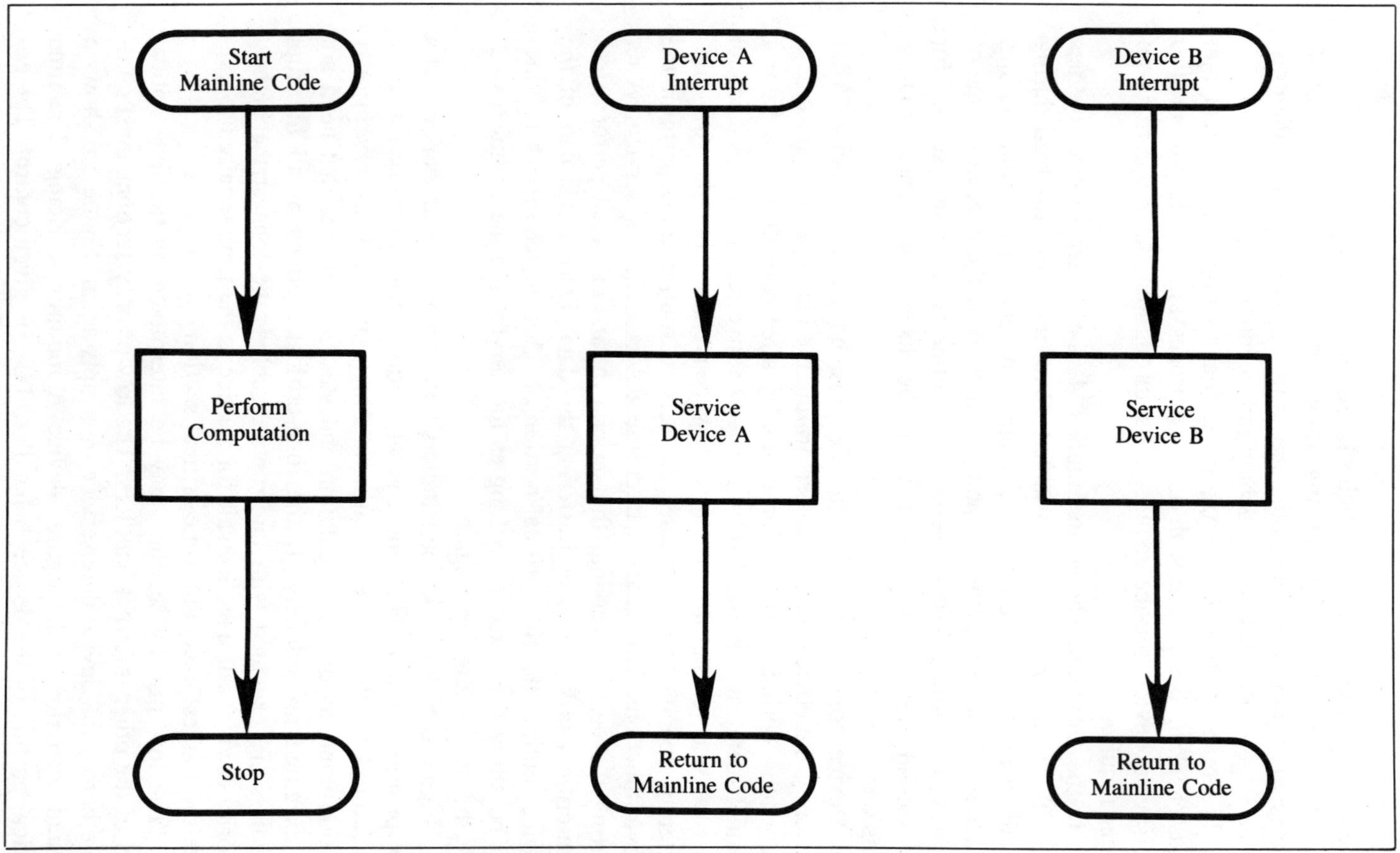

Figure 6.4. A macro flowchart of a program using an interrupt technique to service two devices. In this example, the interrupt service routines run with the interrupt system disabled.

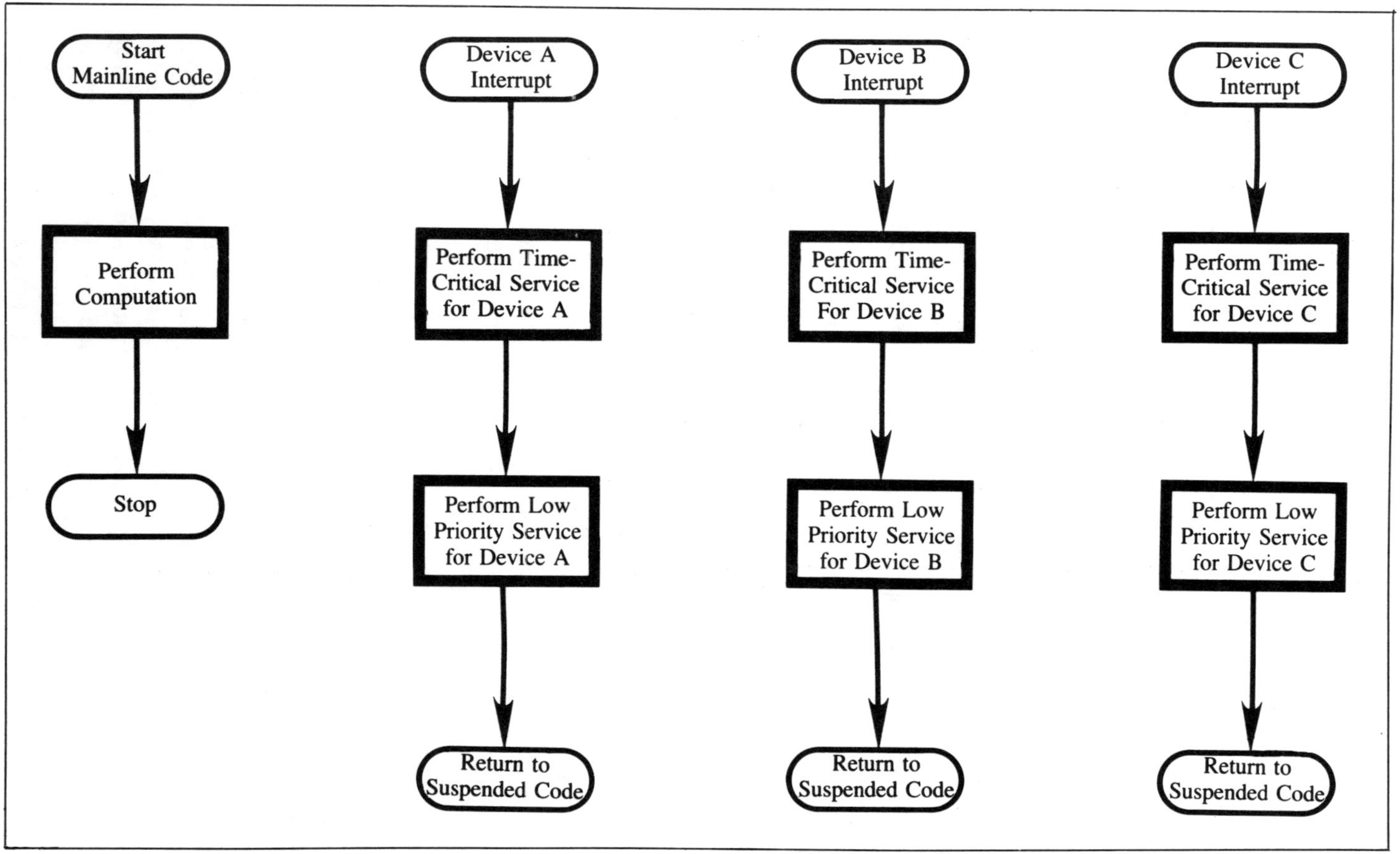

Figure 6.5. A macro flowchart illustrating a program with three interrupt handlers. Each interrupt handler is divided into a time-critical part run with interrupts disabled and a low priority part run with interrupts enabled.

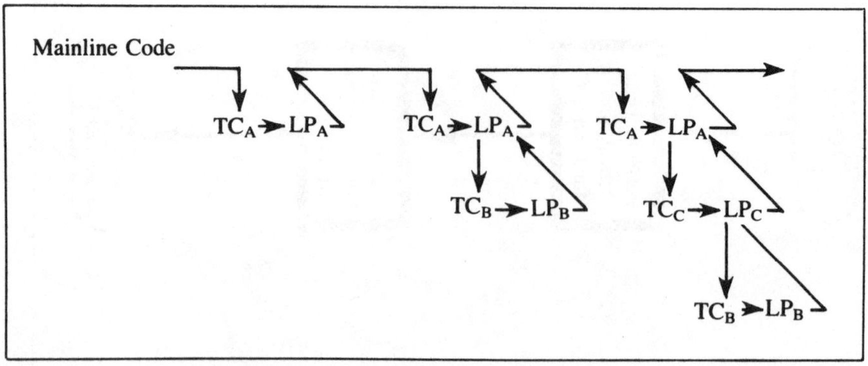

Figure 6.6. A diagram showing a possible scenario of control flow with three device handlers divided into time-critical (TC) and low priority (LP) sections.

tire device handler completes (TC_A and the low priority section, LP_A) and control is returned to the main program.

Later, device A interrupts again. During the execution of TC_A or LP_A, device B requests service. LP_A is interrupted, and the entire device B service routine executes before control is returned to LP_A. When LP_A completes, control is returned to the main program.

Figure 6.6 also diagrams program flow when all three devices require servicing in a short period of time. All three interrupt routines must be executed before device A interrupts again or else the scenario of Figure 6.7 occurs. Before LP_A completes, device A must be serviced again. TC_A and LP_A are executed while the first invocation of LP_A is interrupted. Unless the interrupt routines are very sophisticated, data supplied to or by the device will be in the wrong order, will be lost, or the program will malfunction.

The condition of Figure 6.7 will not occur if the devices are slow relative to the execution time of all the interrupt handlers. If this is not the case, several solutions are possible. Some machines allow the processor to be placed in a state where it will acknowledge interrupts from high priority devices while ignoring low priority devices. In this case, the machine may be in the state to acknowledge all interrupts, no interrupts, or high priority interrupts.

Figure 6.8 illustrates the use of priority interrupts. In the figure, device A, an A/D converter, and device B, a disk drive, are high priority devices. The low priority portions of their interrupt routines can only be interrupted by another high priority device. Device C, a terminal interface, is a low priority device. Its low priority section can be interrupted by the other devices, but its interrupt request is not acknowl-

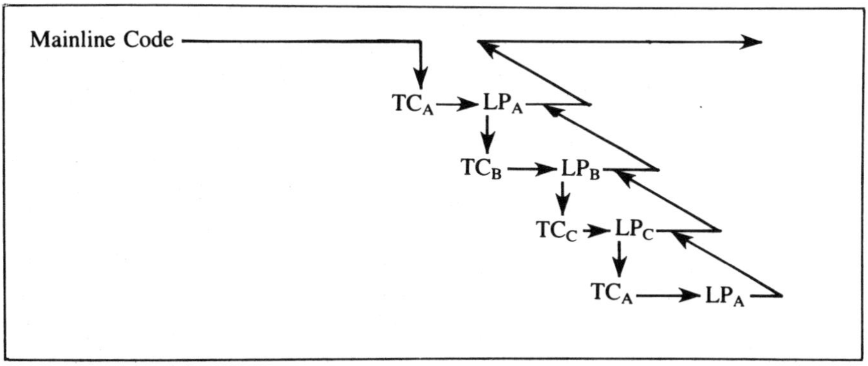

Figure 6.7. A diagram showing control flow where a second invocation of device handler A occurs before the first invocation completes.

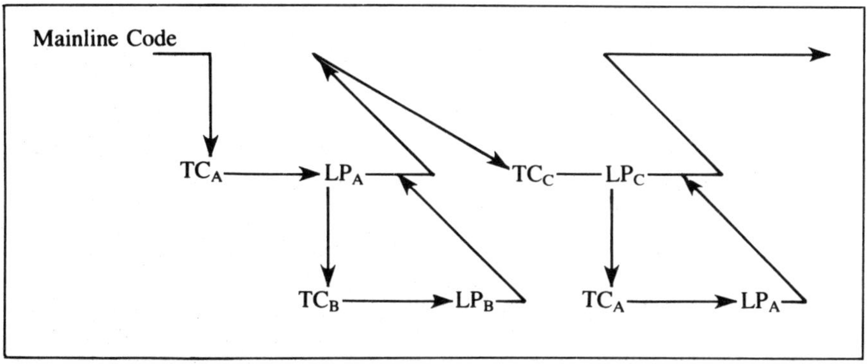

Figure 6.8. Control flow in a system where the device A and device B interrupt handlers run at a high priority. Device C cannot interrupt the device A or device B low priority service routine section, but the low priority section of the device C interrupt handler can be interrupted.

edged while any part of the other handlers are active. This scheme is useful if the service routine for devices A and B are relatively short so that multiple invocations of the same service routine do not occur and if device C interrupts occur at a relatively slow rate.

Many small computers do not allow this interrupt priority scheme for device handlers. Some large scale microcomputers and small minicomputers allow two or three priority levels. When a device interrupts, a priority level is selected as part of interrupt processing. An instruction can be executed in the handler to change this level after time-critical tasks are complete.

The priority levels applied to interrupt routines should not be confused with device priorities when two devices interrupt simultaneously. In this case, the hardware allows higher priority devices to interrupt first.

A second solution to the problem of preventing a device from interrupting its own device handler is to disable the device from interrupting during execution of the device handler. Figure 6.9 illustrates this technique. The low priority section of the device handler can then be delayed from completing if it is interrupted by other devices without being invoked a second time.

With this technique, the device may not be serviced at the optimum rate; however, if the service request is only occasionally ignored for a relatively small period, this technique may be applicable. If the device is inputting data from a high speed device or if data must be supplied to an output device rapidly, there is a limit to how long a device service request can be ignored.

Figure 6.10 illustrates a software solution to avoid the problem illustrated in Figure 6.7. The serializer is a program that executes the low priority section of the interrupt handlers in a first-in-first-out fashion. Figure 6.11 shows interrupt routine control flow with the serializer. When the time-critical portion of an interrupt handler completes, it invokes the serializer. The serializer determines if the time critical code that just completed interrupted another device handler. If it did not, the low priority section of the handler is allowed to run. If another low priority section was interrupted, the low priority section of the current interrupt handler is queued for execution, and the interrupted handler is allowed to execute.

Figure 6.12 is a conceptual flowchart of the serializer. In the simple scheme presented, the queue manipulation part of the serializer must execute with interrupts disabled so that it is not interrupted and given control a second time while it is already active. (Note that when the time critical portion of an interrupt handler gains control, it must determine if it interrupted the low priority section of another device handler, and if so, it must queue the interrupted handler for execution by the serializer.)

The use of the serializer increases the overhead associated with device interrupts. In some real-time operating systems, the function of the serializer is built into the system.

To resume execution of an interrupted device handler, the serializer must restore register values saved by the interrupting time-critical section including the program counter value. To queue a handler section for execution requires that the register values in effect at the time the time-

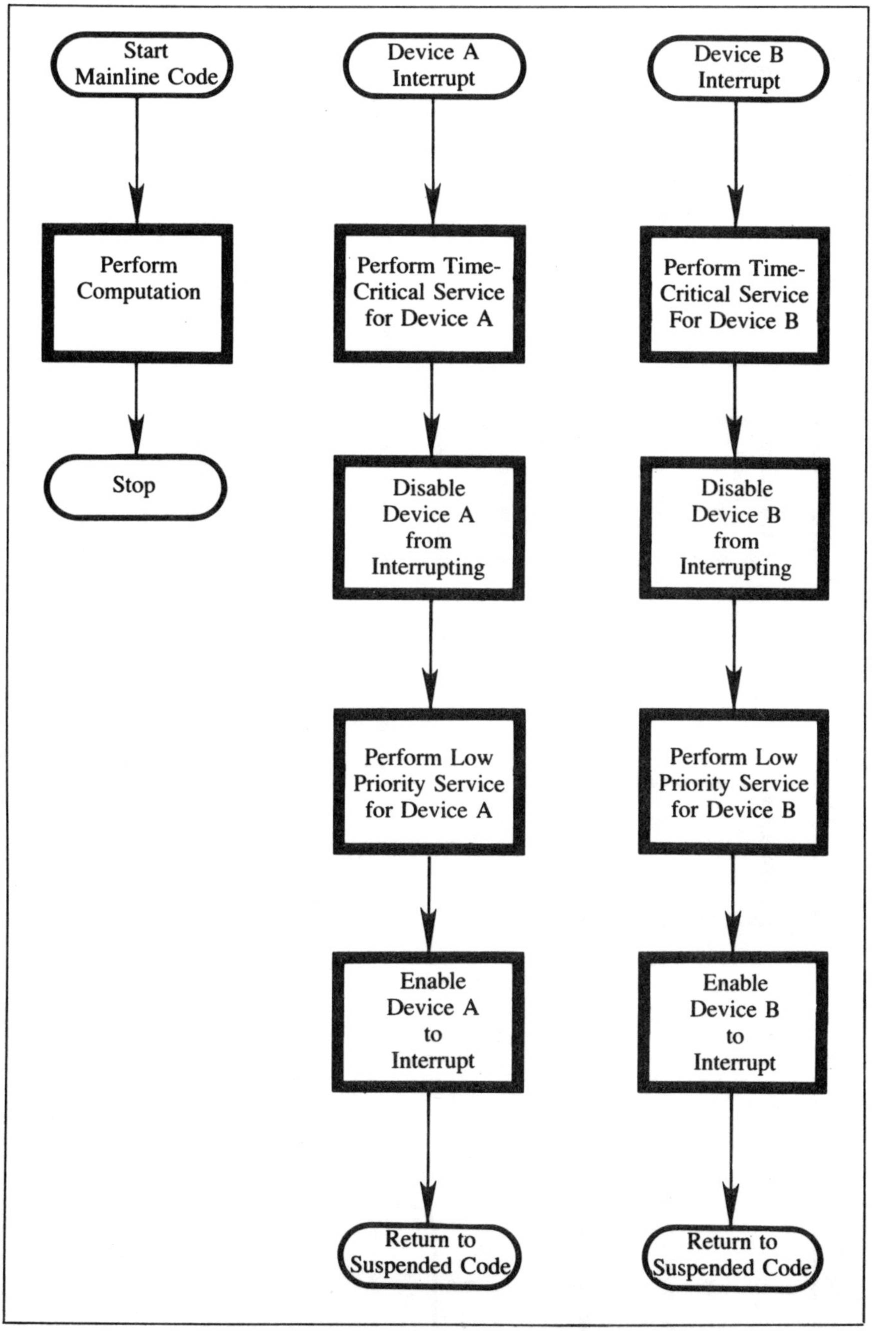

Figure 6.9. A macro flowchart illustrating a technique to prevent the situation of Figure 6.7. The low priority section of each device handler can be interrupted by the other devices but not by the device associated with it.

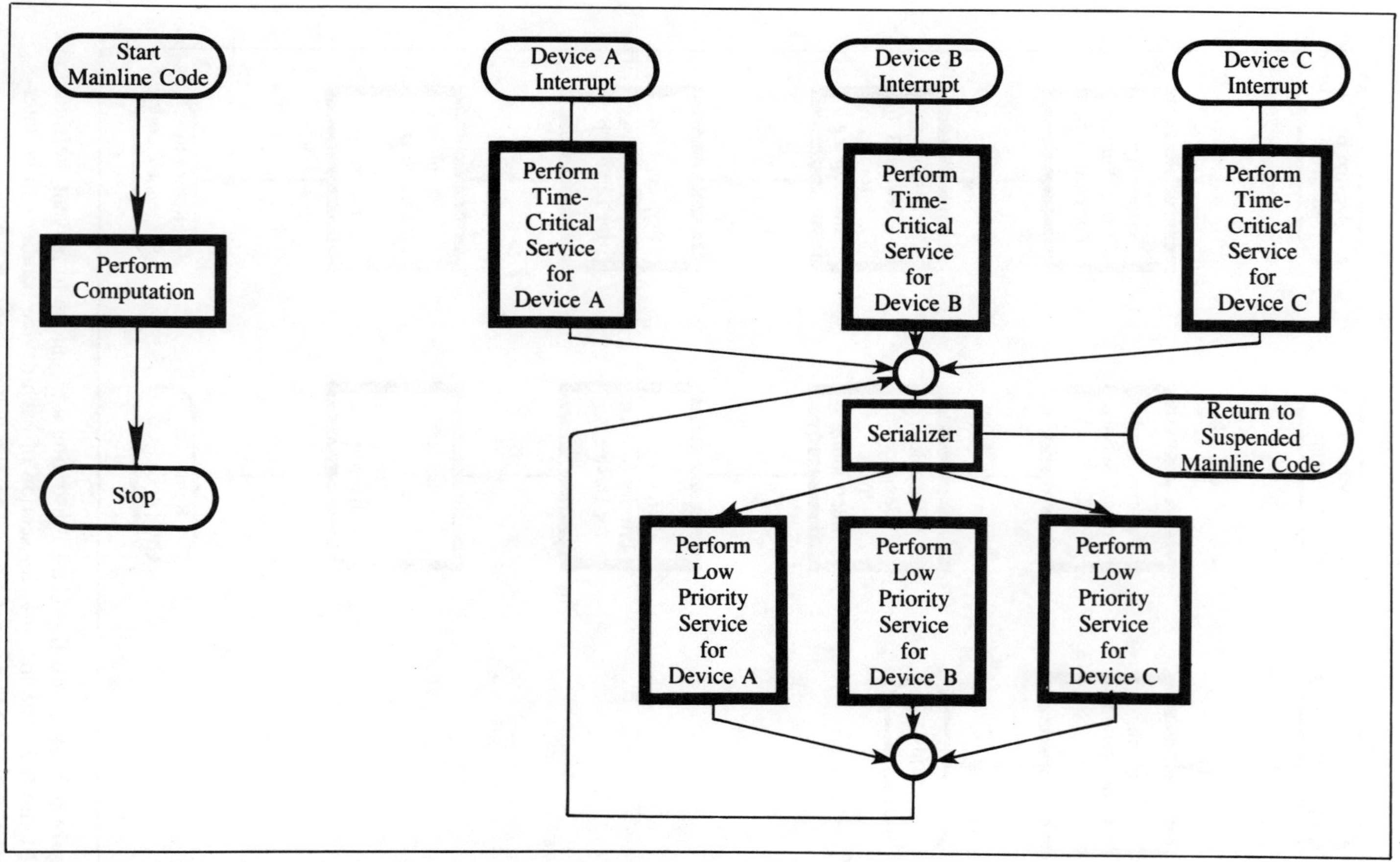

Figure 6.10. A macro flowchart illustrating the use of a serializer.

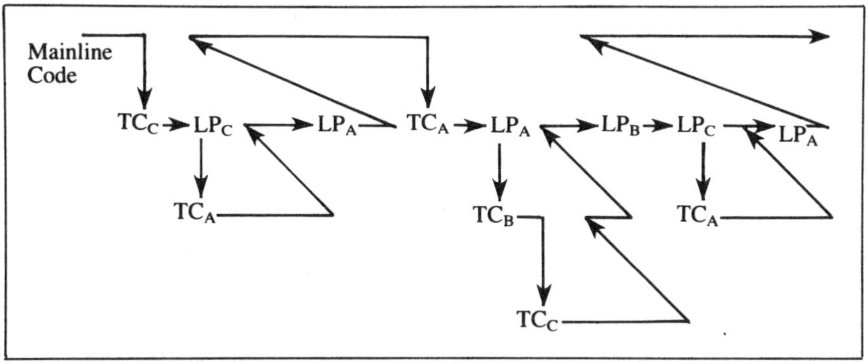

Figure 6.11. Flow of control with a serializer.

critical section of the interrupt handler called the serializer be saved. When it is time to invoke a queued handler section, the saved register values are reloaded, and the saved starting address is placed in the program counter register. When a handler section completes, it returns control to the serializer. If another handler section is queued, it is invoked. If there are no handler sections to be executed, the serializer returns control to the interrupted main program.

Reentrant Device Handlers

The device handlers discussed thus far are designed such that they are not invoked by a device interrupt while a previous interrupt from the same device is being processed. This condition can be enforced by designing the system so that every interrupt routine is guaranteed enough time to execute between device interrupts, by disabling the interrupt request logic of the device during the handler execution, or by using a serializer.

Such a device handler is serially reusable. Each time the handler is invoked, data values in memory are initialized. Other memory locations can be used to save results. An invocation of the handler during the execution of the handler causes data values (e.g. device data and loop counters) to be altered by the second invocation. When control is returned to the first invocation, data values have been altered.

A reentrant or pure code routine is designed so that the code (program instructions) is separated from the data. Any data that cannot be kept in registers are kept in a block of memory separate from the program. The data block is accessed through a register using indirect ad-

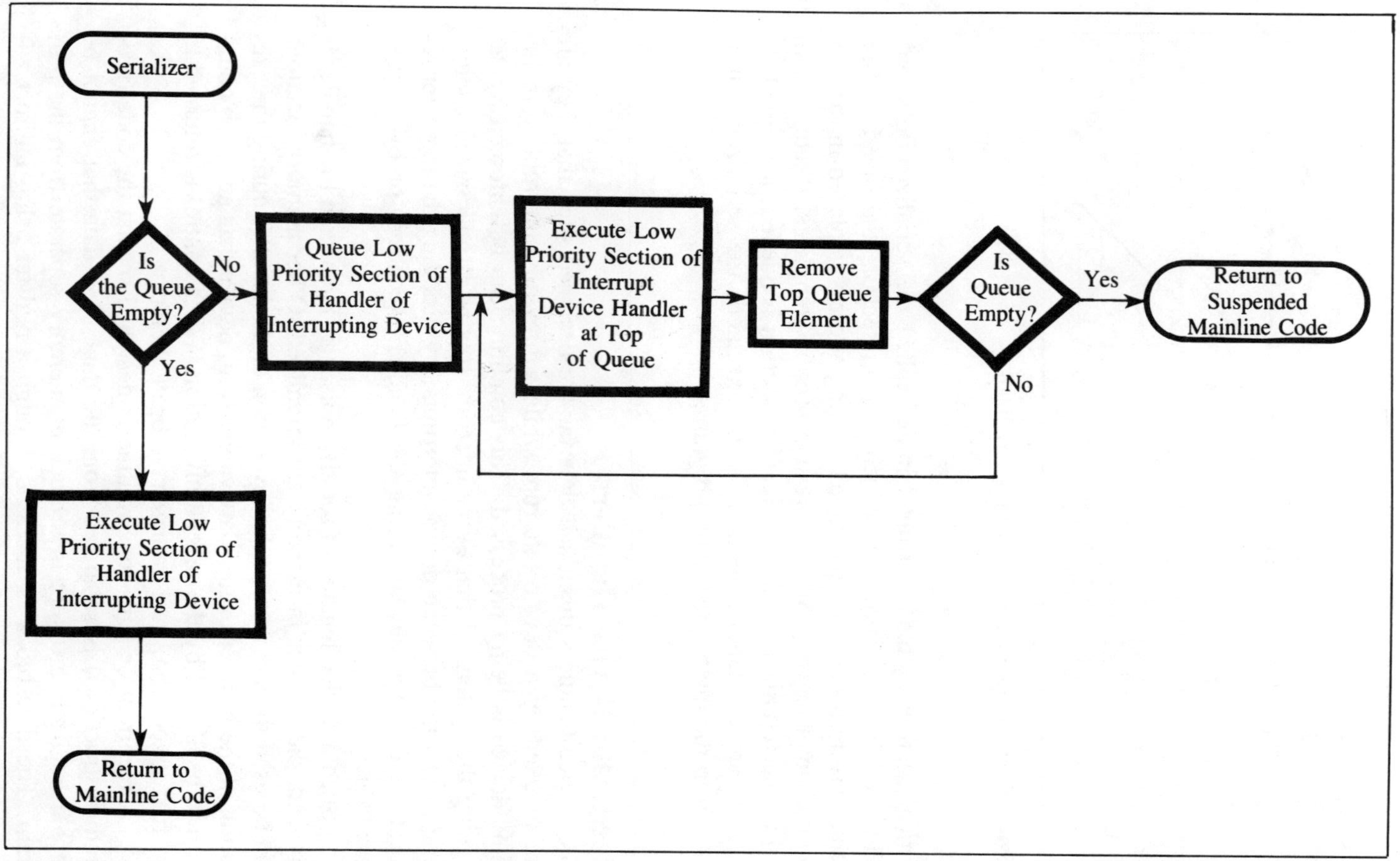

Figure 6.12. A conceptual flowchart of a serializer.

dressing mode. Each data block is associated with a particular invocation of the routine.

A reentrant routine can be interrupted, and a second invocation can occur before the first invocation completes. Because data relevant to an invocation is kept separate from data relevant to other invocations, multiple concurrent invocations are possible. Because data associated with a particular invocation are kept in registers or are accessed indirectly using registers, the normal register save and restore sequence of interrupt processing provides the context switching necessary for reentrant code. A reentrant device handler can be used to service two similar devices without the need for duplicate handlers. A small initialization section for each device associates an invocation with its data.

Figure 6.13 illustrates a reentrant handler servicing two serial interfaces, each connected to a terminal. The handler places characters keyed at a particular terminal in a buffer associated with the terminal, and when a carriage return is sensed, it sets a flag. When a device interrupts and state saving is complete, a register is loaded to point to a memory

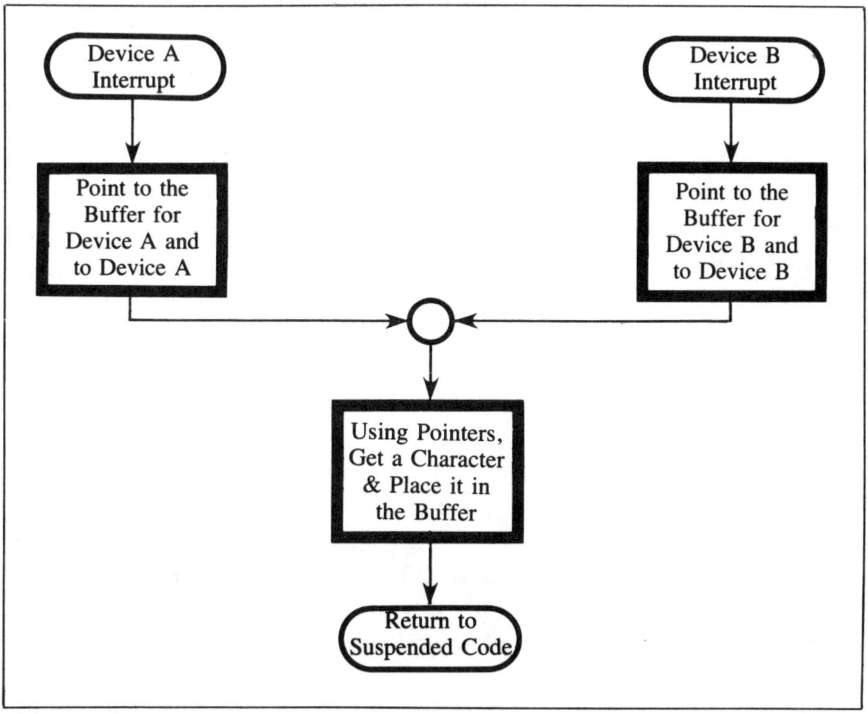

Figure 6.13. A macro flowchart illustrating a reentrant interrupt handler.

area containing the buffer, flag, and control words (e.g. current buffer position and I/O address) for the device. The reentrant handler is then invoked. It accesses the buffer and related information using the pointer register. Any intermediate computational results (such as is needed in updating the buffer pointer and checking for buffer overrun) are either performed in place in the buffer area or in registers. Stack space on machines so equipped can also be used to save intermediate results.

If an interrupt does occur, the buffer region pointer register value is saved. A second invocation of the reentrant handler occurs with a different pointer register value. The data for the first invocation is thus not disturbed by the second invocation. When control eventually returns to the interrupted invocation, the proper pointer register value is restored, and the handler accesses the proper buffer region.

Some machines lend themselves more to the coding of reentrant code than others. Stack hardware, indirect addressing, and the ability to specify an I/O device address in a register are useful features. Machines that have code-modifying instructions (e.g. subroutine calls that save the return address in the first word of the subroutine), limited addressing modes, and I/O addresses that must be coded as part of an instruction complicate the coding of reentrant device handlers. Coding reentrant code on such machines so greatly adds to the overhead of device servicing as to make reentrant routines prohibitive.

Interrupt Routine Communications

Care must be taken when designing control and data communications between an interrupt routine and mainline code. If a section of the mainline code is accessing a memory location and the interrupt routine gains control and modifies the same location, errors can occur.

Figure 6.14 illustrates how such erroneous processing can occur. FLG is a byte storage location that is used to allow one-at-a-time use of some resource (e.g. a buffer or subroutine) by the mainline code and the interrupt service routine. When the flag is one, the resource is available. When it is zero or minus, the resource is in use by either the mainline code or the interrupt routine. Before using the resource, the program section needing it should determine if the resource is available (FLG value is one) and then allocate the resource by making FLG zero. When the use of the resource is complete, FLG must be reset to one to make it available again.

In the figure, Z-80 microcomputer instructions are used. In the main program, the value of FLG is loaded into the A register (LDA A);

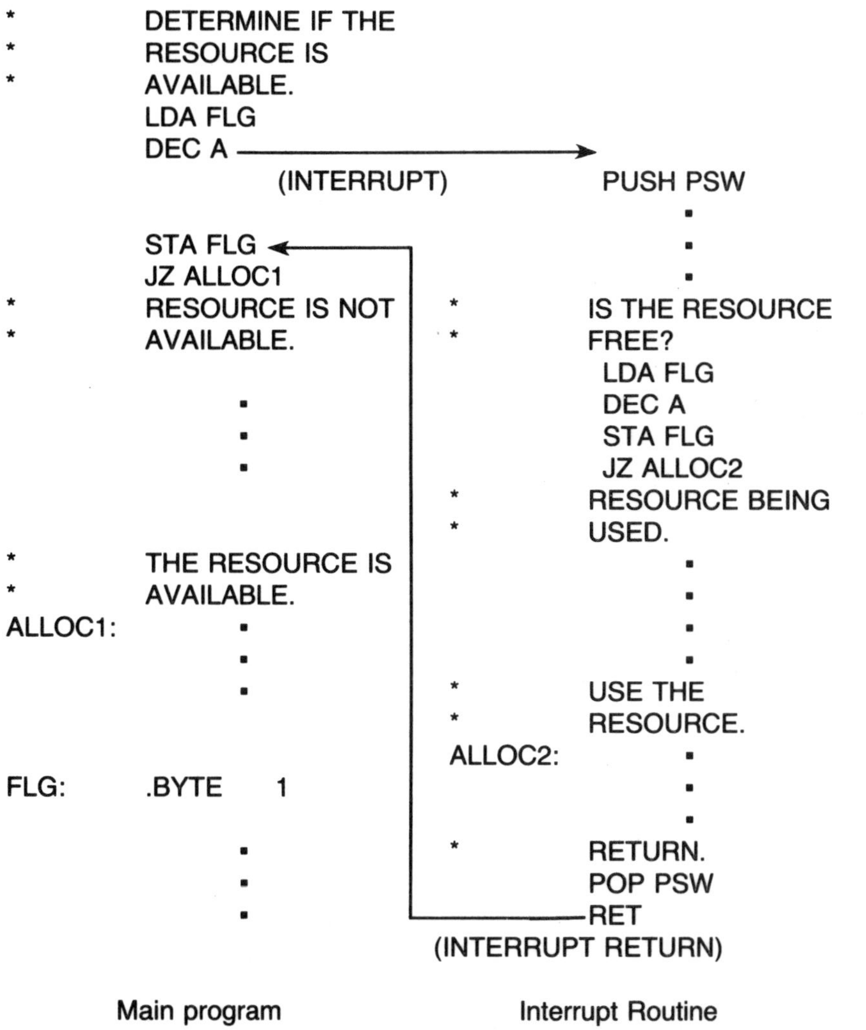

Figure 6.14. Program control sequence in a Z-80 program showing erroneous processing due to the occurrence of an interrupt. Both the mainline code and the interrupt routine allocate a nonsharable resource at the same time.

the A register value is decremented (DEC A); the value of FLG is replaced with the decremented value (STA A); and the decremented value of FLG is tested for zero (JZ). If the decremented FLG value is not minus, access to the resource is allowed, and a branch is made to the program segment that uses the resource. If FLG is made negative by the decrement instruction, access to the resource is denied. FLG is reset to one by the holder of the resource when the resource is no longer needed.

As shown in Figure 6.14, this allocation scheme may not function properly. The mainline code is interrupted by the interrupt service routine immediately after the decrement instruction. The interrupt routine also attempts to allocate the resource. Because the mainline code did not yet place the decremented value in FLG, FLG contains a one. The interrupt routine allocates the resource and places a zero in FLG. Assuming the resource is used by the interrupt routine over several interrupts, the interrupt routine returns control to the mainline code before releasing the resource. The mainline code continues executing after its register values have been restored. The zero in the A register is stored in FLG, and the resource is allocated. Both the interrupt routine and the mainline code attempt to use the resource concurrently, and an error occurs.

The root of the problem is that the testing and value change by the mainline code to a variable shared by it and the interrupt routine is interruptable. Figure 6.15 shows a solution which is to disable interrupts if such a critical sequence of operations can be interrupted by a routine that manipulates the shared variable.

```
DI                  DISABLE INTERRUPTS.
LDA   FLG           ATTEMPT TO ALLOCATE THE RESOURCE.
DEC   A
STA   FLG
EI                  ENABLE INTERRUPTS.
JZ    ALLOC1        BRANCH IF ALLOCATED.
```

Figure 6.15. A Z-80 program sequence illustrating the use of interrupt masking to prevent the interruption of a critical sequence of code.

Figure 6.16 is a similar program for the PDP-11 minicomputer. (See Appendix B for a brief description of the PDP-11 instruction set.) The program directly decrements the FLG value in one instruction. Although this instruction requires several internal steps (read FLG value, decrement the flag value, and store the decremented value in FLG), the sequence of steps is not interruptable. There is therefore no need to disable interrupts in the mainline code section when FLG is tested and modified.

The use of a binary variable such as FLG above (FLG is one or is not equal to one) to communicate between concurrent program sections is common. Such a variable and the rules governing its use (e.g. operations on the variable must be noninterruptable) is called an event flag. The event flag can be used to synchronize resource allocation, signal the completion of an operation, and provide other synchronization func-

```
    .
    .
    .
DECB FLG
BEQ  ALLOC1
    .                              .
    .                              .
    .                              .
                               DECB FLG
                               BEQ  ALLOC2
                                   .
                                   .
                                   .
Main Program                   Interrupt Routine
```

Figure 6.16. A PDP-11 program sequence using the device allocation algorithm of Figure 6.14. Interrupts need not be disabled in the mainline code during the resource allocation code because the decrement byte instruction (DECB) performs both the decrement and test for zero directly on the contents of FLG and cannot be interrupted.

tions. There is no formal definition of what values are used for an event flag. The instruction set of the computer used may dictate the most efficient value. Semaphores are a more sophisticated mechanism for resource allocation. The program segment requesting a resource that is already allocated by another program segment is suspended from executing until the resource is available. Such semaphore functions are found in sophisticated real-time operating systems.

Figure 6.17 illustrates interrupt routine communications using a simple buffer. The interrupt routine reads a value from the device that interrupted; the data is placed in the buffer; and the buffer is then made available to the mainline code.

In the example, a buffer and an event flag are used for communications between the mainline code and an interrupt routine. The program starts a device in interrupt mode and initializes an event flag to one. The flag is then repeatedly tested. The interrupt routine eventually receives a data element from the device. Commonly, it will save the value in temporary storage and restart the device (instructing it to supply data). The interrupt routine will then determine if the buffer is free (flag equals one). If it is not, the mainline code is using the buffer, and there is no storage for the data values without modifying storage locations in use by the interrupted mainline code. This buffer overrun condition must be indicated to the mainline code, possibly by a second event flag or by a word in the buffer after the buffer is free.

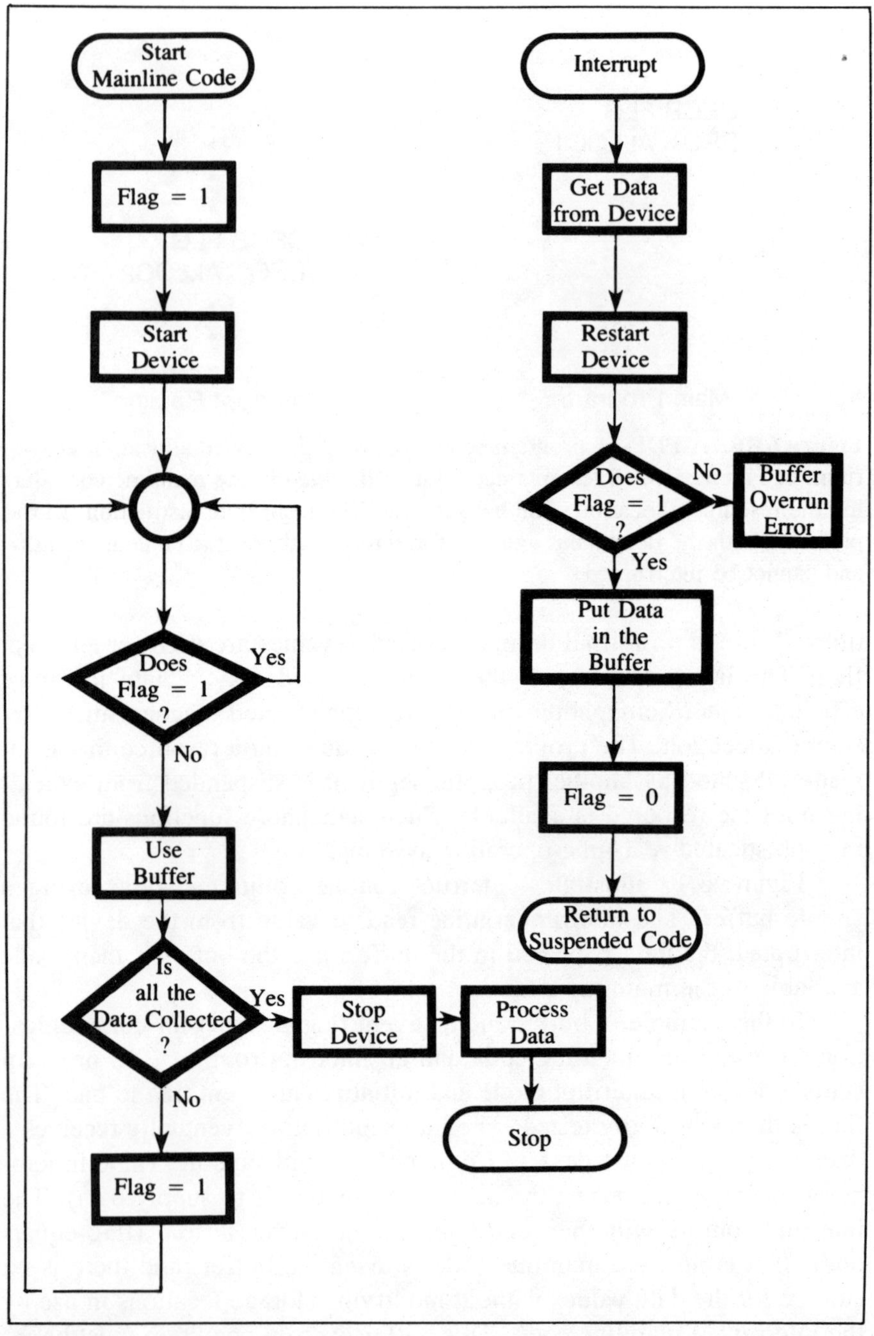

Figure 6.17. The use of a binary valued flag to synchronize mainline code and interrupt code access to a buffer.

If the buffer is available, it is filled by the interrupt routine, and the flag is set to zero to indicate that the buffer may be used by the mainline code. The mainline code processes the data in the buffer and then sets the flag to one, thus indicating the buffer is available to the interrupt routine. Eventually, the mainline code stops data collection based on the data, the collection time, or other events.

Figure 6.18 is an implementation of the Figure 6.17 flowchart in PDP-11 assembly language. Nonrelevant program sections are omitted. The example assumes a device with its control and status register (CSR) at location 176500 (octal) and its data register at location 176502 (octal). The vector address for the device is 300 (octal). Bit 0 (LSB) of the CSR is set to start the device performing some operation (e.g. an analog-to-digital conversion). Bit 6 is set to enable the device to interrupt. When the operation is complete, bit 7 is set by the device which causes an interrupt to be requested if bit 6 is set. When the interrupt is acknowledged, the device clears its interrupt request. Reading the data from the device data register clears bit 7.

```
;       INITIALIZE FLAG AND COLLECTION COUNT.
        MOVB  #1,FLAG          ;SET UP EVENT FLAG.
        MOV   #100.,R0         ;COLLECT 100 POINTS.
;       START THE DEVICE.
        MOV   #INT,@#300         ;SET UP VECTOR AT 300.
        MOV   #340,@#302         ;HANDLER WILL HAVE INTERRUPTS
                                  OFF.
        MOV   #101,@#176500  ;START THE DEVICE. LET IT
                                  INTERRUPT.
;       SUM DATA INTO R1.
        CLR R1
;       WAIT FOR DATA SUPPLIED BY INTERRUPT ROUTINE.
LOOP:   TSTB  FLAG               ;WAIT FOR FLAG=0.
        BNE   LOOP
;       USE THE DATA.
        ADD   BUFFER,R1          ;KEEP SUM IN R1.
;       SHOW THE BUFFER FREE.
        INCB  FLAG
;       LOOP 100 TIMES.
        DEC   R0
        BNE   LOOP
;       STOP THE DEVICE.
        CLR   @#176500
;       PROCESS THE DATA.
```

```
        .
        .
        .
;       INTERRUPT ROUTINE.
;
;       PUT THE DATA FROM THE DEVICE ON THE STACK.
INT:    MOV   @#176502,-(SP);ACCESS DEVICE DATA REGISTER.
;       RESTART THE DEVICE.
        INC   @#176500       ;SET BIT ZERO.
;       IS THE BUFFER FREE?
        TSTB  FLAG
        BEQ   OVERRUN
;       PUT THE DATA IN THE BUFFER.
        MOV   (SP)+,BUFFER
        SHOW DATA IS AVAILABLE.
        CLRB  FLAG
;       RETURN TO MAINLINE CODE.
        RTI
;       BUFFER OVERRUN CONDITION.
OVERRUN:  TST   (SP)+        ;CLEAN UP THE STACK.
        .
        .
        .
BUFFER: .WORD 0
FLAG:   .BYTE  0
        .END
```

Figure 6.18. PDP-11 assembly language implementation of the flowchart of Figure 6.17.

In this example, a single data item is passed from the interrupt routine to the mainline code. The buffer could be enlarged to accomodate a number of data items (e.g. data from several analog channels multiplexed to an A/D converter). The interrupt routine would fill the buffer by processing several interrupts and then flag the buffer as available for use by the mainline code.

The mainline code tests the event flag in a busy wait loop similar to device status checking. If multiple devices are being serviced in a time-critical manner, multiple flags must be tested and device response time problems can occur in a similar manner to status checking devices. (The section describing tasking deals with this problem.)

The method used in the example requires that the mainline code process the data supplied by the interrupt routine before the buffer is needed again by the interrupt routine. If this condition can be met on the average, but bursts of interrupt processing required by other devices in the system occasionally prevent the mainline code from returning the buffer fast enough, two buffers can be alternated in a technique called double buffering. The circular buffer method described below is an expansion of this idea.

The event flag checking technique, when used with double buffering, can be used successfully in time-critical cases where data is moved between two devices. The interrupt routines fill and empty buffers. The mainline code supplies full and empty buffers to the interrupt routines. Figure 6.19 illustrates this technique. An A/D converter fills buffers that are written to disk.

A circular buffer, or ring buffer, is a set of buffers used in a circular fashion. If eight buffers used to form a circular buffer were numbered 1 to 8, the order of buffer usage would be 1 to 8 followed by 1 again. A circular buffer is commonly used to pass data between an interrupt handler and mainline code. In the case where the interrupt handler is supplying data and the mainline code is consuming the data, the circular buffer allows for fast bursts of data-supplier activity or temporary delayed processing by the data consumer. The data consumer must be able to process the data at a rate such that the interrupt handler always has a free buffer when data becomes available. The circular buffer allows for short periods of time when the consumer requires extended computation time, must perform other functions, or is interrupted by another interrupt handler. The circular buffering technique also allows an interrupt routine that supplies bursts of data to be compatible with a data consumer that processes data at a constant rate.

Figure 6.20 shows a conceptual diagram of a typical circular buffer, an actual memory layout, and a sample PDP-11 assembly language version of the memory layout. Pointer GET points to the buffer element that is to be retrieved by the consumer. PUT points to the next free buffer element to be used by the data supplier. Due to the ambiguity that occurs if the buffer is full or empty (in both cases the GET value equals the PUT value), location COUNT is used to hold the number of data items in the buffer.

To add an element to the buffer, first COUNT is checked to see if the buffer is already full. If it is not, COUNT is incremented, the data element is put in the buffer location pointed to by PUT, and PUT is incremented to point to the next free location in the buffer. If PUT then points past the last buffer element, it is set to point to the first buffer element.

If the buffer is full (COUNT value is eight) when a data item is to

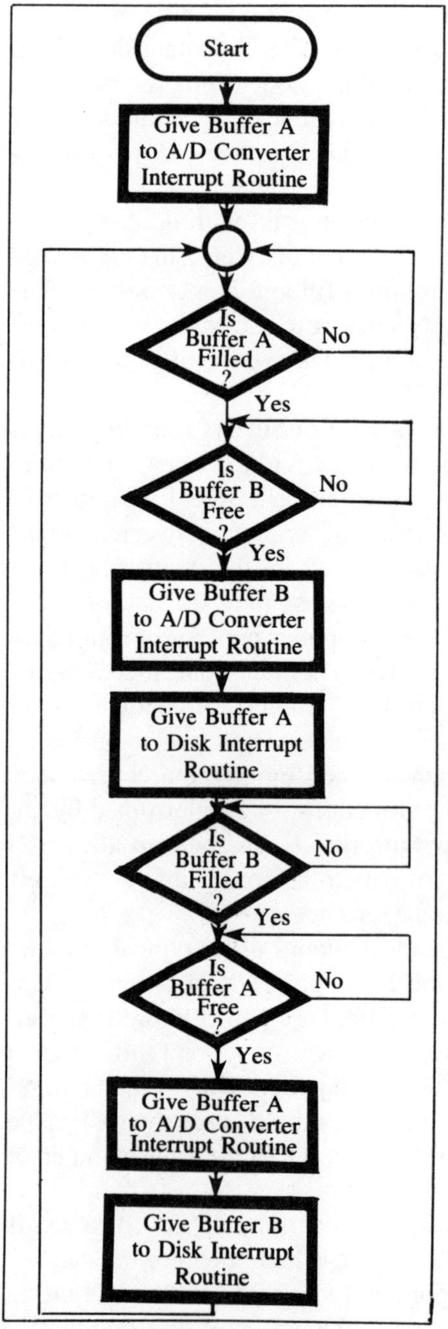

Figure 6.19. A macro flowchart of a program that uses double buffering.

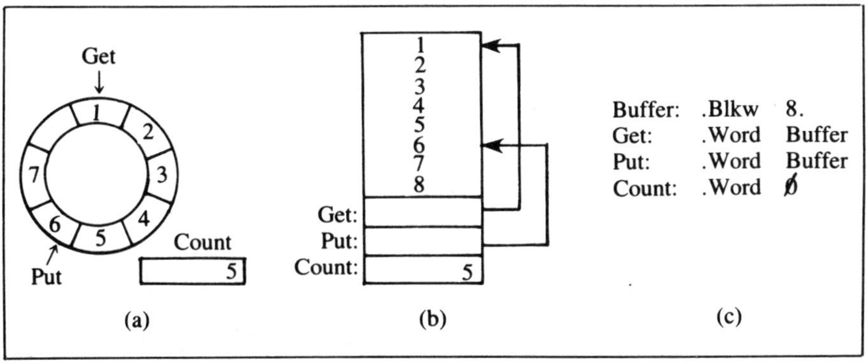

Figure 6.20. A conceptual diagram of a circular buffer (a), the corresponding memory layout of the circular buffer (b), and a sample PDP-11 assembly language version of the memory layout (c).

be put in the buffer, this overrun condition requires special processing. In a simple system, the program typically notifies the operator and aborts processing.

To retrieve data from the buffer, the data consumer must check COUNT to determine if data is available. If the COUNT value is not zero, the data in the word pointed to by GET is retrieved, COUNT is decremented, and GET is incremented to point to the next free buffer location. If GET points beyond the end of the buffer, it is set to point to the first buffer element.

Figure 6.21 shows two reentrant subroutines written in PDP-11 assembly language to insert and remove elements from a circular buffer. The routines may be used by several routines using different circular buffers. When the routines are called, register R0 must point to a buffer control block containing the COUNT, GET, and PUT words along with the address of the first and last buffer elements for use in performing the circular wraparound function.

If RETR is called and no data is available, the carry bit of the PSW is set when the subroutine returns. The calling program can perform a busy wait until data is available. More sophisticated techniques for handling the no data condition are discussed in the following section.

The OVERRUN label is omitted from the example. The processing that occurs during the data overrun condition depends on the system. If the circular buffer routines can be called from an interrupt routine and from mainline code to act on the same buffer, critical sections of the subroutines must be run with interrupts disabled.

```
;               BUFFER CONTROL BLOCK 1.
BCB1:
COUNT1:     .WORD  0                ;ELEMENTS IN THE BUFFER.
GET1:       .WORD  BUF1             ;RETRIEVE POINTER.
PUT1:       .WORD  BUF1             ;INSERT POINTER.
FIRST1:     .WORD  BUF1             ;START OF BUFFER.
LAST1:      .WORD  BUF1+16.         ;WORD PAST BUFFER.
;
;               BUFFER CONTROL BLOCK 2.
BCB2:
COUNT2:     .WORD  0                ;ELEMENTS IN THE BUFFER.
GET2:       .WORD  BUF2             ;RETRIEVE POINTER.
PUT2:       .WORD  BUF2             ;INSERT POINTER.
FIRST2:     .WORD  BUF2             ;START OF BUFFER.
LAST2:      .WORD  BUF2+16.         ;WORD PAST BUFFER.
;
;               BUFFERS.
BUF1:       .BLKW     8.
BUF2:       .BLKW     8.
```

(a)

```
;               MAP OF CONTROL BLOCK OFFSETS
                COUNT=0
                GET=2
                PUT=4
                FIRST=6
                LAST=8.
;
;               INSERT ROUTINE. ON ENTRY R0 POINTS TO A
;               BUFFER CONTROL BLOCK AND R1 CONTAINS THE
;               DATA VALUE TO BE INSERTED INTO THE CIRCULAR
;               BUFFER.
INSERT:     CMP     COUNT(R0),#8.   ;IS THE BUFFER FULL?
            BGE     OVERRUN
            INC     COUNT(R0)       ;COUNT INSERTED VALUE.
            MOV     R1,@PUT(R0)     ;PUT DATA IN THE BUFFER.
            INC     PUT(R0)         ;UPDATE PUT POINTER BY
                                      2 (WORD INCREMENT)
            INC     PUT(R0)
            CMP     PUT(R0),LAST(R0)      ;HANDLE WRAP-
                                            AROUND.
            BLE     NOWRAP1
            MOV     FIRST(R0),PUT(R0)     ;POINT TO FIRST
                                            ELEMENT.
```

```
NOWRAP1:  RTS    PC
OVERRUN:  .
          .
          .
;         RETRIEVE ROUTINE. ON ENTRY R0 POINTS TO A
;         BUFFER CONTROL BLOCK. ON EXIT R1 CONTAINS
;         THE DATA VALUE RETRIEVED FROM THE BUFFER. IF
;         THE BUFFER IS EMPTY WHEN RETR IS CALLED, THE
;         CARRY FLAG IS SET ON EXIT; OTHERWISE, THE
;         CARRY IS CLEARED.
RETR:     TST    COUNT(R0)     :IS DATA AVAILABLE?
          BEQ    NODATA
          MOV    @GET(R0),R1   ;GET THE DATA FROM THE
                                 BUFFER.



          DEC    COUNT(R0)     ;UPDATE ELEMENT COUNT.
          INC    GET(R0)       ;UPDATE GET POINTER BY 2
                                 (WORD INCREMENT)
          INC    GET(R0)
          CMP    GET(R0),LAST(R0)      ;HANDLE WRAP-
                                         AROUND.
          BLE    NOWRAP2
          MOV    FIRST(R0),GET(R0)     ;POINT TO FIRST
                                         ELEMENT
NOWRAP2:  CLRC                     ;CLEAR CARRY.
          RTS    PC
;         NO DATA. RETURN WITH CARRY SET.
NODATA:   SETC
          RTS    PC

                 (b)


          MOV    #BCB1,R0  ;POINT TO BUFFER CONTROL
                             BLOCK 1.
          JSR    PC,RETR   ;GET BUFFER DATA.
          BCS    NONE      ;WAS BUFFER EMPTY?

                 (c)
```

Figure 6.21. PDP-11 assembly language program segments: circular buffer control blocks and buffers (a), reentrant INSERT and RETR (retrieve) routines for the circular buffers (b), and a sample calling sequence for subroutine RETR (c).

Tasking

The interrupt routine techniques discussed thus far are useful for small-scale data logging software. Although several devices may be serviced by interrupt handlers, the mainline code processes data from devices in a sequential manner. It may be desirable to process data related to one device at a high rate while processing data related to other devices only when the high priority task has no data to process. This problem is similar to servicing devices using the status checking technique. Interspersed throughout the mainline code that processes data from low priority devices are checks to determine if the high priority device interrupt routine requires data or has provided data for processing. Due to the complexity of this type of software, this technique should be avoided.

Another technique that can be used to allow data from several devices to be processed in a nonsequential manner is to process data from high priority devices in the device interrupt routine. Data from other devices are passed to the mainline code and processed sequentially. This technique has limited usefulness. The processing performed in an interrupt routine should be relatively short so that the interrupt routine is available for the next device interrupt. If more than one device handler performs a significant amount of processing, device response time is sacrificed. This technique should be avoided except in small systems that have one device that requires a small amount of data processing performed at a high priority.

A tasking operating system is the best general-purpose solution to the problems of providing nonsequential processing of collected data. A tasking system allows a number of concurrent operations to occur. Instead of one mainline program, several tasks are executed.

Figure 6.22 shows an example of a small tasking system. The high priority task receives data from an A/D converter service routine. It performs a data reduction algorithm on each buffer of data, and when a buffer of the reduced data is full, it is sent to the disk interrupt service routine for storing on magnetic media. A second, low priority task communicates with an operator via a terminal. The operator monitors the operation of the system by viewing graphs of the data already written to disk by the high priority task. The low priority task determines the data to be graphed by interacting with the operator, instructs the disk interrupt routine to read the data, receives the data from the interrupt routine, prepares the data for graphing, and displays it.

There are four interrupt routines. The A/D routine fills a circular buffer with data from the converter which is triggered at a constant rate

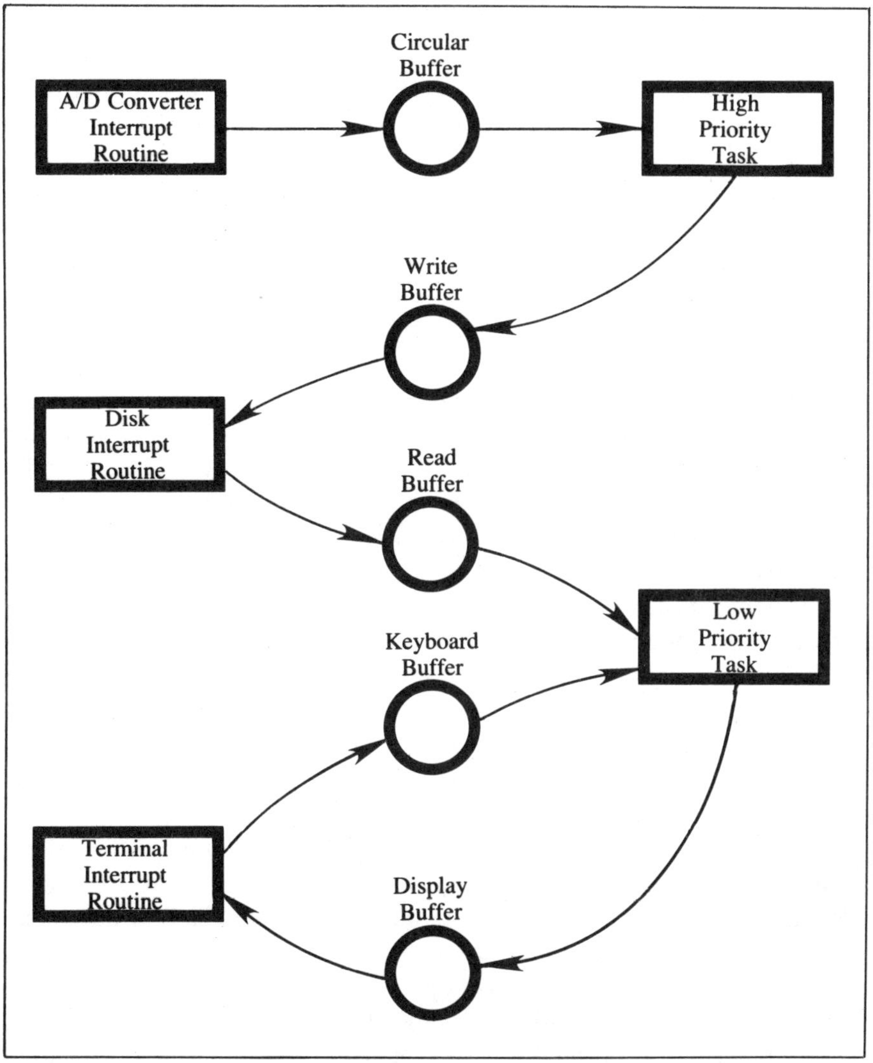

Figure 6.22. A small, special-purpose tasking system. The high priority task inputs data from an A/D converter, performs a data reduction algorithm, and writes the data to disk. The low priority task displays data read from the disk graphically on a terminal based on operator input from the keyboard of the terminal.

by an external clock. The high priority routine retrieves data from the A/D converter interrupt routine and processes it. The reduced data is placed in a buffer for the disk. Each disk buffer element contains storage for the data and the address of the disk blocks to be involved in the operation. The disk interrupt routine gives priority to disk write operations (for storing data) over disk read operations (for graphing).

The disk interrupt routine also fills a second circular buffer with information read from the disk for the low priority task. Two interrupt handlers service the terminal. One handler processes characters keyed by the operator. The other writes characters (including graph instructions) to the terminal display.

The heart of the tasking system is the scheduler. The scheduler is a program that allocates processor time to the tasks. There are a number of methods of implementing a scheduling system. General techniques for use in a small data acquisition system are described below.

Each active task in the system is in one of three states: blocked, ready, or running. A blocked task is in a suspended state waiting for some event or resource. A ready task is waiting to be activated while another task is running. A ready task has all the resources it needs to execute except the processor. The one running task is the task being currently executed by the processor.

When a task is not executing, its state or context must be preserved. The amount of context information saved depends on the system. The most common context information is register values including the program counter and processor status register (state of ALU status bits). When a task is to be placed into the running state, its context is copied into the CPU registers. The context must be saved anytime the running task is suspended.

In a tasking system, event flag operations and circular buffer operations are performed by the operating system. Each task invokes common operating system routines to execute these functions. If a task checks an event flag and the event being checked has not occurred, or if the buffer data is not available in a retrieval operation, the task is blocked and the scheduler is invoked to activate another task. When an event occurs or data is placed in a buffer by a task or interrupt routine, the operating system determines if a blocked task is waiting on the event or data. If the task is waiting for no other resource, it is no longer blocked.

An event-driven scheduler receives control each time an event flag operation is performed and each time a circular buffer operation completes. The scheduler then gives control to the highest priority task that is not blocked. Interrupt routines and interrupt related routines are given higher priority than the set of tasks. Interrupt routines are given control by the hardware. (An interrupt serializer may be used as illustrated in Figure 6.10).

Before an interrupt routine can handle interrupts, some task must initiate the device operation. In the case of an A/D converter, the task passes data collection parameters (e.g. analog gain) to a subroutine that initializes the interrupt handler and starts the A/D converter. In the case of interrupt routines that accept data to be passed to a device, the initialization routine can be invoked by the scheduler when data is placed in the circular buffer and the device is idle. The initialization section is also invoked after the current I/O operation completes if more data is in the circular buffer.

In a simple event-driven scheduler as shown in Figure 6.22, the scheduler must only keep track of the two tasks and interrupt routine initialization sections. If the initialization sections are written such that they are only used by one task, they can be considered part of the task.

The scheduler also has some form of a busy wait which it performs when both tasks are blocked. If the system is designed properly, an interrupt routine will eventually call an event flag or circular buffer subroutine. The subroutine will invoke scheduler processing that can cause a task to become ready.

Figure 6.23 illustrates a more general tasking system. In this system, the scheduler must keep track of a number of tasks, each with its

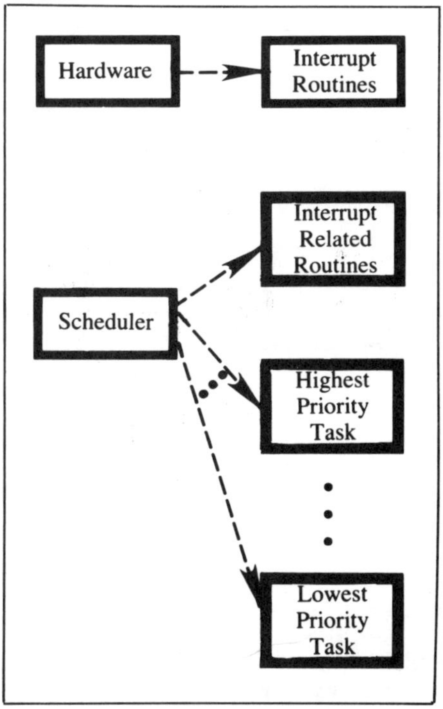

Figure 6.23. A block diagram of a tasking system where each task has a unique priority.

own priority. The scheduler always runs the highest priority task that is ready.

Figure 6.24 shows a tasking scheme where some tasks have equal priority. In this case, the scheduler keeps a queue of tasks in each priority class. Each task is either blocked, on the ready queue, or is running. When an event occurs, the scheduler checks the ready queues in priority order. The first task on the highest priority, non-empty ready queue is made to run. When a blocked task becomes ready, it is placed at the head or rear of its priority ready queue depending on the scheduler design. When a low priority running task is preempted by a high priority task, the preempted task may either be placed at the head or rear of the queue depending on the scheduler design. If a task must be guaranteed high priority execution, it can be placed in the highest priority class alone.

In the queue-based scheduling system, it is possible that some low priority tasks may rarely gain control. If one low priority task performs complex calculations, it may rarely become blocked because it infre-

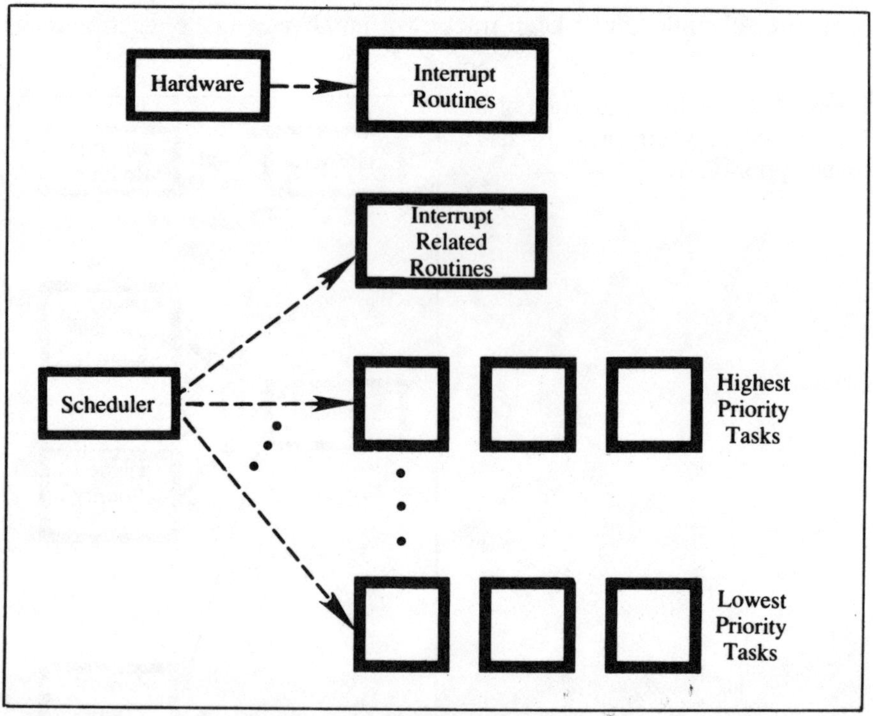

Figure 6.24. A block diagram of a tasking system where there are a number of task priority levels with one or more tasks in each level.

quently performs I/O or event flag operations. This condition causes other low priority tasks to remain in the ready state. One method to insure that all tasks in a priority class are eventually executed is to place preempted tasks at the rear of the task ready queue for their priority class. A second method is to use a clock to invoke the scheduler periodically when it is not being invoked by other events. The scheduler can then allocate the processor based on some algorithm (e.g. preempt any tasks executing for more than one scheduler clock period if the task is not in a high priority class). This method of scheduling is most appropriate in a large-scale minicomputer system that also allows multiuser program development tasks.

It should be noted that a function can be implemented to allow a task in the running state to inquire on an event flag or buffer without being blocked if the resource is not available. If a task has other work to do, it may check on a resource; and if it is not available, the task may perform some other function.

The goal of any scheduling software in a data acquisition system is to ensure that time-critical tasks are serviced in a timely fashion. As complex scheduling techniques increase system overhead, the simplest scheduling algorithm that insures proper system performance is most appropriate. In some cases, the scheduling algorithm is implemented as part of a real-time operating system, and the system designer need only understand the scheduling system well enough to exploit it.

I/O Operation Queuing

The interrupt handlers described thus far either always performed an input or output function or were divided into two sections (one for input and one for output, as in the disk handler of Figure 6.22) and were always associated with a single task. Many real-time operating systems contain a queued I/O system for devices such as a disk drive that can be shared by several tasks. When a task initiates an I/O operation to a queued device, it calls an operating system subroutine. A control block is built for the operation that contains a code to indicate the function to be performed (e.g. read or write), the address of the buffer that will be filled or emptied by the interrupt handler, the task requesting the operation, and the method by which the requesting task will be notified of the completion of the I/O operation. The control block is placed on a queue of functions to be performed by the device. If the queue is empty when a control block is built, the initiation section of the interrupt handler is invoked with the control block information as parameters. When an op-

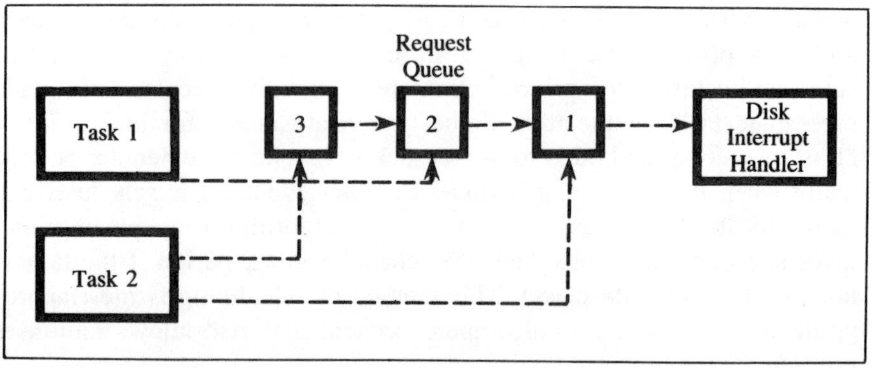

Figure 6.25. Example of queued disk I/O. Task 2 has queued two I/O operations (1 and 3), and task 1 has queued request 2.

eration completes, the requesting task is informed; and if another control block is on the queue, a new operation is initiated. Figure 6.25 illustrates queued disk access.

Tasks can be informed of I/O completion in a number of ways. The task requesting the I/O operation may request that it be blocked until the operation completes. It may associate I/O completion with an event flag that it can check with or without preemption. It may request an asynchronous routine be executed when the I/O completes. (See the next section for a discussion of completion routines.)

High-level Language Use of Operating System Support

If there is sufficient processing power in a system to allow it, much of the data processing software can be written in a high-level language. The advantage of high-level language usage is improved programmer productivity and easier software maintenance. Most high-level languages do not include primitive statements to invoke event flag and other operating system services. These functions are commonly added as system subroutines which are typically written in assembly language and follow a system-defined argument passing convention. Shared variables (e.g. FORTRAN COMMON) can also be used to allow assembly language system subroutines and mainline code to access the same buffer.

A high-level language routine can check event flags, access buffers, and initiate I/O operations by calling system subroutines. Event completion can be passed to high-level language routines by using task blocking, event flags, or asynchronous subroutines. An asynchronous subroutine is a subroutine of the high-level language mainline code that is not invoked by a "CALL" statement but by the operating system when some event occurs. The asynchronous subroutine can perform calculations and initiate new I/O operations. It commonly communicates with the mainline code via shared variables.

When an asynchronous subroutine is to be executed, it is usually executed in place of the mainline code. In a single task system, the mainline task is invoked after the asynchronous subroutine is executed. In a tasking system, all asynchronous subroutines might execute before any high priority task mainline code executes since the asynchronous subroutines are normally associated with the completion of some interrupt event.

Figure 6.26 illustrates high-level language usage in a small real-time system. The FORTRAN task uses an assembly language subroutine to invoke the A/D converter and waits for a buffer to be filled. An asynchronous exit routine receives control when the buffer is filled, starts a new conversion, and makes the data available to the mainline code where the data is written to disk. COMMON variable IFLAG is used as an event flag to inform the main routine that data is available. The asynchronous routine halts A/D conversions when the channel zero value is negative. Variable IFLAG is also used to inform the mainline code that data collection is finished.

An assumption concerning the program is that the A/D converter operates at a relatively slow rate such that the data values can be written to disk and that subroutine COMP can complete execution before the next conversion ends. A second assumption is that the time between groups of samples need not be precise (see the section on precision timing) or that an external trigger is used to synchronize data collection to some time base.

Asynchronous subroutines are sometimes written in assembly language to increase efficiency.

Arithmetic

In real-time applications, efficient calculations are mandatory in many circumstances. All digital computers provide primitive integer operations in the basic instruction set. Integer computations are performed on a limited number of word sizes. Integer calculations requiring values larger than the range of values in the largest integer word size must be handled in software using several integer instructions for each operation involving multiple word operands.

On many small machines, there are no integer multiplication or di-

```
      COMMON /SHARE/ IFLAG,BUFFER(2,16),IBUF
      EXTERNAL COMP
      DATA IFLAG/0/,IBUF/1/
C
C     USE BUFFER ONE FIRST.
C
      ICUR=IBUF
C
C     CALL THE ASSEMBLY LANGUAGE ROUTINE TO START
C     DATA COLLECTION. CHANNELS 0 TO 15 ARE SAMPLED
C     EACH TIME AN EXTERNAL TRIGGER OCCURS. THE
C     COLLECTED DATA IS PLACED IN ARRAY BUFFER, A
C     DOUBLE BUFFER. BUFFER(I,J) HOLDS DATA FROM
C     CHANNEL J-1. I IS THE BUFFER NUMBER (1 OR 2). COMP IS
C     THE COMPLETION ROUTINE CALLED BY THE ASSEMBLY
C     CODE WHEN ONE SWEEP IS COMPLETE.
C
      CALL AD(BUFFER(1,1),COMP)
C
C     WAIT FOR A CONVERSION TO COMPLETE.
C
10    IF(IFLAG.EQ.0) GO TO 10
C
C     ZERO IFLAG SO THAT IT CAN BE USED TO INDICATE WHEN
C     THE OTHER BUFFER IS FILLED.
C
      IFLAG=0
C
C     HAS SAMPLING STOPPED?
C
      IF(IFLAG.LT.0) STOP
C
C     WRITE THE SWEEP DATA TO DISK.
C
      WRITE(9,1) (BUFFER(ICUR,J),J=1,16)
1     FORMAT(16(1X,I4))
C
C     GET READY FOR THE NEXT BUFFER. THE TRIGGER RATE
C     MUST BE SLOW COMPARED TO THE EXECUTION RATE OF
C     THIS LOOP.
C
      ICUR=3-ICUR
      GO TO 10
```

```
      END
      SUBROUTINE COMP
C
C     THIS SUBROUTINE IS CALLED WHEN A SWEEP IS
C     COMPLETE.
C
      COMMON /SHARE/ IFLAG,BUFFER(2,16),IBUF
      EXTERNAL COMP
      DATA IFLAG/0/,IBUF/1/
C
C     WHEN CHANNEL 0 VALUE IS LESS THAN ZERO, FLAG STOP
C     CONDITION.
C
      IF(BUFFER(IBUF,1).LT.0) GO TO 100
C
C     FLAG DATA AVAILABLE.
C
      IFLAG=1
C
C     START A NEW CONVERSION USING THE OTHER BUFFER.
C
      IBUF=3-IBUF
      CALL AD(BUFFER(IBUF,1),COMP)
      RETURN
C
C     FLAG STOP CONDITION
C
100   IFLAG=-1
      RETURN
      END
```

Figure 6.26. A FORTRAN program using an asynchronous exit routine. The program requires that the A/D converter be triggered at a fixed rate by an external trigger and that the sample rate is slow enough so that overruns will never occur. (The latter assumption is rarely valid except in example programs.)

vision instructions. Implementation of multiplication or division by repeated addition and subtraction, respectively, is not recommended due to the inefficiency of these algorithms. Figure 6.27 gives relative efficient algorithms for two's complement multiplication and division. These algorithms are shown implemented in PDP-11 assembly language.

Many instruments produce values in BCD. Because BCD arithmetic

```
;        ROUTINE TO MULTIPLY THE 16 BIT VALUE IN R0 BY THE
;        16 BIT VALUE IN R1 AND RETURN THE 32 BIT PRODUCT
;        IN THE R0, R1 PAIR (R0 IS THE LOW-ORDER PART OF
;        THE PRODUCT). THE OPERANDS MUST BE POSITIVE.
MUL:     MOV   R2,-(SP)        ;SAVE WORK REGISTERS.
         MOV   R3,-(SP)
;        SET UP TO MULTIPLY.
         MOV   #16.,R3         ;LOOP 16 TIMES.
         MOV   R1,R2           ;GET A COPY OF R1 VALUE.
         CLR   R1              ;ZERO HIGH-ORDER PART.
;        MULTIPLY LOOP.
         IF BIT ZERO OF THE R0 VALUE IS ZERO, DO NOT ADD.
MULLP:   BIT   #1,R0
         BEQ   NOADD
;        ADD MULTIPLIER TO HIGH-ORDER PART.
         ADD   R2,R1
;        DOUBLE SHIFT RIGHT.
NOADD:   ASR   R1
         ROR   R0
;        LOOP 16 TIMES.
         DEC   R3
         BNE   MULLP
;        MULTIPLY DONE. RETURN TO CALLER.
         MOV   (SP)+,R3        ;RESTORE WORK REGISTERS.
         MOV   (SP)+,R2
         RTS   PC
```

(a)

```
;
;        DIVIDE THE 32 BIT NUMBER IN R0, R1 (LOW-ORDER
;        PART IS IN R0) BY THE VALUE IN R2. THE QUOTIENT IS
;        RETURNED IN R0, AND THE REMAINDER IS RETURNED
;        IN R1. THE OPERANDS MUST BE POSITIVE. THE DIVIDE
;        ALGORITHM IS CALLED THE RESTORING DIVISION
;        TECHNIQUE.
DIV:     MOV   R3,-(SP)        ;SAVE WORK REGISTER VALUE.
         MOV   #16.,R3         ;LOOP 16 TIMES.
;        DIVIDE LOOP.
;        DO A DOUBLE SHIFT LEFT INTO THE CARRY BIT.
DIVLOP:  ASL   R0
         ROL   R1
;        ASSUME R0, BIT ZERO WILL BE SET.
         BIS   #1,R0
;        SUBTRACT DIVISOR FROM R1. IF R1 IS NEGATIVE, ADD
;        DIVISOR BACK AND CLEAR R0, BIT ZERO.
         SUB   R2,R1
```

```
        BPL   DLOOP          ;R1 IS POSITIVE.
        BIC   #1,R0          ;CLEAR BIT ZERO.
        ADD   R2,R1          ;RESTORE R1.
;       LOOP 16 TIMES.
DLOOP:  DEC   R3
        BNE   DIVLOP
;       RETURN TO CALLER.
        MOV   (SP)+,R3       ;RESTORE R3.
        RTS   PC
        .END
```

(b)

Figure 6.27. PDP-11 assembly language multiplication program (a) and division program (b). These subroutines operate on positive numbers only. Before the divide routine is called, it should be determined if division is possible (divisor is not zero and quotient can be represented in 16 bits).

is basically slow as compared to integer arithmetic, BCD values are normally converted to binary before involved computations are performed. If only a small amount of computation is to be performed, the calculations can be performed in BCD. Many small computers have a decimal adjust command that aids in the implementation of BCD calculations. Because BCD operands are typically too large to be contained in a single machine register, BCD operations are performed by subroutines with operands commonly stored in primary memory.

Many small computers do not contain floating point instructions. If floating point operations are to be performed on these machines, the operations are implemented as subroutines written using integer instructions.

Most floating point numbers are encoded in three parts (see Figure 2.7): the sign, mantissa, and exponent. The value of the floating point number is the value of the mantissa (with sign) multiplied by a selected base raised to the power specified by the exponent. Before addition or subtraction of two floating point numbers can occur, the mantissas must "line up"; i.e., they must have the same exponent. This lining up is performed by shifting the mantissa of the number with the smaller exponent to the right and adjusting its exponent accordingly until the exponents of both numbers are equal. At this point, addition or subtraction of the two mantissas can occur. The exponent of the result is the same as that of the operand with the larger exponent.

Frequently, floating point results are normalized. The mantissa is shifted left until its high-order bit is one. The exponent is adjusted for the shifting. (Normalization is illustrated by most hand calculators with scientific notation format.) If the binary point is assumed to be to the left of the high-order bit of the mantissa, the mantissa is normalized by adjusting the exponent such that the mantissa is greater than or equal to 1/2 and less than one. A normalized value of zero is represented by a sign, mantissa, and exponent with a zero-bit pattern.

To perform floating point multiplication, exponents are added and mantissas are multiplied. The result is normalized. (If the exponent is encoded as an excess-n number, n must be subtracted from the sum of the exponents to retain the excess-n bias).

Floating point division is performed by subtracting the exponent of the divisor from the exponent of the dividend (adding n in excess-n systems) and dividing the mantissas. The result is then normalized.

Implementation of the basic floating point operations requires only the basic integer operations and shifting. Floating point operations can be implemented as subroutines using the basic instruction set or by floating point instructions in advanced machines.

Typically, the base that is raised to the power of the exponent is not two, but eight or 16. This technique allows a small number of exponent bits to cover a larger numeric range. When the mantissa is adjusted, it is shifted in groups of three bits (base 8) or four bits (base 16). Normalization is then accomplished by requiring that the leading octal digit (for base 8) or the leading hexadecimal digit (for base 16) be non-zero.

In most implementations of floating point arithmetic, guard bits are used to extend the size of the mantissa while a primitive operation (addition, subtraction, multiplication, or division) is being performed. When normalization is performed on the result of a primitive operation, some of the guard bits may be shifted left into the mantissa. Any remaining guard bits cause the LSB of the mantissa to be rounded. Without guard bits, the number of significant bits would be reduced (see section on computational accuracy).

In real-time systems, floating point arithmetic may be too slow for a particular application. An alternative to floating point operations is scaled binary arithmetic. Scaled binary operands are typically stored in one integer word. Each scaled binary number consists of an integer value and a binary point (base 2 decimal point) position. The binary point attribute is typically not explicitly part of the number, but is "remembered" by the program processing the scaled binary number. (A general purpose scaled binary subroutine might, however, keep the binary point position of a value in a separate word.)

An n-bit scaled binary number of the form

$$b_{n-1}b_{n-2}\ldots b_m b_{m-1}\ldots b_0$$

has the decimal value of

$$\sum_{i=0}^{n-1} b_i 2^{i-m}$$

where m is the bit position of the bit to the left of the binary point. Figure 6.28 shows several eight-bit, scaled binary numbers and the equivalent decimal values.

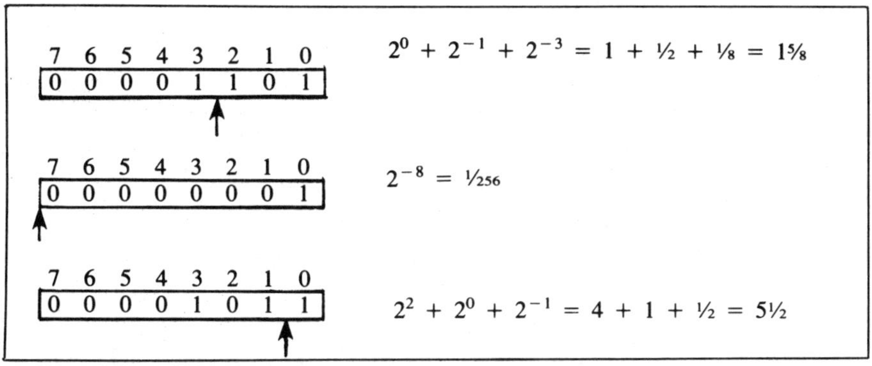

Figure 6.28. Example eight-bit scaled binary numbers. The arrow indicates the position of the binary point.

Before two scaled binary numbers can be added or subtracted, the binary points must be in the same position. If the binary points are not already the same, the numbers are "lined up" by shifting. The operand that is shifted depends on which operand can be shifted without losing significant bits to the left of the binary point. The loss of bits to the right of the binary point should be minimized. A two's complement addition or subtraction operation can then be used to produce the scaled binary result. The binary point is in the same position as with the operands. Figure 6.29 illustrates scaled binary addition.

Scaled operands of multiplication and division need not be lined up before the operations are performed; however, the binary point position of the result must be adjusted. If p_j implies that the binary point is to the left of bit j, then the binary point of a scaled multiplication whose operands have binary points at positions p_q and p_r is at position p_{q+r}. For scaled division, the binary point of the result is at position p_{q-r}. Figure 6.30 illustrates scaled multiplication and division.

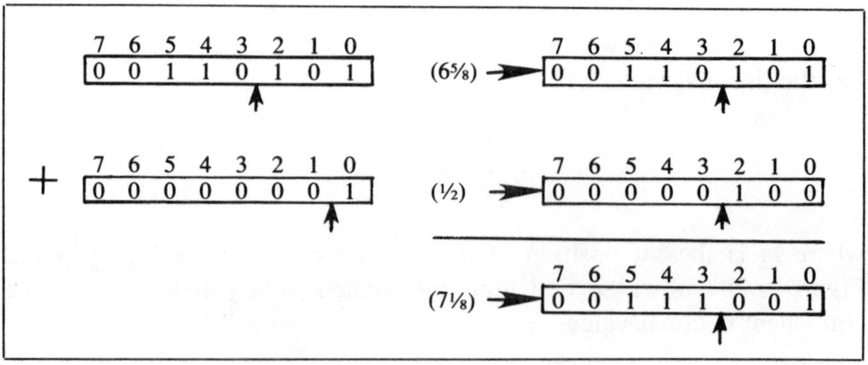

Figure 6.29. An example of scaled binary addition. Note that the second operand is shifted left to line up the binary points.

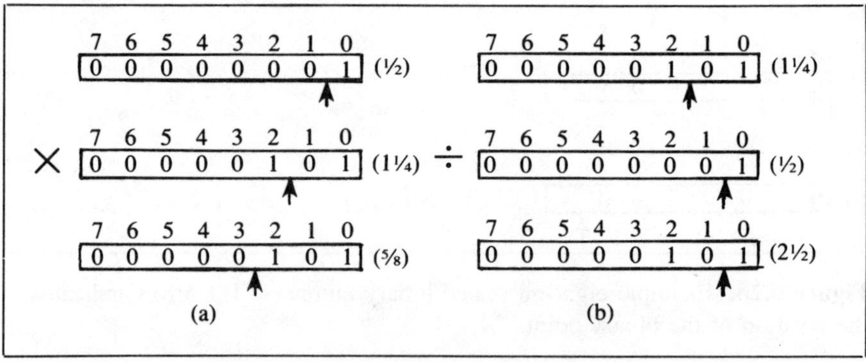

Figure 6.30. Examples of scaled binary multiplication (a) and division (b). Note that in scaled multiplication, the result has the number of binary fraction bits as the sum of the fraction bits in the operands. In scaled division, the number of places to the right of the binary point is equal to the difference of the number of places in the operands.

Scaled arithmetic can also be applied to BCD arithmetic. Although BCD arithmetic is slower than binary, BCD is easier to convert to printable, base 10 format.

General purpose scaled arithmetic can be implemented as a set of subroutines. Each scaled item contains a value portion and a scale portion that indicates where the binary (or decimal) point occurs. Subroutines may be written to always return a normalized value (leading sign bits removed by shifting left).

Scaled arithmetic is useful when dealing with A/D converter values. Most often, the value of the least significant bit is less than one, implying scaling. Scaled operations can be carried out more rapidly than floating point operations which also require a format conversion from the A/D values.

It is usually necessary to convert data in one arithmetic format to another. The conversion of integers between ASCII, BCD, and binary is straightforward. An ASCII digit can be converted to BCD by stripping the high-order three bits. A BCD digit is converted to ASCII by appending the proper high-order bits of the numeric symbols.

A string of BCD digits can be converted to binary by multiplying each BCD digit by the proper power of ten (using binary arithmetic) and summing the results. Binary to BCD is accomplished by successive divisions by ten with the remainders being BCD digits of increasing significance.

Converting a scaled binary number to BCD is more difficult. The integer portion of the number can be separated from the fraction part using shift operations and can then be converted to scaled BCD by successive division by ten using binary operations. To convert the fraction part of the scaled number, the scaled fraction is multiplied by ten repeatedly, with the integer part of each result becoming a BCD digit in the decimal fraction. The integer part of multiplication n becomes the digit in the 10^{-n} place. The fraction part of each result is used in the next multiplication by ten. Figure 6.31 illustrates the technique. After the BCD fraction has been computed to the desired number of places, rounding can be performed. A one is added to the least significant digit in BCD arithmetic if the remaining fractional part is greater than 1/2.

The conversion of a scaled binary number to floating point can be accomplished by shifting the most significant digits into the mantissa part of a floating point word and setting the exponent based on the scale factor and the amount of the shift.

Scaled BCD can be converted to floating point by first converting the integer part to binary and then to floating point. Each BCD fraction digit can be converted to its equivalent floating point value by using a table. The exponent is then set based on the position of the BCD digit with respect to the decimal point. The floating point equivalents of the integer part of the BCD number and the floating point equivalents of the digits to the right of the decimal point are added to produce the floating point equivalent of the BCD number.

The conversion of a floating point binary number to decimal requires that both the mantissa and exponent be dealt with. Given a number of the form $f{\cdot}2^e$, the exponent 2^e can be converted to the proper power of ten by multipying e by $\log_{10} 2$ and rounding to the nearest in-

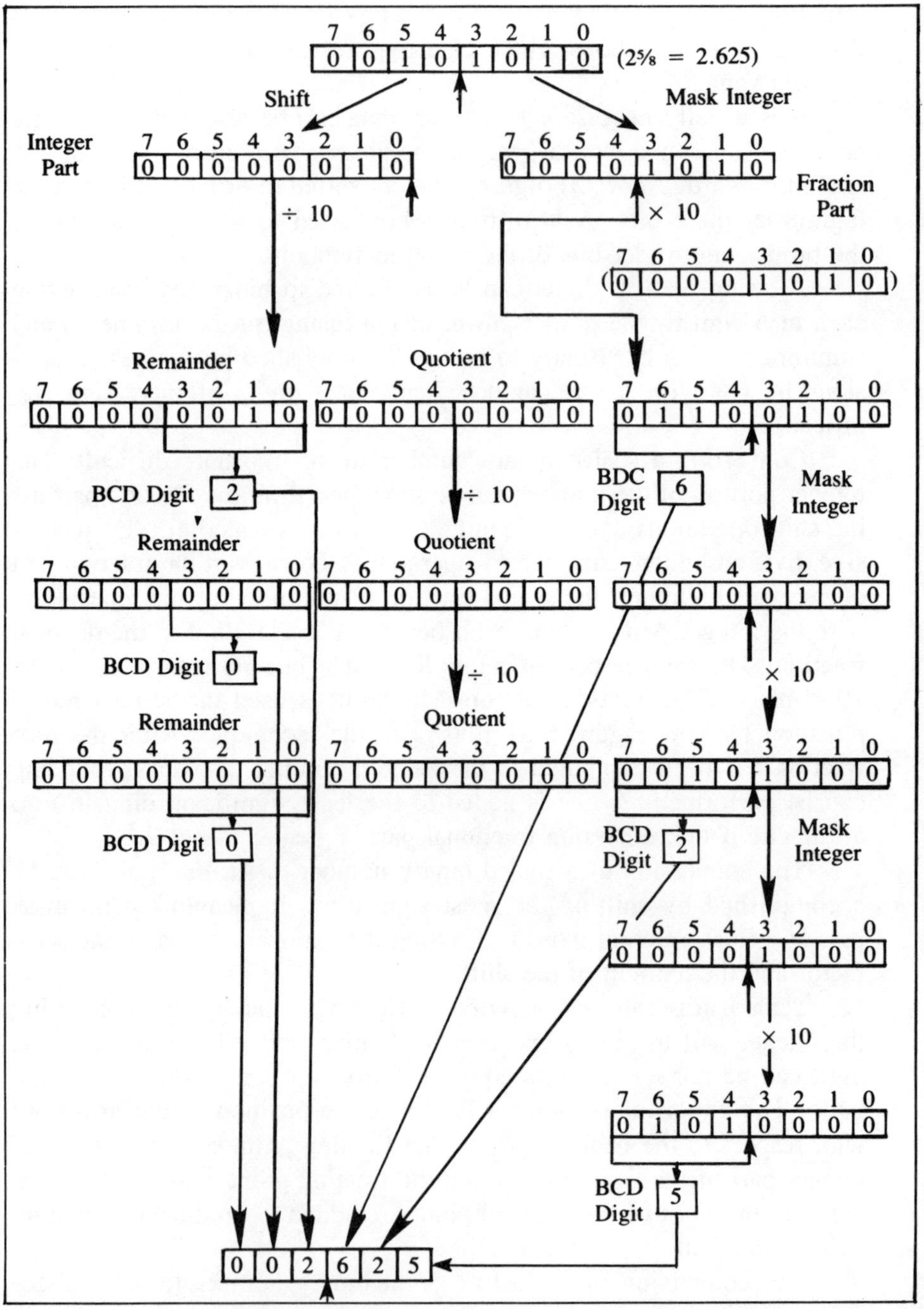

Figure 6.31. Conversion of a scaled binary number to BCD.

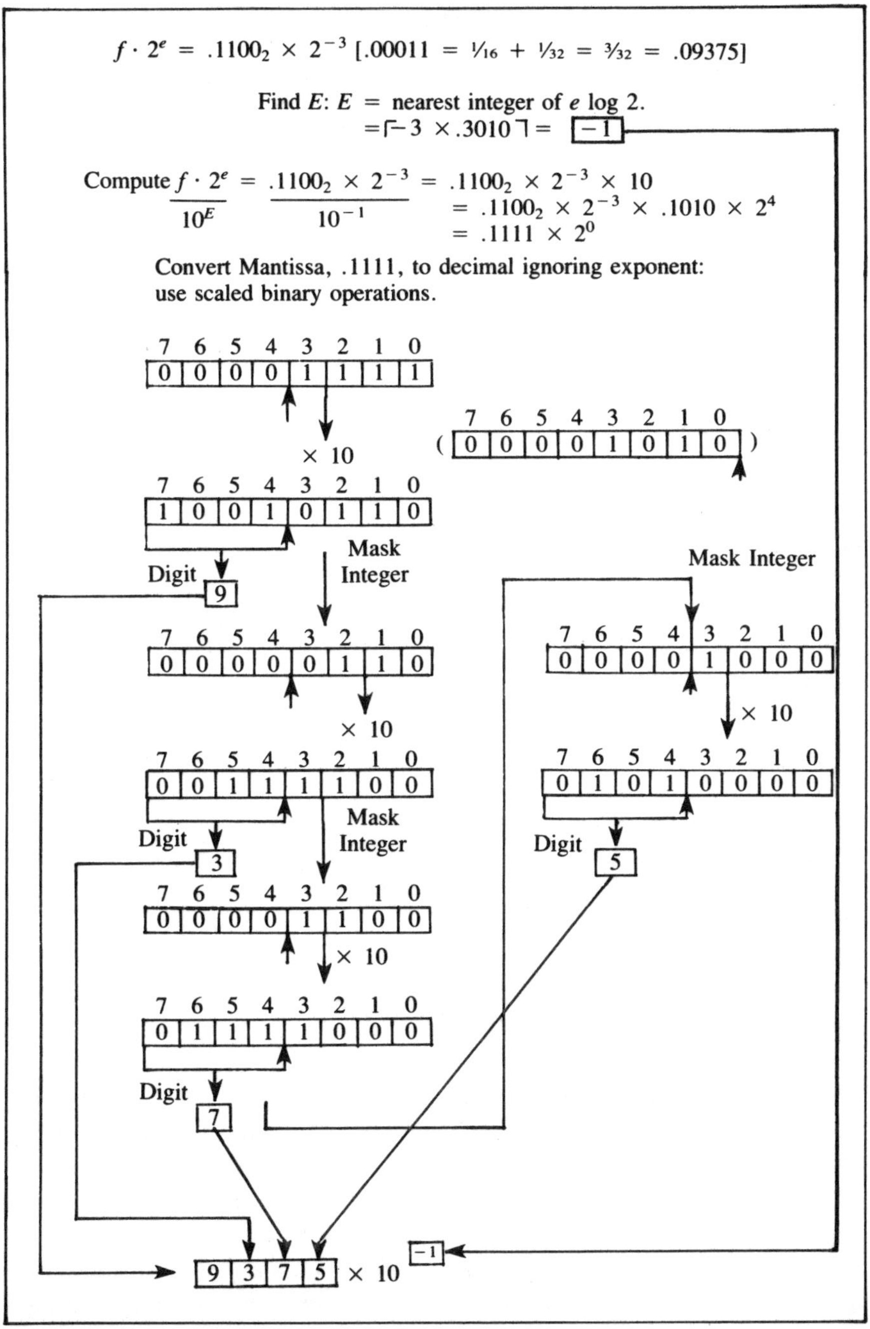

Figure 6.32. A binary floating point number converted to base 10 representation. First the base 10 exponent is computed. 10^E in binary floating point notation is computed using a table lookup. The mantissa of $f{\cdot}2^e/10^E$ is converted to decimal using scaled binary operations.

teger, E. $f \cdot 2^e$ is then divided by 10^E using floating point arithmetic. (10^E is produced from a table or by repeated division.) The mantissa of $f \cdot 2^e/10^E$ is converted to decimal using scaled binary operations. Figure 6.32 illustrates the technique.

Computational Accuracy

The absolute error associated with a quantity is the true value minus the approximate (or measured) value ($e_x = x - \bar{x}$). The relative error is the absolute error divided by the approximation ($e_x/\bar{x}$). Two types of error that affect computation are inherent errors and computation errors.

Inherent errors are caused by the inability to measure a physical quantity accurately. In the discussion of A/D converters, a number of causes of measurement inaccuracies were given. Transducer imperfections and noise add to measurement errors. It is difficult to determine the value of absolute and relative errors due to the need to know the true value of a measured quantity; however, an upper bound on the error should be determined in measurement situations.

Computational errors arise when floating point arithmetic (or scaled integer arithmetic) is used in computations. Floating point arithmetic is discussed because of its wide use and because error analysis of floating point arithmetic is similar to that of other formats that handle fractions. Donald Knuth wrote, "Floating point computation is by nature inexact, and it is not difficult to misuse it so that the computed answers consist almost entirely of 'noise'."[1] Given that a floating point number is represented in the computer with n bits means that only 2^n different numbers must cover the number line from the smallest to the largest numbers representable. Figure 6.33 illustrates floating point accuracy for a four-decimal digit mantissa, two-digit exponent, base ten system (e.g. $.0137 \times 10^{21}$). The best resolution is around zero. As the numbers become larger, there is a larger step between successive representations.

Given any floating point system, irrational numbers cannot be represented exactly. Any value that has more digits than the space allotted for the mantissa also cannot be represented accurately. The result of any computation must be represented in the number of figures allotted to the mantissa. Some computers use a technique called chopping, where digits to the right of the last mantissa digit position are dropped. Another technique is to round the mantissa by inspecting the figure to the right of the last mantissa figure. This figure is held in temporary storage called a guard digit. Rounding introduces less error than chopping.

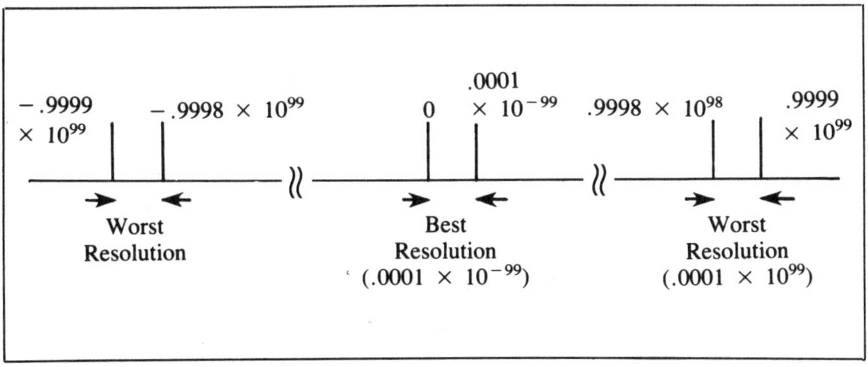

Figure 6.33. Floating point accuracy is best for number representations near zero and gets worse as the absolute value of the represented number increases.

As terms of an expression are calculated, the relative error of the partial results are propagated and possibly magnified. Division and multiplication do not magnify the relative error very much. Subtraction of nearly equal numbers of the same sign or addition of nearly equal numbers in magnitude of opposite signs can introduce large relative errors. If the two floating point values $.1791 \times 10^{20}$ and $.1792 \times 10^{20}$ are subtracted, the normalized result, $.1000 \times 10^{17}$, has only one significant digit. The zero place holders contain no significance but are treated as if they do by the hardware when the number is used in other computation. The relative error of such a subtraction can be large.

Dorn and McCracken[2] make the following suggestions for maintaining accuracy when using floating point arithmetic:

1. When numbers are to be added or subtracted, perform calculations on the small numbers first.
2. Avoid subtraction of two nearly equal numbers, if possible, by rewriting expressions by algebraic manipulation.
3. If nearly equal numbers are involved, use the forms $a(b-c)$ and $(a-b)/c$ instead of $ab-ac$ and $a/c-b/c$.
4. When none of the above rules apply, minimize the number of arithmetic operations.

Care should be taken to ensure the accuracy of results produced by a data acquisition system. A bound on the error can sometimes be determined by applying known (to a small error) physical quantities to the system and analyzing system output. If this technique is not feasible and accuracy is in question, a mathematical error analysis including study of both inherent and computational errors should be performed.

Precision Timing

Real-time clocks are used in data acquisition systems to perform two basic functions. The first function is to keep the time of day or time relative to some arbitrary starting time. This function is useful if collected data must be time stamped or if external events must be timed.

The second function of real-time clocks is to schedule events. Event scheduling can be based on the time of day or on a delay of some time interval. An example of event scheduling based on time of day is a program that must collect solar intensity data at noon each day. An example of interval scheduling is triggering an A/D converter at a constant rate based on an operator defined or predefined sample rate.

In a general purpose data acquisition system, both timing functions may be provided. In a special purpose system, only one timing function may be implemented. Many systems have only one clock; however, diminishing hardware costs make it feasible in some cases to use multiple clocks.

There are basically three types of clocks. The first generates an interrupt at a fixed rate. The second can be programmed to interrupt at a variety of rates and whose internal counter can be read (see Chapter 5). The third type keeps track of the time of day and date. This clock circuitry is normally powered by a battery so that the computer can automatically restart some process after a power failure and still have access to accurate time information.

Use of the calendar/clock is straightforward. The program can read the time of day or date when needed. Most calendar/clocks provide time information in decimal and at relatively low resolution, making their use awkward for precision timing and scheduling. They are useful to set interrupt-driven clocks.

Both single rate clocks and programmable clocks cause interrupts at a constant rate. By counting interrupts, a program can determine when an event occurs with a maximum error of one clock tick. Intervals can also be measured with a maximum error of one clock tick (see Chapter 5).

The time of day function is performed by keeping a count of ticks (clock interrupts) in relation to some known time (e.g. midnight). Although a clock interrupt routine could keep track of seconds, minutes, and hours, normally only a count of ticks is kept. A conversion from ticks to regular time format is performed when needed outside the interrupt routine for efficiency reasons.

Program scheduling is normally implemented using a queue of programs to be scheduled with the program to be run first at the head of the queue. (In simple systems where only one or two programs are scheduled, the queue is replaced by simple program logic.) The interrupt routine compares the current tick count with the time in ticks that the first program is to be scheduled. If the current time count is smaller than the count of the first program, no action is taken. If it is determined that a program is to be scheduled, the routine is activated. In a tasking system, a task is placed on the ready queue. In a small system, the routine may be run as a completion routine, an event flag may be used to signal to the only program in a single program system to run, or current activity may be suspended with the scheduled routine being allowed to run to completion. The clock routine must also determine if several programs must be scheduled at the same clock tick.

If only relative times are implemented and a program is to be run in n clock ticks, the time of the activation of the program is the current interrupt count plus n. This value is placed in a queue element, and the element is placed in the queue at the proper position (smallest schedule time order). If the time of day is used as a reference, the time of day the program is to be run is converted to ticks and placed in the queue. Intervals can be scheduled by computing the time of day the interval will expire based on the current time.

Another type of clock controlled scheduling uses the clock to perform I/O operations at a fixed rate. In the section on A/D converters, a sweep was defined as one sampling of all active channels. One sweep occurs every sample period (operator selected interval determined by the clock). The time between samples in a sweep is normally small (conversion time plus a small software delay for conversion initiation) compared to the sample period (see Figure 4.14).

The first conversion in a sweep is initiated by the clock routine. The remaining samples in a sweep are initiated by the A/D converter interrupt routine at the end of a conversion. The clock routine can initiate the first A/D conversion in a sweep in a variety of ways depending on the architecture of the software. The clock routine can call an A/D conversion initiation routine or possibly invoke it as a task. Some A/D converters can be made to interrupt immediately by setting a bit in their control register. In this case, the clock routine can invoke the A/D converter interrupt routine immediately. The A/D converter interrupt routine then initiates the first sample in the sweep.

Event flags can also be used to allow the clock routine to signal the A/D converter software to start a sweep. In a simple system, the A/D converter software could perform a busy wait until the event flag was activated. In a more sophisticated system, the A/D converter routine would be in a blocked state until the event flag was activated.

If the A/D converter interrupt routine is to execute rapidly, sweep parameters must be computed in advance to reduce the amount of testing and computation in the interrupt handler. At the end of each sweep, the A/D converter interrupt routine can reinitialize data collection parameters in preparation for the next sweep.

Using an interrupt-driven clock routine, events can be timed. Events are normally indicated by some interrupt. The routine responding to the interrupt can read the current tick count to time stamp the event. This technique requires that the tick count be globally accessible or that an operating system function be available to provide the current tick count. To determine an interval between two events, the tick count is recorded when each event occurs, and the difference is computed to determine the interval.

In a small system where only interval timing is required, the clock can be started when the start of an interval occurs along with zeroing the tick count. The tick count is read when the end of the interval occurs.

Sophisticated real-time clocks contain a counter loaded to program the interrupt rate. Everytime the counter is decremented to zero (or overflows by incrementing), a clock interrupt is generated. The interrupt routine counts interrupts at the rate equal to the base rate divided by the number of counts required to zero (or cause overflow of) the counter. If the counter value is one for decrement mode (or the maximum counter value for increment mode), the clock behaves as a simple clock operating at the base counter rate.

If the counter is loaded with a non-trivial value and if the counter can be read, intervals that must be timed accurately can be determined by reading the tick count and the counter value. Programs are scheduled at the interrupt rate; however, intervals can be determined using the base clock rate. Thus the sophisticated clock reduces the system overhead by reducing the interrupt rate.

Inaccuracies in data collection timing can occur in a number of situations. Some clocks must be reenabled after each interrupt within one base clock tick. If not reenabled, the clock counter and interrupt logic will remain idle, and clock ticks are missed. With clocks that continue to count after interrupting, if a clock interrupt is not serviced before another interrupt occurs, the first interrupt will be lost, and a counter overflow will not be counted. If the clock does not have an overrun error detector, the software cannot determine that timing information was lost. Concern for losing timing information is only important in systems where the interrupt system can be disabled for lengths longer than a clock tick.

If clock overrun sensing is available, the software should take advantage of it and report timing errors to the operator. Even if interrupt latency is such that clock overruns should not occur, overrun sensing can be used to insure that the software is functioning as expected.

If the clock attempts to start a sweep before the previous sweep completes, data can be lost. The A/D converter and clock routines should determine if this condition occurs and report data loss. Some A/D converters provide overrun sensing. Such a converter sets a flag in its register if the converter is activated before the data from a previous conversion is read by the computer. If the system lacks this feature, an event flag shared by the clock and A/D converter routines can be used to sense overruns. A software mechanism is also needed to sense overruns with respect to buffer usage.

Data Reduction

A data reduction technique is any algorithm that reduces the amount of data storage required for collected data by extracting meaningful information from the raw data. For example, a peak detection routine is used to reduce a large number of points on an x,y graph to the location of a peak and its amplitude. Figure 6.34 illustrates this example.

Data reduction is normally performed to alleviate storage requirements. For example, it may be necessary to sample an A/D converter at a high rate to prevent aliasing. Sampling at this high rate for a relatively long period will produce large amounts of data. Observers may only be concerned with a waveform of relatively low frequency content. A digital filtering technique can be used to remove other frequency components. With higher frequencies removed, a smaller number of data points can be used to store an accurate representation of the waveform.

A limited number of data reduction techniques retain all the information of the raw data. Such techniques merely pack data into a smaller format (e.g. converting BCD to binary or encoding two limited range numbers into one binary word). Most data reduction techniques imply

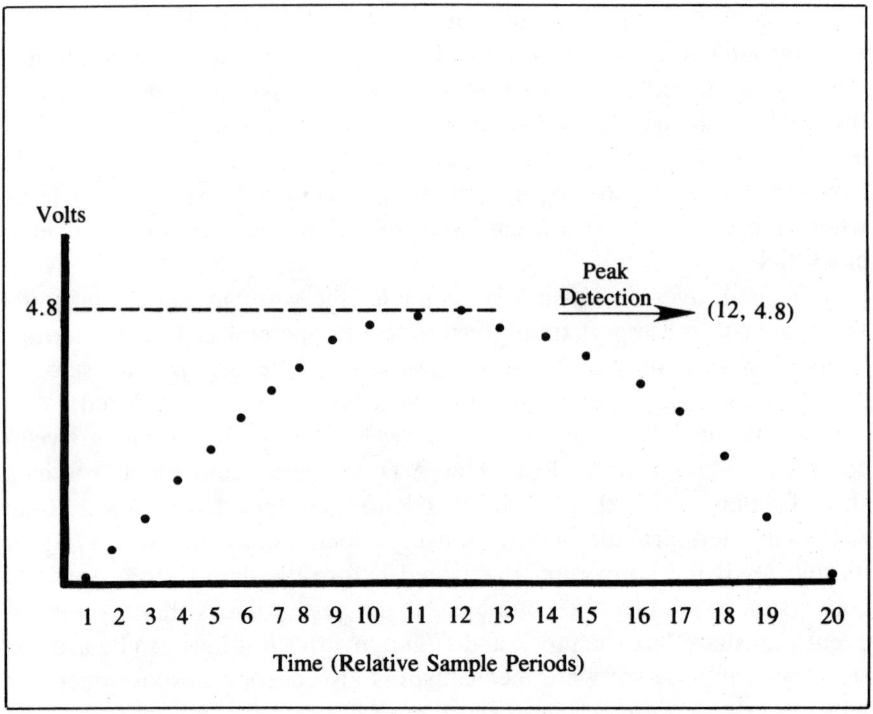

Figure 6.34. Data reduction using a peak detection routine.

that some information is lost by the processing. The reduced data cannot be used to reconstruct the input data accurately, although the missing information may not be useful. Data reduction implies that only some attributes about the data are important (e.g. maximum value) and that the actual input waveform contains more information than is desired or is feasible to retain.

Data reduction can occur during data collection ("on the fly") or after data collection is complete. Data reduction performed during data collection requires extra processing time during collection (possibly limiting the sample rate) but does not require intermediate storage for all of the raw data. More complex reduction techniques are possible if data reduction can be performed after collection.

Data Analysis

A number of mathematical techniques can be used to analyze collected data. Several techniques are discussed in this section. Detailed algorithms are not described as they have been widely discussed in journals and texts. The bibliography can be consulted for appropriate references. Many of the techniques are so widely used that they have been implemented for a wide variety of machines.

Signal Averaging

If a signal is buried in noise (low signal-to-noise ratio), some technique must be used to extract the signal from the noise. Signal averaging is such a technique for a repetitive signal if the noise is randomly distributed.

Assume a trigger is available that can be used to inform the data collection hardware that the signal of interest is to begin. When the trigger occurs, k samples are collected and added to the contents of k successive memory locations that have been initialized to zero. Each time the trigger occurs, k samples are collected at the same sampler rate and added to the proper memory cells. After N groups of samples are collected, the average is produced by dividing the sums by N.

If the noise is random, the probability density function from which the samples added into a particular memory location are drawn is distributed around the true signal value for that particular portion of the signal. As more samples are taken, the standard deviation of the signal average is reduced (it is inversely proportional to the square root of N, the number of samples). The distribution becomes more narrow around the true value as more samples are averaged. The signal-to-noise ratio improves by a factor of the square root of N.

In practice, division by N to produce the average may not be necessary. If the waveform of the signal alone is important, division is not necessary. The summed signal is just larger in magnitude than the original waveform. If a true average is needed, it is sometimes useful to select N to be a power of two so that division can be performed by shifting.

Care must be taken to prevent the partial sum of any channel from overflowing. A common technique is to sum the integer value of the A/D converter into an integer word. In the worst case for a 12-bit bipolar converter summed into a 16-bit word, overflow could occur after sixteen samples. Normally, a larger number of samples can be collected because the part of the sum due to noise is only proportional to the square root of N and because the magnitude of the signal may not use the entire range of the converter.

If it is known that there are large irrelevant peaks in the data where only smaller peaks are of interest, overflow can be ignored for these portions of the waveform. If there is a possibility of overflow in the area of important data, overflow should be detected and reported.

If overflow occurs before enough samples are summed to insure a large enough signal-to-noise ratio, multiple precision arithmetic can be used if time allows and sufficient memory is available. For slow signals or if the interval between signal repetitions is sufficient, floating point arithmetic could be used to prevent overflow.

Another technique to prevent overflow is to scale all partial sums by a power of two using shifting when overflow is detected. Subsequent A/D converter values must also be scaled by the same amount before summing.

Figure 6.35a shows a signal with random noise added. The signal-to-noise ratio is 1/2. Figure 6.35b shows an average of the signal using sixteen samples for each point. The signal-to-noise ratio is 1/2 the square root of 16 (or 2).

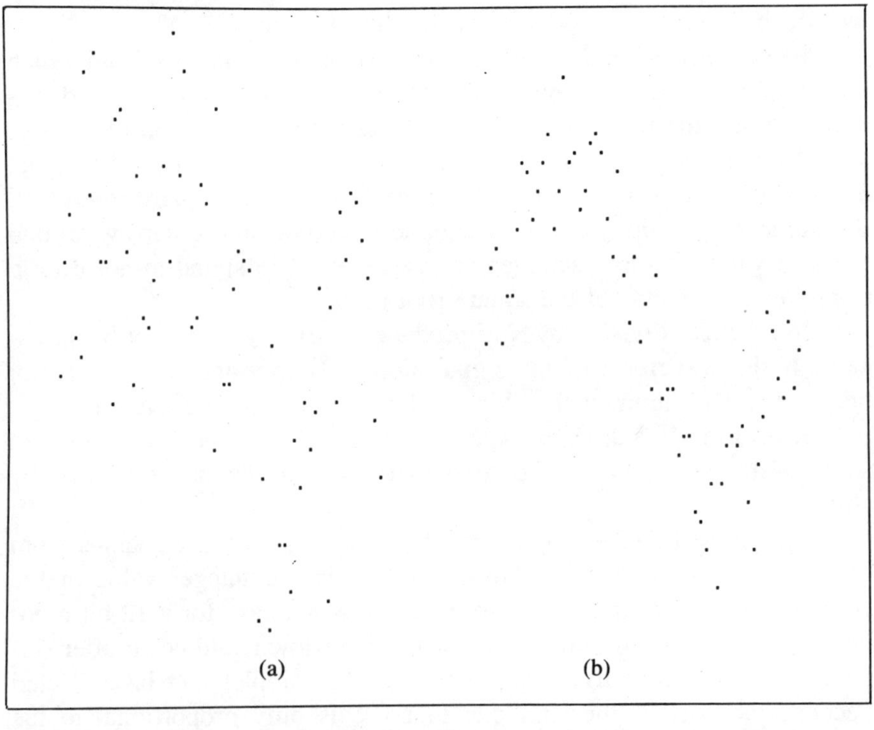

Figure 6.35. Sample of one repetition of data with a signal-to-noise ratio of 1/2 (a) and after averaging 16 repetitions (signal-to-noise ratio is 2). The data without noise is one cycle of a sine wave.

Fast Fourier Transform

Signals sampled by a computer are real-valued functions of time. They are said to exist in the time domain. The same waveform can be represented in the frequency domain where the waveform is represented as a function of frequency and phase. The two representations contain the same information; however, certain characteristics of the waveform that are not usually obvious in one domain are obvious in the other.

It is helpful to present continuous waveforms before discussing signal analysis of the discrete waveforms found in digital computer systems. A continuous waveform can be decomposed into a sum of sinusoidal waves called a Fourier series. Figure 6.36 illustrates some simple waveforms and their Fourier decomposition. Each sinusoidal of a waveform represents a frequency component of the waveform.

The waveform is represented in the frequency domain as a set of complex numbers. The sine wave components are represented as the imaginary part of the frequency domain representation. The real part represents cosine components. The use of complex numbers allows phase information to be contained in the frequency domain. There is also an inverse transformation that allows frequency domain data to be represented as time domain data. Figure 6.37 illustrates some simple waveforms in both the time domain and the frequency domain.

Continuous functions sampled by a digital computer are represented as a series of discrete samples collected over some period. The technique used to transform these samples into the frequency domain is called a Discrete Fourier Transform (DFT). The Fast Fourier Transform (FFT) is a technique for computing the DFT using a digital computer. It is faster than standard DFTs and is more accurate due to a reduction in roundoff errors.

For the FFT to be accurate, the waveform being analyzed must be sampled in a manner such that aliasing is prevented. It must also be sampled such that the number of samples covers either a large number of periods of the waveform or an exact integral number of periods of the waveform. If this condition is not met, a phenomenon called leakage occurs where frequency components of the waveform that are not periodic over the sample interval appear as a band of frequencies adjacent to the actual frequency of the component.

In practice, it may not be possible to sample at exactly an integral number of periods of the waveform. The period may not even be known. The sharp edge of the waveform due to truncation of the waveform in mid-period produces leakage. This error can be reduced by mul-

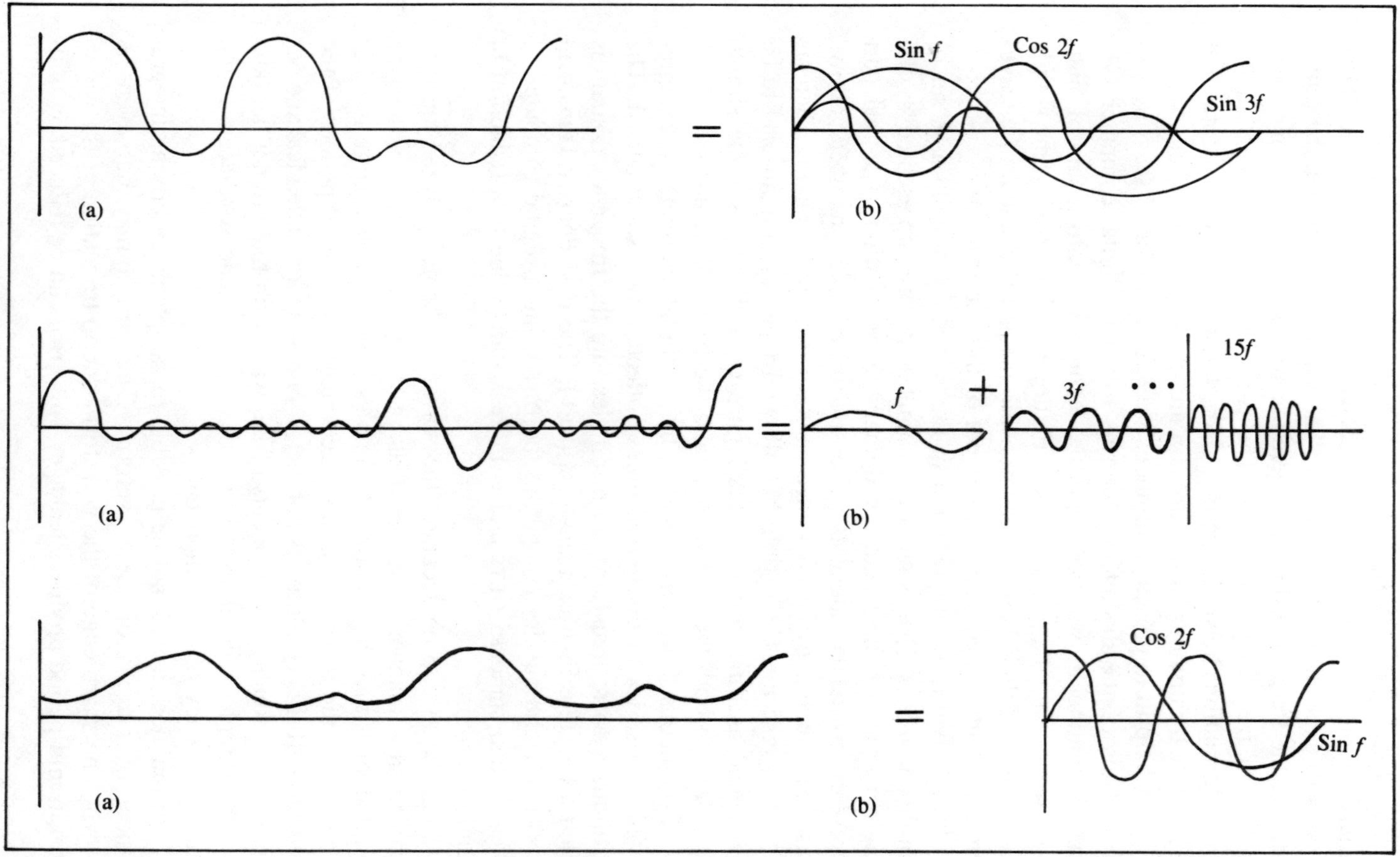

Figure 6.36. Some simple waveforms (a) and their Fourier decompositions (b).

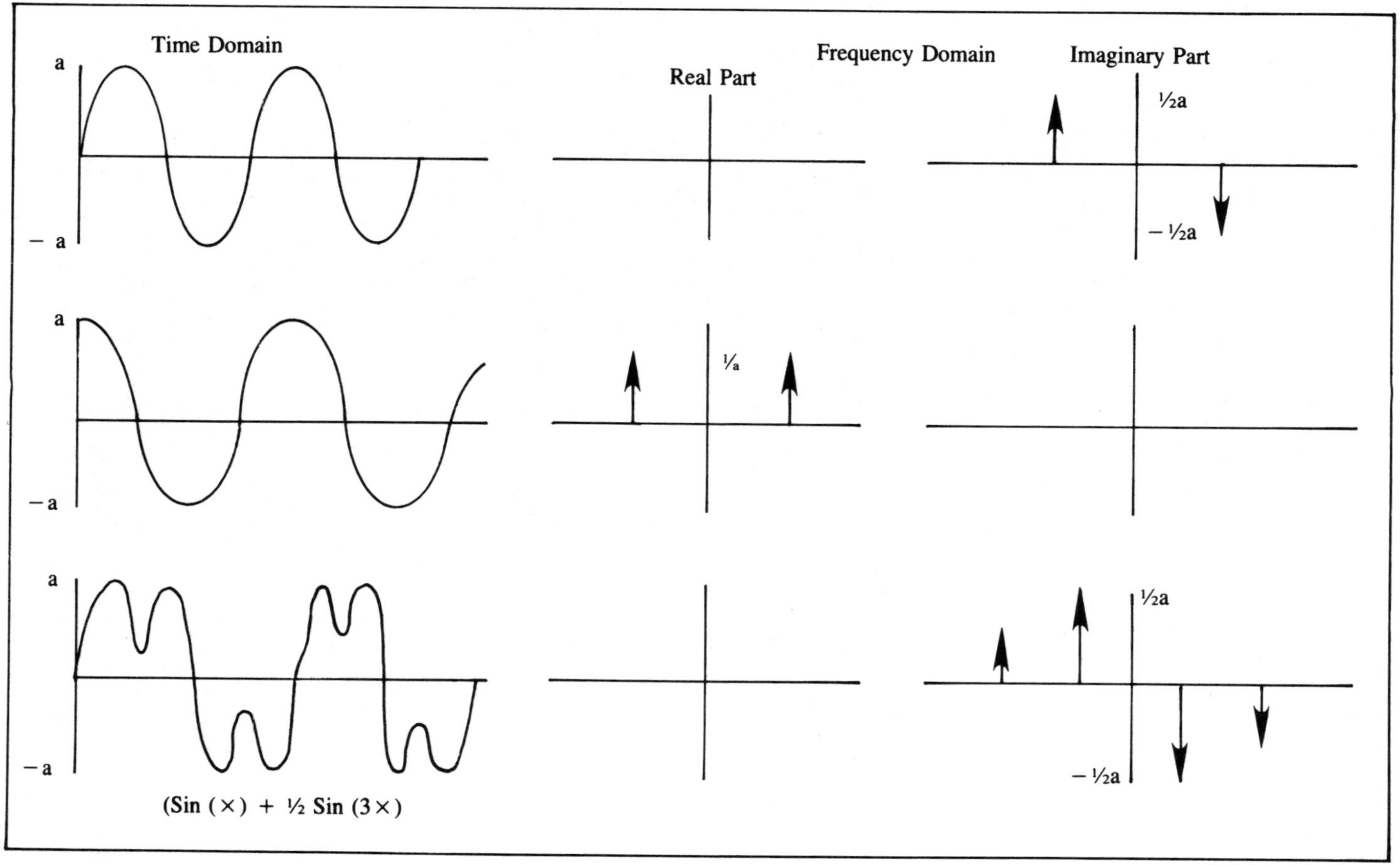

Figure 6.37. Some continuous time domain waveforms and the equivalent frequency domain representations.

tiplying the waveform by a rounded waveform, called a window function, before taking the FFT (see Figure 6.38).

Other window functions can be used to broaden frequency lines in the frequency domain and enhance the signal-to-noise ratio. This technique, for example, has been used with pulsed NMR (nuclear magnetic resonance) experiments to improve the output of the FFT. Phase errors due to delayed sampling (sampling begins at a time other than the beginning of a period) and phase error induced by tranducers can be corrected using window functions.

Once the FFT has been performed, the power spectrum is produced by squaring the magnitude of the FFT output. This operation removes phase information from the data and produces a function of power versus frequency. The power spectrum contains the frequency content of a signal without regard to when sampling begins.

The power spectrum is useful to determine if a signal of a certain frequency is present in the sampled signal. Care should be taken that the observer not attempt to extract too much information from a power spectrum of an unknown, random signal. An average of many power spectrums may be necessary to reduce frequency lines due to random noise.

Digital Filters

It is possible to remove selected frequencies from a sampled waveform in software using digital filters. Although the construction of digital filters is not discussed, algorithms for standard low-pass, high-pass, and bandpass filters are readily available.

The digital filter implemented in software is more flexible than an analog filter. Filter parameters can be easily changed. A number of digital filters can be applied to raw, sampled data; however, data that is collected after being filtered by an analog filter is not available in the raw, unfiltered form.

An example use of a digital high-pass filter is to remove 60 Hz. noise from a sampled waveform. This technique is valid as long as the signal of interest does not contain low-frequency components.

It should be noted that digital filters cannot be used to prevent aliasing. Once a signal is improperly sampled, the folded frequency components due to aliasing cannot be separated from true signal components of the same frequency. An analog filter ahead of the A/D converter can be used to prevent aliasing.

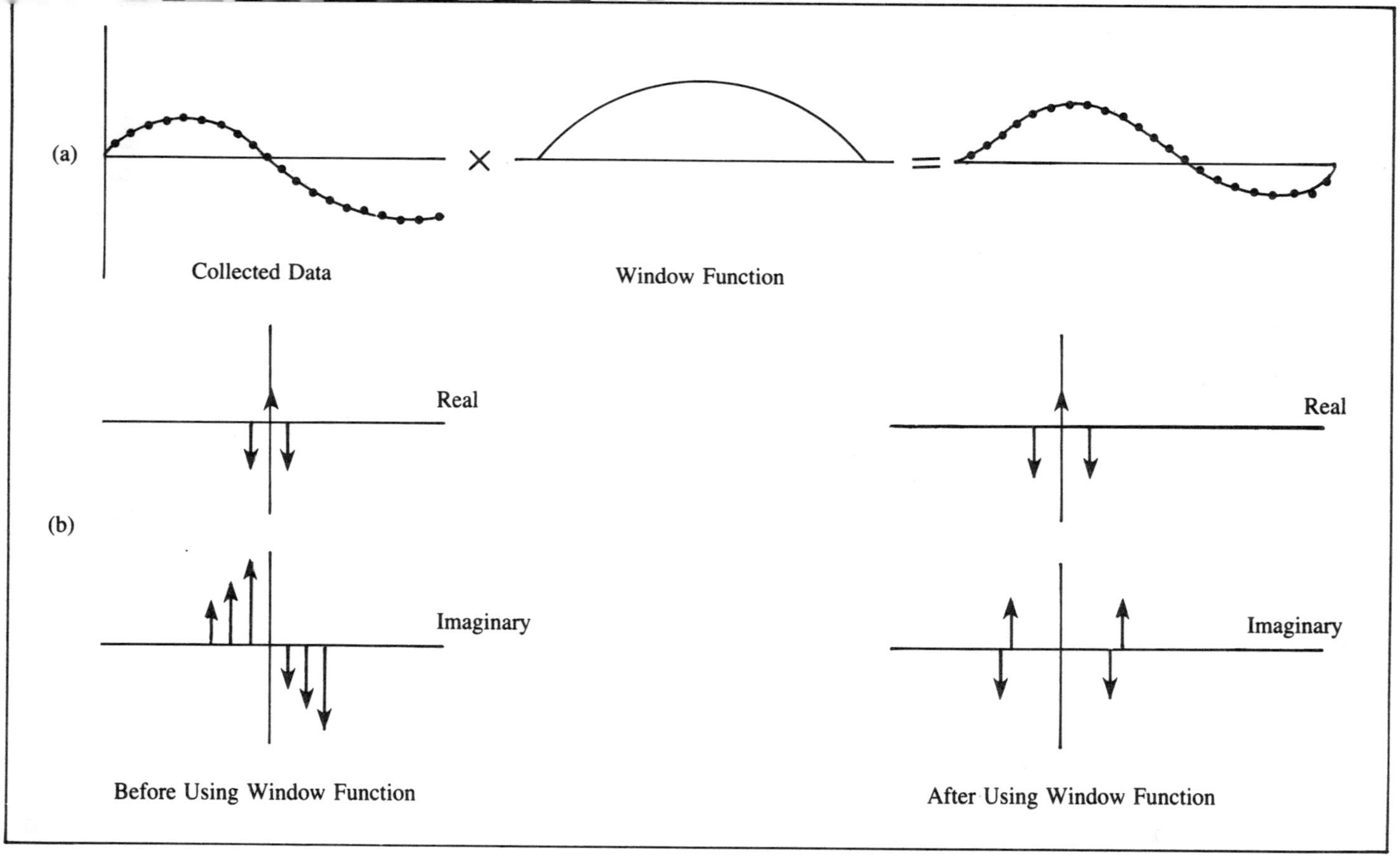

Figure 6.38. A collected waveform that does not represent a complete period multiplied by a window function (a), and the FFTS before and after multiplication by the window (b). Multiplication by the window function reduces leakage due to not sampling an integral number of complete cycles of a waveform.

Correlation Functions

The crosscorrelation function of two signals is the time average of the product of the two signals with one signal shifted in time. The crosscorrelation function indicates the dependence of one signal on another.

The autocorrelation function is used to determine the correlation of a signal value on its past or future values. If the autocorrelation function is periodic, the signal being processed is known to be periodic. When a signal is "buried" in noise, the autocorrelation function is useful in determining the periodicity of the function.

Peak Detection

Peak detection software is used to analyze a signal and provide data such as the position and amplitude of relative maxima and minima in the signal. For example, colorimeters analyze a set of samples and produce

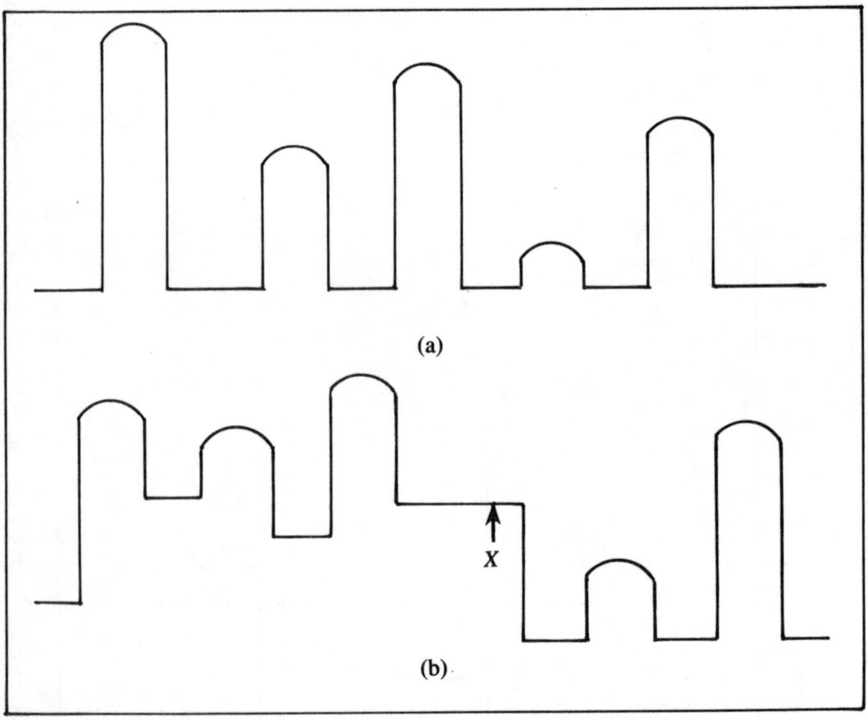

Figure 6.39. Outputs from two types of colorimeters. The first type produces well-defined peaks (a). The second type registers a plateau when an intermediate peak is at mid-scale and is surrounded by a high peak and a low peak (see point *x*) (b).

a set of peaks corresponding to the input samples. The amplitude of the peak for each sample represents the concentration of the chemical for which the sample is being tested. Due to the mechanical nature of fluid sampling, the peaks are evenly spaced. The peak amplitude is the only relevant information and is proportional to the concentration of the chemical tested for. Some colorimeters produce well-defined peaks shown in Figure 6.39a. Others produce plateaus as shown in 6.39b.

Peak detection of the signal of Figure 6.40a is relatively simple. This type of "clean" signal might be provided by an instrument that smoothes its output electronically. Figure 6.40b shows a more typical signal that must be processed by a peak detection subroutine.

In many applications, it is desirable to ignore peaks if they occur below some baseline value. Such peaks are the product of noise. The average baseline value can be determined by the computer by collecting data from the instrument in its quiescent state and computing an average. Data values below the computed baseline value are considered to be noise.

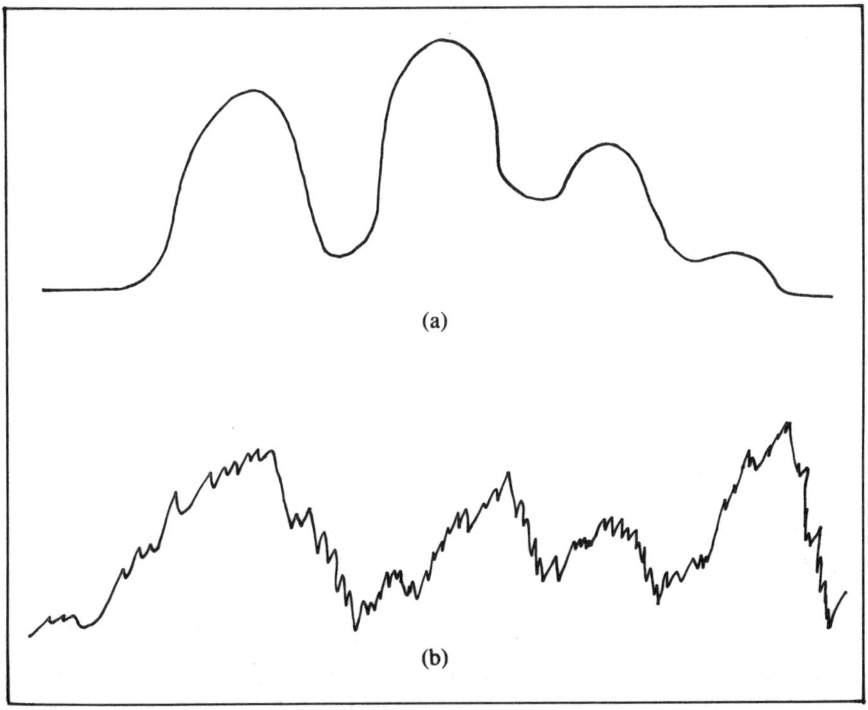

Figure 6.40. A waveform that requires no smoothing before peak detection (a) and a noisy waveform that must be smoothed (b).

If the signal to be processed is noisy, a smoothing technique may be applied. A simple technique is to average *n* adjacent points. The set of averages is the smoothed waveform. If *n* is too large, the smoothed signal will not resemble the input function. The input samples may also be smoothed using curve-fitting techniques.

Peak detection algorithms normally require a certain number of samples increasing in value before a peak will be accepted. A certain number of decreasing samples are required to mark the beginning of the trailing edge of the peak. These thresholds prevent the detection of false peaks caused by noise.

Once the leading edge threshold is met, the peak detection software continues to inspect points until the trailing edge threshold is met. Depending on the data being processed, the software may continue to inspect points until the signal reaches baseline or until another peak begins.

Depending on the data and the peak characteristics desired, the peak detection software may just determine the maximum amplitude of the peak and the sample at which it occurred, or it may actually attempt to define the beginning and end of the peak. The latter technique is necessary if determination of the area under the peak is necessary.

The selection of peak detection parameters (threshold values, smoothing function, criteria for beginning and end of peak) are critical. The parameters must be selected based on the information desired and the signal being sampled.

Calibration of Transducers

A/D converters measure some electrical quantity, typically voltage. In most data acquisition systems, the humans who study the data collected by the computer system are not interested in voltages but in the physical quantities represented by the voltages. Some transducers are calibrated at the factory. The physical quantity that produces a certain voltage output can be determined by applying a formula or by a table lookup.

If calibration information is not available, it can be determined using a calibration program. The operator applies a number of known physical quantities to the transducer. As each quantity is applied, the computer is informed of the value, and the computer reads the resulting transducer output. It is common to repeat the procedure a number of times and produce an average transducer output for each physical quantity used. The table of raw calibration data can then be used as a translation mechanism for translating voltage into physical quantity.

If a wide range of voltages can be produced, it may be desirable to convert the translation table information into a polynomial using a curve-fitting technique such as the least squares technique. The polynomial can then be used to convert voltage into a physical quantity.

Once the calibration table or polynomial has been produced, its accuracy should be verified by applying known values to the transducer, reading the output voltage, applying the transformation technique, and comparing the output of the transformation with the known physical quantity.

In many cases, the absolute value of the quantity being measured is not important, but the change in the value of the quantity being applied is of interest. For example, an LVDT (Linear Variable Differential Transformer) is used to measure how far a wood beam is deflected before it breaks under load. When the LVDT is attached to the beam, it is not practical to adjust it such that it outputs precisely zero volts. If it measures deflection x initially and the beam causes a deflection of y to be measured at maximum deflection, the actual deflection is equal to $y-x$. The output of the transducer is measured before the beam is deflected and the initial output is subtracted from the final reading to produce a voltage that represents the true deflection. This change is then translated to a physical unit of deflection. During calibration of such transducers, it may be necessary to read transducers in their unloaded state and then correct subsequent readings by the initial value.

7

Application of Data Acquisition Techniques

Data acquisition systems are instruments used to collect data from processes and to possibly analyze them. To minimize cost and to ensure proper system operation, the design and implementation of a system should follow a logical path. The designer must have a clear understanding of exactly what functions the system is to perform. He should be knowledgeable as to the expected signal waveforms produced by the process. He must select hardware that will be able to perform the intended function, and he must ensure that the system can tolerate the environment in which it will be contained. Software must be designed and developed to perform the desired function.

After the system has been implemented, the system designer must verify that the system functions properly. This task involves designing appropriate tests, performing the tests, and evaluating the system output under test conditions. Adequate documentation must be produced to make the system usable.

Problem Analysis

The system designer must clearly understand precisely what functions the data acquisition system is to perform. This task involves identifying the signal sources from which the data is to be collected. The output data desired must be specified along with the algorithms required to produce the output based on input signals.

At this stage of the design process, the computer should be viewed as a black box that inputs a number of signals, and based on these signals produces a set of outputs. Initially, it may be useful to ignore computer limitations and specify a set of ideal actions to be performed by the black box. In other words, specify the actions performed by an ideal data collection instrument. This technique is most useful when dealing with individuals who are not computer-oriented or problem solving-oriented.

Once the set of ideal functions are specified, the functions that are impossible with current day technology or that would require excessive cost to implement can begin to be restricted. In many cases, a desired action that is costly can be replaced with only a slightly restricted action.

Input Analysis

There are two general sources of input data to a data acquisition system: human operator input and electrical signals. Operator supplied data, if any, contains information identifying the current run and associated information that cannot be read directly by the data acquisition system. The operator information is merged with the data collected from electrical signals to produce a complete record of the run being performed.

As part of the design, operator input must be identified. Depending on the volume of operator input, an input device must be selected. In cases where only an identification number or a limited number of parameters must be entered, thumbwheel switches connected to a parallel input port may suffice. For an intermediate amount of operator input, a small display panel and keypad may be acceptable. When the operator must interact a great deal with the system or for a more flexible system, a CRT terminal should be used. (See Chapter 11 for more details on the operator interface.)

Analysis of the electrical signals connected to a data acquisition system is a critical task. The first determination is to identify the type of transducer and interface used to access each signal. For digital signals, the number of data lines, handshake, and signal format (TTL, CMOS, etc.) are important details. The type of transducer selected depends on accuracy, range, and cost requirements. The range of analog signals and the accuracy required help determine the class of A/D converter to be used.

The rate at which a signal is to be sampled must be determined. For a general purpose data logger, the maximum desired rate must be selected. If specific analog signals are being considered, sample rates must be selected to prevent aliasing and to allow desired waveform reconstruction objectives to be met. The sample rate selection requires that some general information be known about the signal. The signal-to-noise ratio and the type of noise (random or coherent) should be known.

If the signal to be measured is not familiar to the system designer, he should attempt to obtain information about the signal using available instrumentation such as oscilloscopes, spectral analyzers, and general purpose data acquisition systems. Even signals produced by well understood processes should be viewed to determine noise content. If signal analysis is performed with a data acquisition system and the possibility exists that high frequency signal components are present, anti-aliasing filters should be used when collecting data. If the signal is repetitive, signal components that exceed one-half the sample rate can be detected by recording data with and without the filters and comparing the frequency domain data. This technique allows the detection of aliasing but does not allow the frequency of the ambiguous signal components to be determined.

The amount of analysis of signals performed in the initial design is more critical as the frequency of analog signals and the data rate for digital signals increase. If a general purpose system is being designed, the maximum data rates and sample rates are based on design goals as opposed to the requirements of specific signals.

Once maximum sample rates are determined, interface requirements can be specified with greater detail than in the initial design stage. The presence or absence of common mode noise will affect analog interface requirements. The presence of high frequency components in analog signals that are not dealt with by high sample rates dictates the use of anti-aliasing filters.

Output Specifications

Output from data acquisition systems includes collected data files on mass storage devices, output to terminals, graphics output, data to communications networks, and control information. These outputs can be loosely divided into three categories: data storage, operator information, and control. (Control information is discussed in Chapter 10, data communications in Chapter 11, and storage peripherals in Chapter 8.)

Analysis of data storage requirements involves determining the amount of storage required and the required transfer rate of the storage device. Data format is a consideration in determining the amount of storage and data transfer rate. For example, binary data requires less space and transfer time than printable data but may require special processing before it can be used. The data storage requirements also apply to transmitting data to a separate processor for storage. The amount of data and data transfer rates, along with communications protocol requirements, must be analyzed.

Operator information takes two formats: alphanumeric and graphic. Limited amounts of information may be displayed on special output devices such as lamps. Alphanumeric data can be displayed on small displays or on computer terminals. Computer graphics can be displayed on oscilloscopes, graphic monitors, plotters, or computer terminals with graphics capabilities. Display requirements depend on the speed, amount, and readability of operator output.

Control output, such as controlling the temperature in an environmental chamber, must also be analyzed. The designer must determine the type of control devices and control signals (analog or digital) and other interface characteristics. Data transfer rates must also be determined. The system designer must be careful that feedback loops, where the control value is corrected based on information read from the process being controlled, does not create instabilities (see Chapter 10). In some cases, simple feedback loops may be required just to allow the computer to determine that the control exerted indeed occurs (i.e., the computer can determine when a malfunction occurs in the control mechanism).

Computer Requirement Analysis

After determining system requirements, it is necessary to determine the characteristics of the computer system that will minimally meet the requirements needed to implement the system. Actual selection of the computer hardware is detailed in Chapter 8.

The selected computer and enclosure must be able to function in the environment in which it is to be used. Factors to be considered are temperature, humidity, dust, vibration, and power line quality. If the selected computer system will not operate properly in the required environment, it must be properly sheltered from extreme conditions. Environmental factors must be controlled for all system components (e.g. computer, mass storage devices, and terminals).

Most microcomputer systems can tolerate temperatures during operation in excess of 80 degrees Fahrenheit. If excessive temperatures are expected, either specially designed computer systems must be used or the computer system must be cooled.

Except for specially designed computer systems, computer hardware cannot tolerate condensing humidity. The level of noncondensing humidity tolerated by a computer system can be determined from the manufacturer's specifications. Air conditioning may be necessary to reduce humidity to acceptable levels.

Some industrial and laboratory environments are dusty. Dust can be classified by its electrical conductance. Both types of dust—conductive and nonconductive—can damage mechanical devices. Disk drives are especially susceptible to damage by dust. Conductive dust can cause electrical shorts in computer systems resulting in malfunction or damage. Filtering and sealed enclosures are useful in limiting damage due to dust.

Computer systems can be damaged by excessive vibration. Disk drives are most susceptible to this type of damage. Excessive vibration can be dealt with by using computer equipment designed for such environments and by using shock reduction devices.

Computer systems powered by AC power lines must be protected from power surges. Surge protection devices can be purchased to protect computer equipment. Computers operated near large motors may require power line filtering to remove noise induced in the power system by motors or other large current devices.

Most environmental issues can be solved by isolating the computer in a small, environmentally controlled chamber. This action may require longer signal lines than is desirable due to noise or signal strength conditions. In this case, signal conditioning devices near the transducer may be necessary to drive long signal lines (see Chapter 5). In cases where small computer systems requiring no mechanical peripherals are used, heavy duty systems can be purchased to withstand extreme conditions.

It is advisable to derate maximum environmental tolerances by 10% or more. This safety factor extends system component life and allows expected conditions to be exceeded for short periods without equipment failure.

Response

One of the most difficult computer requirements to quantify is the computing power needed to implement a task. The computer selected to perform a data acquisition function must be able to collect data, process it, and produce the necessary outputs in a limited amount of time.

The computer power needed for adequate response is influenced by such factors as the operating system used (if any), the language or languages used to implement the system, the basic architecture of the machine used, and the peripherals connected to the system. The ability to quantify computing power is difficult if not impossible. For a designer to select a cost effective computer system that will perform the desired functions adequately is an art. The more familiar the system designer is with a number of systems of different capacities, the better able he will be to choose the best machine for the job.

The first step is to identify bottlenecks. Mechanical devices, such as floppy disk drives, are typically slower than the average A/D converter. The ability to collect data from the A/D converter and write the data to floppy disk is typically limited by the speed of the disk. The overhead associated with some file structures can also limit the device throughout. For example, file structures that do not use contiguous space for files require a large number of disk seek operations during file accesses.

In systems where a large amount of processor time is required to analyze data in real time, the CPU may be the bottleneck. Large word sizes, integer multiplication and division instructions, and floating point hardware may be requirements in this type of system.

The system must be able to respond to interrupt rates (or service request rates) defined by the data transfer rates of all devices in use simultaneously. The system designer can estimate average instruction execution time by studying instruction execution times from vendor literature for typical instructions found in service routines. Given an estimate of average instruction time, the interrupt request time, and device data transfer rates, an average number of instructions per service routine can be estimated. The magnitude of this number can help the system designer determine the relative power of a computer. A small number of instructions per interrupt routine implies that the computer can be used for simple tasks where data is collected and stored in primary memory without much processing.

In systems where a relatively large amount of data processing is required, the average number of instructions executed must be divided between service routines and data manipulation routines. If floating point instructions are used in the data manipulation code, the average number of instructions will decrease.

If code is developed in high-level languages (compiled or interpretive), allowances must be made for inefficiencies in the language processors. Operating systems also require a certain amount of overhead (such as clock interrupt support and timing operation support). Familiarity with specific languages and operating systems is the best way to estimate system power.

If standard computer systems are available, test routines driven by test equipment that simulate estimated data transfer rates can be used to benchmark interrupt response rates for interrupt service routines. This technique requires that a certain amount of code be written.

Care should be taken that maximum device data transfer rates not be misleading. Although a particular device may be able to provide data at a high rate, the processor may not be able to perform much processing other than to buffer the data. If the data is to be processed or the device supported at least partially in a high-level language, the device may have to be operated at a slower rate.

When selecting a computer, it is best to choose a machine with more compute power than it is estimated will be required. The extra compute power reduces the effect of compute power misjudgments and allows some expansion of function.

Another factor related to hardware selection is the software development technique used. If code is developed on one machine for a second machine, the hardware resources required for both machines and the hardware needed to move the code from the development system to the target system must be selected. (Chapter 9 includes a discussion of this development technique.)

Storage

The amount of storage needed for a data acquisition system, both primary memory and external storage, must be estimated. Primary memory may also be divided into ROM and RAM for "black box" systems using single board computers with no mass storage. Primary memory contains storage for programs and data. External memory may contain data, programs, or both.

There must be adequate primary memory to contain data collection software and enough data required for real-time processing. If collected data is written directly to external storage, only small buffers are required for data storage. If a real-time analysis routine is used that operates on a large amount of data at a time, more primary memory for data storage is required.

Estimates of data storage requirements are easier to produce than estimates for software storage. The amount of storage required depends on the function to be performed, the languages used to code the function, the architecture of the machine, and the skill of the programmer producing the software. Experience with a particular machine and language is a requirement for the system designer to make good storage estimates.

If execution time is not a constraint, disk storage is available, and the feature is supported, overlays (program segmentation such that only a portion of the program need be in memory at a time) reduces storage requirements (see the discussion on linkers in Chapter 9).

Interfaces

Given a proper analysis of data rates, data format, and noise considerations, specification of interfaces follows logically. Maximum interface data rates should exceed estimated data rates to allow for miscalculation during analysis. Interfaces that may be subjected to traumatic circumstances (e.g. input voltage surges) should include protection features (e.g. fused inputs).

In addition to specifying interfaces, the system designer should decide how input and output signals will be connected to the system. Extreme care should be made when specifying connections for low-level analog devices. Shield connections should be made in accordance with accepted engineering practice (see Chapter 4). Thermocouple connections require special considerations since connections between different metals produce thermal junctions. Signal conditioning circuitry may be needed if a transducer is located at a distance from the interface or if the transducer output does not match the characteristics of the selected interface.

For general purpose systems where the data acquisition system is to be used at several locations, connections to the system should be made such that they can be connected and disconnected rapidly.

System Validation

When a data acquisition system is being designed, a set of validation procedures should also be designed that can be used to verify that the system performs its prescribed task properly. If a noncomputerized system is already being used, the new system can usually be placed in parallel with the old system, and the outputs of the two systems compared. If there is no existing system, other instrumentation can be connected in parallel with the inputs to the data acquisition system. Hand calculations performed on the recorded input can, in many cases, be used to verify system output.

If, due to process complexity or lack of sophisticated instrumentation the above approach is not acceptable, simple waveforms from test equipment or simple circuits can be used to verify system performance under simple input. Depending on the system, this technique may reliably test system performance.

The system should also be tested under abnormal circumstances so that the part of the software that executes when errors occur can be tested.

Project Management

Small systems may be designed, implemented, tested, and documented by a single individual. In this case, the implementor should keep accurate notes on the design and implementation process. The project should be accurately documented so that the system can be used, maintained, and modified by others.

The importance of documenting the design and progress of a single man system cannot be excessively stressed, especially if the project requires many man hours of work. Any event that requires the implementor to be replaced will lengthen the time required to complete the project. If substantial documentation does not exist, the new implementor will require many hours to determine the design and state of the project.

In a project that is implemented by a group, the system designer must proportion the work. Logical divisions for software are major routines and subroutines. The designer typically specifies the input, output, and function of each major routine. He should specify the calling sequence and function of major subroutines. For large projects, procedures to test individual portions of the system should be designed.

Coding standards should be developed such that routines developed by different parts of the group connect in a standard way and are easily understood by the entire group. Documentation standards are important to ensure that routines can be understood easily and that progress by parts of the group can be determined.

The system designer should schedule work such that portions of the system are completed in a logical sequence. Sections of code that are required for the testing of other code should be completed first.

The system designer must supervise project group members to ensure smooth completion of the project. He verifies that coding and documentation standards are followed. He should set reasonable deadlines for completion of the various portions of the project.

If both hardware and software are being developed concurrently, the system designer must provide hardware design specifications to the software group so that code can be written for special devices while they are being developed. Simulation of the devices may also be needed to allow testing of the software prior to hardware completion.

The system designer should also attempt to minimize the effect of hardware changes on the code being produced. What appears to be a simple change to a hardware engineer may spoil a large amount of code. To ensure smooth system integration, the system designer must be knowledgeable, at least to some degree, in both hardware and software.

Final system documentation consists of user documentation, maintenance documentation, and internal software documentation. The user documentation should contain information both on hardware and software and on how to use the system. Since most data collection systems are operated by technicians lacking formal computer training, the documentation should be clear and written in a nontechnical language familiar to the intended user. A liberal number of examples of system usage should be included. The cause and appearance of abnormal conditions should also be included. For a system that is to be marketed, professional technical writers should be employed to ensure clarity for nontechnical users.

The maintenance documentation is produced to allow system software and hardware to be maintained and possibly modified. This documentation includes a description of the data acquisition problem to be solved, the concepts included in the original design notes, descriptions of the software techniques used, software generation procedures, and hardware schematics and design notes. The maintenance guide can be used by both those on the original project as a means of remembering implementation information and others who wish to understand the workings of the system.

Internal documentation (annotation in the software source code) should contain the function of each module (major routine or subroutine), the function of important variables, and comments explaining each step of the procedure. Unusual techniques or hard-to-understand calculations should be clearly documented.

8

Hardware for Data Acquisition Systems

Computers

There are three classes of computers applicable to dedicated data acquisition systems. The first system type, the single board computer, is a small computer system based on a microprocessor that contains primary memory and I/O devices on a single printed circuit card. In this description, single board computer systems are assumed not to have external mass storage. If mass storage is connected to a single board computer, it will be designated as a microcomputer system. Due to the lack of mass storage, program storage is typically in ROM or loaded from a communications interface connected to a larger scale system.

Single board computers can be used for a variety of functions, from simple code converters (e.g. parallel to serial) to more sophisticated functions such as intelligent collection devices that include such features as peak detection. System input may be serial, parallel, or analog. System output is typically a printer, serial interface connected to a host computer, a plotter, or a terminal. The operator interface to single board computers can be as simple as a set of switches and indicators or as sophisticated as a computer terminal. Because of the lack of mass storage, single board computer systems typically are dedicated to a single function. (Network configurations, discussed in Chapter 11, allow single board computers to perform multiple functions.) Some single board computer systems have standard bus connections that allow them to be upgraded into a general purpose microcomputer system with additional memory, interfaces, and mass storage.

Figure 8.1 shows a single board computer system designed especially for data acquisition applications.

The second category of small-scale data acquisition systems is the

Figure 8.1. The Analog Devices μMAC-4000 single board computer. This data acquisition system is specifically designed to be connected to a host microcomputer or minicomputer system by a serial interface. The μMAC-4000 accepts commands from the host system and transmits data to the host system. Data is reported in engineering units when applicable. A number of signal conditioning modules can be configured with the system to make it compatible with a number of transducers. (Photo courtesy of Analog Devices.)

microcomputer system. Such a system normally contains a microcomputer in an enclosure with memory, interfaces, mass storage, and a terminal. Such systems typically are available with operating systems and high-level language translators.

Until recently, most microcomputer systems contained eight-bit microprocessors with no floating point hardware. (Floating point arithmetic is typically performed by subroutines written using integer instructions. Floating point processors that connect to the microcomputer bus are available but not widely supported by high-level language translators.) Eight-bit processors are usually restricted to an address space of 64K bytes. (Memory bank switching systems are available but are frequently not supported by commercial software except for use as I/O buffers for disk operations.) Some or all of these restrictions are not found in newer 16-bit microcomputer systems.

Software written for a particular microprocessor is not necessarily transportable to another microcomputer system using the same microprocessor due to the nonstandard I/O structure created by different vendors. Operating systems that isolate device dependant software help alleviate this problem.

The third type of hardware suited for data acquisition systems is the minicomputer system. The typical minicomputer system contains a processor, mass storage, a terminal, and a variety of I/O interfaces. Primary memory ranges typically from 16K bytes to 256K bytes. Floating point hardware is normally offered as an option. Operating systems and high-level languages are typical.

Some minicomputer systems are offered as complete product lines. Each member of the minicomputer family executes the same basic instruction set; however, some advanced processors in the family may execute additional instructions (e.g. memory mangement instructions). I/O devices are typically compatible with all processors in the family.

Operating systems for minicomputer families can be written to determine the configuration on which they are running and take advantage of extended features automatically. The operating system provides a common operator interface to the system and a common set of services. Software written using the base instruction set will execute on any family member. High-level language software is typically compatible across the line of processors by recompiling the code with proper compiler and link library versions.

Sixteen-bit microprocessors are typically more sophisticated than eight-bit microprocessors and can be used to construct systems that are similar to minicomputers. Some 16-bit processors have integer multiplication and division instructions and memory management instructions. Sixteen-bit processors are typically supported with more sophisticated system software.

The primary advantages of minicomputers over microcomputers are speed and a larger address space. Advanced minicomputers typically have high speed processors, cache memory, and DMA processors for high speed operation. The use of large primary memories allows larger programs and data buffers to be used.

The technical difference between microcomputer systems and minicomputers is in their architecture. In the early days of microcomputers, their performance, I/O structure, and software were inferior to minicomputer systems. As technology increases, these extremely visible differences will disappear. All small-scale computers except those that must execute instructions at an extremely rapid rate will be constructed using microprocessor technology.

The data acquisition system designer should, therefore, choose equipment based on cost, performance, flexibility, and expandability without regard to the type of processor (minicomputer or microcomputer).

Figures 8.2 and 8.3 picture some commercial microcomputers available for data acquisition systems.

Program and Data Storage

Primary memory is used to store program and data for immediate access. Low cost memory circuits are typically volatile; i.e., the memory contents are lost when power is removed from the memory chips. Single board computers typically have nonvolatile ROM for program storage and use volatile memory for data storage. If a single board computer is connected to a communications network, there may be only a small amount of ROM to contain a loader. Programs can then be loaded from the network into volatile memory as needed. (See Chapter 13 for a discussion of networks.)

A special type of ROM, the Electrically Alterable Read-Only Memory (EAROM) is a type of nonvolatile memory chip. Data or program instructions can be read from the EAROM at a rapid rate. The computer can also program locations in the device at a relatively slow speed. The location to be written must be previously erased. The erasure operation is performed electrically; i.e., the EAROM need not be removed from the computer to be erased. Some EAROMs allow selective erasure operations while others require that the entire memory be erased. These devices are

Figure 8.2. The Digital Equipment Corporation MINC-11 (Mobile Instrument Computer). The MINC-11 is built around the LSI-11 microcomputer which emulates the PDP-11 minicomputer instruction set. The system contains a dual floppy disk drive, a graphics terminal, and 64 kilobytes of memory. A rigid disk system and a faster processor that supports additional memory are also available. Laboratory interfaces are optional and include a real-time clock, analog interfaces, and digital interfaces supported in both the FORTRAN and BASIC languages. (Photo courtesy of Digital Equipment Corporation.)

Figure 8.3. The Hewlett-Packard HP 9826 microcomputer based on the Motorola MC68000 16-bit microcomputer. The system includes 64 kilobytes of memory, a CRT terminal, and a floppy disk drive. The amount of memory and the number of disk drives can be expanded. The computer includes an IEEE-488 interface and can accept several types of parallel interfaces. Analog I/O is performed by an optional processor that interfaces to the HP 9826 via the IEEE-488 interface. The available languages include BASIC, HPL (a BASIC-like language produced by HP), and PASCAL. (Photo courtesy of Hewlett-Packard.)

ideal for data logger devices that must save their data for an indefinite period. Once data is written into the EAROM chip, the chip can be transferred to a larger computer system with a compatible EAROM socket where the data can be read and processed.

Systems with mass storage devices typically contain special hardware or small loaders in ROM that read an operating system into volatile memory from the mass storage device.

The amount of ROM and RAM needed for a particular application depends on such items as the amount of data that must be buffered, the computer architecture, and the programming language used.

Slow mass storage devices include cassette units and floppy diskette drives. These media are typically used to store data in applications where speed and quantity of storage is not critical. Although software development using a system with only cassette units is not recommended, floppy diskette systems can be used for program development for a number of applications.

There are two general types of cassette systems for use with computers. The digital cassette unit stores information on a cassette whose speed is held constant by the cassette drive. Audio cassette recording techniques typically use a standard audio recorder and encode binary data as a series of tones. Since the tape speed of small audio cassette recorders is not constant, some audio techniques also record timing information on the tape.

In general, digital recorders are faster, more expensive, and more reliable than audio units, although commercially designed audio systems may be reliable. There are few standards for either recording technique, so care must be taken to select compatible equipment when data written on one machine is to be read by another machine.

Cassettes are suited for storing data produced by a data logger in a remote environment. However, due to the speed and general lack of computer control over the cassette, cassettes are not recommended as the sole mass storage device for program development systems.

Floppy diskettes are characterized by a circular, magnetic recording surface enclosed in a heavy paper sleeve. Floppy diskettes are read or written by bringing a read/write head in direct contact with the recording surface. Diskettes are currently available in eight-inch and 5 1/4-inch sizes. A new microfloppy, which is 3 1/2 inches and enclosed in rigid plastic, is also available. Diskettes may be written in single density mode, double density mode (twice the information on a standard single density diskette), or quad density mode (four times the information of a standard single density diskette). Both single-sided and double-sided systems are available. Both hard sectored (timing information provided by a series of holes in the diskette) and soft sectored (timing information provided by one hole in the diskette and by timing data written on the magnetic media) diskette systems are in use. The IBM 3741 single density, soft sectored recording format for eight-inch diskettes is an industry standard. There is a general lack of standards for other diskette types.

Diskettes typically can store from 100K to 1M bytes, depending on the recording system. Although faster than cassettes, diskettes are slow compared to other disk recording systems. Due to the fact that the record/playback head comes into contact with the diskette, the diskettes eventually wear out. If diskettes are not handled properly, dust and dirt on a diskette can lead to wear of the diskette unit mechanism.

Diskettes can be used to store collected data and can be used as mass storage devices on small-scale program development systems. In data collection systems where large amounts of data must be written to a storage device rapidly, diskettes may not be fast enough. Diskette units must not be subjected to dusty environments, nor environments where they are subjected to heavy shocks.

As technological advances are made, hard or rigid disk drive systems are becoming relatively inexpensive, making them suitable for medium-scale data acquisition systems. Such disk drives are characterized by rapid access and large amounts of data storage (five megabytes and up). The technology requires that the read/write heads be positioned very close to the magnetic media without touching it for an access operation. Since dust and smoke particles between the head and media can damage high density systems, many drives are constructed such that the media and read/write heads are packaged in a sealed unit. In these systems, other peripherals are used to load and backup files on the sealed disk.

Industry standard seven- or nine-track tape systems are rarely found on microcomputer systems. They are available for some small and most large minicomputer systems. Tape drives are typically used in cases where large amounts of data must be stored or moved to large-scale computer systems.

Interfaces and Peripherals

The types of interfaces required for a project are determined by the system design. Data acquisition interfaces are selected based on the transducers and instruments to be connected to the system. Interfaces are also required for terminals and communications links. Interfaces for mass storage devices are typically purchased with the device.

The system designer must ensure that the number and types of interfaces required are compatible with the computer hardware. Power requirements should also be considered.

The availability of software support for a particular device interface should be investigated. If a purchased operating system is to be used, the compatibility of the device and support software with the operating system should be considered.

A variety of terminals can be connected to data acquisition systems. The type of terminal selected for a particular project is based on the function to be performed. Printing terminals are used when a hard-copy record of collected data or system status is required. CRT terminals are typically faster and less expensive than printing terminals. Other considerations include graphics capabilities and cursor addressing. Software support of screen editing and graphics for a particular terminal should also be considered.

Printers should be considered for development systems with CRT terminals. Speed and print quality are two important printer specifications.

Modems for the connection of computers to other computers or terminals located at remote locations are selected based on the distances involved, the transmission rate required, and compatibility requirements. Serial devices using the RS-232C standard and operating at 9600 bits per second (960 characters per second for typical asynchronous systems) can be directly connected at distances in excess of 25 feet. Current loop systems can be used for several thousand feet. Local distance modems can be used with in-house dedicated lines for distances up to several thousand feet at 9600 bits per second. Greater distances using phone lines require modems that encode data as a series of tones. For asynchronous communications, data rates of 1200 bits per second (normally 120 characters per second) over voice grade phone lines are typical.

Real-time clocks produce interrupts (or set status flags) at a precise rate for use in determining intervals of time. Clocks should be purchased based on the timing rates needed and on special features (e.g. ability to externally trigger the clock). The availability of support software and compatibility with a purchased operating system, if used, should be considered when selecting a clock.

Other peripherals, such as small keypads and single line displays for operator stations, must be selected and interfaced on an individual basis. Devices intended for computer usage generally provide serial or parallel access that are easily interfaced.

Comparision and Selection of Data Acquisition Systems

The selection of computer hardware for a data acquisition project is as much an art as a science. The selection process should ideally indicate the hardware that should be purchased to minimize cost and maximize flexibility and performance. In addition to this goal, the questions of hardware and software maintenance and ease of software development should be addressed. The selection process normally must be limited such that hardware selection is performed in a timely and cost effective manner.

Minimization of cost is influenced by development costs, the number of data acquisition systems to be produced, and the expected life of the system. The highest cost item of a one-of-a-kind data acquisition system of any complexity that will be used for a short period of time is the software development cost. Typically, the entire cost of such a project can be lowered by purchasing higher performance hardware, high-level language software to be used in software development, and a system with vendor software-supported data acquisition hardware. On the other hand, if a large number of small systems are to be produced whose life expectancy is long, the hardware cost should typically be minimized. In this case, the high software development costs usually dictated by programming in assembly language can be offset by the hardware savings for a large number of systems.

Another consideration is flexibility and expandability. If the system is to be dedicated to a single function for the life of the hardware, expandability and flexibility are not critical. If the system will possibly be used for another application in the future, flexibility is a consideration. I/O devices should be able to be connected to a number of sources (e.g. analog signals of different ranges). Ease of programming adds to the flexibility of a system to be used in a number of applications.

Expandability is important especially for machines that are to be general purpose in nature. To lessen the possibility of early obsolescence, a general purpose machine should be upgradable in terms of computer power, storage capacity, I/O devices, and a variety of software. Software developed on a nonexpanded machine should be able to be easily converted to run on an expanded machine.

Once future needs, project life expectancy, quantity of systems, and flexibility requirements are established, the system designer can decide if minimal hardware should be used or if a more sophisticated system will be more cost effective over a given period. If minimal hardware is to be purchased, the system designer must determine what class of hardware (e.g. eight-bit single board computer) will meet the design requirements.

If other than minimal hardware is to be selected, the system designer should select the class of hardware that will best meet selected present and future goals. Hardware and software that reduces software development costs, and hardware with flexibility and expandability are selected based on current and future needs.

The system designer must decide if the data acquisition software can be purchased or if it must be developed. If the software must be developed, it must be determined if the software is to be developed on the data acquisition system (typical for one-of-a-kind, short term applications) or if the software is to be developed on a separate machine (typically done when multiple data acquisition systems are to be produced that do not have the resources required for software development).

The initial stages of system design should reveal what class of peripherals will minimally meet the design goals. If future usage of the system is a factor, the system designer may select a class of peripheral that will allow other problems to be solved with the system.

The designer should decide the language or languages in which the software will be developed. He should also decide what operating system features are desirable (unless all device support software will be developed). The selection of software tools will help determine the hardware resources needed.

Once an overall idea of the class of machine and peripherals required to satisfy design and usage goals is chosen, the market can be surveyed to determine available commercial products. Products can be compared by obtaining specification information, manuals, and evaluation systems.

Benchmarks—programs designed to be run on a variety of machines for performance comparisons—are most applicable when comparing general purpose systems. Benchmarks are most suited for rough comparisons of compute power and vendor language comparisons. It is difficult to design and evaluate benchmarks and even more difficult to test data acquisition potential without developing extremely complex benchmarks.

The ability to collect and save data is best compared by estimating interrupt response time and throughput rates by coding simple device handlers. This technique requires a basic knowledge of the machines being compared. By determining the types of actions device handlers must perform to meet design goals, the system designer can roughly code the handlers and estimate throughput rates based on device specifications and instruction execution rates.

This method can provide insight into maximum device throughput rates but fails to indicate performance of data handling between devices for complex software systems. The use of high-level languages greatly complicates execution time estimates.

In practice, the system designer chooses a machine that exceeds his expected compute power needs because hardware requirements involve a great deal of estimation.

Hardware maintenance is an important question in the hardware selection process. If the data acquisition system must be highly reliable, a duplicate system should be available as a backup. Some vendors provide dispatched repair personnel and in-factory repair while others provide only in-factory repair. The cost of board swap options (owner returns defective printed circuit card for replacement), if available, and third party maintenance should be considered. If in-house technicians are available, self-maintenance costs can be determined based on training costs, test equipment costs, and spare parts costs.

Machines that use combined components from a number of vendors are usually more difficult to maintain. If vendor maintenance is used, in-house personnel must first determine which component is failing so that the proper vendor can be contacted.

The availability of a set of diagnostic programs for selected hardware should be investigated. The use of such programs allows in-house personnel to determine system status before summoning repair personnel.

When comparing data acquisition hardware that also will be used for software development, the system designer should also compare development tools (e.g. compilers and debuggers). Items that reduce development time (e.g. screen text editors) are extremely important. Vendor maintenance of software tools, such as the vendor's policy for providing software updates, should be considered in the selection process.

9

Software for Data Acquisition Systems

Software for data acquisition systems more and more represents a large part of the cost of a data acquisition system. Software is either purchased from the computer vendor or third party or developed by the data acquisition system owner. For a large number of applications, complete software systems are not available. The lack of software is due to the large variety of functions that can be addressed using automated systems, the lack of standards for interfaces and instruments, and the lack of flexibility in some commercially available software.

The first reason for a lack of large amounts of data collection software is the large number of diverse applications, and is not directly solvable. Indeed, the overall productivity of man can be increased by the application of computers to more problems. A greater desire to share developed software by the scientific community, software that is more portable between systems, and more mechanisms to allow sharing of software, would greatly increase productivity. Unfortunately, we tend to be content reinventing the wheel rather than pursuing more beneficial endeavors.

Secondly, a large number of computers and instruments contain nonstandard interfaces. Part of the problem is caused by inexpensive hardware that has allowed a large number of vendors of equipment to come into being. The large number of manufacturers and a rapidly growing industry has reduced the application of standards. Not only does the lack of standards increase interfacing costs, it decreases portability.

For example, a program is written for System A that has micropressor chip x. The program reads data produced by a DPM integrated into an instrument. The DPM is connected to a parallel interface designed for System A. System B has the same micropressor chip x; however, the I/O system of the two computers is completely different. System A contains a memory-mapped I/O system while System B uses a dedicated I/O bus. Furthermore, the parallel interface available for System B is more sophisticated than the one for System A and requires initialization software to configure it for compatibility with the DPM.

To run the program from System A on System B requires modification of the program. Depending on the system hardware, on the operating systems of the two computers, and on the language the program is written in, this task may be relatively simple or relatively complex. If the software is a commercial program, the source code may not be available for modification (even if the vendor would allow the transportation of the code under license), and the vendor may not supply the program for System B.

Thirdly, the lack of usable software is in part due to the lack of flexibility designed into some software. System designers typically solve problems specifically instead of solving a class of related problems. In many cases, the more general solution requires only a small amount of additional resource while it can be applied to a larger number of problems.

General solutions typically must be configured in order to be applied to a specific problem. This configuration can be specified by changing part of the program containing configuration data and preparing (e.g. compiling) the new version for execution. Another method is to put configuration information in a file that is read by the program.

For example, a program is designed to record temperature data from a thermistor connected to one channel of a 16-channel A/D converter for 30 seconds at a sample rate of 10 samples/second. After the data is collected, it is displayed on an oscilloscope connected to a D/A converter in the computer.

The most specific solution would not allow the sample rate or data collection period to be modified. A slightly more general solution would allow these parameters to be entered by the operator. The program is still not applicable to a wide range of problems for several reasons. First, only one A/D converter channel is used. (The program could be expanded to allow multiple channels to be sampled.) Secondly, the graphics software could be made more interactive by allowing the operator to pan through the data by viewing enlarged portions of the curve at a time. Other improvements would be to allow the operator to store the data on a mass storage device and to add annotation to the data. The ability to use any one of several popular graphics terminals in place of the oscilloscope would make the software more useful.

There are times when specific software is the appropriate solution. In many environments, however, the use of specific software is too short-lived, while a general purpose solution can reduce overall software costs.

Selecting Available Software

In general, if the software needed to solve a data acquisition problem of any significance is available commercially, the commercial software should be considered for purchase as software development costs for a small number of systems is very expensive. If software must be developed, languages, operating systems, and software tools must be selected.

Sources of commercial data acquisition software include hardware vendors, users groups, scientific groups, and third-party software vendors. Computer vendor literature and technical journals advertise and review software.

When buying any software, the buyer should look for quality and flexibility in the software. Documentation for the software should be of high quality and should be extensive. Consultation on program operation and maintenance of software problems should be available. The purchaser should be aware of the license agreement associated with the purchased software that may limit his ability to copy the software or use it on more than one machine.

Commercial data acquisition software takes two forms: general purpose data acquisition programs and programs for specific applications. Before purchasing software, the system designer should verify that the software is indeed capable of performing the task for which it is purchased. It should be flexible enough to be configured and possibly extended.

General purpose data collection programs can be used in a variety of tasks but, on the other hand, are not applicable to other tasks. Depending on the complexity of the data collection software, it may support only one device or several devices. It will allow the collected data to be stored, but frequently computation on the data before storing is not available. Additional features include transducer calibration software and conversion of inputs to engineering units instead of volts.

Specific purpose programs typically solve a single data collection problem for a specific computer system and specific instrumentation. Care should be taken to determine that the software is compatible with the buyer's system.

If data acquisition software must be developed, a real-time operating system is usually useful except for the smallest systems. A real-time operating system typically includes software support for a console terminal, a mass storage device, and a clock. Clock support usually includes time-of-day processing and event scheduling.

If an operating system is designed especially for a specific hardware configuration, device handlers may also be present for data acquisition devices. A real-time system should allow the user to add interrupt handlers for new devices with relative ease. The system should be efficient to allow devices to be serviced rapidly.

Most real-time systems can also be used for program development. With a small system, development activities may only be performed when data collection is inactive. Larger minicomputer systems may allow concurrent data collection and program development.

The selection of real-time operating systems for a particular computer system is usually limited. One vendor offers three separate systems: a single user system, a multiple user system, and a combination multiple user, real-time/general purpose system. Most other vendors offer only a single real-time system.

Generally, when choosing a real-time operating system, both the system and the hardware are considered as a unit, as most operating systems are not portable. The system designer chooses the hardware and software system that best suits his needs.

When choosing software components (e.g. data logging software, language translators, and graphics software), the system designer should compare similar items based on compatibility with the system, function, and cost. If the actual items are not available for evaluation, the user's manuals should be obtained and reviewed. Vendor claims cannot always be taken literally, especially in the microcomputer domain.

Software Development

Development Techniques

As was previously stated, software development costs are expensive. Techniques to minimize development costs are mandatory. Chapter 7 provides additional information on software development.

The goal of software development is to produce a finished product that performs the desired function, is cost effective, and is maintainable. For software to perform its intended function, it must be well designed and well tested.

Software cost effectiveness is influenced by a number of factors. A vendor who is producing a data logger that will be marketed in quantity can afford to spend more on development as his cost will be distributed over a large number of units. He can afford to produce very efficient assembly language code. On the other hand, one-of-a-kind systems should be developed in high-level languages when possible. In some cases, a hybrid system using both assembly language and a high-level language is the best compromise.

The cost of development can be reduced by using a variety of software tools (e.g. debuggers). A number of such tools are discussed in this chapter.

Maintainability of software requires that the software be designed logically. Clear documentation on the design, use, and internals of the software is a must. All personnel involved should maintain notes during development to reduce the impact of personnel changes during the development effort. All programs should be documented internally as well as in maintenance documentation. If a number of people are working on a project, a documentation standard should be followed by all personnel.

One of the best techniques in developing data acquisition software is modularity. The project is broken down into a number of logical entities. Each entity becomes a software module or program (which may also be divided into modules). Each module can be constructed independently. Modules that require execution of or data from other modules can be tested using simplified test modules and test data.

As modules are completed, they are linked together and tested. Modules can be "linked" by subroutine calls, data files, or common data storage areas. If the interfaces between modules are well defined at the design stage, module connection problems are reduced.

The method used to develop data acquisition software is important. If a machine other than the data acquisition system is used for software development, the development system may be an expanded version of the data acquisition system or it may be an entirely different system with a cross-assembler or cross-compiler. (Cross-assemblers and cross-compilers are language translators that run on one machine but produce code for an entirely different machine. A large time-sharing system can thus be used to produce runable code for a small-scale microcomputer.) If a separate development machine is used, some mechanism must be employed to transfer the runable code from the development system to the data acquisition system. Typically, this process is implemented by the use of EPROMS or data communications links.

If code is being developed on a separate machine for a single board computer that will be used in a stand-alone application, code can be written into an EPROM using an EPROM programming system on the development system. The EPROM can then be transferred to the single board computer. It is recommended that all but the final debugging be performed on the development system. If the development system does not have the same processor as the data acquisition system, an interpreter, a program that simulates the target machine, can be used to test the code. Due to the nature of most interpreters, some timing errors do not surface until the code is tested on the real data acquisition system.

If the code must be tested on the data acquisition system, a small debugger program can also be placed in EPROM to allow program monitoring. If a sufficient amount of RAM is available, it is recommended that the data acquisition program in EPROM be copied to RAM by the debugger before it is run so that minor changes can be made to the program as bugs are found. Typical debuggers require that programs being debugged reside in RAM so that execution can be easily traced.

Code can also be transferred to a target system using a communications interface (called "down line loading"). The target system must have a program to allow it to receive and load programs produced by the development system. This method allows data acquisition software to be easily debugged and changed but requires that the code be reloaded after power failures. Chapter 11 details multiple computer communications.

A useful system combines the two techniques outlined for moving code to the target system. The data link system is best used during program development when ease of testing and modification is important. When the code is to be put into production, EPROMS can then be produced.

After software has been throughly debugged and appears to function properly, testing should continue in order to validate system operation. Validation procedures should be developed during the design stage. Testing should not only test typical software functions but should also test error processing code.

The importance of testing should be viewed in the light of the consequences of inadequate testing. The output of data acquisition systems are used in the field of research and quality control. Invalid data in either area can be disastrous. The problem is compounded by the fact that personnel not intimately familiar with computer techniques tend to place a great deal of significance on computer output even if the output is in error due to poorly tested software.

Development Tools

Software development tools are programs that aid programmers in developing code. The system designer must purchase or develop the tools that best suit the software being developed. A lack of adequate development tools can handicap a development effort just as the lack of a quality oscilloscope can greatly inhibit development of computer hardware.

The major development tool is the language processor. Some projects require that assembly language be used exclusively, such as in single board computer systems with limited memory. Assembly language is appropriate for mass-produced systems where efficiency is a must. Unless absolutely necessary, assembly language code should only be used after much consideration. Generally, an algorithm encoded in assembly language will require a greater development time than the same algorithm in a high-level language. Also, debugging features are usually more sophisticated in high-level language systems.

If the system being used is not limited with respect to memory and CPU power, the best compromise is to construct time-critical code, such as interrupt handlers, in assembly language and the rest of the system in a high-level language. The use of most, but not all, high-level languages requires an operating system. The system designer should also be aware of the overhead associated with the particular high-level language he uses.

High-level languages are divided into two groups: compiled and interpreted. A compiler reads a high-level language program and produces machine code that—normally after being processed by a linkage editor—can be executed directly by the CPU. An interpreter is a program that reads a high-level language program and performs the functions specified by the program.

In most compiled language systems, some interpretation is still needed (such as run-time FORMAT processing in FORTRAN). This interpretation is performed by the run-time package of subroutines that is part of the language system. Most languages can be either compiled with the need for some run-time support or interpreted; however, languages such as APL cannot be compiled to much advantage due to the late binding time inherent in the language (associating of variables and attributes with storage locations).

Code produced by compilers is typically more efficient than programs run by an interpreter. In general, there are two disadvantages of compiled systems. First, to make a program change requires that the program source file be modified, compiled, and the object code processed by a linkage editor (linker). This time-consuming cycle must be performed even when a simple change is made. With an interpreter, the change is made immediately in the primary memory copy of the program, and the program can be immediately run.

Second, compiled code systems do not usually have very good run-time diagnostic features. For example, in many versions of FORTRAN, a subscript error can cause the program to overwrite itself and the operating system, thus making debugging difficult. Error checking and debugging support is more easily built into interpreters.

Even with the advantages of interpreters, the efficiency of compiled code makes compilers more widely used in data acquisition systems. The use of good run-time diagnostics packages can make debugging with compilers similar to debugging with interpreters except for the time required to make modifications. In some cases, a compatible interpreter and compiler can be purchased. Code can be debugged using the interpreter and then compiled for production usage.

The selection of a high-level language depends on availability, cost, function required, and personal taste. A number of popular languages are surveyed here.

FORTRAN is traditionally a compiled language. Although it was one of the first high-level languages developed, it is still widely favored in the scientific community. Typical compilers allow access to assembly language routines via the CALL statement. In typical FORTRAN systems, data may be shared between FORTRAN and assembly language routines using the FORTRAN COMMON statement.

The BASIC programming language has become very popular in many small microcomputer systems. It is traditionally interpreted, although BASIC compilers are available. (In the case of a popular microcomputer compiler and interpreter written by different companies, the compiled code oddly executes slower than interpreted code due to the implementation techniques used.) Most current implementations have a number of extensions over standard BASIC. The extensions are typically not standard across vendors.

Some BASIC implementations allow assembly language subroutines to be called. Usually, the assembly language code must be preloaded before BASIC is run or linked into the BASIC interpreter. In most cases, this mechanism is somewhat limited.

One of the most limiting factors concerning BASIC is its lack of a parameter passing mechanism for subroutine calls to BASIC subroutines. Also limiting is the need to number every statement. As statements are added, old statements must be renumbered. There is, however, usually a mechanism that aids the programmer in renumbering. Lastly, some BASIC implementations allow only single letter variable names. This restriction limits the readability of BASIC code and the number of variables available.

BASIC is best suited for limited projects. BASIC is easy to learn, and an extended BASIC with real-time device support can be used by nonprofessional programmers to quickly write small-scale data acquisition systems.

PASCAL is a block-structured language that is becoming popular in the small-computer domain. It requires that each variable be explicitly declared. It allows the declaration of new data types based on the combination of primitive data types. An extension to standard PASCAL is required to allow a PASCAL routine to call assembly language code. Some versions of PASCAL do not allow the use of independently developed subroutines, thus limiting the use of modular design (subroutines must be imbedded in the program file). PASCAL extensions are rarely standard across vendors.

A subset of the block structured language PL/1 is available for some microcomputers and large minicomputers. The full implementation of PL/1 was designed as an attempt to combine the features of both scientific and business languages to produce a general purpose language. Currently, it is not widely used for data acquisition systems.

FORTH is an interpretive language designed originally for real-time applications in astronomy. It is based on the use of a stack and reverse polish notation. Compared to a traditional language, FORTH appears difficult to read to the uninitiated.

FORTH contains a number of primitive functions. New FORTH subroutines, called words, are constructed using primitive operations and previously defined words. All words are saved as part of the FORTH systems.

FORTH allows a high degree of interaction and relatively high efficiency for an interpreter. Its lack of readability and relative low-level approach may make it inappropriate in many cases.

In some minicomputer systems, only one assembler is available. In the microcomputer domain, there may be several assemblers available for a given processor. In selecting an assembler to be used with an operating system, a macro processor feature is useful to allow system calls to be standardized. Macros can also be useful in generating standard functions such as register saving and restoring for subroutines and interrupt handlers.

If the assembler is to be used with a high-level language, the code from the compiler and assembler must be linked together by a linkage editor, commonly called a linker. The code produced by both translators must be compatible with the linker.

The text editor is an important tool for creating and modifying program source files. Although most interpreters allow program entry and modification directly, a text editor is useful because most interpreters possess only limited editing features.

Text editors are compared in a manner similar to other software. There are a variety of editor types. One way of characterizing editors is into three types: character, line, and screen editors. In a character editor, the cursor can be positioned to any character in the file. The operator performs commands to delete, insert, or change a number of characters at the current character position. Commands are normally provided to delete lines and to advance the cursor by a certain number of lines.

In a line editor, the cursor can be positioned to a particular line. Changes are made in a line by uniquely specifying the part of the line to be modified.

Screen editors display a portion or window of a file on a CRT terminal. The operator may scroll through the file. By positioning the CRT cursor to any part of the screen, direct modification can be made by entering text or deleting characters. Because a number of lines of the file are displayed, the operator sees his changes in context. Because the operator can move the cursor around the screen and make direct modifications, the screen editor is easy to use.

Regardless of the type of editor selected, such functions as the ability to search the file for specified strings, the ability to merge in other files, the ability to output parts of the file being edited to a separate file, and the ability to construct macros of edit commands are useful. A screen editor with these and other features can increase programmer productivity.

The linkage editor or linker is a program used to combine individual program modules into an executable program. Application program modules are combined with run-time support routines by the linker. All input to the linkage editor is in the form of object code with text indicating globally known variables.

In selecting a linker, the prime consideration is compatibility with selected high-level language translators and assemblers. Some linkers allow code generated on a system with mass storage to be produced for a ROM-based system. This feature is the ability to separate code from data.

Another useful linker feature (in conjunction with the operating system) is the ability to process overlays. This feature allows a program to be segregated into parts such that not all of the parts need to be in memory simultaneously. This feature allows programs larger than available memory to be run. The overlay processor reads the portion of the program currently needed from disk. As execution continues and a portion of the program that is not in memory is needed, the overlay processor reads the needed code from the disk, overwriting another segment of code that is not needed at this time.

A typical linker with the overlay feature allows the programmer to segregate his program into sets of subroutines. Selected subroutine sets are designated to share a memory region. Only one set of subroutines assigned to a region is in memory at a time. By specifying subroutine sets to define the overlay, high-level language code can take part in the overlay process.

An interactive debugger is a program that can be linked with an application program and aids the programmer in diagnosing program errors. Debuggers typically allow memory locations to be examined and changed along with instruction tracing, and breakpoints (the ability to enter the debugger when a particular instruction is to be executed). An added feature allows the debugger to be entered when the contents of a particular location is altered.

Typical debuggers operate at a low level, allowing access to memory locations and machine instructions. This type of debugger is useful when debugging assembly language code, but using it to debug a high-level language program requires a knowledge of the code generated by the compiler. Even with such knowledge, the use of such debuggers with high-level language routines is tedious.

When developing high-level language code, the use of a debugger intended for the language is useful. Such debuggers allow tracing and breakpoints targeted to program statements as opposed to machine instructions. Memory locations can be examined and modified using variable names in the high-level language program as opposed to absolute memory addresses. In many cases, high-level language debuggers are not currently available.

When debugging a program with both high-level language modules and assembly language modules, a debugger with access to both types of code is useful. When such a debugger is not available, both an assembly language debugger and a high-level language debugger may have to be used. The fact that such debuggers execute independently of each other reduces their flexibility.

Utility programs, such as screen formatting utilities and data networking programs, must be selected on their compatibility with existing equipment, available functions, and cost. If possible, such software should be evaluated carefully before purchase.

A large amount of software can be obtained for copying fees from users' groups. If the machine for which the users' group exists is used widely in industry, most of the software will be of reasonable quality. Software distributed by a users' group is commonly supplied with source code. Such programs can be modified and extended.

10

Introduction to Computer Control

Presenting techniques used to automatically record the value of physical quantities from a process is the major thrust of this book. However, the ability to measure physical quantities is also used in process control, the automatic control of the physical parameters of a process. In typical process control applications, process signals are measured and—based on the result of the measurements—process parameters are varied to bring about some goal.

Process control can be implemented using analog, digital, or hybrid circuitry. Direct digital control implies the use of a digital computer to perform measurement and control functions.

In general, process control is a more complex discipline than automated data collection. An introduction to process control is presented here. The reader should study further before attempting the implementation of a complex control system.

Interfaces

The parallel interface was discussed in Chapter 5. As was noted, parallel interfaces can be input devices, output devices, or bidirectional with the function of each data line being programmable. Output lines can be used to exert control over the environment when connected to suitable affectors.

The output of a typical parallel interface is a set of signal lines that can assume two possible states. These outputs may be implemented using a standard logic family (e.g. TTL), may be designed for relatively high current switching, or may be isolated using opto-isolators.

If the parallel interface output is not directly compatible with the circuit it must drive, additional circuitry may be constructed to allow connection of the device to the interface. A simple transistor circuit can be used to increase the current handling capability of a digital output. Other circuits can be used to translate between standard logic families.

If the parallel interface used is not constructed with protection circuitry and the possibility of device damage exists, the system designer should include protection circuitry in his design. Resistors can be used to limit current in the output circuit. Opto-isolators can be used to isolate the interface from high voltages.

The parallel interface may be used to control alarms, simple indicators, and displays for communications with an operator. The parallel interface may also exert control over a process by directing devices to perform such functions as opening or closing a valve, starting or stopping a motor, or turning a heater on or off.

A single interface signal can exert binary control over a process. By using more interface signals, more complex control may be exerted. For example, a valve accepts two binary control signals that allows it to be positioned to four flow settings. With a special interface, a parallel interface can control a stepper motor.

Analog control can be produced by a computer using a digital-to-analog converter (DAC). The DAC accepts a binary number from the computer and produces a corresponding voltage at its output. The weighting schemes (relationship of the binary input to voltage output) used for A/D converters are also applied to DACs. See Chapter 5 for a description.

Figure 10.1 shows a conceptual diagram of a four-bit DAC. The switches connected to the resistor network are controlled by bits in a register in the interface. A logic one in a bit position of the register closes the corresponding switch. Due to the construction of the op amp circuit, the inverting lead of the op amp (the summing point) is always held at zero volts. The output voltage is directly proportional to the sum of the currents produced by each of the resistors whose corresponding switch is closed.

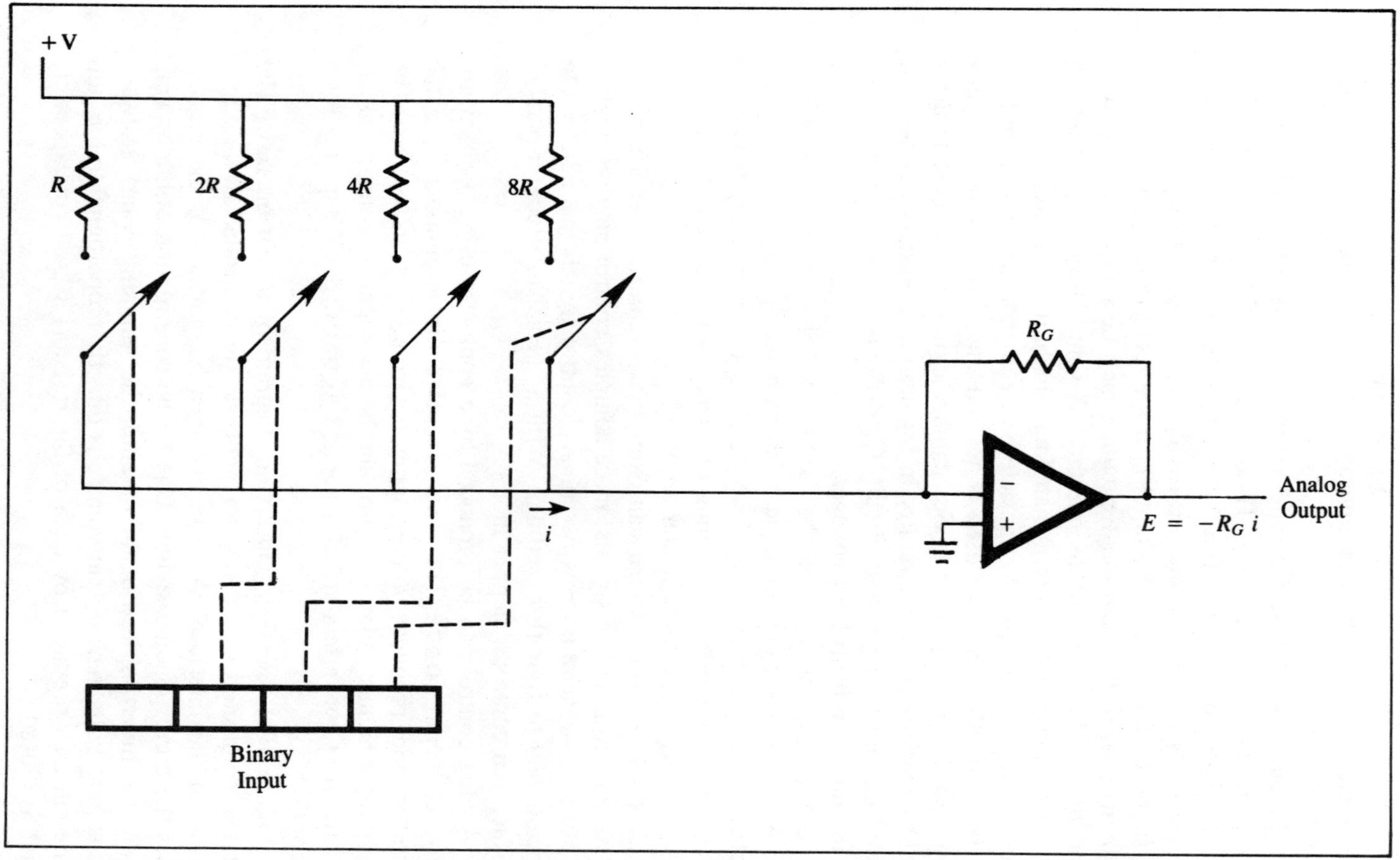

Figure 10.1 Conceptual diagram of a DAC. The potential at the op amp inverting lead is zero due to the characteristics of the op amp configuration. Each closed switch causes V/nR current to be added to i (nR is the resistor value associated with the switch).

There are a number of techniques for deriving bipolar output. One is to offset the output voltage when all switches are open by one-half the most significant bit output value of a unipolar converter with the same number of bits. Since the op amp circuit used in the figure is inverting, with all switches closed the output will be at the negative full-scale output value.

Typical DAC outputs are current limited. Greater current capacity or a greater voltage range can be obtained using external circuitry. Typical DACs produce a voltage that is controlled by the binary input value. The DAC can be used to control current through a load using the circuit in Figure 10.2.

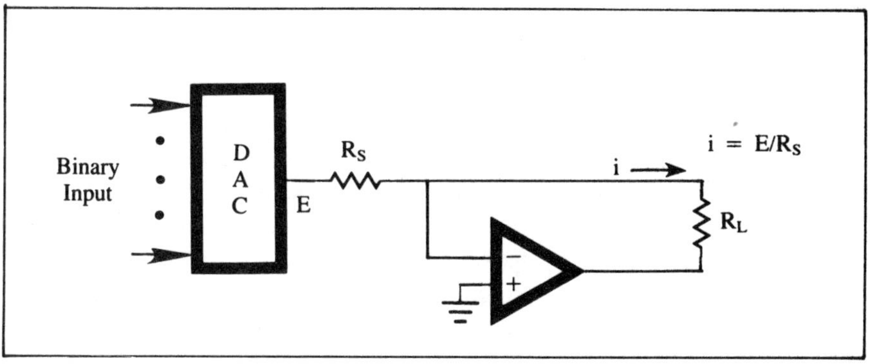

Figure 10.2. Circuit to allow DAC voltage to control the current through R_L.

DACs have similar errors as are found in A/D converters. They have linearity errors where a one-step change in the binary input produces different size output changes at different parts of the range. DACs can be rated as to the maximum drift with temperature and as to the maximum time it takes for the output to stabilize from the time an input change is made.

DACs can be used to vary process variables by an analog signal. A 12-bit DAC can output 4096 different voltages. A DAC could be used to control the speed of a motor or the voltage applied to a heating element.

Digital Control

The word "process," when used in the context of the discipline of automated control, refers to an industrial system. In a very general sense, a process is any physical system that can be monitored and controlled.

There are a number of parameters of interest associated with any process. Process parameters include temperature, speed of motion, pressure, and light intensity. A process control system exerts control over a process to regulate or otherwise modify the values of selected process parameters.

The devices that affect changes in process variables are called control elements. Some control elements are switched on and off to affect control. A heater controlled by a single parallel interface signal is an example of this type of control element. To maintain a constant temperature in some environment, the temperature is measured at some rate; and if the measured temperature drops below a threshold value, the heater is turned on. A variety of algorithms can be used to determine how long the heater should be enabled.

Other control elements can be varied over a range. The speed of a motor that influences some process variable may be controlled by an analog circuit or by a DAC. Although the use of a DAC implies that only a finite number of different speeds can be selected, in many cases a large number of discrete speeds are suitable. Given that the measurement and representation of a parameter like speed in a digital computer is a discrete quantity, discretized control of a significant resolution seems reasonable for most applications using direct digital control.

The use of a control element that is controlled by an analog signal or by a discrete signal with a number of possible values is more complex than using a simple on/off control element. The number of possible algorithms for control increases. Both the amount of time control is asserted and the control element values used are factors.

The setpoint is the operator-supplied or predefined value at which a controlled parameter is to be maintained. During the course of a run, the setpoint value may change, indicating that the controlled parameter is to be changed and maintained at a new value.

There are two types of control systems: open-loop and closed-loop. An open-loop control system exerts control over some process variable independent of the value of that variable. Figure 10.3 illustrates open-loop control. The setpoint is read by the controller. The controller outputs a control signal to bring the controlled parameter to the desired value. A simple open-loop control system to control the light intensity in an environmental chamber using incandescent lights might read the value of the desired chamber light intensity from an operator terminal, and based on previous calibration, output a DAC voltage that would bring the luminescence to the desired intensity.

In some cases, the use of open-loop control may be sufficient; however, there are two major drawbacks. First, calibration of the con-

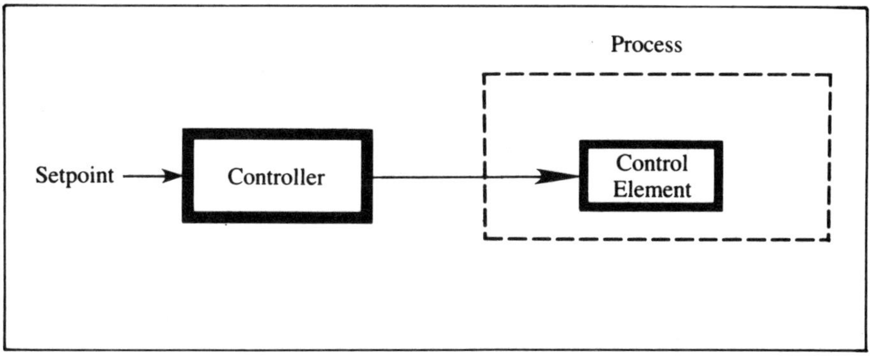

Figure 10.3. Open-loop control diagram.

trolled variable may not be reliable for long periods. In the example of the light intensity controller, the internal resistance of the bulbs changes over time. The light intensity as a function of control voltage changes as the bulbs age.

Second, in open-loop control circuits, the controller has no way of determining if the exerted control actually occurs. An open-loop controller may supply power to a light circuit, but it has no way to determine, other than by operator intervention, that the light circuit is functioning.

The closed-loop control system has a feedback loop whereby the computer measures the process parameter it is controlling. Figure 10.4a is a block diagram of a closed-loop controller. The controller is presented with the difference between the setpoint value and the measured process parameter. This error factor is analyzed by the controller. The control exerted over the process parameter is a function of the current error term and possibly the history of the error term. Figure 10.4b shows a block diagram of a closed-loop controller similar to the block diagram of 10.4a. A digital computer is used to perform the measurement, difference, and control functions.

The setpoint value is shown coming from outside the system as in the case where the operator supplies the desired value of the process parameter. The setpoint may actually be generated by software running with the control software. For example, a computer is to control lights in an environmental chamber to simulate normal sunlight conditions. The part of the program that would change the value of the light intensity desired based on time would use the light intensity value as the setpoint to the closed-loop control program. As the setpoint was

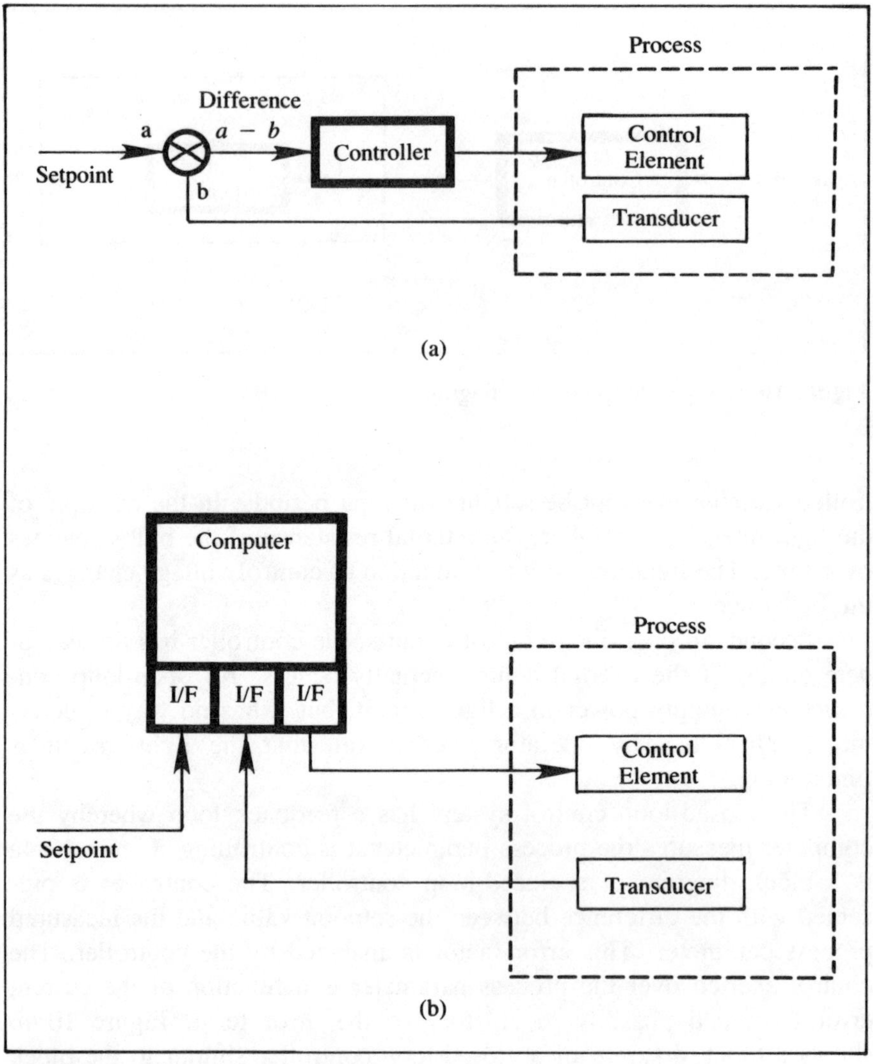

Figure 10.4. Closed-loop control diagram (a) and block diagram of closed-loop control using a digital computer (b).

changed, the closed-loop control program would bring the light intensity in the environmental chamber to the desired value.

An application program could direct a number of closed-loop or open-loop control programs to control a number of process variables. Each control routine would output a value to an interface connected to a device to affect a process parameter. The desired value of the process parameter would be translated to a value that could be used by the interface and connected device.

Control algorithms take many forms. A text on process control should be consulted for details. Some simple examples are given to indicate the flavor of control algorthims.

When the setpoint is changed, the control program exerts control over the process to make the process parameter approach the setpoint value. Figure 10.5 shows the effect of two basic types of controllers (cyclic and damped) on the process parameter. The type of controller used and its response time depends on the process and the parameter being controlled.

As an example, consider that a liquid solution is to be brought to a desired temperature and maintained at the temperature using an heater that can be turned on and off. To produce a cyclic control function, the heater would be enabled until the measured temperature reached the setpoint value. At this point, the heater would be switched off. Al-

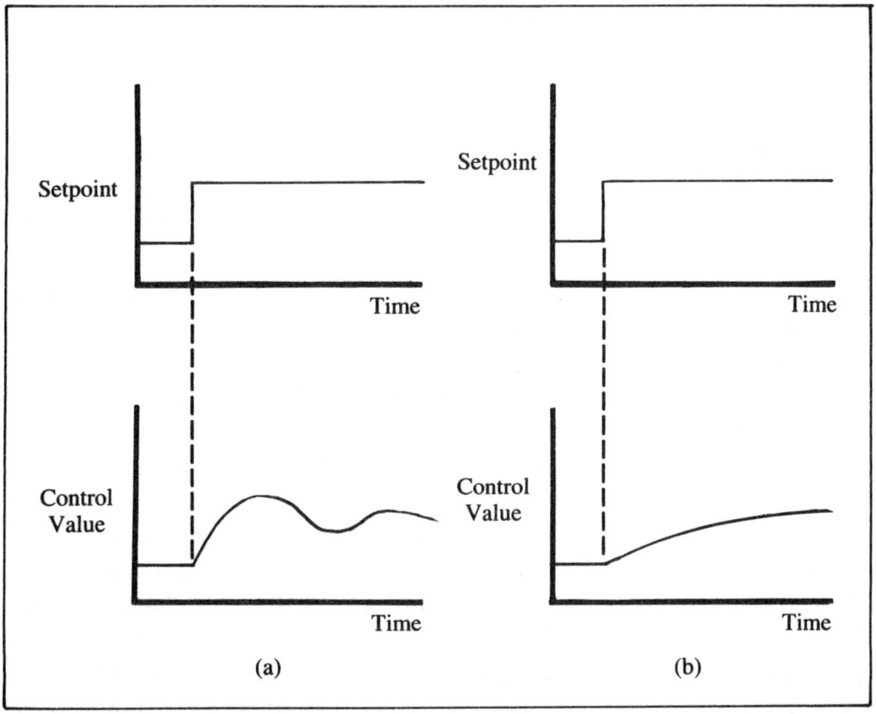

Figure 10.5. Response of cyclic control (a) and damped control (b). (Redrawn from Johnson, *Process Control Instrumentation Technology*.)

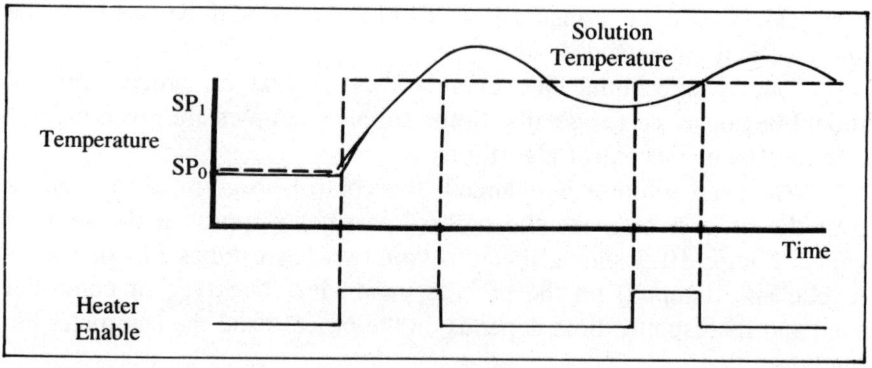

Figure 10.6. Cyclic heater control showing the output of the control circuit (heater enable).

though power is removed from the heater, heat continues to be transferred from the heating element to the liquid until an equilibrium condition occurs, thus raising the solution temperature above the setpoint value. The liquid would eventually cool below the setpoint value. When the measured temperature dropped below some program or operator-defined maximum error value, the heater would again be enabled (see Figure 10.6). Using this control method allows rapid response but causes overshoot.

A second possible control algorithm that produces a damped response takes into account the time lag between the time the heater is turned off and when it no longer significantly raises the temperature of the liquid. The magnitude of the difference in the measured temperature and the setpoint value is used to compute how long the heater will be enabled. The heater will be enabled longer as the difference between the setpoint value and the measured temperature (the error term) increases. When the heater is disabled, the controller remains idle for a period of time proportional to the time the heater was enabled to allow the temperature of the liquid to rise due to residual heat in the heater element. At the end of the delay, the controller again measures the temperature of the liquid and enables the heater if necessary (see Figure 10.7).

After the new setpoint value is obtained, the temperature is measured until it drops below a maximum error value, at which time the damped control algorithm is again applied. This controller does not respond as rapidly to large changes in the setpoint value as the first unit, but it avoids overshoot and produces less error when the setpoint value is in a steady state.

Similar control procedures can be used for control elements that re-

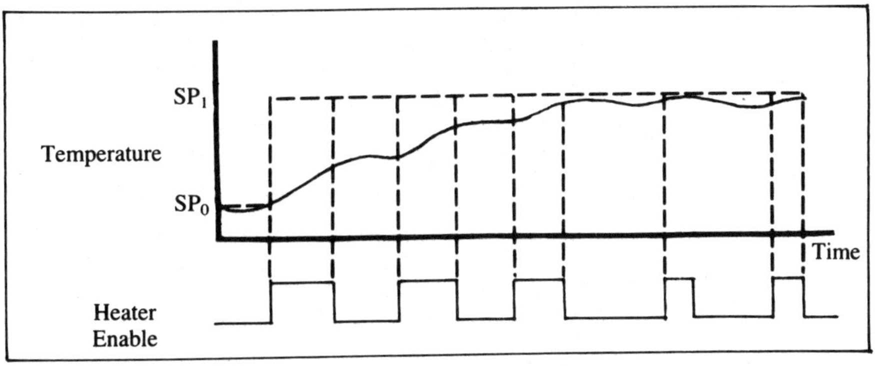

Figure 10.7. Damped heater control using simple digital control.

spond to a larger number of control states to produce cyclic and damped control functions. As an example, assume that a heater is controlled by a DAC. An n-bit DAC would allow the heater to be placed in 2^n states from off to full power. When the setpoint value is changed, maximum heating is used. As the temperature approaches the new setpoint, the power applied to the heater is decreased. A simple technique for implementing this type of control is to use a table of error magnitude versus control value. For a heater controlled by a two-bit DAC, the table structure would be

x = **setpoint − measured**	**DAC value**	**Heater**
$x>e3$	3	Full
$e3>x>e2$	2	2/3
$e2>x>e1$	1	1/3
$e1>x$	0	Off

where $e1$, $e2$, and $e3$ are table values. Based on the error, a DAC control value is selected. For greater errors, more power is applied to the heater. By selecting the error values in the table properly, a useful control function can be constructed.

In closed-loop systems, there exists a chance of instability caused by the feedback loop. If the system is not designed properly, under certain conditions the output of the controller may begin to oscillate. The controller no longer minimizes the error between the process value being measured and the setpoint value.

Instability can occur due to the delay between the time that control is asserted and the time the effect of the control is seen. For example, there is a time lag between the time power is applied to a heater and when a significant increase in temperature is seen.

As a simple example of instability in a closed-loop control system, assume that some process parameter is being controlled. There is a time lag of *t* between the time the controller initiates a change and the time this change is measurable in the process. The controller outputs one of three values. One state causes the value of the process parameter to rise; one causes it to fall; and the third output value produces no control over the process value.

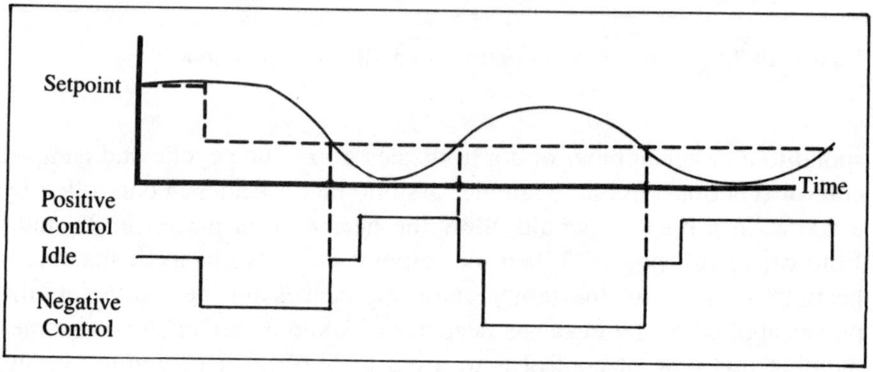

Figure 10.8. Oscillation of control parameter due to poorly designed control system.

As can be seen in Figure 10.8, the controller notes a setpoint change and enables its output to cause the process parameter to begin to fall. The controller continues to cause the process parameter to fall until the setpoint value is reached. Due to the time lag, the controller does not react to the change in the process parameter fast enough to avoid a large overshoot. The controller again corrects for the error in the process parameter by causing it to begin to rise. Due to the time lag, overshoot again occurs. The controller continues to output an oscillating control value. The desired value for the process parameter is never reached.

This example is simplified. The controller could be modified to compensate for the time lag in a number of ways. One method would be to estimate the time required to change the process parameter to the setpoint value. The control output would be enabled (rise or fall mode) for this amount of time before being placed in the neutral mode. The controller would then wait for a period equal to the process time lag before sampling the process parameter and exerting control.

Instability in a real world process control loop would typically be more subtle than in the example. Another factor involved in instability with a direct digital control system is the sample rate used to measure the value of the process parameter. The sample rate must be fast enough to allow the control system to respond appropriately to changes in the process variable being measured.

The stability of a system can be determined mathematically. A detailed discussion of such techniques can be found in a number of process control texts. The designer of a data acquisition system can apply control techniques in a variety of useful ways as long as he takes care that all closed-loop control algorithms are stable.

Open-loop control can be used to vary process parameters over a set of predefined values. The process parameters are modified by the computer, adequate settling time is allowed, data is collected from the system at the current process values, and the program continues at the next set of selected process values. This technique allows data to be collected on the effect of some process parameters when other parameters are varied.

An example of this type of system involves testing the activity of flying insects at different values of temperature and light intensity. Activity is measured by the number of times flying insects break a light beam. In a loop, the computer selects the next values of temperature and light intensity. Using some control technique, these values are exerted in the environmental chamber housing the insects. When the control level is reached, the computer collects a count of the number of insect flights for a predefined period of time and saves this activity value. The loop is repeated for each pair of temperature and light intensity values in the set.

In typical research applications, a failure in a device in an open-loop control output circuit will not be immediately detected by the computer but may be very obvious when the recorded data is inspected. If such failures are rare and the experiment can easily be repeated, open-loop control is valid.

In systems where data is to be collected over a predefined set of process variables where the computer must determine if a control failure has occurred, a simple closed-loop circuit can be used. Once the process parameters have been set and a settling time has occurred, the controlled process variables are read and an error value is computed (setpoint value minus measured value). The computer software does not actually use the error term to correct the value of the process parameter, it determines if the error value falls into preselected error limits. If a control er-

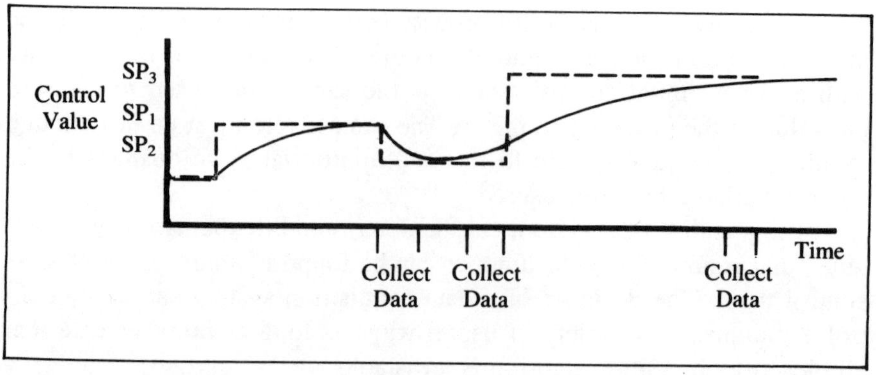

Figure 10.9. Data is collected with the control value at SP_1, SP_2, and SP_3. A closed-loop controller is used to move the control value to the desired value, and then data is collected for a predefined amount of time.

ror is detected, data collection is aborted, and the system operator is notified.

The above control/collection methods are valid only if the control circuits are stable and easily calibrated. If they are not, a traditional closed-loop control system may be involved each time a new element of the predefined value set must be established. The closed-loop control system operates until each process parameter is brought within a predefined limit of the setpoint value. Data is collected for a predefined amount of time, and the closed-loop control system is again invoked. Figure 10.9 illustrates this method for a single process parameter.

11

Data Management and Analysis

Data that has been automatically collected from all but the simplest data sources is rarely very useful in it's raw form. As the amount of data collected from a process increases, the ability of personnel to visually inspect the set of numbers and determine the significance of the data decreases. In many cases, it is necessary for the raw data to be analyzed by software to extract useful information for the operator. A graphic display of the data is sometimes very useful.

The designer of a data acquisition system must be concerned not only with automated data collection but also with data management and analysis. Although he may not directly produce data analysis software, he must consider which software tools will be used for data analysis. The system designer must provide a mechanism for labeling collected data and for merging data collected automatically with data produced manually.

Data Labeling and Manually Collected Data

A typical data collection system acquires data from a number of individual runs. With respect to the data collection system, data from each run is independant. The data from each run may be kept in a single diskette or cassette file. If the mass storage device supports a named file structure, it is useful to name each file in a manner that allows the operator to identify the run. Due to the limited number of characters normally allowed in a file name, it is not always possible to contain useful information in the file name other than an arbitrary run number.

In systems that contain an operator terminal, operator annotation and a time stamp can be contained in each data file. Even a primitive single board computer system can be equipped with a clock/calendar circuit that can be used to add a time stamp to the data file.

If there is no way of labeling a file, either via a file identifier or via records in the file, the operator must keep track of the data files. In this case, there should be a clearly defined procedure for associating data with a run. For example, a data logger records data from consecutive runs on sequential cassette files. The files are referenced by a file number. One method of associating the file number with the run is to have preprinted forms that the operator fills out for each run. The form contains the file number, cassette label, run parameters, and operator comments for each run.

In systems where the operator inputs annotation and manually observed data using a computer terminal, ease of use is a primary consideration. Most modern CRT terminals have cursor positioning features that allow forms to be displayed. Figure 11.1 shows a typical form.

Typical form support software allows the operator to move the cursor from input field to input field by keying the TAB key. The operator can only input characters in an input field. He updates the entire form, possibly correcting typographical errors. When the operator is satisfied with the input, he keys the carriage return key, and the form support software supplies the operator's input to the application code.

Form support packages are available commercially. They can also be developed in a high-level language. The ability of the programmer to design a form interactively and application program access to fields using a symbolic name are useful features.

If form support is not available or requires too many resources for a particular project, simple prompting of the operator can be used. The terminal displays a list of questions sequentially. The operator responds to each question in order. Unlike form-support processing, the operator cannot move the cursor to correct a previous response. To prevent erroneous data from being placed in the record of the run, the operator should be allowed to correct previous input even in systems without forms support. This feature can be implemented by asking the operator

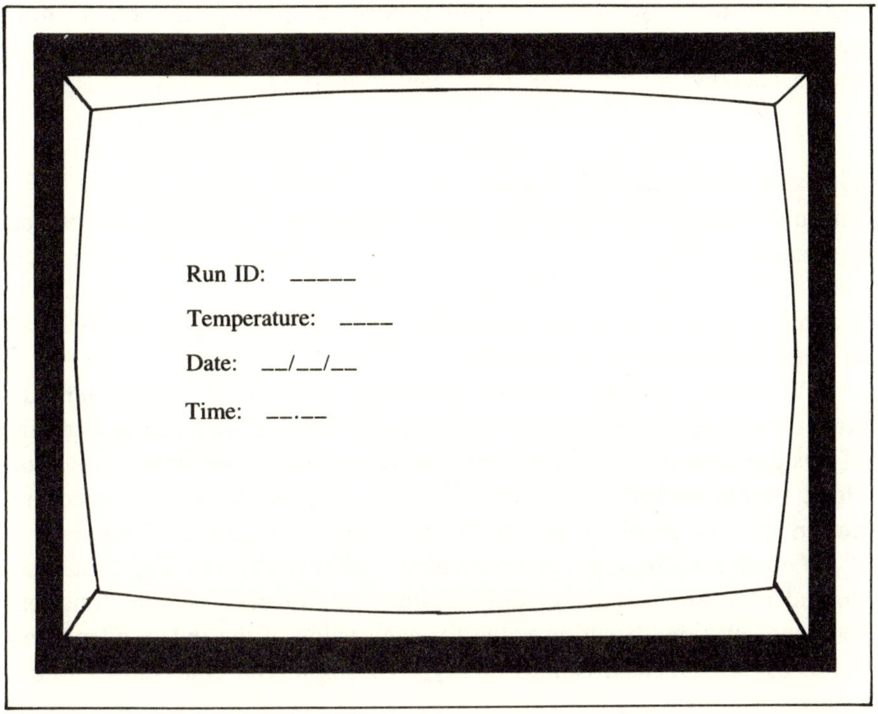

Figure 11.1 CRT screen formatted to allow operator input. The operator can only enter data in fields where underlines occur. Movement between fields is performed using the TAB and cursor keys.

if he is satisfied with the responses he has given at the end of the prompting session. If he is not, either the program again prompts for all the information or allows the operator to symbolically indicate which inputs need correcting.

If the operator must input a number of parameters, it is useful to provide a set of default values. In a forms system, the default values can be placed in the input fields corresponding to the parameters. If the default value is not acceptable, the operator inputs the parameter value of his choice over the default. In a prompting system, the default can be displayed as part of the prompt. If the default value is acceptable, the operator responds to the prompt with just a carriage return. If the default is not acceptable, the operator keys the new value followed by a carriage return. In a system with mass storage, defaults can be stored in a file where they can be changed by the operator.

If a large amount of manually collected information must be entered, the input operation might be performed independently of data collection. In this case, some labeling procedure, perhaps automatic, must be used so that automatically created data files and operator created data files associated with the same run can be merged.

Graphic Display of Data

The use of computer graphics can be useful in a large number of data acquisition systems. Graphics can be used to provide immediate feedback to the operator as to the state of the process being monitored. The graphic display of information is also a useful way to present the result of data analysis to the operator.

When considering the use of computer graphics, the system designer must determine the cost of graphics both in terms of dollars and of system resources. Dollar costs are affected by software costs (purchase or development) and the cost of a display device. Resource requirements for graphics include memory and processor utilization.

Graphics software can be divided into three types. The first type, limited two-dimensional graphics, allows the display of onto functions (one and only one function value for each value of the independent variable). Figure 11.2a illustrates this type of graph. Bar charts fall into this catagory.

The more general two-dimensional system allows the display of any two-dimensional function. Figure 11.2b shows a general two-dimensional graph.

Figure 11.2c illustrates a three-dimensional graph. Because display devices represent graphics on a flat surface, three-dimensional plots are not truly three-dimensional. Depth cues are used, such as displaying

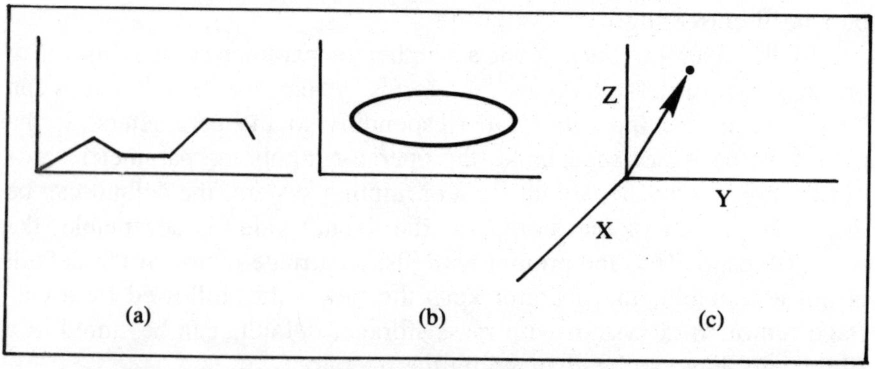

Figure 11.2. A limited two-dimensional graph (a), a general two-dimensional graph (b), and a three-dimensional graph (c).

"distant" parts of the image smaller in size, to give the appearance of three dimensions.

Display Devices

When selecting a display device, the system designer considers a number of factors. These factors include display overhead, speed of operation, soft and hard media, and color capability.

A simple hardcopy or CRT terminal can be used to produce simple graphics. A standard 24-row by 80-column display provides 1920 different screen positions. A simple two-dimensional plot can be constructed using vertical bar and underscore characters for borders and some position centered characters (e.g. an asterik) to mark points (see Figure 11.3). Most hardcopy printers have the feature that characters can be overstruck, adding the capability of multiple contrast shading.

Most hardcopy terminals and some CRT terminals do not allow display on a line after it has been displayed (after the paper has advanced on a hardcopy terminal or after the bottom line has scrolled up on a CRT). However, limited two-dimensional graphs are easy to produce on

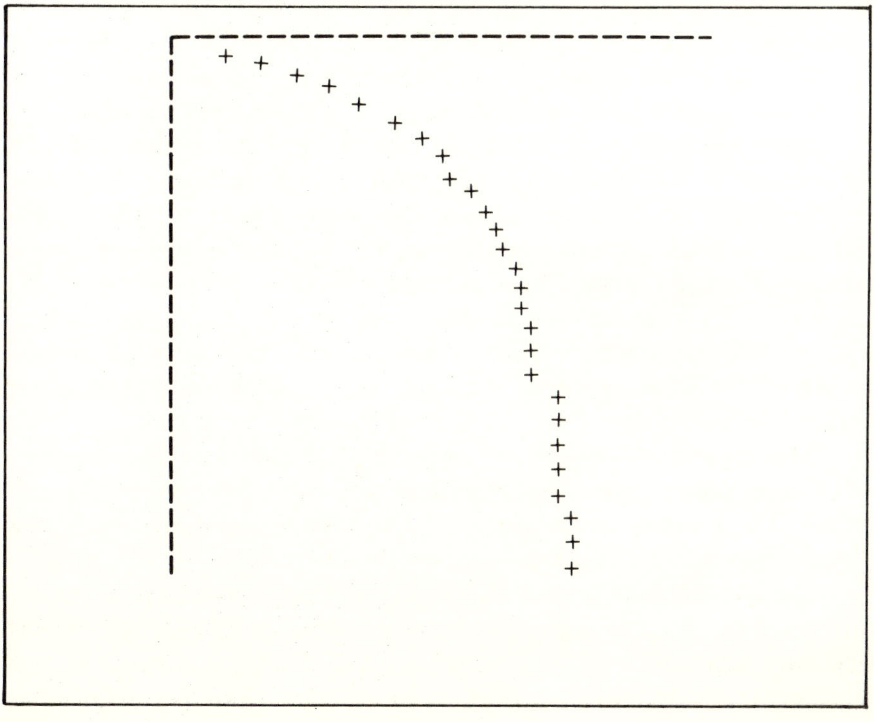

Figure 11.3. A low resolution print plot produced on a hardcopy terminal.

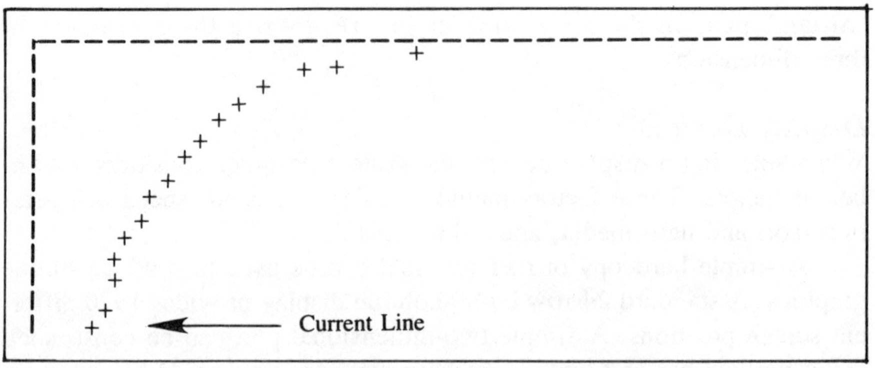

Figure 11.4. Limited two-dimensional graphs can be produced one line at a time with no need to roll the paper backwards on a hardcopy unit.

this type of display one line at a time (see Figure 11.4). For more complex two-dimensional graphs, the entire graph must be stored in memory such that the character to be displayed at each print position is stored before the graph is plotted. The graph can then be produced sequentially.

A limited number of hardcopy terminals allow the paper to be rolled both forward and backward. With this type of hardcopy terminal or with a CRT that allows cursor positioning, two-dimensional graphs can be produced without keeping the entire plot image in memory.

Some terminals offer extended character sets that include not only the standard ASCII character set but also special characters that allow slightly higher resolution plots than when using standard ASCII characters. The extended characters may divide a character position into a number of smaller blocks. Special characters allow combinations of the smaller blocks to be lighted. An additional six characters allow a character position to contain a dot in any of six different positions (see Figure 11.5). Additional characters may also be included to draw graph borders.

The major disadvantage of simple terminal graphics is lack of resolution and a nonsquare display system (typically 24 rows by 80 columns). The primary advantage is relative low cost in situations where high resolution is not needed.

Graphics terminals allow the display of characters and high resolution graphics. A typical graphics terminal allows a 255 by 512 resolution. CRT terminals used for graphics use either storage tubes or refresh techniques. As an image is written by an electron beam, it is retained in the CRT in a storage terminal. One method uses a wire mesh behind the

Figure 11.5. Each block represents a character frame that is the size of a displayed character. Any of six dots in a character frame can be displayed.

phosphor display that retains an image as a set of charges on the mesh. In typical operation, storage tubes do not allow selective erasure of part of the image. Screen erasure is normally done by flooding the screen with electrons, an operation requiring a second or more to perform.

Refresh terminals hold the image to be displayed in a memory unit. Terminal hardware rewrites the screen from memory at a rapid rate. Selective erasure is performed by modifying the display memory.

A graphics terminal may either draw a line as a series of points or as a continuous line segment. If the line is displayed as a series of points (as in most refresh terminals), lines of certain angles appear as stairsteps (see Figure 11.6a). A line drawn by moving the CRT electron beam in a continuous mode from one end point to the other produces a smoother vector (see 11.6b).

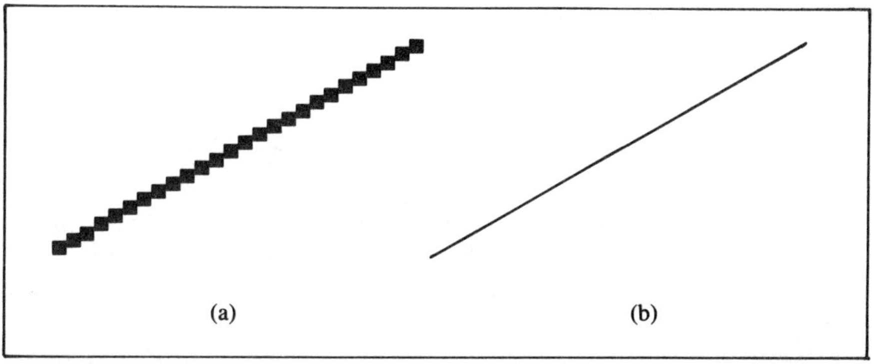

Figure 11.6. A line drawn on a refresh display (a) and a line drawn using analog vector generation (b).

Some graphics terminals have only two intensity levels. Part of the screen is not intensified while other parts are. Other terminals allow several intensity levels. More advanced terminals allow a variety of intensities and colors.

Additional features available on graphics terminals are sometimes useful. A joystick or other device may be used by the operator to input graphics information or to move a graphics cursor to interactively select a point on a graph. Another optional feature allows a hardcopy duplicate of a graphics display to be made. Intelligent graphics devices may perform functions normally performed by the host computer, thus relieving the data acquisition system of performing graphics calculations.

Graphics plotters are devices for producing hardcopy graphs. Traditionally, plotters produce graphs by moving a pen across paper. High-speed electrostatic plotters are also available. Plotter features of primary concern are speed, number of pens (for multiple colors), paper size, and resolution. Most plotters may be interfaced using serial, parallel, or IEEE-488 interfaces.

It is possible for a standard oscilloscope or CRT with control plate connections to be used for plotting. The computer can be connected to the vertical input, and by using the sweep trigger circuits of the oscilloscope, a limited two-dimensional plot can be produced. To produce more complex graphs, the computer must drive both the vertical and horizontal CRT plates. Because oscilloscopes respond to voltages, DACs are used to interface the computer to the oscilloscope.

To produce a flicker-free graph on an oscilloscope requires a large amount of CPU time. A separate refresh processor is frequently used to refresh the display. The use of an oscilloscope as a graphics display device allows the display to be changed rapidly. Unless rapid animation is required, the use of a graphics terminal is usually more suitable.

Graphics Software

A typical graphics package will include a set of primitive operations that may be called from an application program. A simple package may perform functions such as displaying a point and clearing the terminal screen. A more sophisticated package may contain a subroutine that accepts an entire array of data points and draws a graph along with a labeled axis.

If both a graphics terminal and plotter are being used, it is useful to separate device dependent code from device independent code such that both devices can be easily supported.

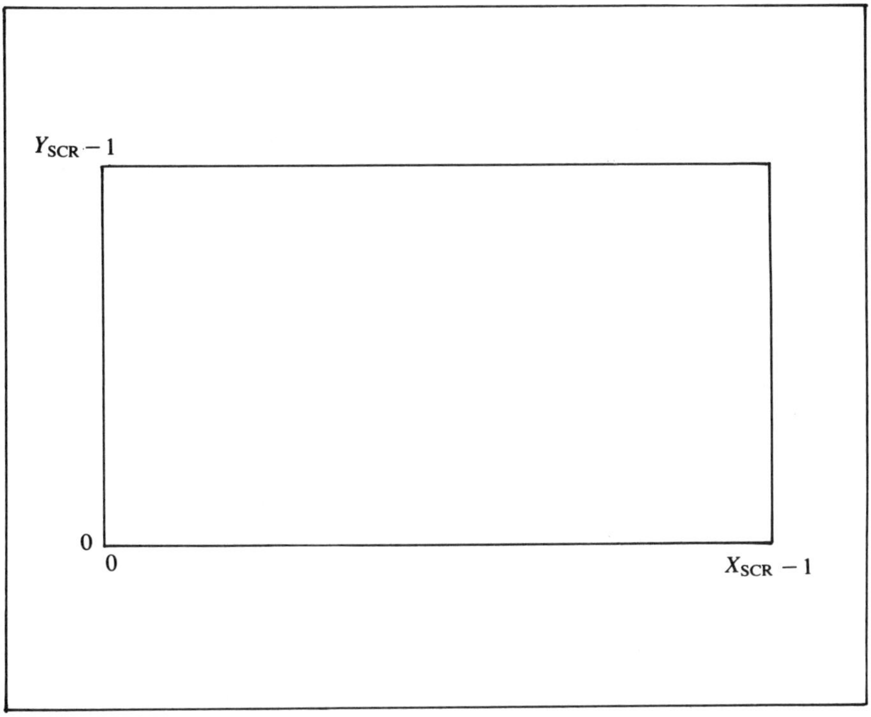

Figure 11.7. Graphics terminal display grid of X_{scr} by Y_{scr} addressable dots.

Plotting Techniques

A display device has a grid of x_{scr} by y_{scr} points, as shown in Figure 11.7, numbered from zero to $x_{scr} - 1$ and zero to $y_{scr} - 1$. To plot a set of floating point values $(x_1,y_1)\ldots(x_n,y_n)$, first the maximum and minimum x values (x_{max} and x_{min}) and the maximum and minimum y values (y_{max} and y_{min}) must be found. Each point (x_i,y_i) must be mapped to a display point (j,k). The mapping is

$$j = \left\lfloor \frac{(x_i - x_{min})}{(x_{max} - x_{min})} (x_{scr} - 1) + .5 \right\rfloor$$

$$k = \left\lfloor \frac{(y_i - y_{min})}{(y_{max} - y_{min})} (y_{scr} - 1) + .5 \right\rfloor$$

This mapping technique can be used directly on most CRT terminals. To use the technique on hardcopy terminals that do not allow the paper to be rolled backwards or on CRT's that do not allow direct cursor addressing, an array of size x_{scr} by y_{scr} can be kept to store point positions until the entire graph is constructed, and then the plot can be drawn from top to bottom from the array. If, as in the case of plots of data against time, the x axis increment is fixed and the function to be plotted is onto, only the y values need be mapped. The x axis is just incremented. If the graph is turned such that the x axis runs vertically, plots on these limited function terminals can be produced without display image storage.

To draw a vector between points (x_1,y_1), and (x_2,y_2), the endpoints are mapped into the display coordinates $[(j,k)$ and $(p,q)]$. As the x display value is incremented from the smaller x display value (for example j) to the larger (for example p), the corresponding y display value can be computed iteratively:

$$y_d = mx_d + b \text{ where } m = \frac{q - k}{p - j} \text{ and } b \text{ is a constant.}$$

$$y_d - y'_d = mx_d - mx_d - m\Delta x_d + b - b$$

$$y_d - y'_d = - m\Delta x_d$$

$$\text{if } \Delta x_d \text{ is one, } y_d = y'_d + m$$

where y_d is the last computed y value and y'_d is the y value corresponding to the last x value plus one. The d subscript indicates display coordinates.

The vector drawing software must check for $p-j$ equal to zero (a vertical line) and produce the set of points (p,i) where i varies from q to k.

With the capability to produce vectors, line plots with axes can be produced. A general purpose two-dimensional plot routine can be constructed using the vector and point plot code. Such a routine would receive a set of points to be plotted. It would first compute the maximum and minimum x and y values. Axes could be drawn and the points or vectors plotted sequentially. If cursor addressing is available, the x and y axis should be labeled with the proper scale and variable identifiers.

An application program can use the two-dimensional plot routine to display raw collected data. A general purpose data collection and display routine should interact with the operator allowing him to view portions of the graph. As parts of the graph are selected for view, the software computes a new scale factor based on the maximum and minimum values of the partial array and displays the graph portion. This feature allows the operator to view parts of the data with greater resolution than is available when the entire graph is displayed.

If a graphic cursor or crosshair is available with the display hardware, the graphics display software can be implemented to allow the operator to select the portion of the current graph that he wishes to plot next. The software can also numerically display the coordinates of the point currently under the cursor in the units associated with the data. This feature allows the operator to read the graph accurately.

The technique used to display two-dimensional plots can be expanded to display three-dimensional graphs. Additional processing is needed to give the illusion of depth and to remove hidden lines (lines that would be obscured in a true three-dimensional world by objects in front of other objects).

Three-dimensional plots of a function of three variables can be produced; however, due to the processing required to generate the illusion of depth, the scale of the graph is distorted. This distortion and the effect of a single view of the graph makes the coordinates of a point on the graph difficult to read. The three-dimensional plot can, however, be used to display curve shape and approximate function values.

The details of three-dimensional graphics software techniques can be found in a variety of texts.

Graphics Software Selection

Most suppliers of graphics devices also supply primitive graphics subroutines to support their devices. If written in a high-level language, these support routines can be made to run on a variety of computers by modifying the code that actually sends and receives display device characters.

In systems with more than one graphics device, it is helpful if a graph can be displayed on all the devices in a system using the same software. This feature requires that graphs be produced in a device independant manner with graph data translation for a specific device occurring at a low software level.

Graphics software should be selected on the basis of features, cost, and resource utilization. Purchased software should perform the needed functions at a reasonable cost. If graphics is to be used in a data acquisition program (as opposed to a postprocessor operating on a file of collected data), it must not consume too many resources so as to impede the function of the data acquisition software.

Data Analysis on the Data Acquisition Machine

Data collected by a data acquisition system is rarely directly usable. It is typically mathematically or statistically processed, combined with manually collected data, and presented in some usable format. Analysis of the data is either performed on the data acquisition system or on another, usually more powerful, computer.

One reason for not processing data on the data acquisition machine is a lack of hardware resources. The data acquisition computer may not have enough memory or compute power needed to analyze the data in a timely fashion. The data acquisition system may not have special hardware, such as a high quality plotter, to produce the desired results.

A second reason that the data acquisition system may not be used to process collected data is the lack of appropriate software. Many statistical packages and special purpose packages require large amounts of memory or have not yet been produced for small computer systems.

A third reason data analysis may not be appropriate on a particular data acquisition system is the need of the data acquisition machine to perform the data collection function without interruption for the period that would be required to perform data analysis. Such a system may possibly only produce a small amount of recorded data but be needed to monitor a process for failure continuously.

If the hardware resources, software, and machine availability are adequate, there are several advantages in processing the acquired data on the data acquisition system. First, the resources of a second machine are not needed. Second, the time and resources needed to transfer the data between the two machines are not needed. In some cases, analysis on a small machine can be faster than on a larger time sharing system that is moderately loaded.

If it is possible to perform analysis on either the data acquisition machine or a second machine, various factors should be considered. Does analysis software exist on either machine? If not, on which machine is it easier to develop analysis software (e.g. what languages are available on the two machines)? What costs are involved in transferring the data between the two systems (see the next section)? Does each machine have the necessary graphics output hardware?

Transfer of Collected Data to a Second Machine

In many cases, it is desirable to move acquired data to another computer system for analysis. Typically, analysis is performed on a machine with more resources than the data acquisition machine. Transfer of data between two machines is performed by a media transfer or electronically.

Media transfer indicates that a storage media that contains data recorded on the data acquisition machine is physically moved to another machine to be read. Typically, the media is magnetic, such as magnetic tape, disk cartridge, or diskette. Less used transfer media include PROMS and cassette tape. If large amounts of data must be moved, either tape or large disks must be used. Floppy diskettes and cassette tape can be used for medium amounts of data. PROMS are suitable for small amounts of data.

For a media transfer to be usable, the media, recording technique, and data format must be compatible between the two systems. Media compatibility refers to the size and type of media. For example, hard sectored and soft sectored diskettes are not compatible. The recording technique refers to the method used to record data on magnetic media. Magnetic tape and single density, eight-inch, soft sectored diskettes are two examples of widely compatible media and recording techniques. Where standards are not widely used, similar media are likely not compatible.

Data format refers to media directory, code, and blocking. If the data format used by two systems is not compatible, a utility program must be obtained or developed to allow one system to read the format of another.

As an example, two different computer systems use standard eight-inch floppy disks with 128-byte sectors. The first system combines the data in four sectors to make one unit of disk storage called a block. The second system uses eight sectors per block. The first system requires that a file be kept in contiguous blocks while the second allows files with discontiguous blocks. Due to the different file structures, both systems have different directory formats.

Since the media and recording techniques are the same, a disk created on one of the example systems can be read by the other, but additional software is needed to be able to format sectors into blocks and to locate the blocks in a particular file. A utility program that reads a foreign disk format must usually bypass high-level operating system file access software and instead perform direct sector I/O. The most difficult step in writing a utility to read and write foreign disk formats is determining the file and directory structure. For some small systems, this information is frequently not fully documented.

Once file blocks can be opened and read, the utility program may have to further decode the file format. For text files, it is necessary to locate the end of each record. The end of record may be marked by one or more characters, by using a fixed length record, or by prefacing each record with a length field. It may also be necessary to convert from one code to another (e.g. ASCII to EBCDIC).

Data can also be transferred between two computers electronically over a communications line. The current standard serial interface is RS-232C (see Chapter 5). This interface specifies the physical and electrical connections. In addition to the electrical and physical interface, the communications protocol must be specified.

A communications protocol is a set of rules governing the flow of information between two or more devices. The protocol indicates how character boundaries are determined. It governs how messages are formed from characters. Error detection and correction procedures are defined. Control of when messages may be transmitted is also part of the protocol.

The simplest protocols exist between computers and local serial peripherals. For example, a digital oscilloscope and computer may interchange data and commands using a simple message structure. On the other hand, the transfer of data from a data acquisition system onto a computer network may be governed by a complex protocol.

The framing of characters is an important protocol consideration since this operation is typically performed in hardware. There are three general framing techniques: asynchronous, synchronous, and bit-oriented protocols.

In asynchronous character transmission, individual characters are framed with start and stop bits. Normally, the line is held at the "mark" state (negative voltage interpreted as a logic one). The beginning of a character is marked by a "space" (positive voltage interpreted as a logic zero) on the line for the duration of one bit time (defined by the line speed). Following this start bit are the bits defining the character (typically eight bits). One, one and one-half, or two stop bits at the mark condition indicate the end of a character (see Figure 11.8).

Asynchronous transmission is typically used for communications between computers and terminals and computers and local devices.

Synchronous transmission does not use start and stop bits to delineate individual characters. A stream of characters are transmitted in sequence. The stream of characters begins with three or more SYNC control characters (ASCII bit code 0010110_2). The receiving hardware samples the communications line as a stream of bits. Each bit time, the last eight bits are compared to a SYNC character bit pattern. When two

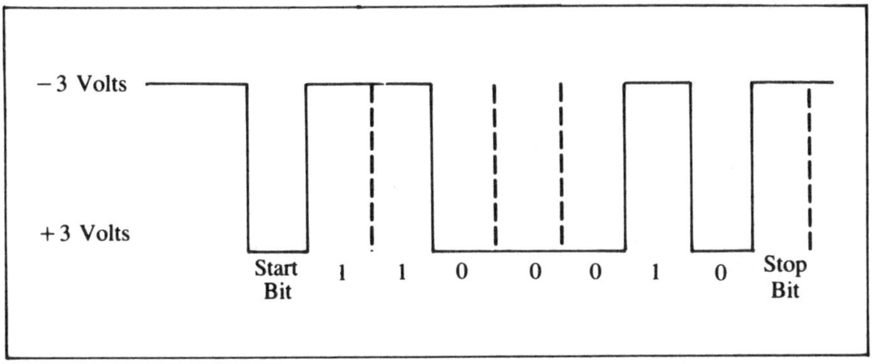

Figure 11.8. The transmission of a character on an asynchronous communications line.

SYNC character patterns are received in sequence, the character boundaries for the message are determined. See Figure 11.9.

For large blocks of data, the overhead required to transmit SYNC characters is not as great as the overhead associated with start and stop bits for each character. Synchronous hardware is more complex than asynchronous hardware.

The ability to send transparent text (any sequence of characters) is complicated because a SYNC character that is the first character in the message is easily confused with the framing SYNC characters. Additional control characters are used to preface control characters that are sent as data instead of their normal control meaning.

Bit-oriented protocols typically use a special bit pattern, such as 01111110_2, as a flag character. This flag character is sent at the beginning and end of messages as a delimiter. The initial flag or flags perform a function similar to the SYNC character in synchronous communications in that they indicate the first bit in a message. The flag character can never be transmitted within a message. If the message being transmitted contains five logic one bits in a row (possibly across character boundaries), the sending hardware inserts an extra logic zero bit after the fifth logic one. When the receiving hardware senses five logic ones followed by a logic zero, the logic zero is removed from the message (see Figure 11.10).

The advantages of bit-oriented protocols are that message synchronization requires little overhead (one character per message) and it is easy to send transparent text. Hardware for bit-oriented protocols is rela-

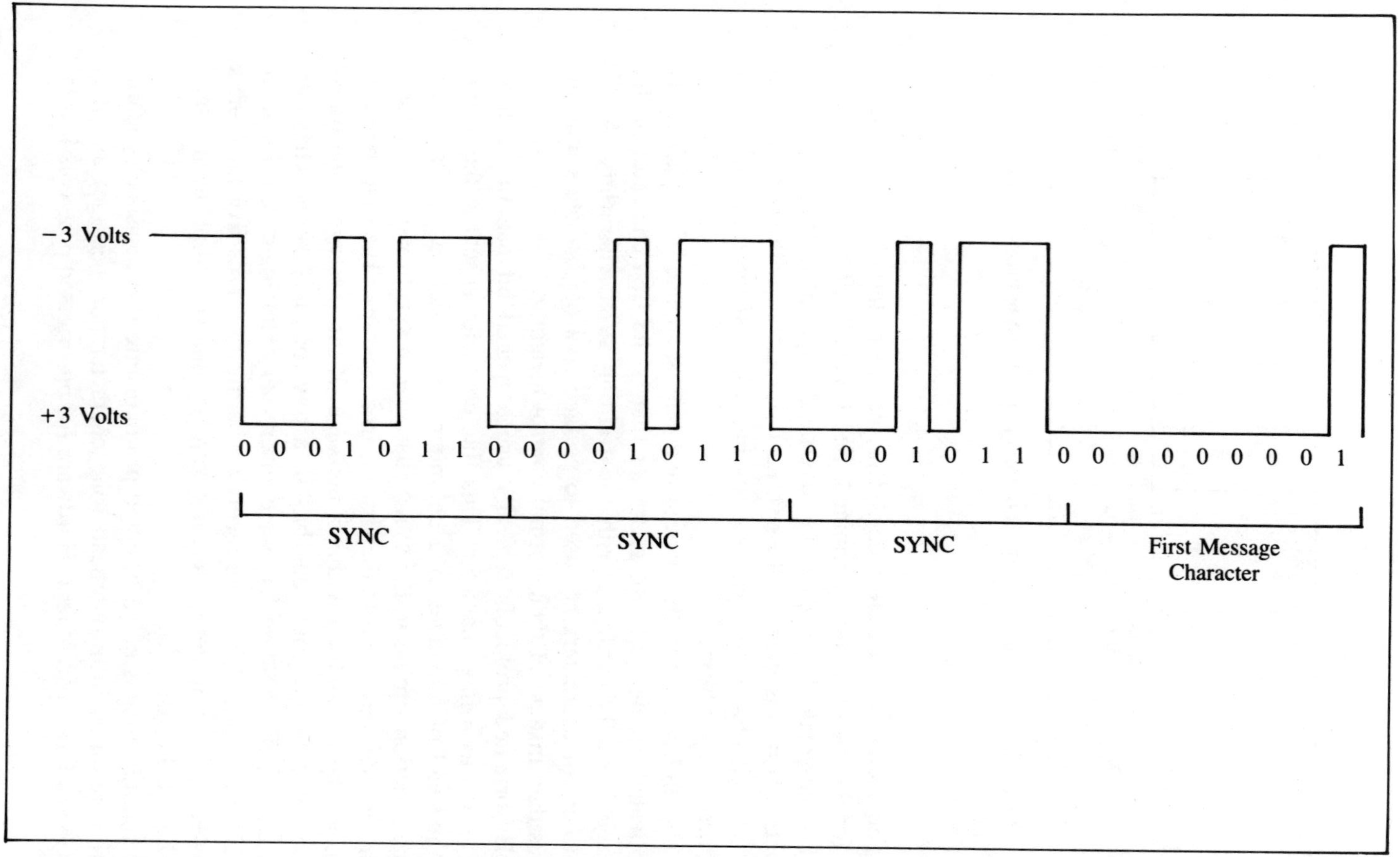

Figure 11.9. Synchronous character transmission using three ASCII SYNC characters at the beginning of a message to define character boundaries.

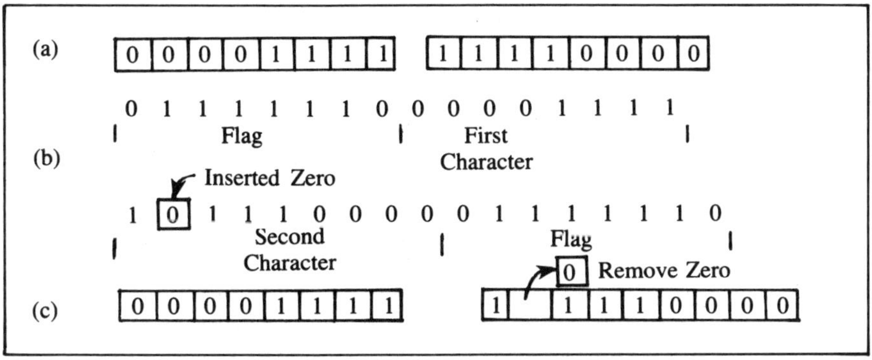

Figure 11.10 Two characters to be transmitted on a bit-oriented line (a), character transmission showing insertion of logic zero to prevent the flag sequence from occurring in the message (b), and reception of the message showing removal of the inserted zero after five logic ones (c).

tively complex. Integrated circuits that perform much of the housekeeping for synchronous and bit-oriented protocols are available.

The use of asynchronous communications between computers and terminals and computers and local devices is not governed by a standard protocol for message formats and control. Four ASCII control characters historically used to control the paper tape reader and punch on a Teletype have been used in a number of ways with asynchronous devices. These device control characters, DC1, DC2, DC3, and DC4, perform the following paper tape functions:

Character	Function	ASCII Bit Pattern
DC1	start reader	0010001
DC2	start punch	0010010
DC3	stop reader	0010011
DC4	stop punch	0010100

These characters are recognized by some cassette units and standalone floppy disk units that communicate via an asynchronous interface. A number of other control characters (nonprintable characters) are used in a variety of ways.

The protocol rules governing messages in synchronous and bit-oriented protocols are more rigidly defined than for asynchronous communications applications. These protocols define message formats, transparency rules, rules governing communications sequence, and error detection and correction formats. Such protocols are widely used for communication between computer systems, between computers and clusters of buffered terminals, and between computers and remote job entry stations.

One important technique used in data communications is error detection. The most common error detection technique involves appending one or more block check characters to the end of each message. The sender uses an algorithm to compute the check character or characters. The receiver applies the same algorithm to the received message and compares the resultant check character or characters to those sent by the transmitter. If the comparison fails, the receiver knows that the message was modified during transmission by noise or faulty hardware.

There are a number of common algorithms for generating block check characters. The goal of such algorithms is to be able to detect errors even when a number of bits in the message have been modified due to noise. Since some of the algorithms require significant computation, it is common practice to provide block check character generation and checking in hardware on the communications interface.

In practice, the most common error correction technique is retransmission. In a typical synchronous communications protocol, the sender sends a message and waits for a reply. The receiver either replys with a positive acknowledgement message indicating that the last data message was received properly or a negative acknowledgement message indicating that the last data message should be retransmitted.

In some cases, noise can cause the receiving station to miss an entire message. To prevent communications deadlock due to lost messages, a timeout technique is used in many protocols. When a station is waiting to receive a message, as defined by protocol rules, the station initiates a timing sequence. If at the end of the preset time a message has not been received, a special message is transmitted, or possibly the last message sent is retransmitted. Message errors or loss due to noise occur infrequently between systems in close proximity. Communications over distances using modems are more likely to exhibit errors.

In many protocols, each messsage contains a sequence number. The sequence number is incremented by the sender each time a message is sent. (The increment is performed using modulo arithmetic based on the number of bits in the sequence number field.) The receiver compares the sequence number in the message with the expected sequence number in order to determine if an entire message has been lost (possibly due to the modification by noise of a character indicating the start of the message). Some protocols allow a number of messages to be received before an acknowledgement is transmitted by the receiver. In this case, a sequence number is transmitted as part of the acknowledgement to indicate how many messages are being acknowledged.

Most protocols allow a station that is busy performing some task (such as reading a record to be transmitted from disk) to send a message indicating that the station is still active but is temporarily unable to transmit data. This technique prevents timeout processing from occurring.

A half-duplex communications session implies that due to hardware constraints or protocol rules, only one station can transmit at a time. A full-duplex systems allows data flow in both directions simultaneously.

Electronic Communications Techniques

The transfer of data electronically between a data acquisition system and a second computer can take place using a simple protocol or a more complicated standard protocol. In either case, error detection and correction techniques are mandatory.

The use of standard protocols for data transfer from a small data acquisition system may not be practical due to the resources required or the lack of commercial software. If suitable software to implement a standard protocol on the data acquisition machine is not available commercially, a significant implementation effort is commonly needed to construct one. The use of a standard protocol on a medium-scale system that contains the resources to support this type of communications and for which communications software is likely available should be considered when practical.

There are primarily three cases where a simple, nonstandard protocol is in order. The first case applies to data transfer between two small-scale systems where neither has standard protocol support available. Second, a simple protocol can be used when one of the machines does not contain the resources to support a complex protocol. Third, a simple protocol is practical when a data acquisition system emulates a terminal connected to a time sharing system for the purpose of transferring data.

Figure 11.11 illustrates the hardware and software components needed for a simple protocol transfer using an asynchronous line. A transfer program resides on each machine and is responsible for the transfer of data. Normally, one of the two systems will assume the role of the primary station and will initiate and control communications.

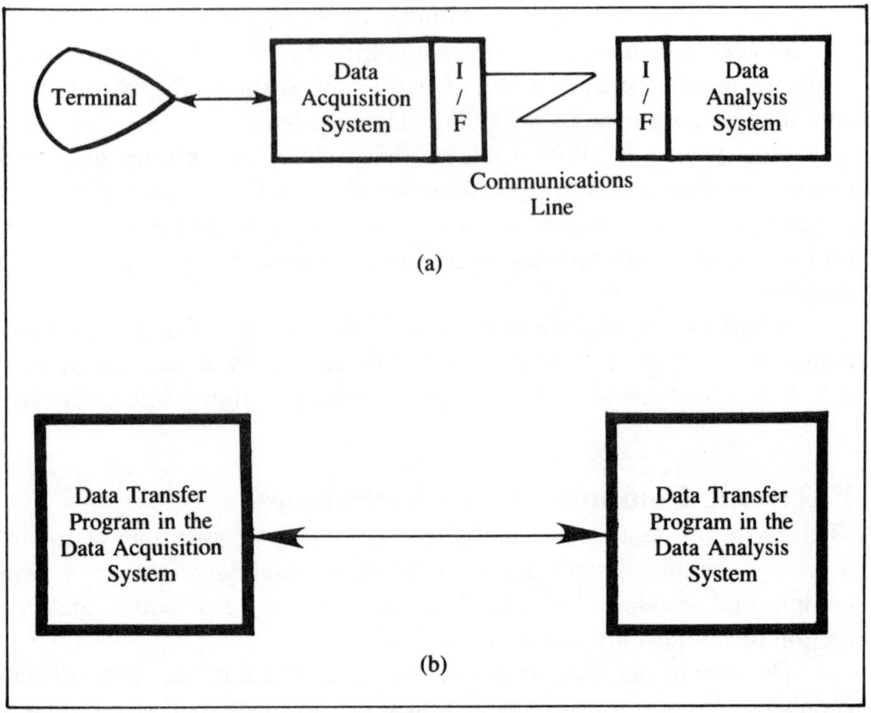

Figure 11.11. Typical hardware needed for data transfer between computers (a) and the interconnection of software between the systems (b).

The following discussion illustrates simple protocol concepts using some sample message formats. These examples are given as illustrations and are incomplete.

Figure 11.12 illustrates a set of hypothetical data and control message formats. Certain ASCII control characters, such as <ETX>[1], are used as message delimitors and therefore cannot appear as part of the data field. If only printable data is to be transferred, this restriction is not severe. If binary data must be transmitted, special character sequences can be defined to allow control characters to be imbedded in the data part of the message.

The check character for a simple protocol should be relatively easy to compute. One such technique is the checksum, which is produced by summing all the characters in the message modulo 256. Since it is possible for the checksum value to be equal to a special control character such as <ETX>, the checksum is converted to a printable hexadecimal representation. A checksum of 00000100_2 would be represented as the two printable ASCII characters 0 and 4. The receiver performs

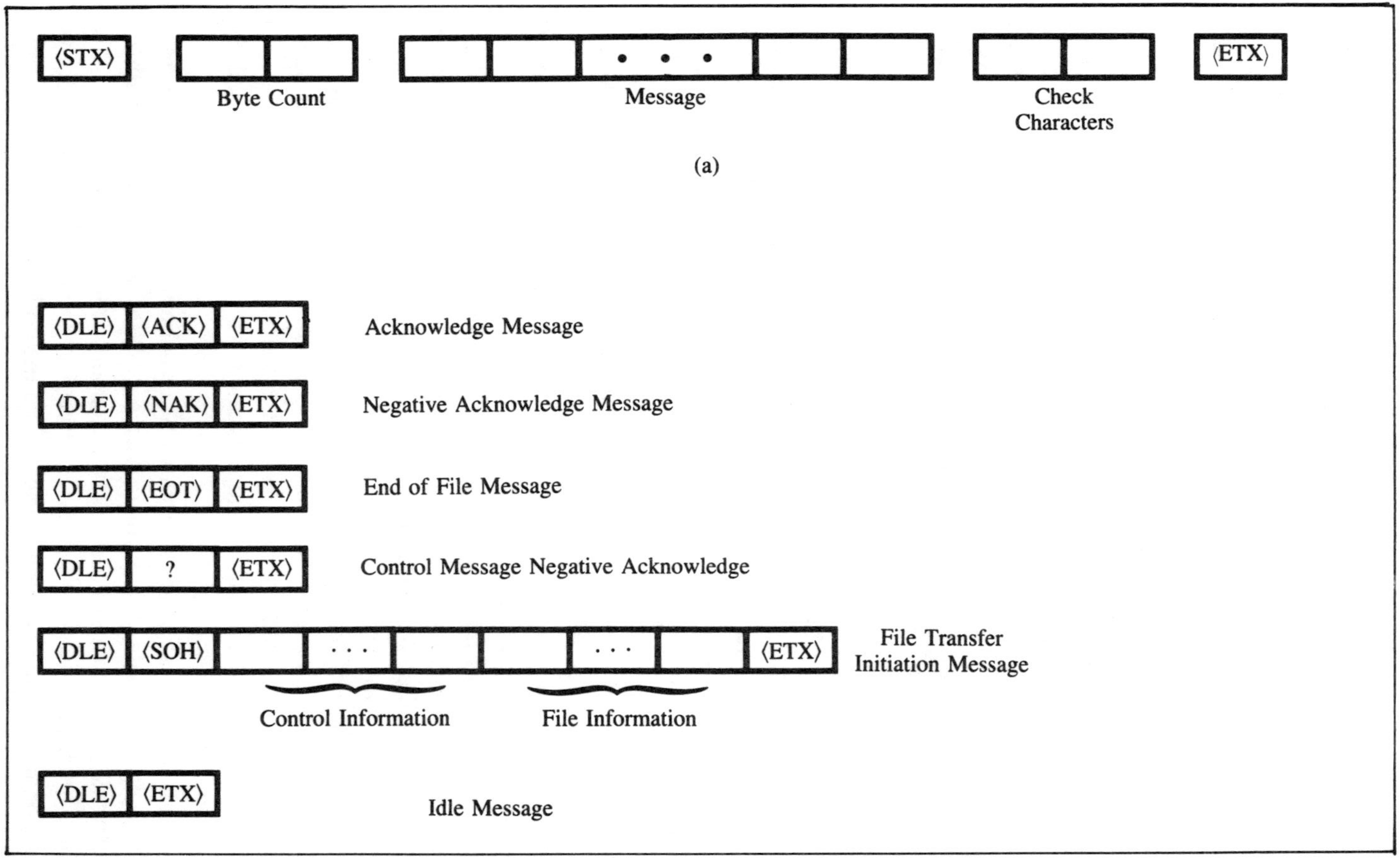

Figure 11.12. The data message format (a) and control message formats (b) of the hypothetical protocol.

the checksum operation on the message characters. It then converts the two check characters in the message to the binary value they represent and compares the result to the computed value.

The use of a checksum does not provide as much certainty that an error will be detected as do other more widely used technniques. Some messages that have two bits in error will be accepted as error free messages. The checksum is easy to compute and affords reasonable error checking in many environments.

When a receiver receives a data message, it responds with an acknowledge or negative acknowledge message. When the sender receives an acknowledge, it transmits the next data record. If it receives a negative acknowledgement, it retransmits the last record. If the sender receives neither an acknowledgement or negative acknowledgement due to a transmission error, it transmits a <DLE> ? <ETX> message that requests the receiver to retransmit its last message.

When the sender has successfully transmitted the entire data file, a <DLE> <EOT> <ETX> message is transmitted. The sequence following the transmission depends on the particular environment. If the two systems are to remain in data communications mode, the systems may transmit idle messages (e.g. <DLE> <EXT>) at intervals until the operator specifies further work. In this case, if the transmitter of the end of file message does not receive an idle message in response but instead receives any other message or receives no message in the time out period, it retransmits the end of file message.

The transfer of a file is initiated by the transmission of a file transfer initiation message that specifies the direction of the transfer (which system is the sender) and the filename involved on the system receiving the start message. Depending on the environment, the primary station may always send the start message or in a more sophisticated environment, either station may start a transfer.

When both systems involved are standalone systems, the operator starts a version of the file transfer program on both systems. By an operator command on one system, a transfer is initiated. On the other hand, the most complicated environment exists where one of the systems is a time sharing system that is communicated with via a port intended for connection to a terminal.

In the time sharing environment, asynchronous ports are designed to accept terminals. Many time sharing systems were designed with no features for support of intelligent asynchronous devices. Due to this fact, intelligent devices may be restricted as to the amount of data that can be transmitted without pause and to the codes that can be transmitted (some control codes such as carriage return may be defined as message delimiters, and others may be discarded). Due to the load on time sharing processers, a data acquisition system may transmit messages faster than the time sharing system can receive and process them. To prevent this situation, a half-duplex environment can be created, as in the simple protocol example, where a single message is transmitted by a station and an acknowledgement or negative acknowledgement must be received before another transmission is made. If timeout intervals are sufficiently long, this half-duplex approach allows both stations to pace each other.

To prevent problems with special time sharing system processing of control characters, the number and selection of control characters used in the protocol should be chosen wisely. A logical choice for the end of message character (<ETX> in the previous examples) is carriage return, because this is the end of message character used by a terminal operator in most systems.

When dealing with a time sharing system, it is recommended that only printable characters be included in the data, byte count, and check character parts of messages. If binary data must be transmitted, it can first be converted to printable hexadecimal characters.

To limit the number of control characters actually used, some of the control characters in the control messages in Figure 11.12 could be replaced with printable characters, e.g., A for <ACK> and N for <NAK>. In the figure, only three characters must be control characters: the start of data message character (<STX> in the figure), the end of message character (<ETX> in the figure), and the start of control message character (<DLE> in the figure). If carriage return is used for the end of message character, it should be possible with most systems to discover two additional control characters that are not treated in a special way by the time sharing system.

A rational approach when designing software for a small system to communicate with a time sharing system is to implement the software to operate in two modes. In virtual terminal mode, the data acquisition system behaves as a terminal, allowing the operator to logon to the time sharing system and to execute time sharing system commands. The virtual terminal should be written in a general fashion such that it does not perform functions not normally performed by a terminal (such as the automatic transmission of a logon sequence). This approach allows the virtual terminal to be used in a variety of situations without the need to modify software.

The second mode of operation is file transfer mode. One technique for switching modes is to use terminal emulation mode to invoke the file transfer software on the time sharing system. The file transfer program transmits a start message similar to the <DLE> <SOH> message of Figure 11.12. The virtual terminal software must recognize the start message and switch to file transfer mode. When the file has been transferred and the end of file message transmitted and acknowledged (possibly by an idle message), the data acquisition software returns to virtual terminal mode. The time sharing system transfer software completes execution, and the time sharing command mode is entered.

Many of the same principles used in writing real-time device handling code (see Chapter 6) can be applied to writing the code to handle interfaces used in a data communications system. The use of interrupt processing to handle devices greatly simplifies software design when more than one device is used by the file transfer program (e.g. a modem and a disk).

Debugging simple protocol software requires special tools. The most useful tool is a line monitor which is a device used to view the messages being exchanged by two stations without disturbing the transmissions. The messages are typically displayed on a CRT.

If a terminal has a special mode where control characters are displayed using special symbols, a simple line monitor can be contructed for use in half-duplex environments. Figure 11.13 shows construction of the simple line monitor. The diodes and resistor essentially form an "or" gate such that characters being transmitted in either direction are displayed on the simple line monitor.

Another useful diagnostic is to have the file transfer software on both stations to display the messages they send and receive. Control

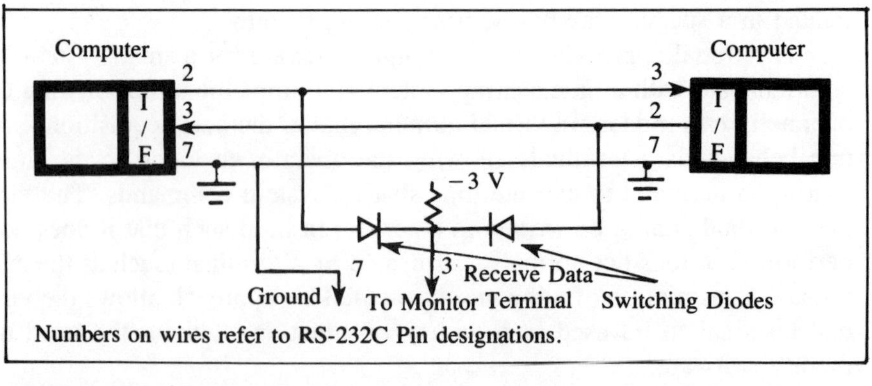

Figure 11.13. Using a terminal as a line monitor in a half-duplex environment.

characters can be displayed as a two-character sequence, such as ∧C to represent ETX (generated by holding CONTROL and keying C on the keyboard of a terminal).

File transfer software should keep statistics as to the number of timeouts, retransmissions, and the number of messages transmitted. If a large number of line errors occur, the communications hardware and line should be checked.

12

Data Acquisition Examples

This chapter contains a number of data acquisition problems and the outline of a possible solution for each problem. It is hoped that the study of these problems will provide some insight into the analysis and solution of typical data acquisition problems.

The reasons for a particular approach are given in each solution outline. Other solutions may be equally practical depending on a number of factors, such as the resources available. The development of new technology may make the solutions less attractive.

Balance/Computer Interface

The first problem deals with a laboratory balance. It is used to weigh ground tobacco samples for analysis. For the particular chemical analysis used, either the weight of all samples must be an accurately measured standard weight or the actual weight of each sample must be recorded and used to correct the output of the chemical analysis by the amount the weight deviates from the standard.

It is easier and quicker for laboratory technicians to fill beakers with enough ground tobacco to approximate the standard weight without actually measuring exactly. It is desirable that the measured weight be recorded automatically to allow rapid weighing and to avoid operator error when recording weights.

As part of the problem statement, an electronic balance is already available with parallel BCD outputs. Data from the chemical analysis is currently being stored on a cassette tape unit that is part of an ASCII terminal. Software exists on the mainframe computer where analysis of the data is performed to read properly formatted cassette tape files from the terminal.

It is desirable to use the cassette unit for storage of balance data for later transfer to the mainframe system. It is also desirable that a set of 40 or less balance readings be retained by the interface circuitry and written to the cassette unit when it is not being used with the chemical analysis equipment. This goal is desirable so that the use of the balance does not tie up the cassette unit.

A diagram of the device interconnections is shown in Figure 12.1. The manual switch in the figure is a commercial switch box for RS-232C cables. While data is being transferred from the balance interface circuitry to the cassette tape, the switch is in position A. (It should be noted that the transfer of 40 balance readings to cassette tape from the temporary storage in the interface circuitry takes less than five seconds). The switch is moved to position C to record data from the chemical analysis device. This process is repeated until it is convenient to transfer a number of data files to the mainframe by using the B switch position for connection of the terminal to the modem.

The block in the figure labeled with the question mark is the circuit or small computer system that must perform two functions. First, the

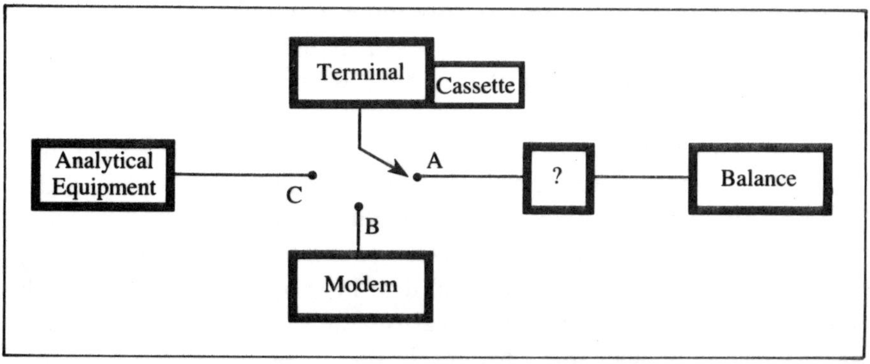

Figure 12.1. Block diagram of the balance interfacing problem.

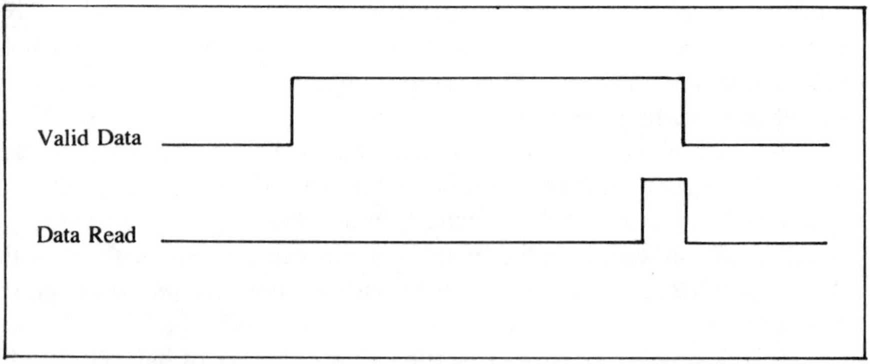

Figure 12.2. Balance interface handshake.

device inputs parallel data from the balance and converts it to serial data for the terminal. Second, the device must store up to 40 balance readings and retain them until the terminal and cassette unit are available. If it were not for the data storage aspect of the device, it is possible that a special circuit could be designed to perform the parallel-to-serial conversion in a manner cost-competitive with a single board computer implementation (cost referring to all aspects of the development). With the data storage requirement, a single board computer appears ideally suited for the solution of the problem.

Figure 12.2 illustrates the handshake involved in interfacing to the balance. In normal operation, four BCD weight digits (16 lines) reflect the current weight. The weight is updated 40 times a second. When the operator has filled a beaker and the weight has stabilized, he presses a momentary contact switch connected to the balance. The balance freezes the current weight value output by the balance and activates the "valid data" line. The valid data line must be sensed by the computer, and the balance data read. Because typically more than one port is required for connection to the 16 BCD output lines, it is mandatory that the balance not change its output during the time the weight value is being read by the computer.

After the weight data is read, the "data read" signal is pulsed by the computer to indicate to the balance that the data has been read, and the outputs can again track the current weight.

The computer interface connected to the balance requires 17 input lines (four BCD digits and the valid data line) and one output line (data read). The solution presented here also requires that a switch be able to be sensed to indicate the operator is ready for the stored data to be transferred to the terminal. Because parallel ports are typically available in groups of eight on eight-bit machines, three input ports and one output port can be used. Polling of the switch and data valid line is sufficient for this system, so no interrupt logic is required.

Figure 12.3 shows the hardware configuration of the single board computer used to interface to the balance and terminal. The reset switch is pressed to restore the system to its power on state. The number of

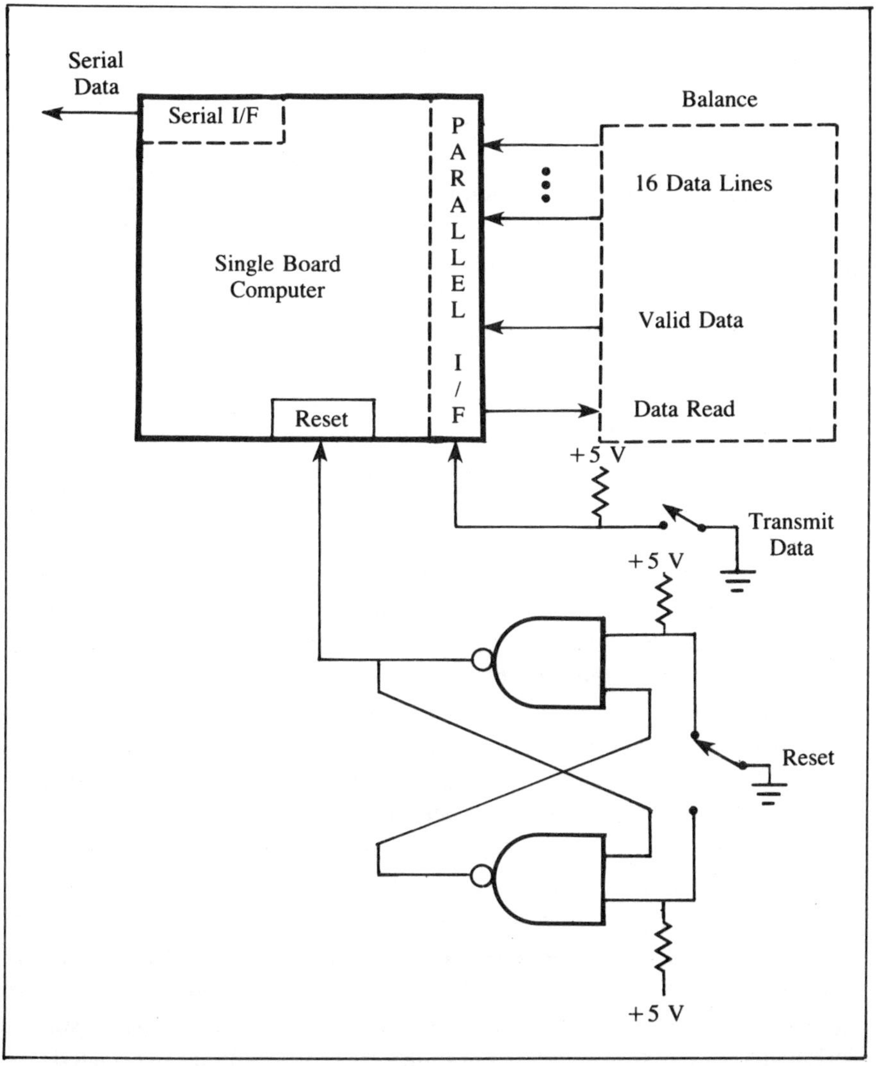

Figure 12.3. Block diagram of the single board computer used to interface to the balance.

stored weights is set to zero, and the computer begins a polling loop, checking for either the valid data line high or the transmit switch closed. If valid data is high, the computer reads the four BCD digits, saves them in memory, increments the number of weights stored, and pulses the data read line. The polling loop is again entered.

If the transmit switch is pressed, the computer transmits the characters to the terminal needed to initiate a cassette-write operation. It then retrieves each weight, converts it to ASCII, and transmits the ASCII characters to the terminal and cassette unit. A line end sequence (such as carriage return and linefeed) is transmitted after each weight or group of weights. After all weights are transmitted, the character sequence to cause an end of file mark to be written on the cassette is transmitted, and the cassette is removed from the write mode. At this point, the operator must push the reset switch on the microcomputer to erase the data in the buffer. If the data were erased automatically after transmitting, a premature activation of the transmit switch or a cassette unit error would cause collected data to be lost. It should be noted that the transmit switch is not debounced. The software must perform the debounce function.

If a power failure occurs before data is written to cassette tape, the data will be lost if the memory of the single board computer is volatile. Data loss due to an occasional power failure is not a major consideration in cases where the data can be easily recreated. In the balance system, if data loss due to power failure had to be prevented, either the volatile memory could be powered by a battery such that information could be retained during power failure or a small adding machine-type printer could be connected to the single board computer to provide a hardcopy backup of the collected weights.

Only due to the simplicity of the problem is the software development investment not a major concern. However, it does require some effort. Typically in a single board computer system, the software is stored in an EPROM. The developer of the balance device must have a means to program EPROMS. The best solution is to use a development system containing a diskette-based operating system with an EPROM programming device. The code for the balance system could be developed and tested on the development system and transferred to the balance system using an EPROM. Testing on the development system requires that either the development system have the same processor and interfaces as the single board computer or that a simulator be used.

In some small systems such as the balance device, the code could be hand-assembled and placed in an EPROM using a manual standalone programmer. This approach is only viable if a debugger is available on the single board computer. For most debuggers to function, the code in the EPROM must first be copied to RAM for execution. Hand assembly and standalone debugging software on a single board computer should only be considered for small projects where primitive development techniques do not add significantly to the overall cost of the project.

Solar Heating Data Collection

In Chapter 1, a discussion was presented of a device that collects temperature data in solar-heated homes. The device must record the temperature in a centrally located room every ten minutes. Five devices are used to record year-round data in five homes.

A thermocouple is selected as the temperature measuring transducer. A type J (iron-constantan) thermocouple is used because of its output characteristics (typically .05 mV/degree centigrade). The output of the thermocouple is linear, a fact that simplifies calibration. The disadvantages of using a thermocouple are its low-level output and the need to provide compensation for the transducer. Figure 12.4 shows thermocouple construction. The measuring junction is formed where the two different metals, A and B, meet. Two reference junctions are formed where metals A and B connect to the signal leads made of metal C. The voltage produced by the circuit is proportional to the difference in temperature at the measurement junction and the reference junction.

To make accurate measurements, either the reference junction must be kept at a known temperature (e.g. placed in an ice water bath) or the effect of the reference junction must be compensated for electronically.

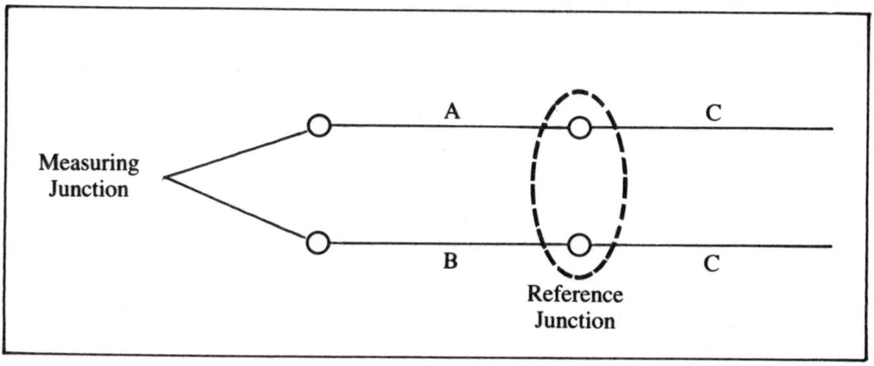

Figure 12.4. A thermocouple constructed of two metals, A and B, and connected to a cable of metal C.

Due to the small number of units to be produced, it is desirable not to invest development time into designing special hardware that can be purchased commercially. It may be useful, however, to construct the system from a number of compatible modules to reduce the cost of hardware.

To avoid the design of special hardware to provide thermocouple reference compensation and to reject noise in the low-level thermocouple environment, a commercial thermocouple conditioning unit is purchased for each thermocouple. The signal conditioning unit inputs the thermocouple output and produces a standard four to 20 milliamp signal. The long signal line capability of the current loop is not required since the recording system and transducer are packaged together. The signal conditioning unit is used because it is a standard component and relatively inexpensive.

The recording system is best addressed by a single board computer. The output of the system is to be recorded on a digital cassette unit. The recorder is interfaced by a parallel interface through which the tape motion and recording can be controlled.

It is desirable to transfer data on the tape to a mainframe computer for processing. Because the tape is not supported on the mainframe, an extra recorder is connected to a disk-based microcomputer system that can transfer data to the host using an asynchronous serial interface. Cassettes retrieved from the monitoring units are read by the microcomputer system, and the data is transferred to the host system.

A time base is required so that the computer can record data at ten-minute intervals and so that a time and date stamp can be recorded with every temperature value. To avoid loss of date and time information during a power failure and to avoid procedural problems associated with entering the date and time manually, a battery-powered clock circuit, using a large-scale integration (LSI) clock integrated circuit, is interfaced to the computer via a parallel interface. The clock IC is designed for such applications and is easily interfaced to a parallel interface.

The single board computer used for this system does not contain an A/D converter. Because the signal conditioner is used with the thermocouple, the A/D converter front-end is not critical. An encapsulated A/D converter is mounted on the prototype area of the single board computer and connected to a parallel interface. The A/D converter module has a high input impedance (250M) and an input range of zero to -10 volts. The four to 20 milliamp signal is converted to a -2 to -10 volt signal by placing a precision 500 ohm resistor in the current loop and measuring the voltage drop across it. See Figure 12.5 for a block diagram of the system.

The system was designed to measure the temperature to an accuracy of two degrees centigrade. The J type thermocouple covers a range of −190 degrees to 760 degrees centigrade. The signal conditioner is designed to convert the voltage produced over the 950-degree range into a four to 20 milliamp range. This range is converted by the 500 ohm resister into a −2 to −10 range. The 12-bit A/D converter divides a 0 to −10 volt range into 4096 parts (LSB is approximately 2.5 millivolts). Mapping the 950-degree temperature range onto an eight-volt range produces a change of approximately 8.5 millivolts per degree. Given that the accuracy of the signal conditioning unit is good and that the 500 ohm resistor is precision grade, the two-degree accuracy can be obtained.

Since the entire range of the thermocouple is not used, a higher resistor value can be selected such that the usable part of the thermocouple range covers a wider part of the A/D converter input range. A resistance temperature detector (RTD) or a solid state temperature measuring device may be more appropriate due to the small temperature range covered. These devices would not require the voltage-to-current signal conditioning unit.

Development time is required to mount and connect the A/D converter and resistor. The thermocouple signal conditioning unit and cassette recorder must be connected to the system. The clock circuit must also be constructed. The entire system and a power supply must be packaged.

Software development should be performed on a disk-based system. Debugging on the single board computer should be supported by a robust debugger. To avoid programming EPROMS during development, the code developed on the disk-based system can be transferred to the single board computer using a serial interface. A console terminal connected to the single board computer is needed during development to communicate with the debugger.

Due to the special hardware, the development of this system is costly. As noted in Chapter 1, the extra development cost might be tolerated in some environments where skilled labor is inexpensive. In a different environment, a set of more costly data loggers might provide a better solution due to savings in development costs.

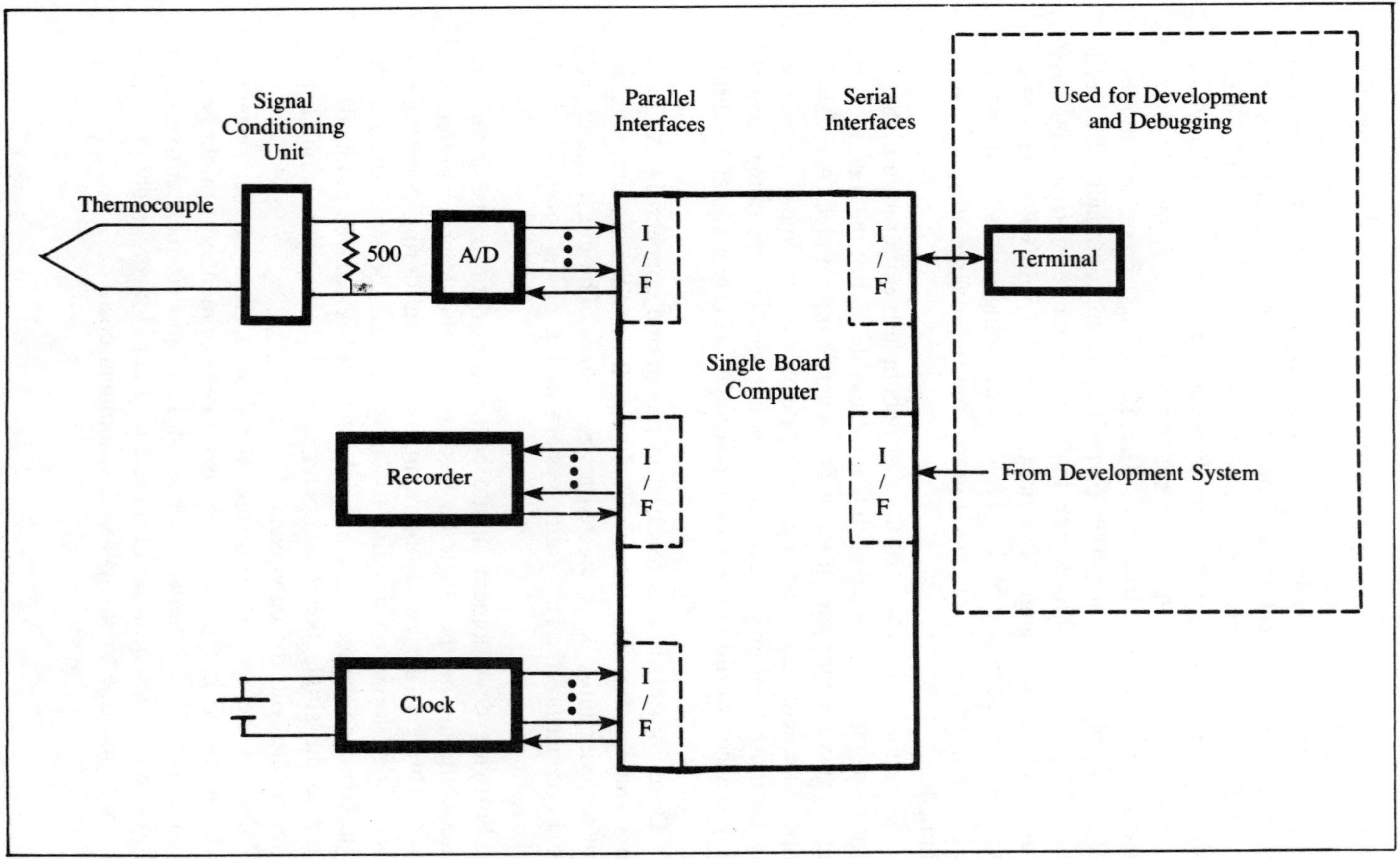

Figure 12.5. Block diagram of the temperature collection system.

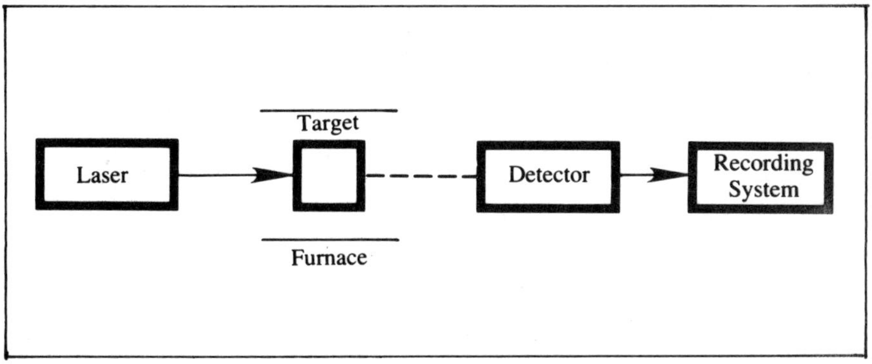

Figure 12.6. Block diagram of the thermal diffusivity system.

Thermal Diffusivity Data Collection Unit

Figure 12.6 diagrams a thermal diffusivity measurement system used in research. A target of some material is placed in a furnace and heated to some temperature, T_0. A laser is then fired at the target, and the rise in temperature at the rear of the target is recorded. The temperature is recorded using an infrared detector. Figure 12.7 shows a typical heating curve.

The value of T_0, the furnace temperature, can assume a wide range of values depending on the particular phase of an experiment. Using one of the available detectors, the temperature range is 550 to 1600 degrees centigrade. If a 12-bit A/D converter were used to measure this entire range, the LSB value would be approximately 1/4 degree (range divided by 4096), limiting the accuracy of the measurement to approximately $\pm 1/8$ degree.

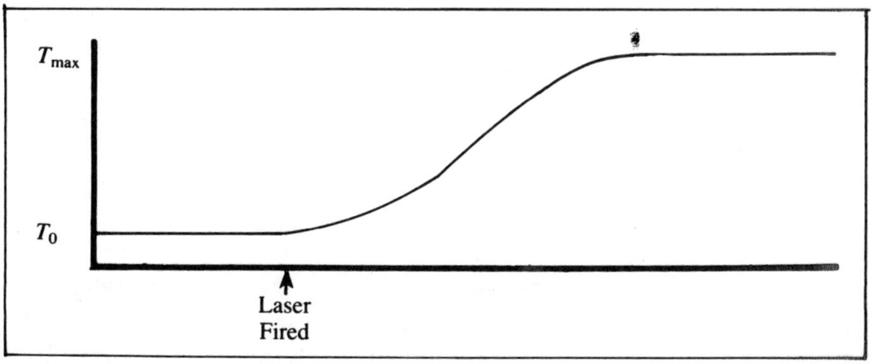

Figure 12.7. Typical diffusivity heating curve.

As shown in the figure, the measuring system only has to cover the range T_0 to T_{max} for a particular phase of an experiment. This range is typically two degrees centigrade. Given that the measurement system can measure the voltage change produced by such a temperature change, it is necessary to compensate for the offset voltage caused by the temperature T_0. If the voltage produced by the detector at T_0 is $V(T_0)$ and at T_{max} is $V(T_{max})$, the input to the A/D converter subsystem should be the voltage $V(T) - V(T_0)$ where $V(T)$ is the voltage produced by some temperature T in the range T_0 to T_{max}.

One technique to produce the desired offset adjustment is shown in Figure 12.8. The output of op amp A is the DAC voltage minus the detector voltage. The second op amp inverts the signal to output the detector value less the DAC value. If the DAC is set to produce the voltage $V(T_0)$, the A/D converter will measure $V(T) - V(T_0)$.

In practice, the target would be heated to some T_0. The data acquisition system would then output an initial DAC voltage and read the A/D converter. Based on the sign and magnitude of the reading, the DAC voltage would be changed and the process would be repeated until the A/D converter reading was near zero to a tolerance set by the errors associated with the A/D converter, the DAC, and the amplifiers.

After the software had zeroed the circuit, the system would begin sampling, and the laser would be fired. Data collection would continue for a preset time, long enough for the transition from T_0 to T_{max} to occur. The target could then be heated to a new initial temperature. The system would again zero the output of the op amp, fire the laser, and collect data.

The system requires no calibration because the important parameters in the research for which the system was designed is the time required for the transition from T_0 to T_{max} and the shape of the curve. The output of some detectors are logarithmic. Software must perform an antilog function on the data so that a standard temperature versus time curve can be presented to the operator.

The circuit shown in Figure 12.8 is a block diagram. The DAC range, A/D converter input range, and gain setting resistors for the op amps must be selected for compatibility in accordance with the output of the detector to allow sufficient accuracy in the measurement. Since the detector is an optical device, vibrations (such as produced by water cooling for the laser) may introduce noise into the detector signal. A low-pass filter may be needed to reduce this noise. A differential input stage may be necessary to reduce common mode noise and to amplify the detector signal.

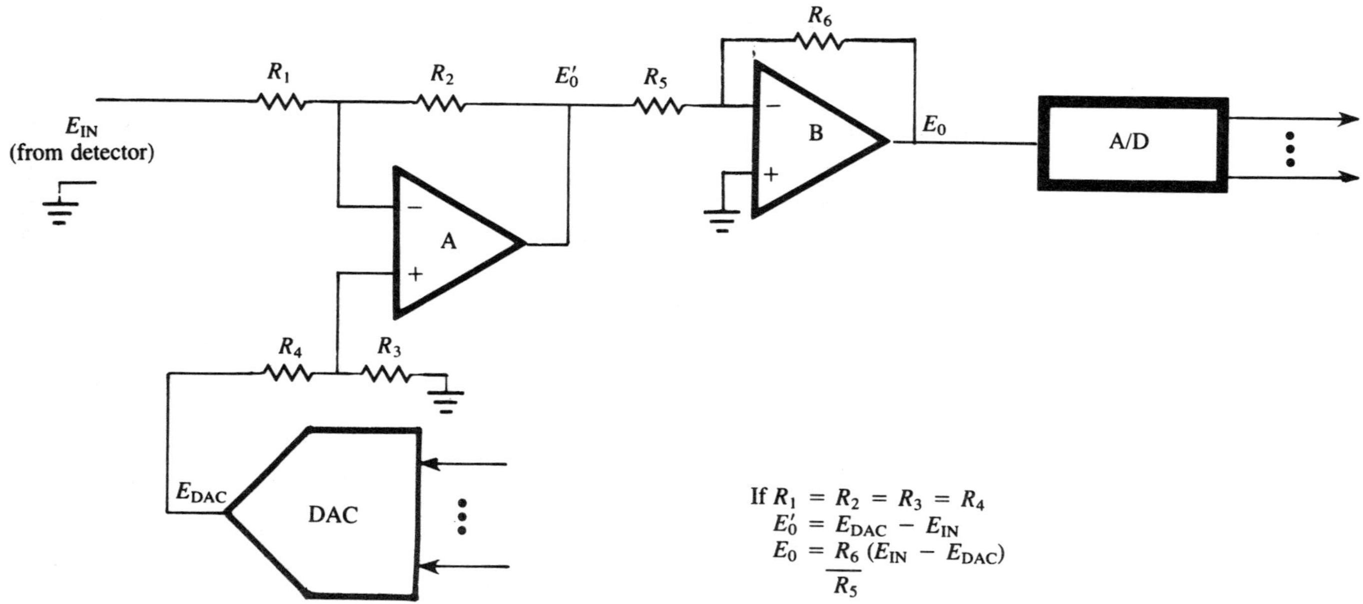

If $R_1 = R_2 = R_3 = R_4$

$$E_0' = E_{DAC} - E_{IN}$$

$$E_0 = \frac{R_6 (E_{IN} - E_{DAC})}{R_5}$$

Figure 12.8. Block diagram of the circuit to allow the computer to zero the offset voltage.

The measurement system should contain a graphics terminal for display of the data. In a typical environment, it is desirable to perform analysis on the data acquisition system. In this case, a small- or medium-sized, disk-based system with a high-level language should be used. A plotter could be connected to the system if it were desirable to have a permanent copy of a graph of the raw data.

Because the software to zero the op amp circuit is not time critical, it can be written in a high-level language provided there is some language mechanism to communicate with the A/D converter and the DAC. The data collection routine that captures the data during the temperature rise may have to be written in assembly language, depending on the machine and selected sample rates.

It should be noted that a complete hardware circuit could be built to perform the offset zeroing function. In this case, the computer would signal the circuit that the offset operation was to be performed. The circuit would perform the offset function using a comparator, control logic, DAC, and op amps. It would then signal the computer that the offset adjustment operation was complete.

The advantage of the complete hardware approach is that the circuit can be used independently of a computer for measurements using a storage oscilloscope. The signal to initiate the offset zeroing function would be controlled with a switch. The output of the circuit, $V(T) - V(T_0)$, could be displayed on the oscilloscope. For some detectors, an antilog circuit would be needed so that the output would be readable. This hardware approach has the disadvantage that the heating waveform must be recorded manually.

The software approach is easier to develop, especially if automatic recording of data is required.

Solid State Physics Experiment

The final example describes a special data acquisition system used for a particular experiment in solid state physics. The system aids in the research of the behavior of the valence electrons of atoms. Figure 12.9 shows a simplified block diagram of the research spectrometer. An electron beam is aimed at a thin target. Interactions between beam electrons and valence electrons cause the electrons to scatter at an angle based on the energy and momentum of the electron beam and the energy and momentum of the valence electron.

The two detector systems are controlled by two voltages produced by DACs that are part of the data acquisition system. The detectors reject

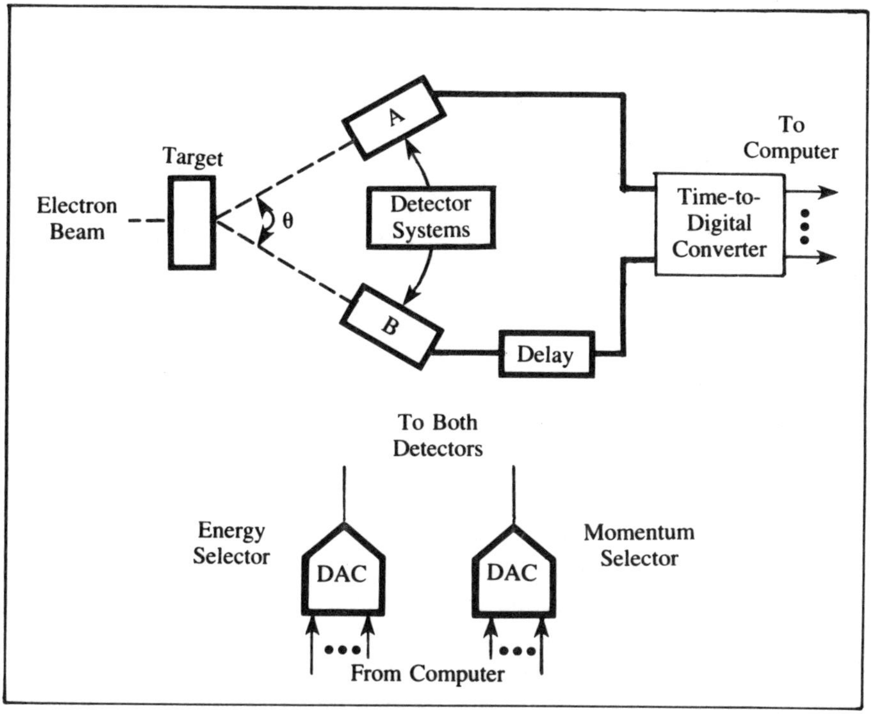

Figure 12.9. A simplified block diagram of the solid state physics research apparatus.

electrons of all energies and momentums except those selected by the DACs. One DAC controls which energy is accepted, and one controls which momentum is accepted. The actual rejection of all but the selected electrons is performed by the magnitude of magnetic and electrostatic fields. The detectors output a pulse for each electron detected.

Data collection is performed by sweeping through a set of operator specified values of energy and momentum. At each pair of energy and momentum, the DACs are set to cause the detectors to reject all electrons except the ones with the selected energy and momentum, and the number of electron pairs (one entering each detector as the result of a collision) are counted. After sweeping the selected values of energy and momentum a specified number of times, accumulating the number of counts at each energy and momentum pair, an array of counts is produced as shown in Figure 12.10. The array cells of energy and momentum pairs with large counts indicate the existence of valence electrons with the specified energy and momentum. The small counts in other cells are due to noise.

Energy

100	52	77	91	118	64	87	51	50	51
10191	87	84	96	117	93	82	92	10211	97
47	9876	51	48	59	60	8976	9076	111	54
68	9047	10987	48	61	84	7654	67	81	21
56	107	61	9900	8765	10091	56	47	35	29

Momentum

Figure 12.10. Example accumulated counts of electron collisions at each pair of energy and momentum values.

The actual apparatus is more complex. Electrons entering the detectors due to a true collision would cause simultaneous pulses from the detectors. Random electrons entering the detectors would cause pulses separated by some random time interval.

A special hardware device, a time-to-digital converter, converts the time between a pulse from detector A and a pulse from detector B to digital format. The pulse from detector B is delayed by 30 nanoseconds which causes the time-to-digital converter to output a value of 30 when pulses caused by a collision occur. The delay is used to allow the operator to inspect the number of events around the 30-nanosecond delay. By graphically displaying counts versus delay for a given energy and momentum, a peak should occur at the time corresponding to a collision. This peak will be near 30 nanoseconds but may vary somewhat due to a number of factors in the apparatus.

The software designed to collect data contains three major components: operator communications, data collection, and graphics. The operator interface uses menus and screens for ease of use. The operator fills in collection parameters, such as the energy and momentum range and the collection time at each cell, on a terminal screen formatted for data entry.

The data collection section sweeps through the set of cells defined by all combinations of energies and momentums from the specified ranges. The cell at which collection is to occur is selected randomly from the cells not yet used in a given sweep. The use of random order reduces the effect of instrument drift.

When a particular value of energy and momentum is selected, the DAC outputs are set to instate the selected values. After an operator specified settling time, data is collected from the time-to-digital converter in interrupt mode for an operator specified amount of time. Each time the time-to-digital converter detects a pulse from detector A followed by a pulse from detector B, it digitizes the time between pulses and generates an interrupt request. The computer reads the time value and increments an array cell corresponding to the time value.

At the end of the collection time, the array of counts is saved on disk, and the process is repeated for the next energy, momentum cell. The entire set of energy and momentum values is swept many times. Each time a particular value of energy and momentum is swept, the counts produced by the time-to-digital interrupt routine are added to counts from previous sweeps for the particular values of energy and momentum. This signal averaging technique improves the signal-to-noise ratio.

The graphics section of the software allows the operator to view the number of events at each time value for a given array representing particular values of energy and momentum (see Figure 12.11). The operator then selects which time channels contain background counts only and which channels contain counts from collisions plus the background value. (The peak near the 30-nanosecond point contains counts from collisions and from background events.)

A large-scale microcomputer could be used to solve this task. A double density floppy disk drive could be used to hold the array of time counts for a range of energies and momentums. Due to the use of screen formatting and graphics, a system with overlay capabilities is necessary if the code is written in a high-level language.

The time-to-digital interface is not readily available for most micro-

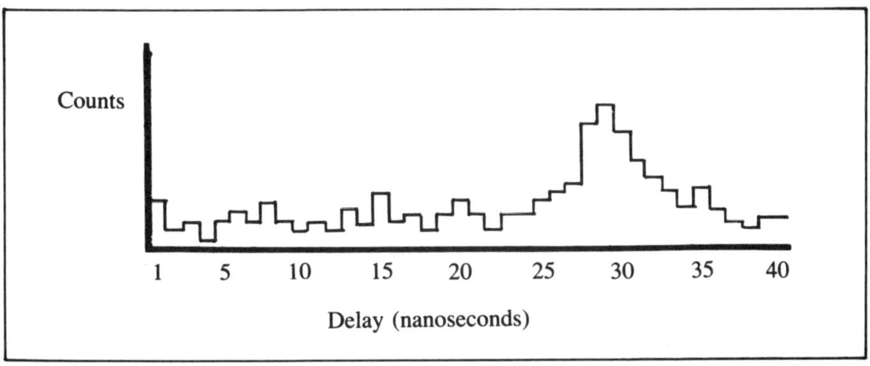

Figure 12.11. A sample graph of counts versus delay between pulses from the electron detectors for a particular pair of energy and momentum values.

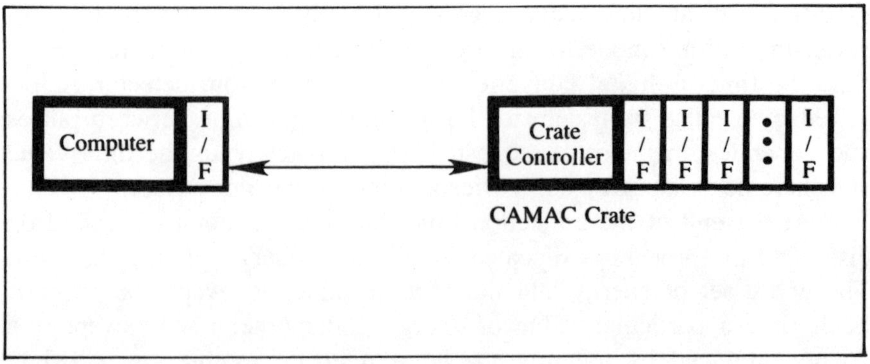

Figure 12.12. Typical connection of a CAMAC crate to a computer.

computers. Such devices are common, however, for the Computer Automated Measurement and Control (CAMAC) standard interface that is used largely in the field of nuclear physics. The CAMAC system is a standard bus and enclosure (called a crate) to which modules, such as the time-to-digital converter, can be connected. The CAMAC bus is connected to a controlling computer using a crate controller module and the computer interface as shown in Figure 12.12. The CAMAC system allows interfaces manufactured by a variety of vendors to be connected to a number of computers. Depending on the crate controller used, the CAMAC crate can appear as a single I/O device to the computer with the modules being selected one at a time, or the CAMAC system modules can appear as a number of individual devices to the computer.

13

Data Acquisition System Management— A Corporate View

Computer-based instrumentation is being used, at an ever increasing rate, due to the hardware technology explosion. In many corporations and universities, systems have been purchased or developed without regard for an overall growth and compatibility plan. The result is that a single corporation might own a variety of systems from a variety of vendors that in general are not hardware and software compatible. Such a situation normally indicates that hardware and software maintenance are costly, effort is duplicated, and the mechanism for transfer of data between machines is limited.

Hardware maintenance is costly in an environment where there are machines from a large number of vendors. It is costly for the equipment owner to stock spare printed circuit cards for each brand of machine. If third-party maintenance is used, the higher costs of providing fast repair on a number of different machines is passed on to the user of the repair service.

Software maintenance, the task of keeping operating systems and commercial packages up-to-date, is more complex in an environment with a large number of different machines. A larger staff must be retained to perform the updates, and a larger number of machines is required for the task.

In an environment where a number of different types of machines are used for data collection tasks, software and hardware development is likely to be duplicated. A graphics package for one machine will typically not function without modification on a second machine. Specially designed interfaces for one machine must be partially redesigned to function with a machine from another vendor.

Due to the lack of standards among vendors, the lack of widely accepted, inexpensive networking systems, and the diversity of the hardware available, the ability to transfer data between machines of different vendors or similar machines with different operating systems is typically difficult. Some of the techniques for data transfer and some associated problems can be found in Chapter 11. The inability to transfer data collected on one machine to a second machine suitable for data analysis is a paramount problem in an organization where equipment is purchased without regard to previously purchased equipment or growth plans.

A number of approaches can be used to reduce the impact of equipment incompatibility. These techniques must be applied on a corporate scale to be most effective.

First, it is necessary to standardize on hardware. In a data collection environment, there may be three classes of machines: single board computers, small floppy disk-based systems, and larger hard disk-based systems. The ideal approach would be to purchase all three types of systems from the same family of computers. In this case, each system contains a software compatible processor although the processors in each class may operate at different speeds. I/O devices would then be interchangeable, except perhaps the single board computers would not be able to connect to standard interfaces.

In the case where a family of computers is not suitable, a standard system in each class could be selected. A typical situation is to select a single board system from one vendor and systems in either disk-based class from a family. In this case, the disk-based systems can probably run compatible operating systems.

By selecting standard equipment, spare printed circuit boards and possibly spare systems can be easily stocked. A hardware failure can be quickly isolated and the failing subsystem replaced. The actual failing hardware can be repaired by return to vendor or other methods at a leisurely rate.

The use of standard processors typically means that the number of software packages and operating systems to be maintained is relatively small, thus reducing software maintenance costs. Software and hardware developed for a particular unit can be used by a wide number of the standard systems. Duplication of effort is thus reduced.

There are some disadvantages to selecting standard hardware. The newest advances in technology are excluded if they are not directly compatible with one of the standard systems. However, since computer hardware advancements are more rapid than the production of software, the purchase of the latest hardware is not always an advantage. The improvements and speed of a new processor are offset by the problems associated with incompatibilities with other systems, lack of software, and software that is not thoroughly tested. Many problems can be solved more effectively with older equipment when all costs are considered.

There must be some mechanism for allowing new equipment to be added to the existing standard. This can be done easily when computer families are used, and improved, faster, and upward compatible processors are added to the family. In other cases, new technology can be surveyed, and a few new products added to the corporate standard. New products are selected on the basis of need, compatibility, and function.

The standard has the disadvantage that some commercial products are not compatible with the standard systems. Desirable software and hardware products may not be available for standard machines. The purchase of instruments with integrated computer systems may also violate the standard. These disadvantages cannot be easily overcome. It may be necessary to violate the standard in these cases and for equipment purchased before a standard is adopted. Such violations should be kept to a minimum.

Data transfer between similar machines by media transfer can be easily accomplished. If the number of different types of machines used is limited, the implementation of a networking system is not as difficult as in an environment with a wide variety of different hardware.

In an environment with several classes of machines with a different standard operating system in each class, software developed for one class typically must be modified before it can be run on a processor in a different class. The use of standard languages and special software development techniques can make software more transportable.

Maximum software portability can be obtained using a language that generates code for a nonexistant standard machine. Each processor that is to run the code produced by the language processor must have an interpreter that simulates the operation of the standard machine. The disadvantages of this approach are performance degradation associated with a machine interpreter and the fact that special hardware must still be supported in a unique way on each machine.

A second approach is to use a standard language, such as FORTRAN-77. Any special language extensions provided by a vendor are not used. Any machine dependant code is localized in a small number of subroutines. The use of assembly language code should be minimized and well documented.

The need for corporate networks for the transmission of data between computers is becoming widely acknowledged. With the use of personal computers for word processing and management work stations, electronic networking is a needed tool. The connection of data acquisition systems to such a network is vital.

An overview of a corporate network is presented to illustrate a number of considerations. This example addresses data acquisition systems and computers used to store and analyze collected data. In an actual network, equal consideration would have to be given to personal work stations.

The network example is intended to address a small corporation or medium-sized university. The ideas presented can be expanded to address other situations. Figure 13.1 shows a conceptual diagram of a data acquisition system data transfer network. The diagram shows a number of small- and medium-scale computer systems (microcomputers and minicomputers) with mass storage devices (diskettes or rigid disks). In a particular corporate strategy, these systems could all be members of a family of computers. Small systems would be used for some tasks, with more powerful systems used where they are required.

The disk-based systems have a communications link to a mainframe time sharing system. Data files can be transferred to and from the mainframe. The mainframe is used for storage of large files, data analysis, and hardcopy plotting and printing.

The remaining connections to each of the disk-based systems are optional. One such unit may be used for data acquisition and control with no connections to single board computer systems. Another system might function solely as a controller of a number of single board computer systems. It may direct and collect data from the single board computers and pass data to the mainframe. A third unit might perform both types of tasks: data acquisition and control along with control of single board computers. Other units might be dedicated to program development. Another unit at this level might serve as a concentrator, being connected to a number of personal computer workstations that must

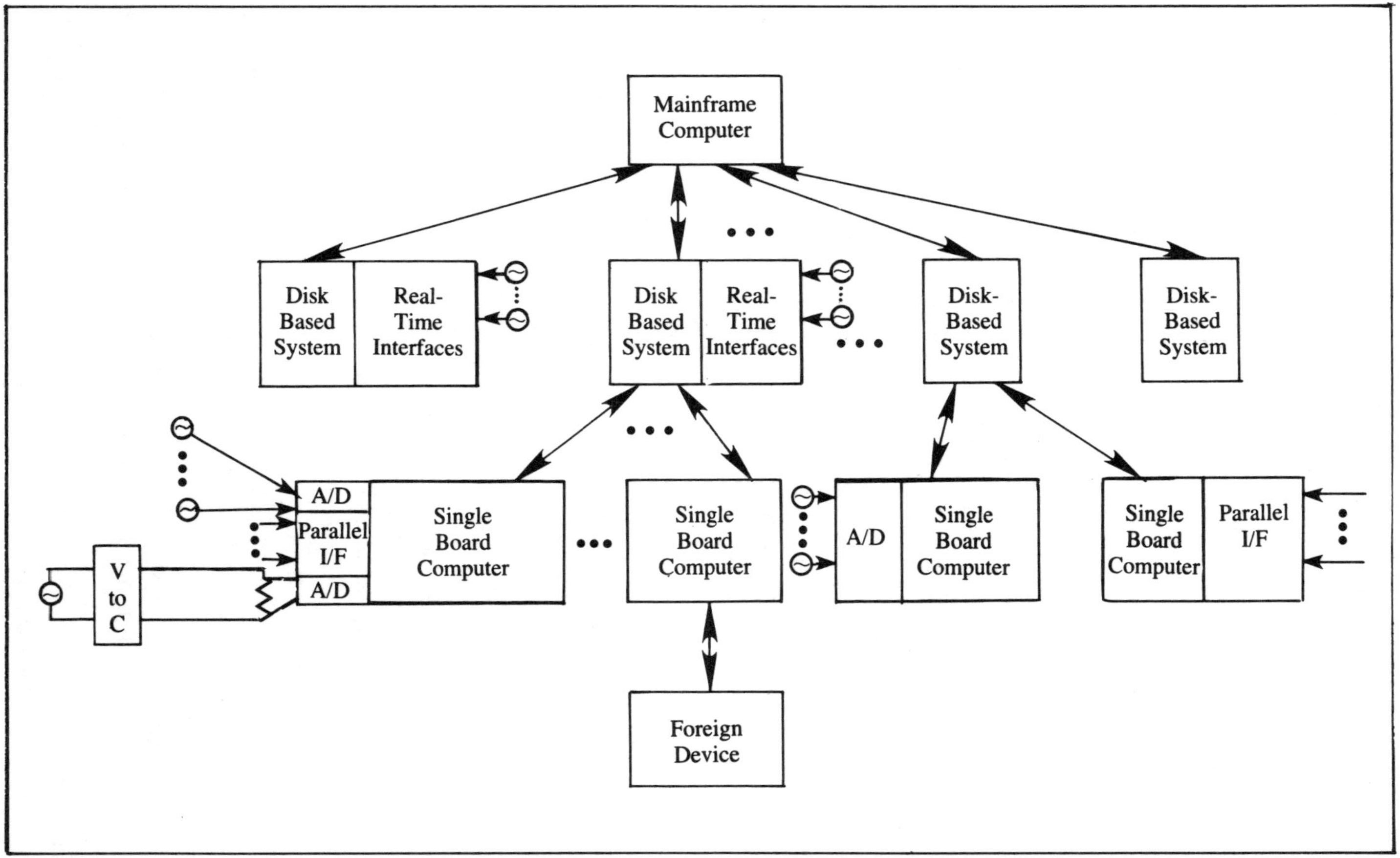

Figure 13.1. Representation of a communications network for support of data acquisition systems.

communicate with the time sharing system. The concentrator is used to offload some communications tasks from the time share system and to reduce the cost of the communications hardware needed.

The single board computers are at the lowest network level. In the figure, a number of connections to each single board computer are shown. Each single board computer would typically be dedicated to a single task and would not have all the connections. A single board computer would either be used for data acquisition or as a protocol converter for connection of foreign devices to the network.

As a data collection device, the single board computer collects data from local transducers using standard interfaces and from remote devices using remote signal conditioners and transmitters (current loop or possibly RS-232C interfaces and short distance modems).

The second use of the single board computers is to serve as protocol converters. In this mode, the single board computer is connected to a computer system that does not support direct connection to the network. Systems that are not members of the standard hardware or instrumentation containing integrated computers may not, by lack of software or memory resources, support direct connection to the network. The single board computer receives data from the foreign devices and retransmits it using the standard network protocol. The network support code in the single board computer is used for any foreign device. Only the code to communicate with the foreign device must be developed.

Regardless of the use of the single board computer, it transmits data to one of the disk-based systems using the network protocol. The protocol used by the single board computer may be a subset of the one used at other levels of the network because of the limited resources of the single board computer. The data exchanged must, however, be transferred in such a way that transmission errors are detected and corrected using a retransmission technique.

The disk-based systems typically store data from a single board computer in a file representing a single experiment or run. The entire file is then transmitted to the mainframe.

The disk-based system may also have the capability to "download" programs to the single board computers. Each single board computer has a ROM containing the code necessary to access the network. The node to which it is connected transmits a program to the single board computer to be stored in memory and executed. This feature allows the single board computer to perform a number of functions depending on the code placed in it. Code modification is more easily performed than in a standalone ROM-based system.

Another approach is to use a single board computer with a processor similar to the disk-based systems. The single board computer runs a small version of the same operating system modified to access the network as a "virtual disk". When the operating system requires disk access, the network driver software is called. The data to be read from or written to disk is actually transmitted across the network. This technique simplifies software development by allowing the single board computer systems to run the same software as the disk-based units.

The actual network requirements depend on the particular corporation or university. The number of mainframes and levels in the network vary. The implementation and maintenance of a local network will be a requirement for all but the smallest organization. Technological advances will both mandate and make possible useful networks.

Appendix A
The ASCII Code

Decimal	Hexadecimal	Character	
0	00	NULL	
1	01	SOH	(Start of Heading)
2	02	STX	(Start of Text)
3	03	ETX	(End of Text)
4	04	EOT	(End of Transmission
5	05	ENQ	(Enquiry)
6	06	ACK	(Positive Acknowledge)
7	07	BEL	(Ring Terminal Bell)
8	08	BS	(Backspace)
9	09	HT	(Horizontal Tab)
10	0A	LF	(Linefeed)
11	0B	VT	(Vertical Tab)
12	0C	FF	(Formfeed)
13	0D	CR	(Carriage Return)
14	0E	SO	(Shift Out)
15	0F	SI	(Shift In)
16	10	DLE	(Data Link Escape)
17	11	DC1	(Device Control 1)

Decimal	Hexadecimal	Character	
18	12	DC2	(Device Control 2)
19	13	DC3	(Device Control 3)
20	14	DC4	(Device Control 4)
21	15	NAK	(Negative Acknowledge)
22	16	SYN	(Synchronous Idle)
23	17	ETB	(End of Transmission Block)
24	18	CAN	(Cancel)
25	19	EM	(End of Medium)
26	1A	SUB	(Substitute)
27	1B	ESC	(Escape)
28	1C	FS	(File Separator)
29	1D	GS	(Group Separator)
30	1E	RS	(Record Separator)
31	1F	US	(Unit Separator)
32	20	SP	(Space)
33	21	!	
34	22	”	
35	23	#	
36	24	$	
37	25	%	
38	26	&	
39	27	’	(Single quote)
40	28	(	
41	29	)	
42	2A	*	
43	2B	+	
44	2C	,	(Comma)
45	2D	-	
46	2E	.	
47	2F	/	
48	30	0	
49	31	1	
50	32	2	
51	33	3	
52	34	4	
53	35	5	
54	36	6	
55	37	7	
56	38	8	
57	39	9	
58	3A	:	
59	3B	;	
60	3C	<	

Decimal	Hexadecimal	Character
61	3D	=
62	3E	>
63	3F	?
64	40	@
65	41	A
66	42	B
67	43	C
68	44	D
69	45	E
70	46	F
71	47	G
72	48	H
73	49	I
74	4A	J
75	4B	K
76	4C	L
77	4D	M
78	4E	N
79	4F	O
80	50	P
81	51	Q
82	52	R
83	53	S
84	54	T
85	55	U
86	56	V
87	57	W
88	58	X
89	59	Y
90	5A	Z
91	5B	[
92	5C	\
93	5D	]
94	5E	^
95	5F	_
96	60	’ (Apostrophe)
97	61	a
98	62	b
99	63	c
100	64	d
101	65	e
102	66	f
103	67	g

Decimal	Hexadecimal	Character
104	68	h
105	69	i
106	6A	j
107	6B	k
108	6C	l
109	6D	m
110	6E	n
111	6F	o
112	70	p
113	71	q
114	72	r
115	73	s
116	74	t
117	75	u
118	76	v
119	77	w
120	78	x
121	79	y
122	7A	z
123	7B	{
124	7C	|
125	7D	}
126	7E	~
127	7F	DEL (Delete)

Appendix B
A Limited View of the PDP-11 Instruction Set

This appendix is intended to serve as an aid for understanding the PDP-11 program segments in Chapter 6. This description is by no means complete. Only the instructions and features of the PDP-11 minicomputer that are required to understand the examples that are described.

The PDP-11 family of minicomputers is produced by the Digital Equipment Corporation. The processors are 16-bit machines. Memory is organized as 64K bytes. (Larger machines in the family may be equipped with a memory management unit to allow access of a larger memory.) The memory can also be accessed as 16-bit words. A word is made up of a low-order byte that has an even address and a high-order byte whose address is one greater than the low-order byte. Instructions are formed using one, two, or three words.

The PDP-11 has eight general purpose registers, R0 through R7. R6 and R7 perform special functions. R6 is also the stack pointer, SP. R7 is also the program counter, PC. A separate Processor Status Word (PSW) register contains the state of ALU flags and the interrupt status.

The programs in Chapter 6 are given in a symbolic format. Memory locations are specified symbolically using one to six alphanumeric characters followed by a colon. Numeric values are specified in either octal (base eight) or decimal. All numeric values are in octal unless they are followed by a decimal point to specify decimal.

Several pseudo-operation codes (pseudo-ops) are used in the examples. Pseudo-ops are instructions to the assembler to perform such functions as the allocation of storage. ".WORD" allocates a 16-bit word and initializes it to the value specified to the right of the pseudo-op. If an address or symbolic parameter is placed in the word, it is placed to the right of ".WORD". ".BYTE" allocates a byte of storage and initializes it. ".BLKW" (block word) allocates a number of words and initializes them to zero. The value to the right of the pseudo-op specifies the number of words to be allocated. ".END" marks the end of a program to the assembler.

The equal sign (=) is used to assign a value to a symbolic name at assembly time. For example, if the address 1000 must be referred to several times in a program, "TAB=1000" can be coded, and then TAB can be used to reference location 1000.

Instructions are specified symbolically with a two, three, or four character operation code. There are zero, one, and two operand instructions. Some instructions can operate either on bytes or words. The word versions of the instructions are specified using a three-character mnemonic. The byte instructions are specified by appending the character "B" to the word version. For example, "MOV a,b" moves the contents of the word specified by operand a to operand b while "MOVB a,b" moves the contents of the byte specified by a to b.

Immediate values are specified by the pound symbol (#) followed by a numeric value or symbolic address. Absolute addresses are specified by the symbols " @ #" followed by an address value or symbolic address.

PDP-11 I/O device registers are memory-mapped in the range 160000_8 to 177777_8. Devices that can interrupt also have a vector address in the address range 0_8 to 400_8. The vector address specifies two words in memory. When an interrupt occurs, the interrupting device identifies its vector address. The current values in the PC and PSW registers are stacked, and the value in the first vector word is placed in the PC, while the second vector word value is placed in the PSW. This mechanism allows the processor to vector to a service routine and change interrupt states in one step. The RTI (return from interrupt) instruction returns to the interrupted code by restoring the stacked PC and PSW values.

A subroutine is called using the instruction "JSR PC,a" where a is the absolute or symbolic address of the subroutine to be called. The PC is stacked, and a branch is made to location a. The RTS (return from subroutine) instruction restores the stacked PC value to return to the instruction following the subroutine call instruction.

Branch instructions are coded as an operation code and an address to which to branch. The unconditional branch, BR, branches under all circumstances. The remaining branch instructions test the PSW flags and branch if the tested condition is true. All of the arithmetic instructions discussed and the MOV instruction set the PSW based on the result of the instruction. BEQ branches if the result of the last instruction that set the PSW flags was zero. BNE branches if the result is not equal to zero. BGE and BLE are branch if greater than or equal and branch if less than or equal, respectively. BCS and BCC are branch if the PSW carry flag is set (logic one) and branch if the carry flag is clear (logic zero), respectively.

There are two zero operand instructions used in the examples. SETC sets the carry flag. CLRC clears the carry flag.

Operands are specified as registers (e.g. "R0"), as immediate values (e.g. "#8."), as absolute addresses (e.g. " @ #100"), and as symbolic names. The operand "−(SP)" causes a value to be pushed on the stack (decrement the stack pointer by two bytes and use the stack pointer value to access memory). "(SP)+" means to use the stack pointer to access memory and then to increment the stack pointer value by two (two bytes to a word). This operand specifies the stack pop operation. An operand of the form "value (Rx)" means to add the contents of Rx to "value" and to use the result as a pointer to specify the operand address. " @ value(Rx)" means that the Rx value is added to "value". The result points to a word in memory that contains the address of the operand.

The last two formats are used in the examples to access control blocks in memory. Rx is loaded with the first word of the control block, and "value" is the offset in bytes to the control block item to be accessed. In the examples, "value" is specified symbolically.

The remaining instructions are listed below. Instructions are specified using the form "opcode op1,op2".

CLR/CLRB	$0 \rightarrow$ op1
DEC/DECB	op1 $- 1 \rightarrow$ op1
INC/INCB	op1 $+ 1 \rightarrow$ op1
TST/TSTB	op1 value sets the PSW flags

MOV/MOVB	op1 → op2
CMP/CMPB	op1 − op2 sets the PSW flags
ADD	op1 + op 2 → op2
SUB	op2 − op1 → op2
BIT/BITB	AND(op1,op2) sets the PSW flags
BIS/BISB	OR(op1,op2) → op2
ROL	op1 is rotated left with the PSW carry flag
ROR	op1 is rotated right with the PSW carry flag
ASL	op1 is shifted left. Bit 15 is shifted into the PSW carry flag. A logic zero enters bit O.
ASR	op1 is shifted right. Bit 15 retains the sign bit. Bit zero is shifted into the PSW carry flag

Programmer annotation is indicated in a program by preceding the comment with a semicolon(;). An entire line is made a comment by

XYZ:	.WORD	5	XYZ refers to a sixteen bit memory location that is initialized to 5.
	BNE	NOT0	If the PSW status flags indicate that the last ALU operation produced a value that was not zero, a branch to the memory location associated with the symbolic label NOT0 is performed.
	MOV	#5,@#300	The immediate value 5 is moved to location 300_8.
	OFFSET = 6		
	MOV	#TABLE1,R0	Place the address of TABLE1 in R0.
	CLR	OFFSET(R0)	Clear the fourth word (bytes 6 and 7) of TABLE1.
		.	
		.	
		.	
TABLE1:	.BLKW	4	

Figure B.1. Examples of symbolic PDP-11 program statements.

placing a semicolon in column one. Comments can also follow instructions and pseudo-operation codes. In the examples in Chapter 6, the reader should be guided by the comments in the programs.

Figure B.1 gives a few examples of symbolic instructions that illustrate the notation used.

Notes

Footnotes for Chapter 1

1. The term "process," taken from the discipline of process control, refers to an industrial system. Process is used in a broader sense in this text to refer to any physical system on which measurements can be performed.

Footnotes for Chapter 6

1. Knuth, Donald E. *The Art of Computer Programming, Volume 2/Seminumerical Algorithms* (Reading: Addison-Wesley Publishing Company, 1969), p. 195.
2. Dorn, William S. and McCracken, Daniel D. *Numerical Methods with Fortran IV Case Studies* (New York: John Wiley & Sons, Inc., 1972), p.94.

Footnotes for Chapter 11

1. ASCII control characters are indicated by enclosing the standard abbreviation of the character between the less than and greater than symbols. For example, <SYNC> indicates the ASCII SYNC character.

Bibliography

Adair, Robert K. *Concepts in Physics*. New York: Academic Press, 1969.

Bibbero, Robert J. *Microprocessors in Instruments and Control*. New York: John Wiley & Sons, 1977.

Blaauw, Gerrit A. *Digital System Implementation*. Englewood Cliffs, NJ: Prentice-Hall, Inc., 1976.

Cooper, James W. *The Minicomputer in the Laboratory with Examples Using the PDP-11*. New York: John Wiley & Sons, 1977.

Diefenderfer, A. James. *Principles of Electronic Instrumentation*. Philadelphia: W. B. Saunders Co., 1972.

Doebelin, Ernest O. *Measurement Systems Applications and Design*. New York: McGraw-Hill, 1975.

Dorn, William S. and Daniel D. McCracken. *Numerical Methods with FORTRAN IV Case Studies*. New York: John Wiley & Sons, 1972.

Gardenhire, L. W. "Selecting Sample Rates," *ISA Journal*, April 1964, 59–64.

Hamacher, V. C., Z. G. Vranesic, and S. G. Zaky. *Computer Organization*. New York: McGraw-Hill, 1978.

Hoening, Stuart A. *How to Build and Use Electronic Devices Without Frustration, Panic, Mountains of Money, or an Engineering Degree*. Boston: Little, Brown, and Company, 1980.

Johnson, Curtis D. *Process Control Instrumentation Technology*. New York: John Wiley & Sons, 1982.

Jung, Water G. *IC Op-Amp Cookbook*. Indianapolis: Howard W. Sams & Co., 1974.

Knuth, Donald E. *The Art of Computer Programming, Volume 2/Semi-numerical Algorithms*. Reading, MA: Addison-Wesley Publishing Co., 1969.

Laboratory Subroutines Programmer's Reference Manual. Marlboro, MA: Digital Equipment Corp., 1981.

Lenk, John D. *Handbook of Controls and Instrumentation*. Englewood Cliffs, NJ: Prentice-Hall, 1980.

Lowe, E. I. and A. E. Hidden. *Computer Control in Process Industries*. London: Peter Peregrinus Ltd., 1971.

Microcomputer Handbook. Maynard, MA: Digital Equipment Corp., 1976.

Minc-11 Book 7, Working with MINC Devices. Maynard, MA: Digital Equipment Corp., 1978.

Morris, Robert L. and John R. Miller, eds. *Designing with TTL Integrated Circuits*. New York: McGraw-Hill, 1971.

Morrison, Ralph. *Grounding and Shielding Techniques in Instrumentation*. New York: John Wiley & Sons, 1977.

Newman, William J. and Robert F. Sproull. *Principles of Interactive Computer Graphics*. New York: McGraw-Hill, 1973.

Oliver, Bernard M. and John M. Cage. *Electronic Measurements and Instrumentation*. New York: McGraw-Hill, 1971.

Ott, Henry W. *Noise Reduction Techniques in Electronic Systems*. New York: John Wiley & Sons, 1976.

Schaum, Daniel. *Shaum's Outline Of Theory and Problems of College Physics*. New York: McGraw-Hill, 1961.

Sheingold, Daniel H., ed. *Analog-Digital Conversion Handbook*. Norwood, MA: Analog Devices, Inc., 1972.

Stearns, Samuel D., *Digital Signal Analysis*. Rochelle Park: Hayden Book Co., 1975.

Vassos, Basil H. and Galen W. Ewing. *Analog and Digital Electronics for Scientists*. New York: John Wiley & Sons, 1980.

Weber, Leonard J. and Donald L. McLean. *Electrical Measurement Systems for Biological and Physical Scientists*. Reading, MA: Addison-Wesley, 1975.

Wedlock, Bruce D. and James K. Roberge. *Electronic Components and Measurements*. Englewood Cliffs, NJ: Prentice-Hall, 1969.

Wolf, Stanley. *Guide to Electronic Measurements and Laboratory Practice*. Englewood Cliffs, NJ: Prentice-Hall, 1973.

Additional References

Foster, Caxton C. *Real Time Programming—Neglected Topics*. Reading, MA: Addison-Wesley, 1982.

Mellichamp, Duncan A., ed. *Real-Time Computing with Applications to Data Acquisition and Control*. New York: Van Nostrand Reinhold, 1983.

Index